The Belle Epoque

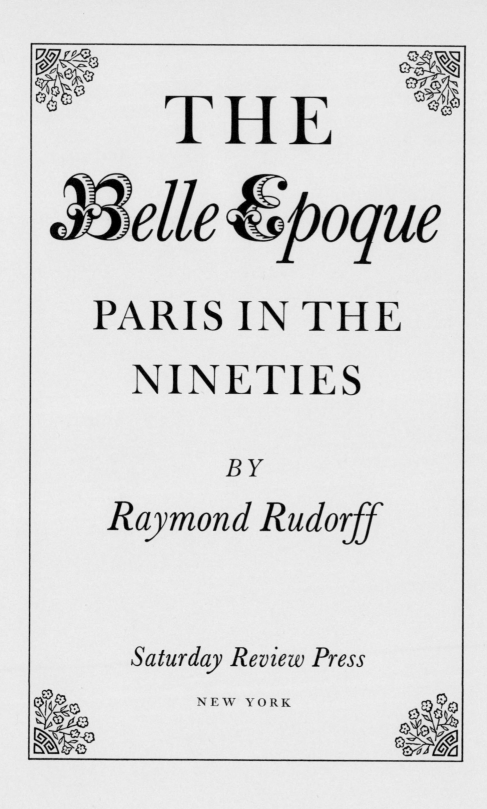

THE
Belle Epoque
PARIS IN THE NINETIES

BY

Raymond Rudorff

Saturday Review Press

NEW YORK

Library of Congress Catalog Card Number: 72–91182
ISBN 0–8415–0225–0

Saturday Review Press
380 Madison Avenue
New York, New York 10017

PRINTED IN THE UNITED STATES OF AMERICA

To
the Memory of
My Mother

Contents

Illustrations

Illustration 24 is reproduced by permission of Archives Photographiques, Paris; 15a by permission of Associated Book Publishers Ltd.; 21b is copyright 1972 The Barnes Foundation, Meryon, Pennsylvania; 27b, 28 by permission of the British Museum; 15b by permission of J. Evers, Angers; 7a, 7b, 10, 16a, 16b, 21a, 22b, 23b, 25b by permission of John Freeman & Co. Ltd.; 1, 3a, 3b, 4a, 5a, 5b, 11a, 12a, 12b, 18a, 18b, 23a, 32 by permission of the Radio Times Hulton Picture Library; 11b by permission of the Mander and Mitchenson Theatre Collection; 29a by permission of the National Film Archive; 20a by permission of Photographie Giraudon, Paris; 4b, 19b, 20b, 25a, 29b by permission of the Victoria and Albert Museum, London.

Preface

IN THE last ten years of the 19th century, Paris became the civilised world's capital of elegant living, pleasure and artistic genius. The decade which had so much charm and gaiety was also one of the most eventful and unsettled in the city's long history. Nostalgic survivors of the period and later generations have fondly looked back at these years as part of what Frenchmen call *la belle époque*—the last of the "good old days" before world wars, revolutions and galloping technological progress transformed the world out of recognition. People who lived at the time, however, called it the *fin de siècle* and the opinion was frequently voiced that the end of the old century was coinciding with the dying of traditional culture and civilisation.

The 1890's were a decade of transition and turbulence in Paris. Just as many aspects of 19th-century life survived the year 1900 for a short time, so others of the 20th century had already appeared before that date. As the century moved to its close, the history of Paris was marked by threats of *coups d'état*, great social unrest, noisy political brawls, both vocal and physical, violent passions and venomous hatreds and a number of spectacular public controversies in the arts. In the 1890's, Paris was terrorised by bomb-throwing anarchists, political extremists called upon the army to take power, the Dreyfus affair split public opinion, and a large number of important artists, writers, poets and journalists openly supported anarchist and radical thinkers calling for the complete transformation of existing society. It was also an intensely creative period in which what we now call modern art was born.

The true face of the 1890's in Paris has been largely obscured by sentimental evocations of the splendours and delights offered by the capital. The *belle époque* has become a legend, romanticised by countless books, memoirs, films and stage shows which have tended mainly to present Parisian life of the time as a heady medley of high living, dinners at Maxim's, elegant *demi-mondaines*, carriages and duels in the Bois de Boulogne, Toulouse-Lautrec and the Moulin Rouge, Sarah Bernhardt in her glory and the gaudy attractions of the 1900 Universal Exposition. Such treatment of the 1890's has risked presenting them to us as a historical museum piece, as far removed from us in spirit and body as the moustachioed gentlemen in frock coats and top hats and the tightly corseted ladies in flowing gowns who stare at us from the faded family albums of great-grandfather's day.

The 1890's were not always as fashionable as they are today. In 1930, the French novelist Paul Morand reacted against the sentimental view of the Paris of his childhood. When he came to look back at it in his book *1900*, he felt as though he were exploring "a sunken continent". He described the period as one which was "faded, delicious and stupid" and concluded that "we have nothing more in common with this epoch . . . I walk through 1900 as through a waxworks". Forty years later, it is possible to see that there is much in common between our own age and the 1890's if we look under the surface glitter which has so mesmerised the nostalgic.

Then, as now, there was widespread disillusion with the political system—especially among the young. Frustrated youthful idealists and fanatics tried their hand at urban guerilla warfare and urged the overthrow of the established social order; there were bomb-throwings, street demonstrations, manifestoes and riots; there was much talk of a gap or a conflict between the generations, and the hippies and drop-outs of today had their counterparts among the young people of the Latin Quarter of the Nineties and in the audiences who flocked to Paris's nonconformist, experimental theatres and listened to poetry in cafés and cellars. Then, as now, there was a large "underground" press; there was an equivalent of psychedelic art, a revival of interest in occultism, mysticism and spiritualism, with attempts to create artificial paradises of the mind through the use of certain drugs. In the young Paris of the Nineties, there was much uncertainty about the future, a reaction against conventional bourgeois attitudes towards life and culture, and a proliferation of groups and "isms".

The 1890's in Paris were also a period of serious high purposefulness and idealism which contrasted strongly with the frivolity and "decadence" which gave the decade such a lurid glamour. While the political revolutionaries and their many sympathisers among Paris's intellectuals and artists questioned the structure of society and called for a spiritual as well as a social revolution to regenerate the world, painters and poets were challenging the very foundations of what had hitherto been regarded as "art". It was a time of passionately expressed ideas and experiments, of extreme preciosity and deliberate eccentricity as the young and creative demanded the right to think, behave, write and make art as individuals. Then, as now, many of the more extreme attitudes assumed and assertions of the individual against society sprang from deep fears that humanity and the individual personality would be crushed or made anonymous by the mass structures of society and scientific development.

This book is an attempt to recreate the spirit, excitement and some of the main achievements of these years when Paris not only gave the world the seductive legend of the *belle époque* but some of the most vital and important innovations in our culture. Although, strictly speaking, the term *belle époque* applies only to the few years following the end of the Dreyfus affair in 1899, it has frequently been extended to the whole of the 1890's. I have preferred it as a title for this book to the expression *fin de siècle*, which has suggestions of old age and decline. A way of life and a century were ending in the 1890's but a new cultural age was dawning and many of its pioneers were some of the most youthful, audacious and experimental spirits ever assembled in one capital. *Belle époque* as symbolised by the gaieties of Montmartre and the boulevards and the gracious living of the well-to-do was only *belle* for a few at the time. But if by *belle époque* we mean a time when the spiritual and artistic life of one of the world's great cities was being renewed and enriched by a spectacular explosion of new talent, then there can be no doubt that the 1890's were a very *belle époque* indeed.

I

1889

IN JANUARY 1889, the highest metal structure in the world was nearing completion in Paris as the city prepared to celebrate a turbulent century of great achievements with a gigantic international exhibition. The occasion was also intended as a celebration of France's Republican system of government but, despite the optimism of the organisers, it looked to many people as if their country's Third Republic was doomed eighteen years after its birth. A few months later, the Universal Exposition was attracting hundred of thousands of visitors and impressing them with its lavish display of the fruits of French genius. Paris was *en fête* and it was easy to forget politics amid the many, varied pleasures the capital had to offer. By the end of the year, the Republic had survived its crisis and all that was left of the Exposition was Paris's newest and most conspicuous landmark: the 984-feet-high Eiffel Tower. It remained as a striking symbol for the new age that began for the city as it celebrated its past hundred years.

The Eiffel Tower was specially designed for the 1889 Exposition and, like the exhibition, symbolised the creativity, vigour and brilliance of France's builders, engineers, scientists, artists and industrialists. It was a sign of French faith in the new scientific age of progress which Jules Verne had forecast and which was fast becoming a reality. Some people could also see the tower as a symbol for the Republic and France's resurgence after her many sufferings. Of all Parisian landmarks, it was the tower which became the symbol of the city all over the world. It soared above the old roofs of the capital like some huge, inverted exclamation mark, a punctuation mark that signified a new phase in Paris's history. In past centuries, the city's poets, writers, architects, painters and scholars had sent French culture radiating outwards throughout the civilised world. Now, the world's tallest tower stood like a beacon in the midst of the great city whose charm, beauty and genius had survived a century of wars, revolutions, *coups d'état*, civil war and a siege. It seemed to invite the rest of the world to come to Paris and there take part in the magnificent new era which was about to begin and of which it was the spectacular herald.

To many Parisians, the Tower was simply a monstrosity. They protested that it was an ugly, vulgar and unprecedented commercial desecration of their beloved city. A professor of mathematics calculated that the tower would inevitably collapse were it to rise any higher than 700 feet. Fear that the iron structure would fall on their heads as well as aesthetic considerations drew strong objections from the inhabitants near the area where the tower was to be built. Gustave Eiffel, the builder, replied by personally guaranteeing indemnity in case of any accident. It was a bold step for the engineer to take and a magnificent expression of self-confidence. Eiffel was France's leading architect in metal. Since 1858, he had been building bridges and viaducts across Europe, composing symphonies of iron like his famous viaduct at Garabit in southern France which have since been recognised as masterpieces of modern design. There was no one better qualified to carry out the project. The idea of a "thousand-feet-high" tower had already been proposed earlier in the century. When the government had decided to hold an exhibition in Paris in 1889, they had invited designs for such a tower and Eiffel's had been the one accepted. It was the spectacular climax to his career and it perpetuated his name.

It was decided that the tower should stand in the middle of the Exhibition, in the Champ-de-Mars near the Seine, between the Trocadéro on the Right Bank and the 18th-century Ecole Militaire on the Left Bank. Work started in January 1887 and, a few days later, a manifesto signed by many of the leading artists and writers of the day was sent to Alphand, the Director of Works for the Exhibition. In what was called the *Protestation des Artistes* they protested against such a "vertiginously ridiculous tower dominating Paris like a black, gigantic factory chimney, its barbaric mass crushing Notre-Dame, the Sainte-Chapelle, the Tour

Saint-Jacques, and the Louvre". Its signatories included the
painters Meissonier, Bonnat and Bouguereau, the playwright
Sardou, the poet Sully-Prudhomme, and the novelist Guy de
Maupassant. The protest was rejected. Work went on and by
April 1, 1888, the first of the tower's three platforms was completed. The second was ready by July 14 the same year, and by
March 30, 1889, the tower was finished in time for the exhibition
despite a last-minute strike, and without a single life having been
lost during its building. The next day it was "inaugurated". Eiffel
gave a party for his workers and invited the municipal councillors
of the City of Paris and some fifty notabilities to visit his tower.
Since the lifts were not yet working, he led them up the stairs
himself. Forty of the dignitaries managed to make the climb up
to the first platform, 190 feet above the ground, and only twenty
succeeded in reaching the little round balcony at the top where
Eiffel solemnly hoisted the French tricolour flag bearing the
letters R.F. in gold and offered a champagne toast while a twenty-
one-shot firework salute was let off from the second platform.
The Tower had come to stay and to become identified, more than
any other single feature, with the city it overlooked.

In France, as in some other countries, the second half of the
19th century was marked by a kind of exhibition mania, more
or less nationalistic in spirit. Since 1867, a universal exhibition
was held every eleven years in Paris until 1900. If Eiffel's Tower
was a symbol for the 1889 exhibition, the exhibition was also a
symbol. That of 1889 was particularly significant since, in the
first place, it commemorated the centenary of the French
Revolution, of which the Third Republic was the direct legacy
and continuation to many Frenchmen. Its opening date was
May 6, the day after the first centenary of the opening of the
States General which was celebrated by another ceremony in the
Hall of Mirrors at the Palace of Versailles the previous day.
The fact that the exhibition was being held in the centenary
year of the Revolution was not to everyone's taste, either at home
or abroad. At the opening ceremony, presided over by the French
President Sadi Carnot, it was noticed that not one of the royal
courts of Europe was represented by its ambassador, with the

sole exception of Belgium. Despite their professed friendship with France, not even the diplomats of Austria-Hungary and Russia were present. Queen Victoria had even recalled her ambassador, Lord Lytton, to London so that he would not have to be present in Paris during the ceremony. Other absentees included many of the leading French aristocratic families, and the inhabitants of the highly conservative and often Royalist *beaux-quartiers* to whom any mention of the Revolution was in the worst possible taste. For the enemies of the French Republic— and there were still many—the Exhibition was simply a gigantic piece of political propaganda and to a certain extent they were right.

Although royal ambassadors might not attend, the Exhibition was also designed to rehabilitate revolutionary France in the eyes of royal Europe. It was to offer a spectacular, visible proof of the strength and assurance of the Third Republic which many people still considered to be as frail as the structure of the Eiffel Tower. In 1889, the Republic had lasted for eighteen years—as long as any regime had lasted in France since the Revolution. A large section of French opinion thought it most unlikely that it could continue to last much longer. Paris had just witnessed a century of revolutionary violence and civil turmoil and it seemed quite possible that before the year was out there would be barricades in the streets again and that Parisians would be continuing the fratricidal struggle that was still unresolved, even after the blood-lettings of 1830, 1848, 1851, and, most terrible of all, the Commune of 1871.

Every political crisis, every scandal that touched those in authority, was eagerly watched by anti-Republicans as a sign that not only the government but the regime itself was ready for overthrow. The Monarchists, divided between the Legitimists and the Orleanists, the Bonapartists and the clerical party, were all hostile to the Republic. The 1880's had seen a mobilisation of the right wing. In 1882, the League of Patriots had been founded by Paul Déroulède, an almost insanely nationalistic author and politician who had fought against both the Prussians and the Commune and who was obsessed by the idea of a great war of revenge against Germany. After being forced by an accident to retire from the army in 1872, he had written some immensely successful patriotic, military songs and had written a hymn *Vive la France* for which Gounod had composed the music for the 1878 Paris Exposition. The aims of his *Ligue des Patriotes* were simple and straightforward: to inculcate warlike fervour in every Frenchman, to regenerate France and to recover Alsace-Lorraine from Germany. The slogan of his party was no less clear-cut and succinct: "Qui vive? France!"

A strong strain of racialism had begun to run through French political and social life. In 1886, the writer Edouard Drumont had published his *La France Juive*, an impassioned anti-semitic work which purported to show that Jewry was corrupting French political, social and commercial life, from the top downwards. It was welcomed by Déroulède's *Ligue* as well as by a number of other militant organisations which would all be labelled as "fascist" today.

In 1887, a huge scandal had caused the fall of the prime minister Rouvier, and even the resignation of the President Jules Grévy when it was found that his son-in-law Daniel Wilson had been trafficking in decorations and particularly in the much-coveted *Légion d'Honneur*. Wilson was a parliamentary deputy and had been an under-secretary in the Finance Ministry. The whole Republic seemed to be tainted with corruption to its enemies, all the more as several generals and ministers were involved one way or another. The ministry had fallen and on December 2, 1887, a large crowd had gathered in the Place de la Concorde to sing *La Carmagnole* outside the Palais Bourbon and cry "Grévy resign!" There had been talk of setting up a revolutionary committee in the Hôtel de Ville, ugly incidents had occurred, the police had charged the mob, there had been casualties and what looked like being the beginning of another Paris Commune had only been averted by Grévy's resignation and his replacement by the "harmless" Sadi Carnot.

Of all capital cities in Europe, Paris was the "reddest". It had a tradition of revolutionary violence and the last week of the Commune had left bitter memories and a legacy which survives to this day. Over 15,000 Parisians, mostly from the working classes, had been shot down by the conservative Versailles government of Thiers. Scenes had taken place that had shocked even conservative Europe. Middle- and upper-class Parisians had stood by and watched as the Marquis de Galliffet and his troops had shot men, women and youths out of hand in the centre of Paris. The poor working-class districts around the Rue Saint-Antoine, the Bastille, Belleville, Ménilmontant and Montmartre remembered their dead and were not disposed to forget or forgive.

The Paris bourgeoisie continued to prosper but they were obsessed by their fear of the Paris mob, of Socialism, Communism and a sudden outbreak of violence against themselves and their property. The growth of the Socialist movement, the fact that an International Socialist Congress had been held in Paris in 1889, and that the suburbs were already acquiring their reputation as the "red belt", all added to their fears. On the other hand, the fiery declarations of certain Royalists and army officers preaching a war of revenge against Germany made them equally nervous. The Republic was weak and liable to be overthrown by some new scandal, the Royalists might attempt to put the Pretender on the throne, and the warlike postures of the army might precipitate another, even more disastrous repetition of the 1870 war. All the good bourgeois wanted to do was to continue to enrich himself and perhaps to buy some handsome country property where he and his family might forget the noise and uncertainty of Paris. His attitude was satirised in the new Chat Noir cabaret by Maurice Donnay in a song called *Adolphe or the Sad Young Man*, the "sad young man" being the incarnation of the bourgeois spirit:

> "La politique le hanta
> Le boulangisme le tenta
> Puis il se fit opportuniste
> Mais il était toujours très triste . . . "

The "boulangisme" that tempted the bourgeois young man was not so much a coherent political movement produced by violent social resentments as one born out of imagination, exaggerated nationalistic feeling and caprice. Looking back, it seems absurd that a shallow-minded army officer with little to commend him except his gift for striking popular martial atti-

tudes and his undoubted sex-appeal for society ladies and romantic *midinettes* should have come so near to providing an alternative
to President Carnot and his Republic.

General Boulanger, who gave his name to the movement, was
the glamorous example of everything a dashing officer was
supposed to be. He was handsome, he had fine whiskers, he rode
a black charger superbly at military reviews, and he had been a
great hit with the public at the Longchamps review of 1886. He
had begun his career by professing "liberal" views, he had been
given office by Clemenceau, the leading Republican radical politician, and in 1886 he had become Minister for War. Like
Déroulède and his kind, he kept trumpeting the need for a firm
stand against Germany and the liberation of Alsace–Lorraine.
He had been idolised for the way he had faced up to Germany
over a frontier incident which had arisen when a Lorraine police
inspector had been arrested on German territory, and his warlike
fervour had made him such an embarrassment to the government that in July 1887 he had been sent to the provinces to take
command of a corps at Clermont-Ferrand. There had been
hysterical scenes at the Gare de Lyon as a huge crowd came to see
him leave, standing dramatically on the foot-plate of a loco-
motive placarded with labels announcing IL REVIENDRA.
Royalist and right-wing propaganda made him out to be a
patriotic martyr sacrificed to expediency by a cowardly and
corrupt government, afraid of the "honest man". The streets of
Paris were enlivened with posters glorifying him and street-
sellers made a small fortune selling red chrysanthemums—his
favourite flower—and handkerchiefs, ties, scarves, plates and
various knick-knacks decorated with his portrait.

Boulanger disobeyed his superiors by returning unauthorised
to Paris in 1888. He was relieved of his army command and was
therefore able to stand for parliament. By the end of the year, he
had been elected to six provincial seats by means of the system
of multiple election, and he had become a leader of a party
calling itself the "Nationalists". It had the usual right-wing programme which aimed at cleansing France of her corruption, and
giving it a Dictator–President in the place of the "decadent and
effete" Republican politicians who had been misgoverning her for

their own private benefit. Boulanger was disowned by Clemenceau, fought a sword duel with the Prime Minister, Floquet, in which he was injured in the neck, and made his way into Paris society. The wealthy and beautiful Duchesse d'Uzès took him up, introduced him into her elegant drawing-room gatherings and made liberal contributions to his party's funds.

The climax to Boulanger's political career came in January 1889 when he stood as candidate in the parliamentary election in the circumscription of the Seine-Paris.

In the three weeks of the election campaign, Paris had gone wild with excitement. Although Boulanger was presenting himself as a Republican candidate with liberal sentiments, he had taken care to reassure both Royalists and Bonapartists. In 1888, the Duchesse d'Uzès had been sent on a secret mission to the exiled Comte de Paris, the Pretender, to tell him that Boulanger was willing to "open the doors of France to him". Boulanger had himself been to Switzerland to make exactly the same promise to the elderly Prince Napoleon. In Paris, the Royalist newspaper *Le Gaulois* compared Boulanger to the battering-ram or cannon-ball which was to make the breach through which the Monarchy was to pass on its way back to power. Since the New Year, Paris was deluged with posters, anti-Republican pamphlets, speeches and processions. Troops of bill-stickers were sent to cover up posters campaigning for Jacques, the leading radical opponent, while crowds marched through the streets ironically singing "Tu dors, pauvre Jacques!" To the brightly coloured posters of Jules Chéret, whose dashing, simple designs had done so much to brighten the walls and hoardings of the city, were added posters showing Boulanger as the Man of Destiny and the Nation's Saviour. In some parts of the city it was even physically dangerous to speak against Boulanger and several well-known Republicans found themselves involved in fisticuffs in Montmartre.

January 27, 1889 was widely expected to be the last day of the Republic. Boulanger had made it a point to establish his headquarters every Sunday evening at a point within equal distance of the President's palace at the Elysée and the Ministries of the Interior and War, so that he might strike at the main centres of government if the need arose. Déroulède had been training his *Ligue* along military lines and it was estimated that he could mobilise some 10,000 armed men within four hours and concentrate them upon any point in Paris within another hour. At the last minute, Déroulède had gone around each Paris *arrondissement* to inspect his groups of "patriots" and there was a widespread rumour that the Paris garrison and fort commanders were ready to support Boulanger should he decide to march on the Elysée and install himself as Head of State. The Republicans could not be confident of the loyalty of the army or the police. Nearly all the barracks in and around Paris had been infiltrated by Boulangist propaganda. NCO's and privates were openly declaring their sympathies and singing Boulangist songs when on leave. It was later learned that even the Presidential guard was commanded by a Boulangist officer. With their usual egotism, Parisians believed that the result of one Paris by-election would decide the fate of all France. The election result seemed a foregone conclusion and even if Boulanger were not to make a *coup d'état* immediately, his party was expected to win the general elections to be held in the autumn and thus inevitably bring in a personal system of government.

The evening of the election, huge crowds gathered in the Place de la Madeleine outside the Restaurant Durand where Boulanger and his supporters were dining while waiting for the results to be announced. Also present were Déroulède, some heads of various sections of the *Ligue*, and the Duchesses d'Uzès and de la Trémoïlle. It was less well known that Boulanger's beloved mistress, Madame de Bonnemains, was also waiting discreetly for her lover in another room.

The election result was impressive. Boulanger was given a majority of more than 80,000 over his nearest rival by obtaining a total of 245,236 votes. It was impossible to preserve order in the streets and boulevards. Carriages were stopped by the crowd and passengers forced to cry "Vive Boulanger!" In the restaurant, Boulanger's companions urged him to make his way to the Elysée in a triumphal procession and take over. Déroulède solemnly told him that the army was for him, the people were for him, the police were for him, France was for him and Europe itself was "only two steps away". But Boulanger refused to march against his President. He would not even show himself to the crowd outside. It was said of him that his nerve failed at the last moment. A more charitable explanation might be that at the last moment a vestige of common sense held him back. The government of the Republic was the legally elected representative of the French people. *Boulangisme* had been a great adventure so far and the adulation of his supporters had gone to Boulanger's head. So far, he had not committed any really serious illegal act. Why then should he attempt to take power illegally, at the risk of violence, when he could be certain of winning it legally six months later at the general elections? His supporters were pushing him too far and too quickly. He reminded his hearers that Napoleon III's Second Empire had been brought to downfall by the circumstances of its origins. There would be no *coup d'état*. Instead, he drove away from the restaurant to go to bed with his mistress. The fickle Parisians knew that they could expect no more grand gestures from him. "Boulangism has begun to slump from this moment," one observer remarked.

The government regained courage. Boulanger was later warned that he could expect arrest and a few months later he fled to Brussels with Madame de Bonnemains. He was condemned in his absence to deportation by the High Court. Déroulède's *Ligue des Patriotes* was declared an illegal organisation, he and his supporters were fined, and in the autumn elections, only thirty-eight Boulangist deputies and 172 conservatives were returned to the Chamber as against 366 Republicans, despite Boulanger's manifestoes to the French people from abroad. In 1891, his suicide on his mistress's grave came as a last sad footnote to the whole tragi-comical affair.

The rise and fall of *Boulangisme* was an astonishing and singularly Parisian episode. The movement was born in Paris and died there. Although Parisians still tended to believe that they could make and unmake regimes, Boulanger was essentially a "paper tiger". One reason why he had appeared such a formidable menace to the government was that neither Carnot nor his ministers realised the basic strength of their regime. Their confidence had been badly shaken. After the "affair of the decorations" in

1887, 1889 had seemed a year of destiny. While work went on at the exhibition site, foreign ambassadors preferred to frequent the *salons* of the Opposition, since they too did not believe that the Republic could last much longer. Although a law had been passed in 1886 forbidding the Royal Pretender to reside in France, the Royalists were a considerable political force. They had been strengthened by the clerical party since Jules Ferry had begun war on the church of France by expelling the Jesuits and other religious congregations in 1880. The idea that France could return to a monarchy seemed perfectly feasible. In 1889, in a book on contemporary Paris high society, a young woman journalist, Juliette Adam, writing under a pseudonym "Count Paul Vasili", thought it worth devoting a forty-page chapter to a description of what the French king's court would be like. Who the French king was to be had still to be decided among the various Royalist factions. Meanwhile, the Duc d'Aumale, the head of the House of Orleans, had made a significant offering to the Republic by giving it his château and art collections of Chantilly—a gift to the French nation.

France was growing more prosperous and more bourgeois. It was also becoming increasingly democratic despite obvious and frequent social injustices. The great war debts owed to victorious Germany had been paid off a year ahead of schedule, in September 1873, after a fantastically popular appeal to the French public to invest in a government loan. France's colonial empire was also growing fast in the 1880's. In 1881, Tunisia became a protectorate, in 1883 a protectorate was established over Annam in Indo-China, in 1884 Tonkin was occupied, in 1885 Cambodia became another protectorate, and France was steadily making territorial gains in Africa.

The regime was becoming bourgeois. The resignation of the President, Marshal Macmahon, in January 1879 in favour of the seventy-one-year-old lawyer Jules Grévy marked the transition from an aristocratic-minded, clerical, military and reactionary government still obsessed by the Paris Commune to a more materialist, democratic and tolerant middle-class government. Although the *grande bourgeoisie* dominated France, the spirit in which they did so was more in harmony with that of the broad mass of the people—particularly the Parisians. Significantly, the 14th of July was first celebrated as a national holiday in 1880.

The 1880's in Paris saw the collapse of many class barriers. The old upper classes and especially the old nobility lost much of their surviving importance in a world which favoured the opportunist, the self-made man, and the ambitious social climber. There were, of course, many scandals, social and financial as well as political. Conservatives saw Jews everywhere; the aristocrats in Paris, living in their palatial *hôtels-particuliers*, deplored a growing disrespect for the old values, the rise of the lower orders, their talent for making money and their skill in acquiring upper-class wives to give them social tone. Guy de Maupassant's *Bel Ami* gave a characteristic and revealing picture of Paris life at the time, with its cynical, clever journalist hero moving from one class to another with perfect amorality and lack of scruples, finally to have his new social status ratified by a smart wedding to the boss's daughter in the fashionable Madeleine church.

Such people had little inclination for Boulangist or Royalist adventures. The rising new rich—who could rise faster in Paris than anywhere else in France—needed peace and a stable regime. Many of Boulanger's supporters had come from the artisan and shop-keeper class, as well as from the army, a section of the aristocracy, the royalists and such extremists as Déroulède. The crowds who demonstrated in the streets of Paris had frightened the government, for they had revived the nightmare of violence in the city. The Republic badly needed confidence in itself and the success of the Exposition gave it reassurance.

The great fêtes of the Exposition and the centenary of the Revolution did much to make Carnot a popular figure with Parisians. Over thirty-two million attendances were registered at the exhibition. Even high society forgot its prejudices to some extent by coming to enjoy itself. The Eiffel Tower was a great attraction and even received a social accolade from smart society when young ladies of the best families discovered how amusing it was to send off little gas-filled balloons with messages attached from the upper platform. Protests against the tower's ugliness became fewer. If ever there was an eyesore at the exhibition it was the enormous Gallery of Machines at the other end of the

Champ-de-Mars which completely blocked the view of the noble façade of the Ecole Militaire.

Royalty and distinguished foreign visitors came from abroad. The Prince of Wales and Thomas Edison climbed the tower and signed the visitors' book; a phonograph was installed in the lantern and artistes from the Paris Opéra made a recording of the "Marseillaise". The Colonial Section illustrated France's recent conquests and offered such additional attractions as the faithful reconstitution of a street in Cairo complete with belly-dancers, and Javanese dancers. The whole event was a clamorous success. The Tower obstinately refused to satisfy the pessimists by falling down and it even paid for itself in the first year of its life. The Republic was safe and a plaster model of the new statue of the Triumph of the Republic was set up in the Place de la Nation in the presence of President Carnot in September. As the pavilions of the exhibition came down in November, Paris had revealed its charms to an unprecedented number of foreign visitors from all over the world. They made the agreeable discovery that the Paris populace was not likely to revolt in the streets at any moment, that Paris was the most beautiful city they had ever seen, and that, of all capital cities, it was the one where a civilised man was likely to enjoy himself the most amid the greatest range of pleasures imaginable.

Since the beginning of the century, Paris had nearly doubled in size. The area of the city remained practically the same between the Revolution and the establishment of the Second Empire. In 1801, it had a population of 548,000 inhabitants. By 1860, Paris had grown by an extent of roughly 400 *hectares* by absorbing the intervening *communes* between the old exterior boulevards and the most recent line of fortifications. Its population had more than doubled and in 1886, according to the latest census, it had reached 2,344,550. The overall aspect of the city had also been transformed since Napoleon I had given it its noble Rue de Rivoli and Louis-Philippe its Arc de Triomphe. It was during the Second Empire that Napoleon III's prefect Haussmann had made medieval Paris into modern Paris by cutting brutally through its centuries-old mazes of narrow streets and alleys with broad new boulevards.

Paris became criss-crossed with new thoroughfares designed partly for reasons of convenience and hygiene, partly because of aesthetic considerations, and partly for political and military purposes.

When the Commune came to its tragic end in May 1871, large areas in the city had been ravaged by fire and artillery. Entire streets were destroyed between the Place de la Concorde and the Hôtel de Ville. The historic Tuileries Palace had gone, the Palais-Royal and the Gobelins were damaged, the Vendôme column had been pulled down by the insurgents, the Hôtel de Ville was reduced to rubble, the Palace of the Legion of Honour and the old Cour des Comptes had also been razed, and large parts of Belleville and Montmartre lay in ruins. But by 1889, the Hôtel de Ville was rebuilt, the Opéra was completed and had been inaugurated, large blocks of flats were built all over the city and there was little to show that Paris had suffered a siege and a civil war.

From the military point of view, Paris was the most fortified capital city in the world. It was virtually a walled citadel, like a medieval city-stronghold. It was protected by an inner *enceinte* consisting of ninety-four sections, each nearly a quarter of a mile long, with an average height of twelve yards and a total circumference of twenty and a half miles. There were bastions, a ditch eighteen feet deep and anything from eighteen to fifty yards wide, sixty-five entrances and, among them, ten openings for railway lines. The approaches to this inner line were defended by a second circle of seventeen forts. Most had been destroyed during the siege of 1870, but they had been rebuilt since with added protective features, and they ringed Paris about two miles from the first line. Yet another circle of forts had been built on the heights overlooking the Seine valley, at a much greater distance from the city, in a seventy-seven-mile-long ring taking in such nearby towns as Versailles, Enghien, Sceaux, Ecouen, Châtillon, Saint-Cyr, Marly and Saint-Germain-en-Laye. Paris was generally esteemed to be impregnable and her fortifications the most advanced in the world.

The city within the first *enceinte* was not so very different in aspect from what it is today. Of the great boulevards, the Hauss-

mann stopped short at the Rue Taitbout instead of linking up with the Boulevard des Italiens, and the Raspail was only complete in sections. What then gave Paris an added charm, long since vanished, was its surprisingly rustic air in many quarters. Montmartre had open spaces, windmills and country cottages, and was still a country hamlet although it had recently become popular with artists and writers. Despite all the horrors it had witnessed in 1871, Belleville, the highest part of Paris, still had the purest air in Paris, the finest views and the greatest rural charm. Cows grazed at Auteuil, market gardens at Passy and behind Montparnasse supplied fresh vegetables for the city, Montparnasse itself looked like part of a quiet provincial town that had been incorporated into the capital by accident, and several other districts retained a most un-metropolitan placidity.

The Seine was more animated than it is today, with its *bateaux-lavoirs* for washerwomen and its *bateaux-mouches* gaily decorated with pennants and streamers. For most Parisians of moderate means, the favourite places for their Sunday outings were just outside Paris, along the river at Neuilly, the Isle of La Grande Jatte, Bougival, Argenteuil, Charenton or along the Marne. It was there by preference that they would spend their Sundays fishing, picnicking *en famille*, dancing in *guinguettes* among the trees and eating the delicious little fried fish from the river. There were fairs and sideshows in the Parc de Vincennes and a general air of simple, popular enjoyment and family pleasure that was lovingly recorded by writers and painters of the time.

But for the true city-lover, the tourist, the dandy, the man-about-town and the pleasure-seeker, Paris's most attractive feature were her magnificent, spacious, tree-lined boulevards. For many Parisians the boulevards *were* Paris. They were the quintessence of the city and it was there, as nowhere else, that the life of the city could be observed at its richest, its most varied, its most colourful and its most exciting. The Paris boulevards provided a perpetual entertainment and made the city unique. Songs were written about them, they inspired writers, the most elegant cafés were situated on them and they fascinated foreigners. Once the foreign visitor had arrived in Paris and taken possession of his hotel room, there was no question where to go once he

had visited the Exposition and made the ascent of the tower to marvel at the panorama of Paris. Pigalle, Montmartre, Saint-Germain and Montparnasse were not yet tourist magnets, and the Mecca for the tourist consisted of the boulevards near the Opéra, the Capucines and the Italiens, and the Avenue de l'Opéra. It was there, in a relatively small area, that the greatest and most fashionable cafés were situated, the Grand Café and the Café de la Paix on the Capucines, the Café Anglais on the Italiens and the Café de Paris on the Avenue. The tourist could sit for hours watching the never-ending procession of fellow idlers, dandies of the day, journalists and society personalities, and the great ladies of both the *monde* and the *demi-monde* displaying the latest fashions.

Unlike London, Paris did not yet have its underground railway system and the streets and boulevards were every bit as crowded and certainly livelier than they are today. All of human life was to be seen along the boulevards. It could be seen at its most elegant along the Boulevards de la Madeleine, the Capucines and the Italiens, at its more mixed along the Boulevards Montmartre, Poissonière and Bonne-Nouvelle (*Baedeker's Guide* for 1889 advised families against frequenting the cafés on the *north* side of the Italiens and Montmartre "as the company there is far from select"), and at its most raffish, popular and working-class along the Boulevards Saint-Denis, Saint-Martin and Beaumarchais towards the Bastille. To walk the full length of the *grands boulevards* from west to east was a heady, exciting experience in the most beautiful pleasure-giving capital in the world.

The exchange stood at twenty-five francs to the pound. A cup of coffee and a glass of brandy from the graded *carafon*, which the waiter would often bring and leave on the table, were less than a franc. In 1887, Augustus Hare informed his fellow-countrymen in his book *Paris* that "nowhere is existence cheaper than at Paris for those who know how to manage. A bachelor who does not mind mounting five pairs of stairs may have a charming little apartment for about £1 a week." He also stated that a well-furnished room with "breakfast, lights and attendance" in one of the smaller hotels seldom cost more than thirty shillings a week and recommended the chain of the Restaurants Duval, or

bouillons as they were known, where you could have an excellent dinner with coffee and a glass of brandy for between 2 francs and 2 francs 50 centimes. *Baedeker's Guide* for 1889 estimated that one should be able to limit one's expenses to fifteen to twenty francs a day but warned that Paris, ''where luxury is raised to a science'', might well be one of the costliest cities in Europe.

The English still held pride of place among the big spenders from abroad. Diplomatic relations might be in an almost permanent state of strain between the two countries, but English visitors could be sure of being well and efficiently catered for in Paris. They tended to stay in the great hotels along the Rue de Rivoli or the Rue Castiglione, the Meurice, the Brighton, the Rivoli, the Saint James and Albany and the Oxford and Cambridge. They could rely on their English tea and breakfasts, there were two English pastrycooks' establishments in Paris and if they suddenly succumbed to nostalgia for honest English fare they could dine at such English restaurants as Richard-Lucas in the Place de la Madeleine, Austin's in the Rue d'Amsterdam and Hill's on the Boulevard des Capucines. If they were afraid of catching a sudden chill they could go to 23, Boulevard des Italiens and buy Dr. Jaeger's ''sanitary woollen clothing''. If they found the cafés too noisy for their taste they could drink at one of the new-style Anglo-American ''bars'' that had recently opened in the city. The first was the ''Eureka'' at number 2, Rue des Mathurins. It had been founded by Henry Ridgway, a famous dandy and sporting man and the friend of all the leading Paris Anglophiles. He had specially brought over a barman from London and his English visitors could always be certain of finding themselves at home there and of being able to meet someone with whom they could discuss racing form and the latest club gossip from London.

Ladies went to the great fashion houses of Worth or Laferrière and gastronomes went to the Grand Véfour in the arcades of the Palais-Royal, Lapérouse by the Seine, or Ledoyen on the Champs-Elysées. If they wished to catch a glimpse of *tout-Paris* of 1889, they could take a cab after dinner for a cup of chocolate at the suffocatingly fashionable café-restaurant Chévillard at the Rond-Point des Champs-Elysées. But on the whole, when they had done

their round of sight-seeing, most foreign visitors would congregate after dinner at the cafés around the Rue Scribe and the Rue de la Paix, then the centre of high fashion and boulevard life at its most splendid. In the daytime they might go further afield and join the leisurely throng of Parisians making their way up the Champs-Elysées towards the Bois de Boulogne, the favourite playground of the upper classes.

The Avenue des Champs-Elysées was not the brash and commercial thoroughfare it has since become. It was green and picturesque, with great private mansions scattered among the trees, including the sumptuous *hôtel-particulier* that had once belonged to La Paiva, one of the greatest of all the *demi-mondaines*, the palatial town residence of the Duchesse d'Uzès, on the site of the present Claridge's hotel, and the noble mansions of the Duc de Trévise and the Duc de Massa. The Avenue was still the best address in Paris for the aristocracy of wealth but it had a more intimate, popular charm thanks to its numerous sideshows, its stalls selling toys and gingerbread, its Punch and Judy shows, its children's roundabouts, its miniature carriages for children, drawn by goats, its cafés and its highly fashionable summer circus where the most snobbish children in Paris would be taken if they behaved themselves. After the Rue de la Paix, it was *the* place where one might watch the high mode of Paris and see the most celebrated representatives of the two aristocracies of money and blood appearing in public.

Every morning and every afternoon at about five o'clock in the season, passers-by and the curious could watch riders and coaches coming out from the streets of the Faubourg Saint-Honoré and from across the river to ride along the beaten-earth avenue towards the Bois in a glittering cortège which included high-born dandies and their female counterparts, the beautifully costumed *amazones* like the Baroness Adolphe de Rothschild who always rode escorted by two grooms wearing cockaded top hats. Duels were still being fought in the Bois, amorous intrigues would be discreetly planned there and every morning the *amazones* would gallop between the Porte Dauphine and the Champ des Courses to stop at the Pré Catelan for refreshment and to exchange gossip.

Electricity gave Paris an added splendour. 1889 was not only the year of the Eiffel Tower but the beginning of Paris as the "Ville Lumière". The first electric lights went on in the Place du Carrousel, the Parc Monceau and on the Buttes Chaumont. Most theatres, department stores, railway stations and the Palais Royal were lit up by the *fée électricité* as it was nicknamed. The main monuments of the city and the exhibition were also lit up by electricity for the celebrations of the centenary. To the more fortunate Parisians it was yet another reason to feel proud of their city and to the others it could have been a sign of the better life to come. Socialism and science would combine to redress the social inequalities that still aroused so much bitterness and rancour beneath the surface glitter of Paris in the glorious year of the Centenary.

Since 1789, the main changes in the exterior physiognomy of Paris occurred during the two Empires. The social face of the city had also been changing. The areas least touched by the great architects and Haussmann's surgery were those where the greatest poverty and squalor were still to be found. The districts around the Bastille, the Gobelins, the Rue Saint-Antoine and the Halles, that *ventre de Paris* as Zola had called it, were in an almost medieval state of decrepitude and poverty and inhabited by the direct descendants of the people who had fought in the revolutions of 1789, 1848 and 1871. Ill-lit, stinking narrow streets and alleys still ran down towards the Seine in the centre of Paris and in the suburbs new slums were beginning to fester as Paris's immigrant population increased. In his memoirs, the Duc de La Force recalled how his mother, one of the patrons of the *Oeuvre des Faubourgs,* would visit the slums in the Ternes district between Paris and Neuilly to give alms and comfort to the needy. Such scenes were not rare. A great number of charitable organisations were founded by society ladies who would often make a point of putting on their very best afternoon wear before going on their missions—perhaps to show their less fortunate fellow-citizens that the upper classes had not forgotten them. Their attitude was often patronising and inevitably such activities became admirable pretexts for elegant social functions. Charity was fashionable and practically every great family in Paris was patron of its own special organisation for the relief of the needy.

Before the Revolution, the old Paris nobility had lived in their palaces and mansions in the Marais district, that area between the Boulevard Sébastopol and the Bastille, north of the Rue Saint-Antoine and south of the *grands boulevards*. They lived in the midst of the people who rose against the regime they represented and who howled for their blood during the Terror. By the mid-19th century, the old aristocracy and the new "upper classes" had moved away from what was becoming an increasingly insalubrious district. They congregated in newer districts in the west of Paris while many of the fine old 16th- and 17th-century *hôtels* were neglected and fell into disrepair. Balzac had observed that the *grande bourgeoisie* and the aristocracy were occupying private mansions mostly in the areas of the Rue Saint-Honoré and the Faubourg Saint-Germain while the other social classes tended to mix horizontally and separate themselves vertically, each living according to his station and means on one of the levels of the new blocks of flats put up during the great building boom of the '50's and '60's.

In a typical block of rented flats, known as an *immeuble de rapport*, the well-to-do *bourgeois* would live with his family in a large flat with as many as ten rooms, on the ground or the first floor. Above him would live one of his higher-graded employees, higher still, an artisan or a worker, and still higher, up in the attics, the servants, the seamstresses and the poor students. But as the bourgeois became richer he might leave the building to look for a more select and private residence in one of the newly fashionable districts like the Plaine Monceau. While workers and peasants from the provinces came into Paris and swelled the populations of the "red" suburbs, the very rich, the well-to-do and the titled congregated in the *beaux-quartiers*.

Of all the *beaux-quartiers*, none was more jealously kept as the preserve of the old aristocracy in Paris than the Faubourg Saint-Germain, the Left Bank district facing the Louvre and the Tuileries Gardens and extending behind the Chamber of Deputies towards the esplanade of the Invalides. The aristocracy of wealth might live in the Faubourg Saint-Honoré, opposite, on the Right Bank, or on the Champs-Elysées. But the *crème de la crème* of Paris society, the last surviving representatives of *ancien régime* Paris, the descendants of France's oldest princely and ducal families, lived in the austere but elegant mansions of the Rue de Lille, Rue de l'Université, Rue de Varenne and Rue de Grenelle among the embassies and ministries. In 1889 they represented all that was most conservative and die-hard in Paris.

Life in the Faubourg Saint-Germain was stiflingly exclusive. As "Paul Vasili" observed in *La Société de Paris*, published in 1890, "One of the peculiarities of Paris society is the impenetrable secrecy in which it wraps itself". The old families, the Lévis-Mirepoix, the Noailles, the Talleyrand-Périgords, the Brissacs and the Gontaut-Birons, lived according to a strictly observed ritual. The ruling spirit was that of the family. To a large extent they were already a fossilised relic of a past society, and as their political and social power declined, they became increasingly obsessed by their genealogies and the need to maintain a kind of *ancien régime* ideological purity. They were the people who closed their shutters on the 14th of July, who stayed away from the Exposition, who refused to put out tricolour flags for the Centenary celebrations and who remained aloof while the rest of Paris enjoyed itself in the open. The only Republican celebration they could permit themselves to attend, if they were not already out of Paris by that time, was the annual military review at Longchamps where General Boulanger had cut such a dashing figure in 1886, winning over the Paris populace and inspiring the song *En r'venant de la revue*. Otherwise, when they were not holding court in their discreet *salons*, they would escape to the country, to hunt and to spend holidays at the select resorts of Trouville, Dieppe or Luchon in the Pyrenees. They did not really like Paris, for, to them, everything outside the Faubourg was vulgar and *parvenu*. Although they were generally Royalist in their sympathies and might dream of a Restoration, they knew that the new age was not going to be *their* age. They were so conservative that even electricity was too modern for them and many noble households continued to use petrol lamps rather than the new lighting system.

One of the top names in Paris high society in 1889 was the aged Duchesse de Maille, a kind of unofficial mother figure who had been receiving her worshipping flock every Sunday afternoon for the past thirty years. She was stout and imposing, was known for her dictatorial manners, her blunt speech and occasional severity. She ruled over a vast brood of relatives, grandchildren and charitable societies and occasionally appeared in the streets of Paris in a huge, old-fashioned landau drawn by one of the finest teams of horses in the city. Like the Duchesse, the other descendants of France's oldest families devoted much of their time to family gatherings and stiff receptions in their drawing-rooms. One of the most magnificent *salons* was that held by the Duchesse de Polignac in the Hôtel de Crillon (now the hotel of the same name) overlooking the Place de la Concorde or, still, the Place Louis XV to the really conservative. The Duchesse had all the virtues expected of such an aristocratic hostess. She had the right kind of beauty with just that hint of noble sadness appropriate to one obliged to live in something as vulgar as a Republic. She was delicate-featured, gracious, queenly, a devoted wife and mother, and her life had never been touched by the slightest hint of impropriety.

The institution of the *salon* was born and most greatly flourished in the 18th century. It continued throughout the 19th century and still had an important part to play in the literary, artistic and political life of the city. But the majority of aristocratic *salons* were very dull indeed. "Vasili" gave a depressing description of the *salon* of the Comtesse de Lévis-Mirepoix, a singularly cold and cheerless woman with a husband considered haughty even by the standards of the Faubourg: "Flattering though her receptions may otherwise be, they lack the charm of kindness and simplicity. Her visitors have the vague impression of having entered some classical shrine of good manners and social virtues, and feel that they are generally called upon to keep up, by their presence, conversation and general behaviour, the tradition of good company." The same might be said of a good many other such gatherings. The reigning atmosphere was much the same with guests going through the wearisome forms of social behaviour with a precision and a conformity which seemed to be a last reflection of the courtly, soulless ceremonial imposed by Louis XIV on his long-suffering courtiers in his later years at Versailles.

Not all the great households were so grimly solemn. There were splendid parties and balls, scandals and love affairs. But every slip was noted and remembered. Everyone was expected to conform and originality was not a quality in great demand. The code of manners was hostile to anything in the least unexpected and conversation was of a uniform, excruciating dullness. If the company were especially Royalist-minded, one might enquire after the exiled Comte de Paris or discuss the chances of a Restoration but otherwise the main topics were the weather, the latest birth, death or wedding, and some eminent person who was safely dead and buried.

Life in the Faubourg revolved around receiving guests and paying visits. It had been the custom to pay friendly social calls in the hour immediately after lunch. At three o'clock, carriages would be ordered, the ladies would put on their afternoon, visiting dresses and drive off to see their lady friends and chatter about clothes, children and charities. English-style tea-parties were becoming very popular and were known as "five o'clocks", with society ladies loading their tables with novelties and delicacies from the best London stores.

By 1889, it was fast becoming the custom to pay calls only on certain appointed days. Servants went from one house to the next, leaving their masters' visiting cards. Formal calls would be made between three and seven in the afternoon. Every great household would have its "at home" one evening during the Lent season but they were no more enjoyable. The younger and more high-spirited guests regarded them as an irksome bore. You were expected to exchange some stiffish conventionalities with your host for some fifteen minutes before leaving and it was remarked that there was something indecent in the haste with which certain guests would attempt to discharge their duty before rushing out for their carriages to take them where Paris was really enjoying itself.

The great Faubourg families had little to contribute to the culture of the time, even though they might pay lip-service to the arts. "Vasili"'s comment on the society of 1889 is interesting:

"Having lost its former grandeur, the French aristocracy became in turn interesting, charming and puerile; it is now simply insignificant. It is very rare to meet in society any person possessed of real originality. As a rule, when a member of the upper classes devotes himself to science or literature, he makes it a point to dwell simply on the trifles dear to society, for fear of arousing spite, jealousy or indifference. On entering a drawing-room, he leaves his intellectual accomplishments behind him—a proof of good taste much appreciated by the upper classes." In the 18th century, the great intellectual *salons* had flourished among the aristocracy but by the late 19th century the cultural *salon* was to be found in less exclusive circles of society. The Faubourg Saint-Germain was generally hostile to artists and writers, no matter how fashionable or well established they might be. "Protect art —never artists" was the motto of one wealthy nobleman and it was a sentiment that was widely shared. A few Faubourg *salons* were open to the occasional author such as Paul Bourget, but if he had ventured to talk of literature it would have been regarded as very bad form.

There were a few notable exceptions but the literary and artistic *salons* that counted were outside the Faubourg. One of the more interesting members of this most conservative of "sets" was the old Princesse de Metternich, a fascinating grandmother who, after leading a life of pleasure, had turned to art and become a passionate Wagnerite, with strong and sometimes disconcerting opinions on literature, painting and politics. The Comtesse de Pourtalès was also known to have cultural inclinations but by far the most scholarly, intellectual and cosmopolitan aristocrat of all was Count Eugène-Melchior de Vogüé. He had made himself an expert on Russian literature and performed an inestimable service for French culture by bringing such writers as Tolstoi and Dostoievski to the attention of French readers for the first time. Perhaps the most colourful younger member of the old aristocracy was Count Robert de Montesquiou, the fanatical admirer of Baudelaire and Mallarmé who toyed at writing poetry himself, belonged to a literary group known as *les déliquescents*, and who had given Huysmans the model for Des Esseintes, the "decadent" hero of *À rebours*. But his spiritual home lay outside the Faubourg, among circles where a *salon* was not merely a place in which the relics of the *ancien régime* came together to pretend that the Revolution had never taken place.

The stiffness and nostalgia of the Faubourg was in direct contrast to the prevailing spirit of Paris. If there was a representative of the aristocracy who really did take part in the social-cultural life of Paris it was the aged Princesse Mathilde, the niece of Napoleon I. She kept open house for dandies, painters and writers but, of course, she was merely a member of the First Empire nobility and the older set could hardly consider as being one of themselves a woman who could remark that if it had not been for her famous uncle "she might still be selling oranges in the streets of Ajaccio".

There was a movement in Paris towards greater freedom and social mobility. Even the old aristocracy of blood was beginning to mingle with the newer aristocracy of money and a rich banker might now find himself regarded as a good marital prospect by circles which would have remained closed to him a decade earlier. At a slightly lower level of society, it was possible for the adventurer, the literary or artistic bohemian of a certain education to make his way. What most Parisians seemed to want more than anything else was to be amused and there was a future for anyone who could be amusing. There was change in the air— too much for some people.

Edmond de Goncourt, still chronicling literary and artistic life in Paris nineteen years after the death of his brother, morosely remarked in his 1889 diary that "in the Paris of today, the Parisian and the Parisienne have begun to become rare beings in this semitic or Auvergnat or Marseillaise society, following the conquest of Paris by Jewry and the South. The truth is that Paris is no longer Paris; it is a kind of free city in which all the thieves of the earth who have made their fortunes in business come to eat badly and sleep with the flesh of someone who calls herself a Parisienne". His racial prejudices were deplorable but it is pleasant to think that had he lived somewhat longer than he did, he would have seen a new conquest of Paris by the poor but talented of the earth who were to give his beloved city an unprecedented cosmopolitan lustre and primacy in the arts. Paris *was* " a kind of free city":

in the past it had radiated culture and civilisation outwards; now, it was to draw into itself some of the greatest talents in the world outside.

There were to be no more violent political revolutions in the city. The coming revolutions were to be of the spirit, in the arts, in the letters, in the theatre. Paris was to become the international artistic and intellectual capital of the world. Its culture and life were to be nourished and reinvigorated by adventurers and bohemians from many different countries. Out of this influx there would emerge a new Paris, with a charm, a diversity, a richness and a fascination far exceeding anything that could be imagined when the Exposition opened.

Conditions were right for a new flowering of Paris. It was sensed at the time that it was one of the freest cities on earth. Again and again, writers and visitors to Paris in the late 1880's and '90's commented on the atmosphere of freedom they found there. They found that it was in Paris that the most complete freedom could be enjoyed, it was there that people could most be themselves and express themselves. They could live as they liked, dress as they liked, write and paint as they liked among a people with a passion for novelty, whether it was the latest sporting craze like bicycling or the latest literary *ism*. It was a place where they could be ignored, attacked or applauded by some of the wittiest, most heartless, cynical, enthusiastic and sophisticated city dwellers in the world. There was freedom of the press, freedom to express even the most outrageous political convictions, freedom to create and innovate, and freedom to look forward with the highest hopes.

In 1889, André Gide began his *Journal* with a single entry, dated *autumn*. The young aspiring writer described how he and his friend since school-days, Pierre Louÿs, ascended to the sixth floor of a house in the Rue Monsieur-le-Prince to look at a room in which they planned to hold their literary reunions. They came to a large unfurnished room under the roof, with a view "over the roofs of the Ecole de Médecine, over the Latin Quarter, grey houses as far as the eye could reach, the Seine and Notre-Dame in the sunset, and far away in the distance, Montmartre, barely visible in the rising mists of the evening". There, wrote Gide who had still to publish his first book, "we both dreamt of the life of a poor student in just such a room, with means enough to be free to work. And at one's feet, before one's table, Paris. And of shutting oneself up in there with the dream of one's masterpiece, and only to come out again with it finished.

"The cry of Rastignac's[1] as he looks down on the city from the heights of the Père Lachaise: 'and now! . . . *à nous deux!*' "

A nous deux! The challenge was to be repeated many times in the next quarter century. A new age and a new revolution were beginning in Paris, unnoticed by its citizens. But even while they were maturing, the city was entering into the "Nineties", a period which certainly had its fair share of troubles and turmoils but which had such vitality, such charm and such colour and abundance of pleasure that it has since become known to nostalgic Parisians as *la Belle Epoque*.

[1] Rastignac was Balzac's young hero who came to Paris from the provinces to make his fortune. He first appears in *Le Père Goriot*, looking at the city for the first time from his attic window, defiantly crying: "Paris, à nous deux!" ("Paris, it's between you and me now!")

II

THE PLEASURE CAPITAL

LIKE THE Nineties elsewhere, the 1890's in Paris now conjure up images of pleasure and gay abandon. In 1887, in his book *Paris,* Augustus Hare already wrote that "pleasure at Paris becomes business; indeed, a large portion of the upper classes of Parisians have no time for anything else". That Paris was first and foremost a Mecca for frivolous sensualists with money to spend seemed confirmed to the eyes of the many foreigners who came to see the 1889 Exposition. No other great world capital seemed to cater so efficiently and with such devotion to the needs of the pleasure-seeker. At the same time as the Exposition, the fall of *Boulangisme* and the rise of the Eiffel Tower, Montmartre became the centre of Paris entertainment. In 1889, the Moulin Rouge opened its doors, the great red wooden sails of its windmill above the entrance began to turn and an entire decade in the city's life began to pass from history into myth.

Montmartre, *la butte sacrée,* was not only a place of pleasure but of pilgrimage. It was the sacred hill of Saint Denis, the first bishop of Paris and the traditional site of his martyrdom. The 417-feet-high eminence had a turbulent history. Henri of Navarre had bombarded the city from its heights, in 1589, shortly before becoming King Henri IV. A last desperate battle had been fought there against the Allies in 1814. Montmartre had been a commune outside the administrative area of Paris until 1860 when it had been annexed by the capital, and in 1871 it had become a symbol for the rebellious Commune when mutinous soldiers had murdered the generals Thomas and Lecomte before seizing the cannon stationed on the heights from the National Guard. Four years later, the hill was chosen as the site of the symbol of national reconciliation: the Sacré Coeur. By the end of 1889, long before the neo-Byzantine, neo-Romanesque basilica had been completed, the foot of the *butte* had become a new Mecca to pleasure seekers and a new Babylon to the censorious.

The highest part of the hill was a picturesque spot in 1889. A few of its many windmills still survived, wine had been made until recently from a vineyard on its slopes, and its *maquis*, a large patch of open ground that was dotted with small cottages and gardens, gave it an undeniably rural air. In the late 1880's painters in search of peace and good air had begun to migrate to the hill and by 1870 it was already the home of a flourishing artists' colony and a popular rendez-vous for writers, journalists and "Bohemians". A more popular attraction was its dance hall perched high up near the summit, the Moulin de la Galette, which Renoir had painted in 1876 but for most Parisians the centre of attraction was the Clichy and Pigalle area at the foot of the hill in Lower Montmartre. Ever since the 18th century, the district had been notorious for its great number of *cabarets*, taverns and dance halls and other drinking establishments. Until Lower Montmartre had been incorporated into the city of Paris in 1790, wine merchants going through the barriers into the capital had been forced to pay high tolls, even on inferior wines. The natural result was a large number of wine shops and *guingettes* where thirsty Parisians might drink more cheaply than on the other side of the barrier. With the wine shops there came a floating population of prostitutes, thieves and smugglers, tricksters, conjurers, pimps and singers, gypsies and dancers. By the late 19th century, the district was a centre of Parisian night life with its dance- and music-halls and its *café-concerts* where working men could hear an assortment of traditional songs on such themes as wine, women and political events. On October 6, 1889, a new era began for Montmartre as the Moulin Rouge opened its doors for the first time and made the *can-can* world famous.

The *can-can* had been born during the Second Empire. It was one of those dances which seemed to resume the gaiety of an age, like the Charleston of the Twenties. After the Franco-Prussian War and the Commune it had survived to a certain extent among the working classes who called it *le chahut*, a word signifying din and rumbustiousness. Rumbustious the new *can-can* certainly was. It was not a dance for the elegant and the sophisticated, and one of its first homes was the Moulin de la Galette.

The Moulin was a descendant of the Second Empire *bals musettes*. A wooden barrier separated the dance floor from rough wooden tables where customers drank the speciality of the house: pitchers of mulled wine. It was certainly not a "respectable" establishment, being an authentic working-class haunt with a public largely composed of working girls and working men on a spree together with an assortment of pimps, prostitutes, petty thieves and local toughs. On week-days it was particularly raffish and more than one underworld feud had been settled by a quick knife blow in the dark streets and winding lanes around it. On Sundays, however, the Moulin de la Galette had a more innocent air of festivity as young apprentices, white-collar employees and their sweethearts came up to the Butte for a sample of popular pleasures and a pleasurable suggestion of low life. Those who danced there did so solely for their own pleasure and occasionally the brassy orchestra would play Offenbach's champagne-light, frothy *can-can* tunes and the dancers would do their own im- provised version of the quadrille with much lifting of grubby skirts and petticoats. This was the *chahut*—an expression of hila- rious high spirits rather like an 1890's version of a "Knees up Mother Brown" in a Cockney pub.

The *chahut* was also to be seen at the Elysée-Montmartre, another descendant of one of the many dance halls just outside the city walls. It was no more fashionable than the Moulin de la Galette at first, for when it opened the upper classes of Paris society had not yet discovered the joys of slumming among the dance halls and *café-concerts* of Montmartre. But with its garden where nature was embellished with mock palm-trees made of zinc it had a certain charm. Polkas and waltzes would be danced there to the accompaniment of a brass band and an accordion while an ancient guardian, Du Rocher or "Father Modesty" as he was better known, would stroll among the couples to prevent any excessive immodesty. Ironically enough, it was there that the most immodest of dancers sprang out of obscurity.

The band-leader at the Elysée-Montmartre, Dufour, had had the genial idea of reviving the Second Empire quadrille which was

a splendid excuse for high kicks and a display of swirling petticoats and knickers which were not always as white as could be
desired. The dance was a difficult one for the general public,
demanding a high degree of training and great physical agility and
assumed the character of a spectacle. It was danced by girls
alone, without male partners, and although the basic steps are
easy to describe there was much scope for improvisation, depending on the imagination and vitality of the dancer.

As the band struck up, the girls would come out to the centre
of the dance floor, start with a few relatively simple steps and then
work up to a frenzy, spinning around like tops, turning cart-
wheels sometimes, and punctuating their gyrations with the
famous high kick, the *port d'armes* ("shoulder arms"), when the
dancer would stand on the toes of one foot, holding the other
foot as high as possible with one hand. The other main feature
of the *chahut* was the *grand écart* or "splits" when the dancer would
make a spectacular finish by sitting down on the floor with both
legs stretched out absolutely horizontally. It was a noisy, stamping dance, it was earthy and animal, performed to a rough-and-
ready clientèle in an atmosphere of tobacco smoke, sweat and
cheap perfume and, in the person of one dancer known as La
Goulue, it became highly erotic.

Her real name was Louise Weber and she was born in about
1865. Her curious nickname which literally meant "glutton"
came from her habit of greedily sucking every last dreg from
glasses and, no doubt, from her voracious appetite for food and
sexual pleasure. She had been a washer-girl, an artists' model
and a dancer from her 'teens. A genuine child of the streets, she
wandered from café to café, dance hall to dance hall, and with
her cheekiness, her boisterous high spirits and animal vitality
she soon became a well-known figure in the district. She seems
to have been abominably spoilt from an early age since her earthy
sexiness and frank vulgarity had brought her champagne, money
and other favours from the richer customers at the dance halls.
In the mid-Eighties she was performing as one of the leading
dancers of the *chahut* at the Elysée-Montmartre and it is not
surprising that the dance that made her famous should have
been the one that best allowed her to display her high spirits and

anatomy. There is no better description of her in her early years than that of an eye-witness Georges Montorgeuil, a talented journalist and chronicler of Paris in the 1890's:

"Pink and blonde, about eighteen years old, with a wilful, vicious and ruddy-hued baby face, a nose with quivering, impatient nostrils, a nose of one sniffing after love, nostrils dilating with the male odour of chestnut trees and the enervating bouquet of brandy glasses, a mouth gluttonous and sensual, a look shameless and provoking, a milky-white bosom freely escaping from her corsage, such was the little washerwoman who had rediscovered the *can-can* as though by instinct . . . she was the pretty girl unaware of any modesty or constraint."

Refinement of any sort was unknown to La Goulue. She was heavy and coarse, "more Flemish than Parisienne" as one onlooker remarked, devoid of any real wit, ungainly and clumsy in her manners except when carried away in the tumult of the *chahut*. For all this, she was fascinating and helped to create the great sexual myth of Paris in the "Naughty Nineties" when the city became the world capital of erotic pleasure. High spirits, high kicks, dance halls like the Elysée-Montmartre and the Moulin Rouge, and the fleeting glimpse of perhaps two inches of bare feminine flesh between stockings and frilly knickers played a vital part in spreading the myth of "naughty Paris". At a time when women were covered from head to foot and encased by corsets, petticoats and flowing undergarments, such a display as that provided by La Goulue was sensational. How erotic she appeared to her contemporaries was described by Montorgeuil again:

"She dialogues with desire whose progression she reads among the flaming glances darted at her . . . She provokes by the display of bare flesh or that, at any rate, which may be divined amid the turbulent swirl of her underclothes as she purposefully allows a glimpse of a large sample of her naked skin between garter and the first fold of her petticoat by lifting her leg . . . The invitation is brutal, blunt, without feminine grace, almost bestial, in this fleshy girl as she outlines the lascivious meanderings of her sullied imagination with a twist of her limbs and an abrupt swirl of her hips. The apotheosis of this rhythmic merry-go-round in which loins and midriff are used in turn is a last audacity when, bending double, the better to stress her lewd intention, she insolently flings back her petticoats to make a callypygean display of her behind."

La Goulue's dancing partners at the Elysée-Montmartre were quite as curious if not as extrovert. One of the best known was Grille-d'Egout, a more modest women who was delicate and even somewhat refined in her appearance. She was neither pretty nor unattractive and her repulsive nickname, which meant "gutter grating", was given her by the journalist Henri Rochefort who had been particularly impressed by her jutting jaw and mouth with projecting canines which made him think, when it was open, of "two bars against a pink-shadowed hole". She was better spoken and behaved than La Goulue whose coarse boisterousness she seemed to condemn, and her style of dancing was correspondingly different. Where La Goulue was frantic and seemed to go into an orgasmic ecstasy at the climax of the *chahut*, Grille-d'Egout was precise, dignified and almost intellectual. Together they were a sensation. An even more curious foil to La Goulue was provided in the shape of the incredibly bony, angular Valentin-le-Desossé, a male dancer who, with La Goulue, was to find immortality in Toulouse-Lautrec's paintings and sketches.

Valentin's real name was Renaudin and he was a respectable bourgeois whose brother was a notary and who himself owned a wine shop in the Rue Coquillière in the centre of Paris. Dancing was the great passion of his life and his gaunt physique and supple style had earned him the nickname of "le Desossé", the "boneless one". He would spend every evening at Montmartre where he was always in demand as a dancing partner and there he would dance with his peculiar genius and unwavering decorum until he was a well-known figure. He was usually to be found at the Elysée–Montmartre and sometimes even at the Moulin de la Galette. With his striking appearance and the top hat he always wore he was almost as much of an attraction as La Goulue with whom he eventually formed a rather mysterious liaison. For him, "there was no other dancer than La Goulue—for the waltz I mean. The quadrille is nothing but a *chahut*". Nonetheless it was the *chahut* that brought the crowds to Montmartre and it was against the background of the dance that the legend of Montmartre was formed. One who both helped to form the legend and became part of it himself was the dwarf of genius, Toulouse-Lautrec, who haunted Montmartre as though possessed by the district. He seemed to live for the noise and vulgarity of its cabarets, its bars and music halls and could be seen night after night at his specially reserved table at the Elysée-Montmartre and later, the Moulin Rouge, drawing in his sketch-book, stumping around the hall, ordering drink after drink. He would invite his favourite performers to join him during the intervals before going out into the night to wander like a restless ghost in search of another bar or cabaret as though the only life that mattered to him and all the colour, vitality and strangeness of Paris were to be found in the few streets and squares of Montmartre.

Another architect of the fame of Montmartre was the impresario Zidler. With his Moulin Rouge, a Parisian attraction became a world attraction. He had begun his working life as a butcher before entering the world of entertainment. In the early Eighties he had sensed that the centre of Paris's geography of pleasure would henceforth be Montmartre and he had realised the possibilities of the revived *can-can*. There was a vast new clientèle to be attracted from the nearby *café-concerts*, cabarets and music halls and he knew that only some good "public relations" work was needed for the *tout-Paris* and the more respectable public to come to an establishment that would give them the *quadrille naturaliste* in an atmosphere of authentic Parisian vulgarity. What were needed were new surroundings which would be free of the more raffish public which prevented the socially prominent from frequenting Montmartre. He went into association with the brothers Oller, two leading impresarios, and opened two establishments, the Hippodrome and the Jardin de Paris, but he was not satisfied. What he needed was a new café-dance hall in which the *chahut* would be the main attraction. The "stars" were already to be found at the Elysée-Montmartre: all he needed was a new home for them.

He found his site in 1889: a disused dance hall, the Reine Blanche, with a garden facing the Place Blanche in Pigalle. He called in the painter and illustrator Willette to provide the decorations and it was Willette who had the brilliant idea of crowning the façade of the new building with a giant mock windmill with bright red sails that could be made to turn. The interior had a large dance floor surrounded with galleries where the spectators could sit and drink; in the garden he set up a huge plaster elephant which he had acquired from the Exposition and which contained a tiny stage in its belly. He strung fairy lights between the trees and constructed an open-air extension for the main bar. From the moment when the sails of Willette's windmill began to turn, the Moulin Rouge was a huge success. With its curious assortment of attractions, its garden with the hollow elephant in which the belly-dancer Zelaska gave performances, its pastiches of an old Norman cottage and a Spanish palace, the Moulin Rouge had an appeal that drew every social class. At last, the *tout-Paris* had been given the opportunity to enjoy the "real Montmartre" with no loss of dignity and the delicious sensation of participating in the most democratic of Paris pleasures.

Zidler successfully recruited not only La Goulue, Grille-d'Egout and Valentin-le-Desossé (who remained an unpaid performer) but a whole company of dancers with such picture-esque appellations as Rayon d'Or, Cri-Cri, la Sauterelle and Nini Patte-en-l'air. Nini "foot in the air" was one of the older members of a group which had been lured away from the Elysée-Montmartre, much to the owner's dismay. A short, thin, wiry little woman with haggard features and dark, glittering eyes, she taught the *chahut* to others and danced with a kind of controlled frenzy, her foot quivering as she held it high in the *port d'armes* as though charged with a surplus of electric tension. When new girls were hired, Nini would give them lessons in a nearby house where lodging was also provided. There, they would go through their paces and learn the art of the high kick and the "splits", with lectures on just how high they might raise their petticoats without being unseemly. They had to be as strong as horses if they were to survive the course. One dancer, Jeanne Faès, died after severe internal injuries from doing the splits, and another dislocated her knee. While they trained, the house would be besieged by a crowd of gentlemen-callers, would-be "protectors" with various propositions, impresarios and curious hangers-on who would squeeze past the door into the corridor until they were sent packing by Nini's shrill voice.

Grille-d'Egout made the *chahut* more socially acceptable. She lived with her family and talked to her pupils about dancing while stressing her preference for white underclothes, frilly petticoats and tight-fitting panties with the tops of stockings fixed to the garters so that no bare flesh might be detected since "les femmes qui montrent leur peau, c'est sale".[1] She taught a kind of drawing-room *can-can* in which petticoats were not supposed to fly any higher than the knee. Her most distinguished pupil was the actress Réjane who introduced the Moulin Rouge version of the *quadrille naturaliste* into polite Parisian society by demonstrating it before a select private assembly.

In the meantime, the undisputed star of the Moulin Rouge *chahut* was La Goulue, who drew the crowds with her own less inhibited version of the dance. In a short time the Moulin Rouge had become the main tourist attraction in Paris. Night after night, the Place Blanche was packed with carriages from the elegant districts of Passy, Neuilly and the Faubourg Saint-Honoré. Hordes of local costermongers and their girls, artisans, shopgirls, clerks, ladies of the town, American and British tourists besieged the hall as the great red sails of the windmill turned above their heads and inspired at least one well-known song:

> "Moulin Rouge,
> Moulin Rouge,
> Pour qui mouds–tu, Moulin Rouge?
>
> Pour la Mort ou pour L'Amour
> Pour qui mouds–tu jusqu'au jour?"

This was the great period when for people throughout Paris, France, Europe and the world the Moulin Rouge became a synonym for Montmartre, Montmartre a synonym for Paris and Paris—another word for Pleasure. The Moulin Rouge gave immense impetus to the diffusion of a great erotic myth—the myth

---

[1] "Women who show their flesh—that's dirty."

of a naughty, free, uninhibited city of *frou-frou* and champagne, of
the wild music of the quadrille which seemed to urge rich and
poor alike to forget their cares and live for love and laughter only.
Montmartre with its "bohemians", its poets and painters and
singers and flaring lights of its gas jets and electric signs exerted
a powerful fascination upon the minds of a generation and has
continued to fascinate novelists and film-makers ever since.

The reality was more down-to-earth. There was little in common between the lavish imitation of the *can-can* offered by the
modern Folies Bergère and the cinema and the real Moulin
Rouge with its not so glamorous ladies who danced with more
gusto than choreographic precision. It was a somewhat rough-
and-ready dance hall with a variety of entertainments including
popular songs and music-hall acts. The climax of the evening was
when its wooden floor shook under the stamping feet of the
dance girls in an atmosphere of smoke, noise and the brassy blare
of the band. The girls who performed were not chosen for their
looks but because they were strong and their appeal—or rather
that of their dancing—was direct, unabashed and crude. There
was no false glamour and no barrier of footlights to set them in
another dimension from their audience. When the girls came
out on to the floor, the audience would surge forward and crowd
in upon them for a glimpse of an inch or two of naked flesh. The
attitude of many of the spectators was, as one French writer has
remarked, more that of the naughty schoolboy than the seeker
after eroticism.

There was certainly as much hypocrisy in Third Republic
France as there was in Victorian England, but there was also a
strongly surviving tradition of public enjoyment of physical
pleasures and suggestions. A comparison between English and
French popular illustrated journals and newspapers of the time
reveals the relative lack of prudery in France and a willingness
to enjoy a good, Rabelaisian belly-laugh. *Gil Blas Illustré*, *Le Rire*
and other papers were full of "sexy" cartoons and jokes about
erring husbands, respectable gentlemen caught in compromising
situations, wives in bed with their lovers and innumerable
advertisements for "rejuvenation pills", cheap contraceptives
and treatments for venereal diseases. Humour on the stage was

often bedroom humour which might be vulgar but which could also be raised to a high level of comedy and touched with genuine wit.

Indicative of the Parisian public's readiness to appreciate an honest Rabelaisian spectacle was the success of the amazing *Pétomane*. In all the history of popular entertainment there has never been anything like him. When he hired him, Zidler gave yet another proof of his flair for attracting stars. According to the singer Yvette Guilbert, a sad-looking pale-faced man had come one day to see Zidler and had confided that nature had endowed him with an unusual gift. Joseph Pujol, as he was named, had an "aspirating anus" which allowed him to take in air through his posterior and to break wind at will. He claimed that he was a phenomenon and that, if given a chance, he would be the talk of Paris. After he had given a demonstration of his talents which included "playing tunes" and blowing out a candle from a distance of one foot, he was hired on the spot and billed as:

LE PETOMANE
The only man who pays no author's royalties.

His confidence in himself was not misplaced. He became a sensation and reduced audiences to hysteria as he performed on the stage in the plaster elephant in the garden of the Moulin Rouge. There was no fraud: doctors examined him and wrote learned reports on the elasticity of his anus and newspapers described his act in glowing terms although they sometimes found it a little difficult to find suitably polite terms that would not offend the susceptibilities of their more prudish lady-readers.

Joseph Pujol began his triumphant career in 1892 and continued to perform with few interruptions until 1900, also giving a number of highly successful performances abroad. Few people were shocked and the laughter of his audience was so loud that it could be heard a hundred yards away from the Moulin Rouge. He was so famous that the King of the Belgians even made a special trip to Paris to hear him.

Meanwhile, back on the dance floor, La Goulue had been joined by another fascinating dancer who was also to join

Toulouse-Lautrec's gallery of picturesque personalities. She was known as Jane Avril and of all the girls who danced at the Moulin Rouge she was the most "classy" and the most enigmatic.

If La Goulue might be said to have been the heart of the Moulin Rouge quadrille, Jane Avril could be said to have been its soul. Zidler had invited her to dance for him but she had refused all remuneration on the grounds that she had less pleasure in dancing when paid for it. As it was for Valentin-le-Desossé, dancing was a kind of private obsession for her. She was another of those meteor-like phenomena who suddenly sprang fully-fledged out of obscurity to make their own contribution to the fascinating legend of the Nineties before receding into oblivion.

She was half French and half Italian and her father was said to have been an aristocratic Italian playboy. From her early youth she had had a passion for dancing and had run away from home to haunt the Paris dance halls, from the Bal Bullier in the Latin Quarter to the Jardin de Paris on the Right Bank. Her languid beauty, red hair and pale face appealed to such Parisian celebrities as Paul Fort, Mallarmé, Barrès, the humorist Alphonse Allais and Toulouse-Lautrec who was, perhaps, her most devoted admirer. She was nicknamed La Mélinite and Jeanne la Folle, because of her mania for dancing. With her refinement and air of gentility she was a perfect foil to La Goulue. Although she had made her début at the Elysée-Montmartre, she had found its vulgarity and general "tone" to be unpleasant, later declaring that "women with a shameless air danced there in a way I found indecent, arm in arm with book-makers who looked like butchers or worse ... I did not like the place. I preferred the dancing at the Moulin Rouge". But the high-kicking quadrille was too indelicate for her. Instead, she gave improvised solo performances, swaying dreamily to the strains of sentimental waltzes and songs and executing complicated patterns of steps with a wealth of sinuous movements which seemed to foreshadow the intricate curvilinear rhythms of the Art Nouveau style. To the Englishman Arthur Symons, the critic and poet who had felt the lure of Paris so strongly, she suggested the decadence of the *fin de siècle* on which he was such an expert. He was a frequent visitor to the

Moulin Rouge and other Paris night-haunts, knew Toulouse-Lautrec well, and had met Jane Avril in the spring of 1892 when she was dancing at the Jardin de Paris. Her appearance had greatly impressed him and he later wrote of her as being "young and girlish, the more provocative because she played as a prude, with an assumed modesty, *décolletée* nearly to her waist, in the Oriental fashion. She had long black curls around her face; and had about her an air of depraved virginity." Being inclined to see much of Paris in the lurid light of that "decadence" in life and art for which he was a leading spokesman, he went on in the purplest of his very purple prose to represent her as a kind of perverse genius. She was a Salome-like apparition, a "creature of cruel moods, of cruel passions; she had the reputation of being a Lesbian . . . an absolute passion for her own beauty". As for La Goulue whom Toulouse-Lautrec drew with such compelling truthfulness, she loomed large in Symons' imagination as a "Messalina, a monstrous beast, a Vampire . . . a creature of incarnate degradation".

Messalina or not, La Goulue's vanity was to lead her to an early decline. Sensing that she was the "star" of the Moulin Rouge, she soon gave herself the airs of a prima donna and became careless of scandal. Apart from her rather strange liaison with Valentin-le-Desossé, she was rumoured to be conducting a Lesbian affair with a dancing girl who had come with her from the Elysée-Montmartre. As if to illustrate her contempt for all the fine gentlemen who came to gaze lecherously at her while she danced, she took to walking around Montmartre in the daytime, leading a tame goat by a leash. During her brief but dazzling career, she had been consecrated by Toulouse-Lautrec whose painting of *La Goulue entering the Moulin Rouge* had been exhibited by Zidler who had also bought the painter's *Danse du Moulin Rouge* in 1890, hanging it in the foyer.

The great golden age of the Moulin Rouge lasted for five years. The Elysée-Montmartre had been unable to compete and had closed down. The Prince of Wales visited the Moulin Rouge "incognito" and had been followed by foreign princes and grand dukes and celebrities in every walk of life. Zidler hired a fleet of omnibuses to take his distinguished patrons from the Moulin Rouge, once the quadrille was over, to the Jardin de Paris. Then, in 1894, he left the Moulin Rouge after cancelling his contract with the brothers Oller and from that moment the magic of his establishment began to wane. The *chahut* continued to be the main attraction; La Goulue was still performing; crowds continued to make their pilgrimage to the Place Blanche, but something had gone. It had simply become "commercialised". Zidler had been in love with the Moulin Rouge, which was his most successful creation. He recognised the fact that his stars were not there for money alone and it was something more than the gaudy appeal of his dancers that had fascinated a genius like Toulouse-Lautrec who would sit late every night sketching busily while Zidler let the band play for a quarter of an hour after closing time so that the dancers might practise and improvise for their own pleasure.

Zidler soon regretted his decision, but too late. The Moulin Rouge became a highly successful institution and inspired imitations all over the world but like many institutions it had become complacent and unoriginal under its new manager, Joseph Oller. Soon afterwards, Jane Avril left to go to the Folies Bergère, the Moulin Rouge's foremost rival for gay spectacle in the Paris of the 1890's. La Goulue stayed for another year. Her conceit was now unbounded: she had her own carriage, she was frequently photographed in various poses, and on one famous occasion she had insolently addressed the Prince of Wales—by then a devotee of Paris—by calling out: "Hey, Wales! It's you who's paying for the champagne!" In 1895 she left to strike out on her own and by the end of the century was a circus performer in the lion's cage. A few years later she was a gross and prematurely aged ruin, practically penniless despite her previous large earnings.

Like the Moulin Rouge, the Folies Bergère became world famous. It had begun its life as a *café-concert* under the Second Empire in May 1869. After an uneven early period, it had been taken over by two successful clowns, the brothers Isola, and had been transformed into one of the first modern "music halls" of Europe, complete with variety shows, conjurers and clowns, jugglers, acrobats, singers and dancers. In 1886, under the management of a Monsieur and Madame Lallemard, it became the birthplace of the modern type of revue, with a series of "star turns" and acts linked together by commentaries and introductions by a compère. The famous performers who appeared there ensured its reputation and it played an important part in the history of light entertainment by encouraging the tendency towards an international form of variety. As far as the Folies Bergère was concerned, there were no language barriers. The foreign visitor was made to feel completely at home and performers were invited from many different countries. Parisians were attracted by feeling that they were participating in a truly cosmopolitan entertainment by seeing artists and acts which had been seen by the public of the world's other great cities. It was was also a kind of club, a "theatre which is not a theatre, a promenade where you may sit down, a spectacle which you are not obliged to watch, with two thousand men all smoking, drinking and chattering and seven or eight hundred ladies all laughing, drinking and smoking and offering themselves as gaily as you could wish".[1] The spectacular "girlie" shows for which the Folies later became famous were not yet a feature of the establishment. Instead "as soon as the curtain goes up, an overture, a polka, is played . . . and then, should you wish to look, you may watch in succession an India-rubber man, English songstresses, a crazy velocipedist, seven acrobats, three clowns, a juggler etc. etc." It was only much later that the Folies Bergère specialised in "leg-shows" and became a kind of temple of high-class strip-tease raised to its apotheosis by the beauty of the girls and the lavishness of the décor.

The first strip-tease, for which Paris was long considered the home, took place more by accident than design in the Place Blanche during the noisy annual students' ball and carnival, the *Bal des Quat'z'Arts* in February 1893. During an impromptu "beauty contest" between artists' models and girl friends, a young lady named Mona leapt naked on to a table amid great applause. The incident gave rise to a scandal and a near-riot and, after the intervention of the much hated Senator Béranger, Paris's self-appointed custodian of morals, a prosecution. The condemnation and the light fine imposed by the magistrate led to riots in

[1] Camille Debans, *Plaisirs de Paris*, 1889.

earnest in the Latin Quarter. Student demonstrations led to a sudden explosion of violence the like of which had not been seen since the Commune. Fighting broke out between students and police in the Place de la Sorbonne; the Prefecture of Police was mobbed; troops were called in to assist the police and shots were fired, one student being accidentally killed. The immediate result of the whole affair was the dismissal of the Paris Prefect of Police and the process of unveiling portions of the female figure for commercial profit and public pleasure being carried a step further.

The new kind of spectacle seems to have started in 1894 in a modest little music-hall-cum-cabaret, Le Divan Fayouac, in the Rue des Martyrs. It consisted of a short sketch entitled *Le Coucher d'Yvette* (Yvette goes to bed). There was no question of allowing a completely naked woman to appear upon the stage, nor was there very much actual baring of flesh, but there was a very obvious appeal to the audience's imagination. The general pattern for such shows was the same for Yvette as it was for her numerous imitators: a plumpish lady in voluminous costume would slowly rid herself of a variety of garments while winking at the audience or pretending coyness until she was left in a shift whereupon she would climb into a bed. Such French "naughtiness" proved a great success and established a *genre* of entertainment that was repeated by small cabarets in Paris and the provinces, the degree of suggestiveness in the performance depending on the degree of local prudishness. One of the most famous such acts, at the Casino de Paris, was by a performer called Angèle Hérard whose pretext for disrobing was that she was suffering from an itch, presumably caused by a flea which she proceeded to hunt by much shifting and shedding of undergarments. Such acts also led to a flood of saucy postcards and "albums". Picture-postcards with such titles as *The Bride at Bed-time*, *The Maid takes a bath* and *Madame at her toilet* were produced in tens of thousands and still turn up in antique and junk shops on both sides of the English Channel. Similar themes inspired some of the earliest silent films "for gentlemen only" and amateur photographers in Paris made small fortunes as they rigged up their studios as boudoirs in which complacent ladies would perform their bed-time ritual as they waded through a mass of petticoats, or reclined in bed smiling invitingly at a moustachioed gallant.

All this was very far from the accusations of Satanic immorality and *fin de siècle* "decadence" which horrified puritans and titillated the imaginations of foreign visitors and provincial Frenchmen. The books of the so-called "decadents", the novels of Huysmans, Rachilde, Barrès and Villiers de l'Isle Adam, with their preoccupation with themes of sadism and sexual aberration, were read by a limited public but helped form a widespread picture of Paris as a sink of iniquity or a Mecca for the votary of erotic and forbidden pleasures. A clandestine pornographic press flourished in Paris but apart from highly obscene and erotic publications and reprints for connoisseurs and collectors, most of the pseudo-pornographic "yellow-backed" novels that were available to foreign tourists in Paris were naïve and repetitive. The "daring French novel" that the English or American tourist brought back in his suitcase as evidence of French lubricity might either be a genuine work of literature by one of the "realist" or "decadent" writers or a titillatory saga of the cavortings of a wealthy and eccentric "milord" among an assembly of heartless governesses or exotic female flagellants. Although such books flirted with taboo subjects, in their style and attitudes they were not so very different from the more respectable and worldly novels of "Gyp" and Paul Bourget who wrote of adultery and seduction and gave their theme a veneer of superficial "psychology". Nonetheless, the fact that adultery featured so conspicuously in French plays and novels convinced many foreigners that Paris seethed with immorality and was a haven for the debauchee.

By the second half of the 19th century, French writers had been dealing with sex with increasing frankness, often in the name of "realism" which could represent an ideology, a crusade and a literary movement. But each victory of the realistic school was generally only won after a battle. The difference with the more hypocritical and prudish Anglo-Saxon world was that at least it was possible to give battle in the first place. Emile Zola's novels were attacked in England as disgusting but his novels together with such naturalistic works as Goncourt's *Elisa*, several of Maupassant's tales and even Flaubert's *Madame Bovary* had not gone unassailed in France. The movement towards freedom in literature gained impetus steadily towards the end of the century and its reverberations abroad had, at one level, given a picture of a remarkably cynical and amoral society.

France was a secular republic without a royal family to give an example of middle-class stability and respectability. The church was open to violent attack and even persecution, and a popular cynicism, encouraged by a century of political turbulence and scandals, encouraged the man in the street to regard immorality in high places as a matter of course. But as far as the almost legendary French *amour* went, the *belle époque* was only *belle* for a small minority. A dedication to eroticism, adultery and illicit love was not for the bourgeois and if we read such popular novels as those of Paul Bourget, the writer of the "Physiology of modern love", we have the impression that such "modern" love was reserved for the upper strata of society—a luxury for the happy few like *cordon bleu* cuisine. Paris was certainly less puritanical in the Nineties than England or the United States but, even so, tolerance had its limits. Oscar Wilde would not have been prosecuted in France but it is significant that during his brief stay in Paris after his imprisonment he was never taken up by Paris society, literary or otherwise. The witty boulevardier, journalist and chronicler Jean Lorrain was a well-known pederast but had to behave with extreme circumspection. Divorce was permitted by the legislation of the Republic and infidelity on the part of both sexes could be condoned or laughed at but only among a small, sophisticated set.

The great erotic legend of *fin de siècle* Paris was partly fostered by those who had a commercial interest in its propagation. It was incarnated in the persons of the great *cocottes* or *grandes horizontales* who carried on the traditions of the Second Empire courtesans. On a more frivolous level, the legend was encouraged and maintained by witty boudoir farces in the manner of Feydeau. In Paris and elsewhere, 1890-vintage eroticism was to a large extent a matter of stage setting and trappings. The *cocotte* or *femme fatale* had her place in society as long as she behaved in the manner expected of her, and she required appropriate surroundings to heighten her sexual fascination. A striking illustration of the mania for exotic decoration as a setting for sin is provided by the famous photographs of Sarah Bernhardt reclining in the midst of semi-Oriental luxury, against a stagy background of tiger skins, velvets and silk hangings, like a panther lying in wait for its prey in a claustrophobic, incense-heavy atmosphere. The age was one that was highly receptive to sexual suggestions. The fetish of the female leg, ankle and bosom which was so pronounced in the late 19th century, the frankness of well-known writers, and the florid, flowing lines of interior designs and furnishings which were to reach a paroxysm in the *art nouveau* style all played an important part in giving the French Nineties an aura of intense eroticism.

The writings and theories of the "decadents" only reached a limited number of readers but their reputation had both shocked and fascinated a wider public. Their expressed desire to experiment with new sensations, their interest in what was bizarre and exotic and the fact that they seemed to be encouraging the individual to enrich his sensual experience through art, drugs, absinthe and unconventional behaviour encouraged belief in the moral wickedness of the Nineties. Such a tendency was by no means confined to France but it was Paris that had provided the centre for the "decadent movement". The innocent frolics at the Moulin Rouge and other places of entertainment, the publicity which was given to well-known courtesans, the frankness of singers, writers and caricaturists and a vague conception of Paris as the centre of a moral decadence encouraged by immoral artists and writers made the city appear a new Babylon to many curious foreigners. In addition, the growth of the Socialist movement, anti-clericalism and the apparent impunity with which artists and intellectuals flouted middle-class propriety dismayed many moral-minded Parisians.

In 1891, Léo Taxil, a literary turncoat and *agent-provocateur* who had used his pen first to unmask clerical "conspiracies" and then the machinations of Freemasonry, shocked the respectable even more with his book *La Corruption fin de siècle*. He gave graphic descriptions of the immoral depths to which Paris society had allegedly sunk and his book contained sensational references to the vogue for Lesbianism that was supposed to be spreading among Paris society ladies. It was well known, he wrote, that

THE PLEASURE CAPITAL   63

devotees of Sapphic love made rendezvous or recruited new
members along the Champs-Elysées. He told his fascinated
readers that such women were easily recognisable for the "*tribade*
in search of her kindred has a distinctive sign: the magnificent,
curled, bedecked, prettified and sometimes even berribboned
poodle which accompanies her in her outings, whether on foot
or by carriage". Lesbian "academies" flourished in Paris and it
seemed that apart from the Champs-Elysées, favourite meeting
places for the cream of the Lesbians' set included the Allée des
Poteaux in the Bois de Boulogne between ten and twelve in the
morning, and a certain restaurant in the centre of Les Halles.
Toulouse-Lautrec had depicted the very real Lesbianism that
existed among the inmates of Paris brothels and although bars
and clubs for homosexuals of both sexes were to be found in
Paris as in all great cities, it is questionable whether the perversion
existed on the scale alleged by Taxil. But the subject did enjoy
a certain vogue for a time and had intrigued a number of writers
including Pierre Louÿs who gave it a certain risqué *chic* with his
Songs of Bilitis, a collection of pseudo-Sapphic verses, and his erotic
novel of Antiquity, *Aphrodite*.

Taxil's "revelations" concerning male homosexuality were
more sensational still. Paris high society was corrupt, Frenchmen
were losing their old-fashioned masculine virtues, corruption
extended to even the most elegant social functions and as for
the famous masked balls held at the Paris Opéra—well "they are
nothing else today but great festivals of pederasty". The more
orthodox forms of sexual activity were represented at one end
of the social scale by the *cocottes* and at the other by the Parisian
prostitutes who haunted the pavements and the foyers of music
halls, and that long-enduring and once almost homely institution—the Paris brothel.

The part played by the licensed *maison de tolérance* in 19th-
century French social life has been described by Maupassant,
painted and drawn by Toulouse-Lautrec, exaggerated by Taxil
and other moralists, and virtually ignored by social historians.
For a variety of reasons, some of which were related to the rapidly
growing tourist boom, and others to the attention they had received in the novels of well-known writers, the great brothels of

64

fin de s
an ess
and w

Pros
was in
or the
ladies
and m
New Y
their v
pravity
declare
"the n
the Re
Club, f

By 1
à la mod
somew
such es
the nu
In 1892
covery
closes we
than th

A fact
phenom
version
custome
subject
and its i
in Paris
tion was
Paris Sû
replaced
of comn
Café du

Eiffel and his Colleagues
Salute the Completion
of the Tower

¹ Brothe
set above

Boulangisme: Voting Papers
for the 1889 Paris Elections
are taken to be counted

Haussmann's Paris: Boulevard des Capucines

Old Montmartre

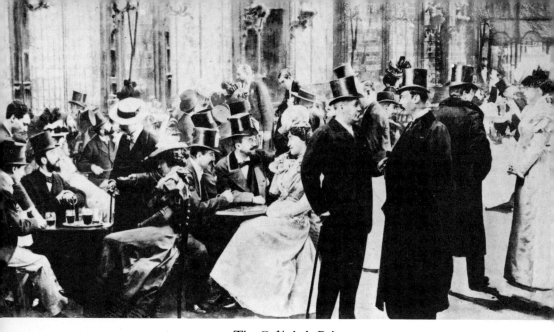

The Café de la Paix

1895 Fashions from the House of Worth

Riding in the Bois de Boulogne

The Paris Slums: Rue de Bierre

The *Chahut* at the Moulin Rouge

La Goulue and Valentin-le-Desossé
drawn by Toulouse-Lautrec

Ladies of the Street

An early Striptease

The Poetry of the Pavements:
A Steinlen Illustration
for a Song Sheet

A Shadow Show at the Chat Noir

visitors and many had an upstairs room where clients might retire with the partner of their choice after the brief preliminary negotiation had been conducted over a beer-stained table. The serving girls often dressed with such freedom that in 1889 the Paris Préfecture felt compelled to issue a circular requesting *brasserie* proprietors to see that their employees wore longer skirts.

For the more discriminating roué or curious traveller there were a number of more select addresses to which he might pay a discreet visit. Some houses were so luxuriously appointed that they became famous as a new kind of Arabian Nights pleasure palace. Moralists of the day pointed out that touting for these establishments was becoming increasingly open and frequent. A single gentleman sitting at a pavement café could hardly sip his coffee undisturbed without some waiter, street urchin or passing cabbie slipping him a pink-tinted and often scented visiting card with a name followed by an address and the hint "*tout confort*" or "discretion assured". Some were more eloquent, promising such delights as "*tableaux vivants*" and all the refinements of "modern science".

The whole period, from the Eighties to the First World War, was a golden age for some Paris brothels which catered to a distinguished and cosmopolitan clientèle. One of the best known, number 6, Rue des Moulins, was famous for being the home for a time of Toulouse-Lautrec who had painted each inmate in turn and boasted to friends that his address had a "very large street number. A very large number indeed." He had long been a frequent visitor to Paris brothels ever since he had first taken lodgings on the Boulevard de Clichy only a few yards away from the notorious Perroquet Gris which was demolished in 1892. His documentary turn of mind, the fascination that Paris popular and low life had for him, his deliberate rejection of his family background and his need for consolation for his deformity led him to some of the great Parisian *maisons closes* which he painted with as much enthusiasm as the circus or the music hall. He was not alone in depicting such subjects, for in 1899 the artist Georges Bottini held a well-attended exhibition of water colours of *Bars et Maisons closes*.

The sumptuous furnishings of some of the higher-class establishments were a matter of pride for their owners and much talked about. For all his apparent disapproval, even Léo Taxil could not refrain from describing such interiors. One was "said to be the most famous in Europe; people visit it out of curiosity: it has a famous grotto and rooms furnished in the taste of various countries of the world with a Scotch room, a Russian room, an Italian room, a Spanish room, a Chinese room, an Indian room, a Persian room, a Negro room etc." Another authority, Monsieur Macé, author of *La Police Parisienne*, described one of these aristocratic *lupanars* with a pen worthy of a Huysmans:

"The *maisons de tolérance* established not far from the Bourse and the Palais-Royal have been furnished with the greatest fantasy. As you penetrate into their interiors you are dazzled by the glitter of cut glass, by the profusion of gilt and the brilliance of the illuminations.

"Each *retiro*, decorated with rich and sumptuous hangings, has a comfortable luxury of which the particular and original character is a reminder to the foreigner of some intimate corner of his absent homeland. Among such curiously furnished rooms we must mention one transformed into the cabin of an ocean liner. The walls, lined with canvas, carry ropes and pulleys which hold up open sails which serve as curtains. The bed, placed in a net, has the form of a hammock and is suspended by ship's rigging. The result is that the rolling motion of a ship is produced each time the person stretched out on the bed makes the slightest movement . . . In the midst of this ship's apparel, the voyager may imagine that he is making an agreeable crossing.

"The darkened chamber also merits special mention. Lit by electricity it contains a bed framed by black curtains with gold fringes and tassels. Rays of light with changing tones are directed on to a sky-blue ceiling in the centre of which may be seen soaring Eve in the costume of the Earthly Paradise."

He was not exaggerating—for the interior decorations of many of the top *maisons closes* were a faithful reflection of the florid opulence and gaudy medley of tastes which characterised much of the art and interior decorations of the period. Luxury and vice went hand in hand. The mistresses of such well-endowed establishments were rumoured to live like princesses and their rooms were filled with *objets d'art*, gilt mirrors and candelabra, and paintings. Number 14, Rue de Monthyon had huge mirrors, carpeted floors, Louis XV chairs and sofas and a famous *Salon des Lords*— doubtless for the reception of the wealthy English. Number 6, Rue des Moulins contained a fantastically ornate wood-panelled room in a mixture of mock-Tudor and mock-Gothic styles, and a richly carved mahogany shell-shaped bed with the head-board crowned by a half life-size naked girl looking down at the happy occupants. It was said to have once belonged to the courtesan La Paiva.[1] But perhaps the most famous and spectacular of all these temples of pleasure was the Chabanais in the street of the same name.

It had been founded in 1878 by an enterprising Madame Kelly who had the advantage of being on friendly terms with many of the most important members of the Paris Jockey Club, and it became almost an extension of that snobbish institution. A sign in the vestibule announced that it was "a house of all nations" and during the years of its existence before the First World War it was one of the most famous brothels in Europe, catering to an illustrious clientèle from all over the world.

Once the visitor had been admitted into its opulent reception room with its antique furniture, gilt and inlaid panelling and 18th-century paintings, he had the choice of going with his partner to the Japanese, Spanish or Directoire rooms or the astonishing "Moorish" room in imitation of the Alhambra at Granada, the Chambre Louis XVI with painted medallions in the style of Boucher, or its extraordinary "Pompeian saloon" for which Toulouse-Lautrec had painted some medallions. Finally, as an added attraction for those drawn to the "English vice", it had "the prettiest torture chamber in Paris".

Some features mentioned by Léo Taxil might well have been inspired by the fertile imagination of one of the "decadent"

[1] Just how opulent were such interiors was proved on October 30, 1946 when the contents of the Rue des Moulins establishment were sold at an auction conducted by M. Maurice Rheims. The catalogue included sculpted wooden caryatids and the contents of "Gothic, Louis XIII, XV and XVI, Napoleon III and Chinese bedrooms".

novelists. If we can believe Taxil, one of the leading Paris *maisons closes* contained a "funerary chamber" for would-be necrophiliacs:

"The walls were lined with black satin and strewn with tears of silver. In the centre, a very luxurious catafalque with a lady lying inert in an open coffin, her head resting on a velvet cushion. Around her, long candles in silver holders, incense-burners and livid-hued illuminations. The lustful madman who has paid ten *louis* for this séance is then introduced. He will find a *prie-dieu* on which to kneel. A harmonium, placed in a neighbouring closet, will play the *Dies Irae* or the *De Profundis*. Then, to the strains of this funeral music, the vampire will precipitate himself upon the girl simulating the deceased . . . "

With such lurid accounts being provided, it is not surprising that Paris should have assumed the aspect of a capital of vice, a haven of immorality and forbidden pleasures of which the uninhibited frolicking at the Moulin Rouge and other pleasure-palaces was but the tip of the iceberg, the visible tenth of the licence lurking behind the façade of the city. But whereas such accoutrements of sin helped to create the legend of a wicked *fin de siècle* Paris, the more humdrum vice and degradation of the meaner streets and districts provided material for a new form of popular art that often became a poetical evocation of the poorer life of the city as it moved towards the 20th century.

The "realist" tendency in French literature had led many writers to turn to humble, everyday, working-class themes. The popularity of themes of low life had become particularly pronounced by the 1890's. Writers of varying degrees of talent and with progressive social opinions made ready use of such themes even though their work might often be attacked for its concentration on the seamy side of life. The figures they chose to illustrate the more picturesque side of proletarian life were naturally the *clochard*, the out-of-work and the poor girl compelled to solicit on the streets rather than the honest but dull working man and his hard-working housewife. The new heroine was the prostitute; the new hero the tough *apache* to whom she gave her heart.

Such themes were frequently susceptible to sentimentalised

and unreal treatment by indifferent writers, but by a happy chance their popularity coincided with a remarkable renaissance in the art of the French song and the "artistic cabaret". They inspired a number of sincere and unaffected ballads and songs which often reached a high artistic level and represented a genuine "poetry of the pavement". This new source of poetic inspiration brought forward a small number of talented singers and composers who created a new *genre*, half-way between poetry and popular song, and established a tradition in popular entertainment which has been recently represented by such great performers as Edith Piaf and Georges Brassens.

The *chanson réaliste*, as it was called, was inspired by the reverse side of the *Belle Epoque*. To say that the Paris of the *chahut*, high-class cocottes, elegant wits and fashionable ladies, music halls and popular balls, had a darker side may seem a truism. Nevertheless, to a greater degree in Paris than in many other European cities, a large mass of the population lived in near-desperate poverty in a climate of hope and bitterness which was given a peculiar tension by the memory of a hundred years of revolution and social struggles and a foreboding that further violence and struggles might be imminent. This was the spirit that inspired the drawings of artists like Forain and Steinlen, the bitter caricatures in some famous periodicals, and the abrasive social satire of writers like Octave Mirbeau and Georges Darien. It also found its expression in the new little night clubs and sophisticated cabarets that had been springing up in the city since the 1880's.

That the humbler aspects of Paris life were able to find expression in popular entertainment was due to the revived institution of the artistic and literary "cabaret" and the *café-concert*. Appropriately enough, it was Montmartre which became the home of the new song after becoming the centre of Paris entertainment after dark.

In the 1880's, the *café-concert* was a permanent fixture in Paris life. It was above all a café where a mixed and often rowdy public might hear popular singers for the price of a drink or two. The difference between the *caf' conc'*, as it was usually known, and the music-hall was often tenuous. Rough stages might sometimes be set up in the café and performers would alternate between one establishment and the other. Most of the leading music halls and *caf' conc's* were to be found in the northern sector of the city and, in particular, on and around the Boulevard de Strasbourg and the Porte Saint-Denis, while the Jardin de Paris and the Ambassadeurs in the Elysées district catered for a smarter clientèle who would never go to anything as "vulgar" as an ordinary *café-concert*.

At their best, the variety halls and *caf' conc's* offered lively, full-blooded entertainment comparable to that of a good London music hall of the same period, with songs, dramatic and comic monologues and recitations predominating. Many of the more modest and working-class *caf' conc's* were scattered throughout the Pigalle area and the *grands boulevards* and gave new singers the opportunity to make their professional debut before audiences who were not slow to show their feelings one way or the other.

The art of the French song had fallen into decadence after the Second Empire. Most songs were crudely vulgar or over-sentimental, being unredeemed by any wit or charm. Singers made their name by braying out the latest patriotic jingles, treacly romances or else risqué songs of the *frou-frou* type, accompanied by a wealth of innuendo and stage winks and grimaces. Then, towards the mid-Eighties, the traditional French song began to revive, thanks to such talented composers and singers as Jules Jouy and Xavier Privas. They had of necessity begun their careers in the *caf' conc's* but their talent and more sophisticated approach brought them before a more discerning public.

Like many of the Paris *chansonniers*, Jouy wrote his own numbers and displayed an original, sincere spirit in songs which contained frequent references to working-class life and which often had political and satirical overtones, while Privas specialised in the more sentimental type of ballad. With other singers who showed talent in the composition as much as the rendering of songs, they were drawn into the orbit of the new cabarets that were being opened and it was there that their art received the accolade of intellectual and artistic appreciation.

Until the early Nineties, much of the most sophisticated and essentially Parisian entertainment that the city had to offer was to be found in the Chat Noir. It was one of the first *cabarets artistiques* and had been created by Rudolphe Salis, a former art-student and "bohemian".

Salis was born in Châtellerault, a small and probably a very dull country town in the department of Vienne, and like many another young Frenchman of the provinces he had felt the pull of Paris. Unwilling to follow the profession of his father who was a sweet-seller, he had succumbed to the myth of Paris "Bohemian" life and went to the city to be a painter. He attended classes at the Beaux Arts school for a time and enjoyed himself immensely but he cannot have been very serious in his intention to be an artist since the withholding of his allowance by his father brought him back home. After marrying and making at least a show of settling down, he returned to Paris, this time with a little more money at his disposal. He was now more determined in his purpose which was to open an "artistic" cabaret and provide a meeting-place and an entertainment for artists, writers, poets and fellow-"bohemians". He was inspired by the examples of two such cabarets, the Grand' Pinte and the Nouvelle Athènes which were already enjoying a local if restricted popularity. He further realised that as Montmartre and its adjacent area were becoming focal points for artists and intellectuals as well as for pleasure-lovers and tourists, a cabaret run on the right lines would be almost certain of attracting a large clientèle.

In December 1881, he opened his cabaret on the Boulevard Rochechouart, not far from the Place Blanche, in disused premises which had formerly belonged to the postal service. He decorated it rather showily in the early 17th-century style known as "Louis XIII", with copper pots and pans, old weapons, pewter, and dark oak chairs and tables. While the work of decoration was in progress, a stray black cat had been found on the pavement outside and, in addition to being adopted at once, it gave the cabaret its name. It must also have brought Salis luck, for the day before the Chat Noir was due to open he had had a marvellous stroke of good fortune.

Salis had been to the Grand' Pinte where he had met the poet Emile Goudeau who was the president of a society with the peculiar name of *Les Hydropathes* which had just lost its home. The

Hydropathes were a group of poets, musicians and artists, many of whom had belonged to the Symbolist movement or one of its many offshoots. They had been meeting in the heart of the Latin Quarter, on the first floor of a small café-restaurant which had shut down suddenly. Salis at once performed the remarkable feat of bringing the whole group across Paris to the Chat Noir and convincing them that it was just the new home they needed. With a clientèle that included the well-known illustrator and painter Willette, the humorist Alphonse Allais and such important poets as Charles Cros, Albert Samain and Jean Richepin, success was assured from the start.

Salis had begun his enterprise with the aim of attracting a limited and "arty" public but his Chat Noir was soon filled every night with a greater public than any he had dreamed of. People found the place attractive and amusing and it became famous throughout Paris. In a short time Salis was publishing the *Chat Noir* as the official journal of the establishment, with poems supplied by his customers. Talented singers and performers were invited and they, in turn, attracted still more talent. The Chat Noir became a fashionable late-night resort for Paris society, particularly on Friday evenings, and it eventually became obvious that the place was too small. Salis moved his cabaret to larger premises in the Rue Victor Massé nearby and had it decorated in a fancier, pseudo-historical style of the period of François Villon, the beggar-poet whose spirit the place claimed to be maintaining.

Although the Chat Noir was becoming rather self-conscious with its members and Salis himself addressing each other and distinguished visitors with courtly reverences and long-winded, fantastic titles, the main spirit was resolutely anti-bourgeois and anti-conventional. Actors and singers kept up a stream of mockery and invective aimed at society, politicians, the rich and the *demi-monde*, often to the great delight of the same classes they were attacking. It was there that the new type of mocking, seditious and rebellious song was encouraged. Although romantic and sentimental ballads like *Les Petits Pavés* and *Le Fiacre* became popular there, and have remained so ever since in France, songs of everyday life and social protest were also becoming frequent. Society ladies, foreign tourists, bankers, playwrights and journalists found themselves attentively listening to songs of a world of which they knew little except, perhaps, through the books of Zola. Typical of the new "realistic" songs of the time which could be heard at the Chat Noir was one entitled *Un Vieux ouvrier*, the lament of a homeless workman without a job:

> Les chiens perdus ont des fourrières;
> Les cygn's, des boit's sur leurs bassins;
> Les rodeurs de nuit, des carrières,
> L'bagn' sert d'hotel aux assassins . . .
>
> La nuit au poste, les roussins
> Ont d'quoi s'coucher sur leurs derrières,
> Les architect's, pour un tas d' saints,
> Ont creuse des nich's dans des pierres.
>
> Eh ben, moi, pauvr' vieux ouvrier,
> Parc' que j'ai pas d'quoi travailler,
> J'peux mem' pas ronfler comm' Gavroche.
>
> Bah! J'm'en fich' d'avoir pas d'foyer,
> Car si j'ai pas l'rond dans ma poche,
> Au moins, j'ai pas d'terme à payer.[1]

Such songs, with their use of popular jargon and the argot of the streets, were a great novelty.

But although poets and singers first brought the public to Salis's club, the attraction that most contributed to the great fame of the Chat Noir in the Nineties was its shadow show—a kind of precursor of the cinema. It was the result of Jules Jouy's inspiration. To accompany some of his songs, he had the idea of illustrating them by means of cut-out puppets and silhouettes whose shadows would be projected on to a transparent screen

[1] Stray dogs have their holes / swans have shelters by their ponds / Night prowlers have their quarries / And jug's a sort of hotel for murderers. / By night at the station the cop / has something on which to flop / and architects for a heap of saints / have dug niches in the stones. / Ah well, poor old workman that I am / since I haven't means to work / I can't even kip down like Gavroche. / Bah! I don't give a cuss if I haven't a home / for even if I haven't a penny / at least I haven't any rent to pay.

while they were being manipulated. After some early experiments, it was decided to present an animated shadow-show with music and a spoken, running commentary by a compère. One of the most successful and ambitious of these shows was a Napoleonic saga designed by the artist and caricaturist Caran d'Ache. Such an ingenious form of entertainment became an even greater attraction than the songs that were sung every night and, until 1897, the "shadow theatre" at the Chat Noir rivalled the Moulin Rouge as one of the foremost tourist attractions in Paris.

The great period of the Chat Noir came to an end in the mid-Nineties. During its lifetime, it had given great impetus to the growth and establishment of other artistic cabarets in the Montmartre district and as early as 1888 a schism in the Chat Noir group had led to the foundation of a rival establishment. Rudolphe Salis had brought his younger brother Gabriel to Paris to assist him, together with Gabriel's wife. Gabriel and Rudolphe, and their spouses, had quarrelled over the management of the club and various members had taken sides. In 1889, Gabriel left the Chat Noir and took over the lease of the now defunct Grand' Pinte, transforming it into the cabaret Ane Rouge. A painter was called in to decorate its walls with large panels including one of a crucified red donkey. Artists from the neighbourhood were invited to exhibit their works there and with Gabriel himself singing a repertoire of old popular and traditional songs, it flourished until 1898, a year after Rudolphe died and the Chat Noir had shut down for ever.

One of the singers who appeared at the Chat Noir was to become the most illustrious representative of the new tendency in the French *chanson réaliste* and a Parisian legend in his own lifetime. He was Aristide Bruant, another great character of the period whose name is inseparable from the Paris of the Nineties when his well-known silhouette appeared on the walls of Paris in the posters of Toulouse-Lautrec.

Bruant was born near the town of Sens in 1851. Even as a child he had shown promise as a singer and after a chequered early career, which included a spell as a *franc-tireur* in the Franco-Prussian War and as a regular soldier, he had come to Paris to work for the railways. It was during his early years in the city that he had begun to explore the city and, in particular, the life of the poorer, outlying districts. He got to know the Paris of the *zone*, the sad wasteland of the outer boulevards and the fortifications, the Paris of the little corner *bistrot* with its assortment of picturesque regular clients, the cheap eating-shops, the cafés where laundrywomen and concierges would go after work and the lean-to's and shanties where *clochards* and the workless led a near-hopeless existence. He noted down and memorised the rich, slangy language of the people around him and, with the aid of a friend who worked for a police inspector, he explored the more dangerous world of the thieves' den, the street prostitute and her pimp, the thief and the swaggering *apache*. After frequenting some of the dance halls and *caf' conc's* in the working-class districts of Ménilmontant and Belleville, he started to write his own songs and sing them before predominantly proletarian audiences.

Like other singers, Bruant found that he could only make his début in the *café-concert*. Until about 1885, his repertoire mostly consisted of sentimental, humorous, patriotic or military songs, occasionally interspersed with a satirical reference to politics or a note of social comment, addressing his rough and ready public as equal to equal:

> Entre nous, j'trouv' que la grand' classe
> Pourrait s'occuper de c'qui s'passe
> sur l'pavé.[1]

Like every other self-respecting *chansonnier* of the time, Bruant had sung at the Chat Noir. He had met and become friendly with Jules Jouy, who had taken him to see Salis, who had agreed that Bruant should sing in the cabaret where he could sell his songs in lieu of remuneration. It was there, before a select audience, that Bruant's style underwent a transformation and that he emerged as the foremost singer-poet of the "other Paris", the city of the common people and the underworld. Many of his

---

[1] Between ourselves, I think the upper classes
Might take the trouble to see what passes,
on the streets.

songs had topographical titles after the districts which had inspired them—*à Batignolles, à la Villette, à Ménilmontant*—and he created a new folklore for the poorer Paris *faubourgs*. He sang at the Chat Noir and Les Ambassadeurs but after Salis had moved to the Rue Victor Massé he raised a loan and broke out on his own.

He returned to the Chat Noir's first home, took over the lease and opened his own cabaret, christening it Le Mirliton. It was a sparsely furnished establishment with a few sticks of furniture, a piano and a counter and it became the home of the most sensational one-man show in Paris. To begin with, his public had been scanty but after berating and insulting a customer who seemed to be poking fun at him and who returned the following night, apparently not in the least offended, Bruant discovered the formula for success: the more he mocked and swore at his middle- or upper-class patrons the better they loved it and they came back for more.

Unlike the Chat Noir with its lavish décor and Salis's penchant for ridiculous high-sounding titles and flummery, Le Mirliton remained a simple cabaret where people sat on chairs and benches to savour a genuine sample of working-class humour, wit and coarseness. As it had become popular to go slumming in Montmartre, well-known writers, actors, dandies and elegant ladies came to Bruant's cabaret. He treated them all with sovereign contempt. Anyone allowed into Le Mirliton after first knocking on the door would be greeted with a chorus of:

> Oh! la! la! Cett' gueul', cett' binette!
> Oh! la! la! Cett' gueul' qu'il a![1]

Then, before they had had time to regain their dignity, Bruant would stare rudely at them, hands on his hips, and apostrophise them as *salauds!* and *tas de cochons!* After inviting those already present to contemplate the pitiful faces of the newcomers, he would send them off to a far corner of the room to huddle in what was called the *Institut*, a space reserved for late-comers when all other seats had been taken.

With his thick black hair, high forehead, burly figure, fierce

[1] Oh! la! la! What a mug, what a phiz!
Oh! la! la! What a mug it is!

eyes and bitter smile, Bruant was an impressive figure who commanded respect. He invariably wore the same costume for his performances: black corduroy jacket and trousers, a bright red flannel shirt, black neck-scarf and black boots. He fully believed in audience participation. Before reciting one of his songs, he would gaze disdainfully at his audience for a few moments and then annouce the title of his next number: "Now, I'm going to sing you à Saint Lazare!" After a dramatic pause, he would repeat: "A Saint Lazare!" and then exhort his listeners to join in: "As for you, herd of camels, try to bray together in tune, will you?" He would usually sing from ten or eleven at night until two in the morning, walking up and down or sometimes standing up on a table as he did so. One visitor to Le Mirliton in its heyday was Arthur Symons:

"It was small, with wooden walls, and a few long plaques in high relief covered one wall, representing wild dancers, a sort of Bacchanalia à la Bullier, with mythological touches. Pictures were all about: an affiche of Les Ambassadeurs striking in its sardonic and striking way. Queer things hung from every corner; and along the ceiling, swords, carved images, and other odd ornaments. There was an inner room into which the initiated sometimes retired. On the stroke of eleven Bruant entered . . . He was clean shaven with a powerful face, hair brushed down, fine features, a certain dignity and occasionally a genial smile. He sang his own songs to his own music, in a loud and monotonous voice and without emphasis, always walking to and fro."

The critic Jules Lemaître paid more generous tribute to the quality of Bruant's voice for he declared it to be "the most cutting voice, the most metallic voice I have ever heard; a voice of rioting and the barricades which could dominate the roaring in the streets on a day of revolution; an arrogant and brutal voice which penetrated into your soul like the stab of a flick-knife into a straw dummy".

Bruant was accompanied by a pianist while two other singers, known as Chopinette and Alexandre, sang in his place when he took a break. The only drink in the house was beer and, as time went on and Bruant's popularity grew, the price went steadily up. The great period of Le Mirliton ended in 1897 when Bruant

left Paris to tour France and became co-director of the *café-concert*
l'Epoque on the Boulevard Beaumarchais, near the Bastille. In
May 1898, he stood as a radical candidate for the Belleville circumscription during the general elections, but he polled a mere
502 votes, coming last on the list. He later retired to the countryside, leaving behind him the cabaret Aristide Bruant which
flourished for a time on his reputation. His fame had grown to
such proportions that in 1896 his assistant Alexandre had left him
to plagiarise his act. He had opened a cabaret in the Rue Pigalle
and advertised himself as "le Bruyant Alexandre", copying his
master's costume and calling himself his "pupil". Bruant sued
and won his case but showed little rancour towards his former
employee. In 1924, at the age of seventy-three, Bruant made a
triumphal return to the Empire music hall where the Paris public
showed that they had not forgotten him. The following year he
died.

So much for Bruant's successful career. We must now come to
the songs he wrote and see what it was that made them absolutely
unique in the history of the French poetic *chanson*.

It had been said of Bruant that "all things considered, he had
the soul of a bourgeois *salaud*".[1] For all his declared contempt for
the middle classes, we may well imagine that Bruant's pose was
calculated to impress the public and fit in with the general
spirit of his songs, for he was a good business man as well as an
artist. But his desire to shock and provoke middle- and upper-
class audiences was shared by other artists of the time and there
is no reason to doubt that he did have very strong political and
social convictions. This was not enough, of course, for Bruant
was no mere "left-wing" singer. He was a poet in his own right
and his songs had genuine literary merit and were admired by
such discerning literary figures as the poets François Coppée and
Mallarmé.

His songs were written to be sung before small, intimate
audiences and any artificiality or forced sentiment would have
been inevitably exposed given the conditions of their presentation. Many were written in the *argot* of the working class and the

[1] F. Borgex, *La fin d'un siècle*, Paris 1953.

vernacular of the outer districts and slums which Bruant had so well explored. His best compositions were distinguished by simplicity, poignancy and truthfulness. There was no glossing over the sad facts of life and none of the sentimentality that delighted English music-hall audiences when they went to hear "Cockney" songs. Whether his songs were bitter, trivial, humorous or brutal they always remained vivid and sincere. Often, they were inspired by the life of the streets and the tribulations of the homeless and out-of-work, but although they were full of distress they were not in the nature of laments or cries for pity. It was in songs of the *apache* and the urban outlaw that Bruant particularly excelled. To some extent, he represented the tradition of François Villon and the spirit which animated his songs of thieves, prostitutes and pavement Romeos was that of the real-life protagonists of the dramas he recorded in verse.

Such themes were not new for the picaresque rogue or social outlaw had already acquired a certain literary respectability and the idea of reviving the Villon type of ballad had already been anticipated. In 1876, the poet and playwright Jean Richepin had published his collection of "beggars' songs", the *Chansons des Gueux*. Although he may well have intended them to be "popular" pieces, they illustrated all the pitfalls awaiting a literary-minded author who endeavoured to create a poetry of the people from above rather than from inside. The language Richepin used was one compounded of archaisms and a hopelessly erudite *argot*. They remained lifeless and devoid of any of the vigour that comes from the direct observation of real life whereas the language of Bruant was a living one which had been welded into powerful poetry.

When people came to hear Bruant they were not visiting the Mirliton to hear a message or to have their social consciences stirred but to hear the authentic voice of the "other side". Bruant's success in establishing the new *genre* in French song, or "sung poetry" as we may call it, made an important contribution to the cause of "naturalism" in French poetry and the Paris folklore of the "little people" which has been continued in recent years by the films of Renoir and Marcel Carné, the poetry of Prévert, the songs of Piaf and Juliette Greco.

Like Salis, Bruant also published a review for which the title was the name of his cabaret. *Le Mirliton* appeared irregularly at first and then became a successful weekly, each number containing a new song and an illustration on the front page by Steinlen who became famous as the graphic interpreter of Bruant's poetry. Steinlen came of an artists' family in French-speaking Switzerland and as a young man he had been deeply impressed by Zola's novel *l'Assommoir*. Zola's picture of plebeian Paris had drawn Steinlen to the city and particularly to Montmartre where his sympathies had brought him into contact with Bruant whose colleague and accredited illustrator he became.

Bruant's songs have survived in publication. Besides appearing in *Le Mirliton* and the paper *Gil Blas Illustré* which specialised in publishing popular songs with illustrations, his songs became published in two volumes, both titled *Dans la Rue*. One song, *à la Villette*, the story of a typical "teddy boy" of the time, is worth reproducing *in extenso* for not only was it one of his most popular numbers but it gives us a good idea of his unforced, ballad style. The song is supposed to be sung by the girl friend of a young *apache*, the most handsome in the quarter, and it ends on a note of inevitable tragedy. Like many of his kind, the hero ends up in prison and the last time his sweetheart sees him he is lying, stripped to the waist, with his head held in the *lunette* under the knife of the guillotine in the open square in front of the prison of La Roquette where all public executions took place at the time:

A la Villette

Il avait pas encor' vingt ans
L'connaissait pas ses parents,
On l'app'lait Toto Laripette
à la Villette.

Il était un peu sans façon,
Mais c'etait un joli garçon:
c'était l'plus beau, c'était l'plus chouette
à la Villette.

. . .

I'm'aimait autant que j'l'aimais,
Nous nous aurions quittés jamais
Si la police était pas faite
            à la Villette.

Q'on l'prenn' grand ou p'tit, rouge ou brun
On peut pas en conserver un:
I's'en vont tous à la Roquette
            à la Villette.

La dernièr' fois que je l'ai vu,
Il avait l'torse à moitié nu,
Et le cou pris dans la Lunette
            à la Roquette.[1]

Another singer of the "poetry of the pavements" in the Nineties was Gabriel Randon, known as Jehan Rictus, but whereas

[1] An attempted translation must inevitably remain an unsatisfactory approximation of the original. However, a rough equivalent would be:

He wasn't even twenty yet
His parents he never knew,
They called him Toto Laripette
            at la Villette.

He was a bit rough in all his ways,
But still he was a handsome lad.
He was the best-looking, he was one of the best
            at la Villette.

. . .

He loved me and I loved him,
We'd never have left each other
If there'd never been the police
            at la Villette.

Take them big or take them small, red-hair or dark,
There's no keeping any of them.
They all end up at La Roquette
            at la Villette

The last time that I saw him
His chest it was stripped bare
And his head held fast in the *lunette*
            at la Roquette.

Bruant's shrewdness had brought him recognition and prosperity, Randon was to remain a tragic outcast and rebel all his
life.

His whole life was one of poverty and suffering. He was born
at Boulogne in 1867 and had lived for a time as a child with his
family in England before coming to Paris at the age of eleven
with his mother. For reasons which remain obscure, he ran away
from home at the age of sixteen and worked for a time as an
errand boy. Then, from 1883 until 1889, he suffered the first of
the many desperate periods of abject poverty which were to scar
his life. He had been a puny youth, so thin that he had been nick-
named *Fil de Fer*. It is a wonder that he did not die in the years he
was living the life of a *clochard* in Paris, wandering from one
district to another, starving and in constant fear of arrest for
vagabondage. During one terrible winter, that of 1888-9, he had
slept outside in the streets and doorways almost every night until
he collapsed and was taken to hospital, where he was kept until
the following spring.

A post as assistant clerk was found for him in the Paris Town
Hall, in an office headed by the poet Albert Samain. It was there
that the boy's vocation for poetry was recognised and encouraged
by Samain. In the years of his wanderings as a penniless vagrant,
Randon had become passionately interested in the life of the
Middle Ages and, in particular, in the poetry of Villon which
had seemed to him to epitomise the spirit of the common people
of Paris. Randon's self-identification with the beggars and rogues
of the Middle Ages, his long acquaintance with hardship and the
life of the *clochards*, and his extensive knowledge of Paris *argot* and
popular diction inspired him to attempt the creation of a new
"poetry of the people". Until the 16th century, he claimed,
poetry in France had been composed for everyone to enjoy:
there had been no difference between the language of poetry and
that spoken by ordinary people. He aimed at giving poetry back
this universality and he wrote verses and songs in a French he
described as "being strewn with ancient and modern words like
garlic in a joint".

Had Randon been content to confine himself to writing he
would probably have taken his place as a minor poet in a few

anthologies of French verse, but he also wanted to communicate directly with a public, believing that the true function of poetry is to be recited or sung. He gave himself the medieval Christian name of Jehan, adding "Rictus", a word which means a grimacing smile, more of pain than of humour; and with Samain's encouragement he made his début in a Latin Quarter artists' and poets' club, La Bosse, before moving on to Montmartre where he gave recitals at the Chat Noir and the Quat'z Arts cabarets.

He began by being fairly successful with a series of song-poems called *Soliloquies of the poor man*. Audiences found his slangy style impressive but occasionally obscure. Like Bruant he was a spokeman of the life of the Paris streets and slums:

"Above all, the Paris suburb dweller has a love of the picturesque, a gift for imagery, and a genius for banter, whence his extraordinary eloquence. He speaks a true poet's language. You must, since your childhood, have wandered, suffered and starved in Paris and its faubourgs and suburbs to really understand the profound humanity of the popular language, its joy, its colour and, even, its music . . . "

But there was little joy in his appearance and his recitals. He was a strange sight to the sophisticated audiences of the *cabarets artistiques* as he half-sang, half-recited his poems of poverty and homelessness, written in his peculiar kind of *argot*, in his sad and toneless voice. Very tall and very thin, with long bony arms and hands, a long, haggard face with sunken eyes, reddened eyelids, a drooping moustache and straggling, ill-kempt beard, he must have seemed the very embodiment of the tragic wanderer of the Paris streets, as in his *Nocturne*:

> A chacun son tour le trottoir,
> J'vas dans l'silence et le désert,
> Car l'jour les rues les pus brillantes
> Les pus pétardier's et grouillantes
> A Minoch' sent gu'des grands couloirs,
> Des collidors à ciel ouvert.
>
> J'suis l'Empereur du Pavé . . .
> j'suis l'baladeur . . . le bouff'-purée,

Le rod-la-nuit ... le long-ruisseaux,
Le marque-mal à hueul' tirée,
Le mâche-angoiss' ... le caus'-tout haut.

. . .

Et d'Charonne au quartier Monceau,
Au milieu du sommeil des hommes,
Me v'là seul avec ma pensée,
Et ma gueul' pal' dands les ruisseaux!"[1]

Jehan Rictus also gave recitals of the works of other poets, including Gérard de Nerval and Samain, and once even appeared at a soirée in the rooms of the painter Gauguin in 1895. But even though he was defended and admired by such a notable fellow-poet as Mallarmé, his performances disconcerted and mystified other critics. After an early measure of success as a novelty and a curiosity, Jehan aroused the jealousy of other *chansonniers*, from whom he stayed aloof, and the hostility of cabaret-owners. He was too difficult for them, too uncompromising and too touchy. His hatred of what he called "salon poetry" and his bad-tempered reaction to any hint of criticism discouraged those who might

---

[1] To each in his turn, the pavements,
I walk in silence and in a desert,
For i'th' day the finest streets
The fullest of din and crowds
At mi'nigh' are only great hallways,
Corridors open to the sky.

I'm the Emp'ror of the Pavement,
I'm th'roamer ... the mash-chewer,
Th'slink-at-nights ... th' along-the-gutters,
The out-of-sorts, the long-mug,
Th'anguish-chewer ... the talk-to-himself.

. . .

And from Charonne to the Monceau quarter,
In the middle of men asleep,
Here I'm alone with my thoughts
And my pale mug down there in the gutter!

otherwise have helped him. The trouble was that he was too much the crusader and the fanatic for him ever to succeed in establishing himself as an entertainer or an artist with an audience. Excess of suffering in his youth had left him without a sense of humour.

After his first poems had been published by the *Mercure de France,* he cut himself off from company, went into seclusion and devoted himself to his stark, slangy poetry in an obsessive endeavour to renew French poetry through a return to everyday language "of the people". An almost mystical sense of mission possessed him increasingly until his death in obscurity in 1933. From some of his writings and semi-didactic verse, it is clear that he saw himself as a kind of apostle of the French poor and proletariat but the tragedy was that there were none to listen to him any longer.

A more successful performer who also did much to popularise songs of low life and the Paris streets was the Algerian-born *caf' conc'* singer Eugénie Buffet. She was a gaunt and eccentric young woman with a stormy private life, who had once been sent to prison for a fortnight after expressing her Boulangist sympathies somewhat too vociferously for the authorities. She was particularly successful at dramatic song-recitations in which she played the part of the Paris *pierreuse*, the tart of the poorer districts who had become one of the leading stock characters in the folk lore of *fin de siècle* Paris.

Eugénie Buffet had discovered her true vocation after a visit to Le Mirliton and had made her début at the *café-concert* La Cigale near the Place Pigalle in December 1892. She sang two of Bruant's best-known *faubourg* songs, *à Saint Lazare* and *à Saint Ouen*, and was such a hit that she was given a contract at once. Always specialising in the rôle of the *pierreuse*, she afterwards sang at the Gaîté-Rochechouart, one of the most important music halls, and Les Ambassadeurs where one of her most appreciated numbers was —appropriately enough—called *Sérénade du Pavé*. She also sang some of Jean Richepins's more natural compositions. After seeing her, the poet noted that "her voice is not to be catalogued. It is unlike anything you may hear at lyric theatres or concerts, or even at *café-concerts*." But, without a doubt, the most unusual and least catalogue-able voice of the decade was that of Yvette Guilbert.

Like all performers of genius, Yvette Guilbert belonged to that race of artists who defy all classification and comparisons. She was one of the great phenomena of the period and although she made her name in a *genre* which had already become established, she succeeded in something which neither Bruant at his finest nor Eugénie Buffet had succeeded in doing: although her songs were essentially Parisian and as such not easily comprehensible to foreign audiences, she was equally successful in communicating her art and the essence of the Parisian spirit to audiences abroad, in London and New York.

Yvette was born in Paris in 1867, into a poor family. She had at first trained for the stage and her first and unsuccessful appearances on a stage had been at the Bouffes-du-Nord music hall and the Théâtre des Nouveautés in 1887. Two years later, she had obtained engagements as a singer in Lyons and then in Paris at a number of theatres, including the Eldorado music hall where she sang the usual kind of *caf' conc'* repertoire with uneven success. She then moved to the more respectable and staid Eden where she specialised in "clean and wholesome" songs and sketches. She was gradually establishing a reputation and in 1890, after leaving the Eden, she was taken on by Zidler at the Moulin Rouge where she sang every evening before the dancing began.

She still had not quite found herself as an artist or discovered the vein of song in which she was to distinguish herself but she was fast acquiring valuable experience, particularly in the art of miming and dramatic suggestion. One of her early famous numbers was *Miss Valérie*, a comic little ditty about an English maid who coolly turns down the repeated advances of her French employer, and she sang in an imitation-English accent which delighted the public. But all the time, Yvette Guilbert was moving towards a "realism" in song that was inspired by the realism in literature of Zola, Goncourt and Maupassant. As she later wrote in her *Memoirs*, these were days in which "my only aim was realism; I tried to do in song what they had done in fiction. These ideas were gradually taking shape in my mind."

She spent one summer looking for the right kind of song for her repertoire and came across the songs of Xanrof including his famous *Le Fiacre* and *Les Quat'z' étudiants*. Using Xanrof's songs as the foundations for a new style, she went to Belgium where she was a sensational success. She even revealed her own gifts as a song writer with one "realistic" composition, *La Pocharde*, in which she acted the part of a drunken woman.

Back in Paris, she returned to the Eden where *La Pocharde* was equally successful notwithstanding the mournful predictions of the manageress who was convinced that the new type of song had no future.

In a short time Yvette was in great demand among the important Paris *café-concerts* and music halls and she began to attract a more select and discerning audience after a literary critic and editor, Réné Maizeroy, had written a glowing account of her in the weekly *Gil Blas*. Thereafter her life as an artist was an unbroken success story. Zidler had told her that if she hoped to establish herself completely she would have to "go down" into the city from the heights of Montmartre and this she proceeded to do, but already she was fast becoming a new idol and drawing the *tout-Paris* to Montmartre, whose spirit she seemed to incarnate.

From the Moulin Rouge she would go on to sing at the Divan Japonais later in the same evening. Although it was a cramped little cabaret, she could sing a different kind of song to a different public and found it far more artistically satisfying than the Moulin Rouge. In later life, she recalled the difficult physical conditions in which she had to sing:

"Imagine a little café-hall of the provinces with a low ceiling and in which some hundred and fifty or two hundred people could be crowded at a pinch. It was there that people came to sing.

"There was a platform set at the back of the hall, about a metre and a half from the floor, which obliged me to take care not to lift my arms unless it was absolutely necessary for then, my hands would hit the ceiling—a ceiling up to which the heat of the gas-lit footlights rose so fiercely that it was like putting one's head into a suffocating furnace!"

Other singers could only stand it for about ten minutes but

Yvette would remain there for an hour at a time, singing to an audience which included painters, sculptors, men of letters and journalists. The Divan Japonais was managed by an amateur poet, Jehan Sarrazin, known as "the poet with the olives" since he would recite his verses while holding a small barrel of olives which he would sell wrapped in sheets of his own scribblings. The atmosphere was sometimes noisy but always good-hearted. Yvette remembered how Madame Sarrazin would sit at the cash desk and keep an eye on the clientèle, her spectacles perched on the end of her nose, or else serve drinks while a boy stood by her husband to help him as a chucker-out if necessary.

But when Sarrazin would shout for quiet and announce that "Mademoiselle Guilbert is going to sing some songs for us" there was always quiet. It was in such unassuming surroundings in an atmosphere typical of the Bohemia of Montmartre that Yvette Guilbert perfected her "realistic" style before audiences who understood and encouraged her. She never forgot her debt to Montmartre:

"It was in the Divan Japonais that my artistic consecration began. And Montmartre has kept my heart. At the Divan I sang the songs of Xanrof and Bruant. For the public they were a revelation; for it was there, for the first time, that they escaped from out of their confines, the Chat Noir, and through me became popular throughout the world."

Yvette's admirers included such brilliant personalities and talents as Willette, the cartoonist, the poster-artists Léandre, Forain and Steinlen, the singer Maurice Donnay, her composer Xanrof and, of course, Toulouse-Lautrec. Journalists including Maizeroy, Georges Montorgueil, Catulle Mendès and Arthur Meyer, director of the influential *Le Gaulois* newspaper, were also regular visitors and helped to make her famous in Paris. Another important friend was the tragic actor Sylvain who would come from the Comédie Française to hear her, bringing with him some of his pupils so that they might learn from her technique of recitation.

Fashionable Paris and high society heard of her and wanted to see her. As they did not go to anything as vulgar as a music hall or a cabaret, Yvette was invited to the small Théâtre d'Application where she proved just as much a success as in the Divan Japonais. She was invited to sing before a private gathering in the house of the publisher Charpentier and she was praised to the skies by an illustrious band of writers which included Zola, Alphonse Daudet, Pierre Loti, Octave Mirbeau and Jean Lorrain. Her art was one that transcended all social frontiers. She was probably the best-loved entertainer in Paris and so greatly worshipped that crowds would follow her from the Moulin Rouge to the Divan Japonais and then accompany her cab when it drove her home late at night. The public soon realised that she was no ordinary singer of *caf' conc'* songs and some intellectual admirers urged her to go on the legitimate stage, declaring that among her gifts she had that of a great tragic actress.

The kind of *chanson* that Yvette Guilbert raised to such artistic heights was unlike the usual lyrical ballad or *chansonette*. Words counted for more than the musical line and her ability to project a personality and to evoke an atmosphere or a mood were far more important than her actual musical ability. Although she sang songs that were of slight poetic or musical worth, almost everything she sang became "something special". After he had heard her sing one of her "realist" songs, no less a literary giant than Edmond de Goncourt wrote in his *Journal* that she had shown herself to be "a great, a very great tragic actress who causes your heart to constrict with anguish". Similar opinions were voiced in London after Yvette had made a very successful appearance at the Empire Theatre in May 1894, and she went on to tour New York where she was no less appreciated.

Although a lot in her songs was too French to be understood, she was a sensation and quite unlike anything the English or American public had ever seen in their music halls. Bernard Shaw had seen her perform to an audience at the Savoy and had realised the vast difference between her and even a talented "popular singer", observing that "there is not a trace of the rowdy restlessness and forced 'go' of the English music-hall singer about her". The aesthetes of the *Yellow Book* found much to fascinate them in her art and in a long article devoted to her claimed that it was "in the beautifying of the terrible that lies the supremacy of her art".

The critics of the *Yellow Book* were right for there certainly was an element of the "terrible" in her art and in her poetic evocations of a Paris which had been given such prominence in the books of Zola. At the same time, her chameleon-like personality enabled her to render comic and sentimental songs with equal effect. She could radiate an air of beauty and hold men enchanted but she was anything but a physical beauty. She was tall, even gawky, and had a habit of craning her neck forward as she sang. The pen portrait that Jean Lorrain gave of her makes a worthy accompaniment to Toulouse-Lautrec's famous sketches.

"She is tall—oh, so tall and thin—oh, so thin! Her chest is of a chalky whiteness and her figure slightly rounded but she has no bosom to speak of and her chest is quite extraordinarily narrow. She has long—too long—thin arms clad in high black gloves that look like flimsy streamers, and a bodice that seems about to be slipping off her shoulders . . . the great originality of this very modern singer lies in her almost rigid immobility, the 'English' appearance of her long, thin, overgrown body and the absence of gestures which is in strong contrast to the almost diabolical rolling of her eyes, and the grimaces and contortions of her bloodless face."

Lorrain's description of her might almost be that of a Japanese mask. He was certainly exaggerating her appearance which readily lent itself to caricature but there was no exaggerating the effect she produced on her audiences. Goncourt had called her a *diseuse* and he was right, for even though she followed the melodic line of a composition the result was more in the nature of a semi-musical dramatic recitation and mime than a song. She was at her greatest in songs which allowed her to make use of her dramatic gifts. Two of the most famous both had tragic themes and made an immense impact on the public.

The first, *La Soularde*, was widely held to be her masterpiece. It had been suggested by her and written by Jules Jouy. The subject was a homeless old woman lurching through the Paris streets in a drunken, exhausted stupor. Yvette Guilbert created a picture of this human wreck in a few lines, as incisive as those of a sketch by Steinlen:

Dés le matin, on peut la voir,
Sur le pavé, sur le trottoir,
Cheminer, la mine haggarde,
    La soularde.

Un ancien châle à mêm' la peau,
Coiffée d'travers d'un vieux chapeau,
En marchant, tout' seule, à bavarde,
    La soularde.

. . .

Chien égaré cherchant son trou,
Parfois, allant sans savoir où,
Loin de la barrière ell'se hasarde,
    La soularde.[1]

The song ends with mocking passers-by and children throwing rotten vegetables and rubbish at the crazy old woman as she staggers past them. The end made a very deep impression on the critic of the *Yellow Book*, who tells us how the performance struck a foreign audience at the time: "At the end of the verse . . . Yvette Guilbert throws her head back and breaks the final syllable of the refrain *La Soularde* into a cry of two notes. It would scarcely be too much to call this the greatest moment that has ever been brought off in executory art. It takes your breath away."

The other great song was equally tragic in spirit. *Ma Tête,*

[1] From morning onwards you may see her
   On the street, on the pavement,
   Making her way with haggard face,
      The drunk old woman.

   An ancient shawl next to her skin,
   An old hat askew on her head,
   Walking alone, muttering to herself,
      The drunk old woman.

   . . .

   A stray dog looking for its hole,
   Sometimes, going she knows not where,
   Far beyond the walls she wanders,
      The drunk old woman.

rather like Bruant's song *à la Villette*, is the story of a young *apache* who haunts the *zone* on the outskirts of Paris. He is popular with the girls, smart and well dressed and a typical "teddy-boy" of the Nineties who lives by charming women and robbing the well-off. He lives for the moment only, defiant of any organised society, without guilt, and fatalistically accepts the probability that he will end by being guillotined one grey morning:

> Faudra qu'j'attend, blême et vanne,
> L'instant suprème de la guillotine,
> Alors un beau jour on m'dira:
> C'est pour c'matin, fait's vot' toilette;
> J'sortirai, la foul'salu'ra
> 　　　　Ma tête![1]

Such a song had a macabre and intense effect on French audiences. Capital punishment was still carried out in public and both the tall uprights of the guillotine and the figure of the executioner, Monsieur de Paris, cast their long shadow over the popular imagination. To imagine the effect of the song we must go back in time and imagine ourselves among a Paris audience, held spell-bound by a pale thin woman with long black gloves and immensely expressive gestures, slowly dragging out the words of the final verse, halting after *la foul' salu'ra* and then, after a pause, gasping out the final words *Ma tête* in an atmosphere of electric tension.

Small wonder that such a performer could fascinate very different publics and become a legend. Yvette Guilbert sang in the same style until the early years of this century and then changed completely, appearing in 18th-century costume to sing traditional songs of an earlier age. But although she brought the same amount of genius to her new repertoire, her greatest achievement had been to raise the realistic type of French song

---

[1] I'll have to wait, pale and dead-beat,
　For the supreme moment of the guillotine,
　When one fine day they'll say to me:
　It's for this morning, make yourself ready;
　I'll go out and the crowd will cheer
　　　My head!

to the level of an art, taking it out of Montmartre and then Paris
to give the world another expression of the spirit and genius of
the city in its *Belle Epoque*. She was one of the first great international "stars" of modern times and of all the singer poets of
the Nineties she performed the greatest services for what must
henceforth be considered an integral part of the living culture
of that time.

III

THE ARTISTIC REVOLUTION
PART I

ON AUGUST 23, 1890, a twenty-year-old painter and writer on art called Maurice Denis wrote in a small Parisian art review that "a painting, before being a warhorse, a naked woman, some anecdote or whatnot, is essentially a flat surface covered with colours arranged in a certain order". It was a revolutionary statement for the period. Later, Denis remarked that he saw the year 1890 as a "turning in the road of art". To a very large extent, he was right. The 1890's in Paris and the first decade of the 20th century were one of the most fertile periods in the history of Western art. In the Nineties, some of the most important battles between traditional conceptions and new theories in art were fought in Paris and the foundations were laid for what we now call "modern art". But even when young Denis was making his statement, which later became famous, there were few signs that Paris was about to become the world's leading centre for artistic innovation.

Paris was already famous for women's fashions, for its brilliant high society life, its gastronomy and all the entertainments that created the legend of the *Belle Epoque*; but, at first sight, it seemed to have little to offer in the way of new art.

The kind of painting, sculpture, furniture, interior decoration and architecture in favour with most Parisians who could afford them was distinguished by academic traditionalism, a nostalgia for past styles and a total lack of imagination. In the paintings which the prosperous bourgeois admired in exhibitions or hung on his walls, the emphasis was on a nearly photographic realism and on subject matter. A painting had to be "well done" and the subject represented had to be "picturesque", "dramatic" or "moving". Most of the paintings produced were narrative scenes, historical or military, sentimentally contrived incidents from everyday life, portraits or illustrations of Greek and Roman legends, the last being good pretexts for representations of the nude. Such paintings were no different in style and spirit from those that could be seen in homes and art galleries and in thousands of engraved reproductions in Berlin, Vienna, Brussels, Rome or London. Where Paris differed from other capitals was in its attraction for art students from all over the world—lured to the city by its Bohemia and uninhibited student life—and in the exceptional degree of official respect paid to the most popular artists.

The last three decades of the 19th century in Paris saw the apotheosis of the great masters of what is now known as "official", "Salon" or "academic" art. The art they produced faithfully reflected the standards, tastes and ideals that prevailed among France's middle and upper classes, and in return for their paintings they were lionised in society and honoured by the state.

The works of most of these painters have long been forgotten or if they are occasionally resurrected it is because of their curiosity value, their "quaintness" or because of the light they throw on the social history of the time. But the life and civilisation of the late 19th century cannot be fully appreciated if we ignore them because such works were more typically representative of the society that produced them than those of the revolutionary artists. The *chers maîtres* of the *Belle Epoque* are as much part of the background of 1890's life in Paris as the horse carriage, the Second Empire-style architecture of the boulevards, the bustles and frills of elegant ladies and the general air of comfortable opulence that older generations have recalled with much nostalgia.

The governments of the Third Republic decided that, like Louis XIV and Napoleon III, they too would be great patrons of the arts. It was a chauvinistic age and in promoting art they felt that they were promoting France's prestige as a great, powerful nation which had fully recovered from the humiliation of defeat by Prussia in 1870. The kind of painting they admired and encouraged was grandiose, huge and always resolutely realistic in style. It was the equivalent of the officially sponsored architecture of the time and the civil servants in the Ministry of Fine Arts were lavish in giving commissions to officially approved artists to decorate buildings of public importance.

The painters who were called upon to cover the walls of such buildings as the Sorbonne and other university premises, the Law Courts, the Panthéon, the Hôtel de Ville and the various *mairies* were invariably those who had undergone academic training under the older masters at the Ecole des Beaux Arts. They were the painters who had won the Prix de Rome which entitled them to stay at the Villa Medici in Rome which was the official Italian residence of the French Academy, and who steadily exhibited at the official Salon of French artists every year. The works they produced for the official patrons may still be seen today. They are like giant illustrations for old-fashioned school history books, and mostly consist of historical scenes like *The Massacre of the Barbarians by Hamilcar*, in the Sorbonne building, or such allegories as *Truth leading the Sciences and shedding her Light over Mankind*. All these great frescoes with their painstaking, detailed scenes and determined optimism are perfect examples of that pompous, grandiloquent painting now given the derisive name of *pompier* in France. Similar monumental compositions were also admired in the Salon exhibitions which played such an important part in social life, and in museums which bought them for the State.

The officially sponsored artistic life of Paris was centred around the yearly Salon which was held in the premises of the Palace of Industry on the Champs Elysées. It was a meeting place for fashionable society, it was there that all that was recognised as French art was displayed, and it was there that painters could hope to sell their works to collectors and attract the attention of wealthy, influential patrons. It was in the Salon that a new painter could make a reputation, gain the esteem of the critics, and win his first medal, thus starting along the path that led to important state commissions, official decorations and perhaps membership of some august body like the Institute of France. Few one-man exhibitions were held. There were less than a dozen art galleries of any importance before 1900. Dealers were few, and for any painter or sculptor to break into the market, find favour with

Aristide Bruant at Le Mirliton

Yvette Guilbert drawn by Toulouse-Lautrec

The Birth of Venus by Bouguereau

André Antoine at Work

From a *Théâtre Libre* Programme

PROGRAMME DU Théâtre LIBRE

Ce blanc Pierrot assassiné,
N'est-il pas l'Idéal sans tache
Que la Réalité s'attache
A frapper d'un poing obstiné?

Qu'importe! Pierrot vit encore,
Et du plus pur sang de son coeur
Jaillit toujours l'Espoir vainqueur
Fleur de pourpre qui le décore!

Rodolphe Darzens

oct. 1888 -

Francisque Sarcey

Verlaine at the Café François Ier

A Headline from *Le Père Peinard*

Ravachol on Trial

Dynamite in the Chambre des Députés
Anarchist Celebrities: The Editorial Staff of *L'Endehors*

Alfred Jarry

Joséphin Péladan by Desboutin

From Léo Taxil's *Les Maîtresses du Pape*

'Diana Vaughan' in Palladist Uniform

collectors and eventually see his work sold in thousands of steel-engraved reproductions, the prizes awarded by the Salon juries were all-important.

The Salon exhibition would be inaugurated by the President of the Republic in the morning, in the presence of numerous officials and artists. In the afternoon, the private view or *vernissage* would be held. This was the great day for Paris's leading fashion houses who would launch their newest styles. All the great names in Paris society would attend. After the President had performed the opening ceremony and dutifully toured the rooms with his retinue, uttering a few ritual phrases of appreciation here and there, artists and officials would go to the elegant Restaurant Ledoyen nearby for lunch before returning to meet their friends and admirers. The Salon would be crowded by generals and academicians, politicians and journalists. Celebrities from all walks of life would turn up to admire and be admired, and to pay homage to what was generally believed to represent the summit of the French artistic genius.

For days after this event, magazines and newspapers would publish long columns devoted to the exhibition, describing each of the main "novelties" in detail and lavishing praise on the leading favourites.

The painting on view in Salon after Salon was all basically the same and seemed destined to continue unchanged indefinitely. The works that Paris society of the later 19th century expected to see and admire were a collection of costume pictures illustrating such dramatic events as the murder of Julius Caesar or the Fall of Babylon, nudes in the approved Graeco-Roman manner, sentimental scenes of daily life, domestic incidents, landscapes and battle scenes, these last being especially popular and mostly inspired by incidents in the Napoleonicand Franco-Prussian wars. Such pictures were not expected to be adventurous or experimental since it was taught and it was believed by most people that the purpose of French art was to instruct, adorn, edify and exalt.

The "masters" were practically regarded as public servants. They believed it was their duty to maintain the traditions of French civilisation. Technical skill was considered all-important.

The picture had to be based upon careful drawing in the classical manner and the colouring had to be orthodox and realistic. The figures had to be lifelike and the more carefully rendered detail the artist could cram into his composition, the more likely he was to be admired and praised for his "realism". As it was believed that there was only one way to paint a picture, as taught in the academies and art schools, the originality of a painting tended to depend upon the artist's choice of subject. When, in 1878, one of the most popular painters of the day, Henri Gervex, created a sensation at the Paris Salon with a picture called *Rolla*, it was not on account of any radical innovation in pictorial technique. It was simply because the subject—a lover gazing at the naked body of his mistress sprawling on an unmade bed—was considered to be "daring". Twenty years later, the situation was basically the same: to be successful, a painter was expected to be a meticulous draughtsman, to use conventional colours, to pay as much attention to the smallest detail as to the main figures in his composition, and to choose an "interesting" subject.

Academic art seemed to have come to the end of its road. Most of the critics, the public and buyers generally agreed that French art had reached an ideal state and was destined to continue as before, with each new generation of artists faithfully adhering to established styles and standards. Art was a system and, for those who conformed to the system and became popular, the rewards were great. Once a painter was well established, he led a comfortable life. The most successful artists lived like princes in great mansions in the most fashionable parts of Paris, magazines published photographs of them in their huge studios, they were welcome in high social circles and were given important commissions and honours by members of the government and civil service. They virtually monopolised the art market, dominated the exhibitions and became members of juries at the Salon. No matter what they painted, the successful painters all shared a common feeling that they belonged to the same caste. An academic or Salon painter was a member of a club with clearly defined and unchangeable rules. They were public figures and established, officially approved representatives of their nation's culture.

There was no question of the artist being a man outside society, a rebel shut away in his studio struggling to express a personal emotion or view of life in an idiosyncratic manner which disregarded the way other artists painted and the methods by which art was taught. They were at peace with a society which they served and which honoured them in return, and they earned vast sums.

The academics had learned how to paint in a certain manner and—perhaps even more important—they knew exactly what they were expected to paint. The idea that an artist could change his style and technique, mature and transform his art as he followed the impulsions of his genius was alien to them. Similarly, the idea that the officially accepted attitude to art could be stultifying, outmoded or reactionary never occurred to most artists and critics. They would have been deeply hurt if anyone had called them either reactionary or unimaginative.

When one of the most notorious of the Salon painters, William Bouguereau, spoke in 1885 to the five Academies of Paris at their annual meeting in the building of the Institute of France, he was being perfectly sincere when he said:

"One is born an artist. The artist is a man of a special nature, who has a particular sense which is to see form and colour spontaneously, together, in a perfect harmony . . . One must first love nature with all one's heart and soul, and be capable of spending hours before it, studying and admiring it. Everything is in nature. A plant, a leaf, a blade of grass are objects for infinite and profound meditation."

Cézanne might have agreed with his words but had one of his landscapes been shown to Bouguereau, the latter would have been horrified. Yet there were many upholders of Salon art who deeply believed that it was progressive in spirit. In one of the many large albums of reproductions of French paintings that were published at the time, Les Maîtres de l'Art français, the author repeated the prevailing official opinion of contemporary painting when he said that "it has rediscovered life which is the first condition of art; it has widened the framework of painting; it has enfranchised it from deadly and superannuated prejudices. Our revolutionaries have, all in all, done useful work and now that their exaggerations are a thing of the past, lofty tendencies have prevailed, and French art continues its triumphal march while becoming more intimate, more truthful, more human.

"From this point of view above all, our painters conform to their time which is distinguished by a special horror of convention, whatever it may be. Man now sees himself or seeks to see himself as he is."

The "revolutionaries" must have been the Impressionists or perhaps the "ultra-realistic" Courbet who had been reproached for his exaggerated naturalism. Among the artists mentioned in the book as being among those "who conformed to their time" are Falguière, Bouguereau, Meissonier and Carolus Duran, all prominent representatives of late 19th-century Salon art at its most conservative.

Each of the most famous painters who reigned supreme in the Paris exhibitions and drawing-rooms in the 1880's and '90's had his own speciality. The collector of battle scenes would buy a painting by Meissonier or Edouard Détaille; Cormon provided scenes of prehistory; Jean-Paul Laurens supplied sumptuous historical scenes when not busy on one of his innumerable commissions, painting walls and ceilings in official buildings; the admirer of nudes would address himself to Bouguereau, and the celebrity in search of a portrait painter would try to arrange sittings with Bonnat. Other great names in Parisian art were Carolus Duran, Carrière, Gervex, Roll, Besnard, Rochegrosse and Gérôme. Every one of their conscientiously painted but un-original works was an event when it appeared on view before the public and the prices paid for them were enormous. They were acclaimed as the masterpieces of French art at the time, and as continuing proof of the genius of the idols of establishment painting, the "dear masters", who upheld the nation's cultural prestige in the eyes of the world.

For years, the supreme figure in this world of academic art was Meissonier who specialised in military subjects and reconstructions of famous battles. He was so highly regarded that French generals would manoeuvre troops and stage cavalry charges before him in order to help him compose a painting. Meissonier had risen from humble origins, being a grocer's son, and began his long and successful career in 1836 when he first attracted attention in the Paris Salon. For the rest of his life, he demonstrated the immense material awards a painter might expect if he applied himself to winning and retaining the approval of both the government and society.

Meissonier had sold his painting of two 17th-century bravos drawing their swords at each other in a quarrel, *La Rixe*, to Napoleon III for the unprecedented sum of 150,000 francs. Years later, one of his most passionate admirers, the collector Chauchard, paid 840,000 francs for his *1812*, the famous picture of the tired Napoleon retreating from Moscow. Many of his other works fetched hundreds of thousands of francs and he made many thousands more through the sale of steel-engraved reproductions of his most famous pictures. It was said of him that his signature alone was worth that of the Bank of France. Naturally, the government honoured him and in 1889 he was awarded the Grand Cordon of the Legion of Honour. He was an extremely vain man and in 1890 he founded a rival Salon together with several other famous painters since he could not obtain the coveted post of President of the Salon of French Artists, that seat being already occupied. The private viewing at this new Salon was the glorious climax to his career since the President of the Republic came to it, accompanied by the Republican Guard in full dress uniform who blew a fanfare of bugles as the painter stepped into the Salon. Meissonier's death in 1891 was an event of international importance. The German Kaiser send his condolences and the funeral procession in Paris included trains of artillery.

Meissonier was successful because he gave the French public exactly what it wanted and could understand. He satisfied its jingoism with his huge battle scenes and reminders of the glory of French arms, and he also satisfied their demands in art with his photographic precision, his technical virtuosity and his attention to detail. He always took great pains to ensure the accuracy of his compositions and made use of models. In his *Recollections of a Picture Dealer*, Ambroise Vollard gave an amusing description of how this king of Parisian painting worked in his studio. Vollard happened to be visiting Meissonier's studio with a successful horse- and dog-painter called John Lewis Brown. They found the painter's assistant at work in a corner of the vast studio:

"Armed with a rake like a croupier's, he was engaged in levelling, on the floor, a layer of sparkling white powder that looked like boracic acid."

" 'I'm preparing', he said to Lewis Brown, 'the field of battle that M. Meissonier is about to paint.'

"He opened a box and took out guns, little trees, ammunition wagons, soldiers and horses, which he ranged in battle formation in the frosted square. Taking a spray, he pressed the rubber bulb and projected a cloud of liquid gum over the whole of the little army, which he dusted afterwards with a powder of duller white . . . Meissonier came in:

" 'Brrr!' he said, casting a glance at the work of his assistant, 'what a fine winter landscape! It almost makes my fingers ache . . . ' "

Another spectacular example of the way an artist could prosper and become a public idol was Edouard Détaille who had studied in Meissonier's studio. He also painted battles and military pageants and became so highly regarded that no critic dared to criticise him on pain of being called unpatriotic since Détaille was glorifying France's martial past at a time when militarism was a passion widespread throughout France. Each of his painstakingly painted set pieces was an event when it was presented to the public and his reward followed the familiar pattern: glowing praise from politicians and civil servants, the Grand Croix of the Legion of Honour, membership of the Institute of France, a sizeable fortune and a palatial mansion.

Such history painters who had won gold medals in the Salons could be sure of collecting lucrative commissions from the Paris municipality and local authorities. One such was Fernand Cormon in whose studio Toulouse-Lautrec worked for a time. His painting *Cain* had brought him success at an early age and he had won a gold medal at the Salon when aged only twenty-five before continuing his triumphant career by specialising in such prehistoric scenes as *The Funeral of an Iron Age Chieftain* or *Hunters in the Ice Age*, and by being invited to decorate public buildings. Jean-Paul Laurens, who also collected every honour that an artist could hope for, dealt with later historical subjects, showing a marked predilection for execution scenes, and added to the number of vast frescoes that remain in Paris as a reminder of what art meant to most people in the late 19th century. Even more spectacular was Georges Rochegrosse. He was to painting what Cecil B. de Mille was to costume films, with his reconstructions of the *Fall of Babylon* or the *Pillage of a Roman villa by the Huns*, and he was a popular favourite until the early years of this century. Another painter much in demand as a public-building decorator was Alfred Roll who dealt in more up-to-date subjects but who became so over-whelmed by commissions that he saved a number of young students from penury by farming them out.

Sex of a certain kind also had its part to play in Salon painting. The master of nude painting was Bouguereau, who remains notorious and is ridiculed in France today for his spectacularly bad taste. His huge, oily compositions teem with nudes in a variety of falsely modest poses which border upon the porno-graphic in their uneasy compromise between the demure and the suggestive. Bouguereau was never wholly accepted by the critics, but for nearly half a century he dominated nude painting in the Salons with his *Bacchantes*, *Water Nymphs* and *Venuses* which provided pleasant titillation for the respectable public who were extremely receptive to all such erotic suggestion. Bouguereau ended his career as a member of the Academy of Fine Arts and holder of the medal of Commander of the Legion of Honour.

Most of such paintings were too large and expensive for the majority of collectors. Many people bought genre scenes by artists who specialised in sentimental or amusing scenes, still lives or pictorial snapshots of city life. The *frou-frou* aspect of Paris life was well represented by Henri Gervex, the author of the controversial *Rolla*. He was a dandy, a well-known society per-sonality, and he specialised in portraits of pretty ladies, nudes and scenes of high-society activities. Other scenes of contemporary life were the speciality of Jean Béraud who delighted the public from 1880 to 1900 with such pictures as *The Promenade of the Folies Bergère*, *The Racecourse at Longchamps* and scenes at the Moulin Rouge. Although his pictures are certainly inferior artistically to anything by Toulouse-Lautrec or Degas, he had at least the merit of recording the pleasanter side of Parisian life at the time with photographic fidelity. Several of the lesser-known genre painters had a definite charm which has been rediscovered today and given them a new vogue. They were honest craftsmen who did their work well and displayed a limited but nonetheless genuine talent within the strict confines of their art.

The most fashionable portrait painters were Léon Bonnat and Carolus Duran until the Italian Boldini revolutionised society portraiture with his brilliant and dynamic—also very showy— "whiplash" style at the end of the century. Bonnat was the official portrait painter of French Presidents of the Republic and ladies of the very highest high society. He would demand and receive fees of thirty or forty thousand francs while Duran, whose prices were equally astronomical, specialised in painting ladies of both *le monde* and the *demi-monde*. Georges Clairin also made his name as a theatrical portraitist as well as a history painter and for a long time was a close friend of Sarah Bernhardt whom he painted in her main rôles.

Corresponding to the "great stars" in the painting world were "stars" among the wealthy collectors. One of the most famous was Alfred Chauchard, a self-made millionaire who became owner of one of Paris's most important department stores, the Magasins du Louvre. He was tremendously influential, tremendously conceited, and the living embodiment of the most reactionary and unimaginative taste of the period. Although he knew nothing about any kind of art, he had a mania for collecting pictures. His lack of education and his cultural stupidity were well known in social circles but he was a leading "character" at every Salon and a power to be placated.

Chauchard was particularly fond of paintings which told a story and of military subjects, and his god was Meissonier. Whenever Chauchard's tall, bearded figure was seen in the Salon, there would be a sudden hush among the public. Even the most famous painters would defer to him as he ponderously inspected the display, occasionally shaking hands, solemnly passing judgement on one of the year's "novelties" or remarking to the critics and journalists who followed him that "this year the Salon is of exceptional quality . . . What a pity that weeks are needed to see it all! Too much talent! Too much . . . "

Despite the wealth of talent that he saw around him and his love for Meissonier, the buying of new works presented a problem to Chauchard. Unable to pick the masterpieces himself, he employed scouts who earned a commission on anything they bought for him. He filled his mansion on the Avenue Velazquez with the most conservative academic paintings after making sure that each work had its authenticity guaranteed. He gave lavish dinner parties which were famous. After he had regaled his guests with oysters, trout, game, *foie gras*, salads garnished with truffles and the finest wines, he would take them on a tour of his house. They would dutifully admire his dull landscapes, his much-prized *Angelus* by Millet, his countless anecdotic paintings, battle scenes, nudes by Bouguereau and views of Venice which were churned out by the popular "picturesque" painter Ziem who rarely left his Montmartre studio. If Chauchard was satisfied by his guests' reactions, he would end the evening by giving them medals struck with his effigy. If they were on sufficiently intimate terms with him, he would even make them confidants to his other great passion: the design of his mausoleum and plans for his funeral.

With the academic painters and such collectors dominating the Parisian art market and public taste, it was extremely difficult for any truly creative, independent-minded and innovating artist to make a reputation and a living. If a newcomer wished to enter the privileged circle of painters who earned fortunes and were awarded official honours, he would have to conform to the system which had been established. He would have to learn a conventional idea of artistic beauty which was taught in the art schools "as one teaches algebra", as the architect Viollet-le-Duc once remarked. He would work under an academic master who preached the virtues of "classical" drawing and composition and he would take his works to be inspected by the Salon jury each spring and abide by their judgement. He would have to learn how to please the public, never to provoke or disconcert it. Above all, he would have to learn the importance of never puzzling the spectator. A painting was not supposed to be "difficult", to make the viewer think or to contain any significance not immediately apparent to the simplest mentality.

Such art had become static. The "dear masters" were believed to have raised painting to a state of perfection. Once an aspiring new artist had reached their level, it was difficult to see in what way he could progress any further. Art had become an officially approved system. It had been so advantageous and profitable to painters like Meissonier, Gérôme and Bouguereau that they were determined to maintain it until Doomsday, and by the 1890's it still appeared dominant. It was defended not only by the Salon artists themselves but by most newspaper critics, members of the Institute, art teachers, advisers to dealers and civil servants in the government. They all saw themselves as absolute experts on what was and what was not Art and they were popularly and officially recognised as such. The result of their dictatorship over public taste was that in the 1890's most of the painting on display in Paris was substantially the same in spirit, style and content as that which had been seen in the 1870's. Even in the first years of the 20th century, such an authoritative guide book as *Baedeker*'s was telling the visitor to Paris that "a survey of CONTEMPORARY PAINTING may be obtained by visiting the Hôtel de Ville, the Sorbonne, the Mairies, the Luxembourg, the annual Salons and the smaller exhibitions".

Such a situation was not without its critics. It was fiercely condemned by Octave Mirbeau, a journalist and writer on art who was one of the few to campaign for a new kind of painting and to point out that it was not in the Salons that fresh and original talent was to be found. Writing in the *Echo de Paris* in May 1892, he said:

"Painting has put art to flight. You no longer see it in the exhibitions which have now become the great vomitoriums of universal mediocrity, nor in the sales where the inexpressible bad taste, the overwhelming ignorance and the intellectual platitude of contemporary art are so crudely displayed.

"Twenty artists suffice to immortalise the great epochs of art. We have them, these twenty privileged beings who are as worthy of admiration as the most illustrious geniuses of times past. But who would dream of recognising them among this deafening pell-mell? They themselves, disgusted by this increasingly all-invading, increasingly degrading promiscuity, move away and shut themselves up. And far away from the hubbub, solitary and happy, they are working at things we do not understand."

Mirbeau was right. France did have a number of truly great and original artists who worked "far away from the hubbub" of Paris's fashionable art world. While academic art fossilised in the complacent atmosphere of the Salon and leading art galleries, a revolution was taking place in French painting and gathering momentum towards the final decade of the century.

The revolution in French art was a gradual one. Two of its pioneers had been Courbet and Manet in the 1860's. They were both rebels and non-conformists who preached an anti-academic approach in art to their followers. Their frank realism and refusal to bow to the standards maintained in the Salon aroused great hostility and provoked public scandals as in the case of Manet's famous *Olympia* when he refused to respect the conventional, "classical" way of painting a nude.

The example set by Courbet and Manet was followed by the painters who became known as the Impressionists and who continued the revolution. It was marked by bitter struggles and violent controversies in Paris where, as the art historian John Rewald has remarked, "all the great battles of art were fought" in the 1880's and 1890's. But even as they were being fought, few people realised the significance of what was happening outside the cosy world of academic art. Even so, from the late 1870's onwards, it was possible to see the new tendencies in art in two or three Paris galleries and in exhibitions held by the non-conformist artists themselves.

As in great political revolutions, one of the main features of the revolution in painting in late 19th-century France was the formation of successive small groups of artists bound together by commonly held ideas and aims and by the elaboration of various "isms" such as Impressionism, Neo-Impressionism, Pointillism, Synthesism and Symbolism. Although the revolutionaries behind these "isms" often varied greatly in their styles, methods and aspirations, a number of characteristics distinguishing them from the academics was common to them all.

The mere existence of such groups and "isms" was a sign that something conspicuously lacking from academic art had returned to painting: thought and the urge to discover and experiment. In Salon art, it was as hard to discover original ideas behind the works on view as it was to define any different "schools" or tendencies in painting. Works were displayed by painters of historical scenes, battles, domestic life, classically rendered nudes and portraits, but the "dear masters" all had the same fundamental ideas about art and the same approach to it in practice. Whether they were painting a huge picture representing the fall of ancient Babylon, a Paris street scene or a girl holding a bunch of flowers, their ways of tackling the problems of pictorial representation were basically the same. It was significant and revealing in this respect that when journalists reviewed the annual Salon shows in lengthy articles, they mostly contented themselves with describing the subject matter of the paintings.

Another characteristic dividing the revolutionaries from the academics was that the former were not tied to Paris as were the latter. The Impressionists, the painters of the Pont-Aven group, and the great individual geniuses like Van Gogh, Gauguin and Cézanne, did much of their most important work outside the capital. They were not society figures like Meissonier or Gérôme, they were not interested in obtaining official titles and posts, and although some of them tried to display in the Salon and all of them wanted to have their works sold by the galleries and art dealers they did not depend on Paris society for their prestige. For an academic painter, to leave Paris to work in the provinces was unthinkable. The popularly and officially acclaimed masters had become thoroughly Parisianised. It was only in Paris that they could establish their reputations and make all the social contacts so necessary for them to obtain important commissions such as portraits of notabilities and the decoration of public buildings. The Salon was in Paris and was the centre of the French art world. It was only there that the academics could win the approval of civil servants, collect honours and generally enjoy the social and material awards of their success.

When the new painters did work in Paris or visit it for any time, their favourite place of assembly was usually the café. It was both a natural and a convenient place for them to exchange ideas and make plans for the future. The entire cultural history of Third Republic Paris is filled with references to various cafés which became centres for meetings, debates, the drafting of manifestoes, the preaching of "isms", the recruitment of allies and followers and the organisation of exhibitions. Courbet had met Boudin and Monet at the Brasserie des Martyrs during the Second Empire and it was there that he preached his theories and urged young painters to break with the past, follow their instincts and study reality with a new vision. The meetings which led to the forma-tion of the Impressionist group took place in the Café Guerbois at the end of the 1860's and the first Impressionist exhibition in 1874 had been planned as the result of meetings in the Nouvelle Athènes café. Other cafés became headquarters for new groups, and some were even used for exhibitions with the consent of cooperative proprietors.

Another feature of the artistic revolution was the independent group exhibition in Paris. As the new painters had broken or ignored the rules and conventions of the established art world they could expect little recognition or encouragement from that quarter. The only way in which they could exhibit the results of their discoveries and experiments was by holding their own ex-hibitions jointly and this is precisely what they did. Between 1874 and 1886, eight Impressionist exhibitions were held in Paris. In May 1884, an "anti-Salon", the *Salon des Artistes Indépendants*, was organised by a number of artists which included Seurat, Signac, and Gauguin. The *Salon des Indépendants*, as it became known, had no jury system, was open to all who wished to display their works in it, and became an annual feature of Paris's non-conformist art life.

All these exhibitions aroused great hostility among the major-ity of the critics, the public and the Salon painters. They were seen quite rightly as a challenge to the Salon system and all that it represented. They encouraged a belief that there was a deliberate plot to subvert art and beauty as they were commonly understood and they did much to intensify the atmosphere of controversy which surrounded each new tendency as it emerged. To the academics and their supporters, the Impressionists and those who followed the path of non-conformism that they had blazed were anarchists, madmen and unscrupulous adventurers who sought to bluff the public. They were seen as enemies of the "purity" of French art.

The first of the great battles between conservative art and innovation had broken out in 1874 when the first Impressionist exhibition opened in a set of studios which had belonged to the photographer Nadar, on the Boulevard des Capucines, a year after the Salon had rejected works by Pissarro, Monet, Renoir, Cézanne and Sisley. The name Impressionist was given to the group by a journalist after seeing Monet's much derided *Impression: sunset* and had been accepted by the artists taking part in the show. Violent attacks were made against the paintings shown and the war that had broken out continued to rage throughout the 1880's.

All the revolutionary artists painted differently from the academics and it was the fact that they were so *different* in the first place that provoked so much hostility against them. The mass of the public did not want anything different in art, and when they saw it, they were not prepared to make the effort to understand it.

Whereas the academics mostly painted in their Paris studios, the Impressionists went out into the open air of the countryside and painted as though they had never seen any other landscape paintings before in their lives. For the academics, there was only one way to paint a landscape. But, for the Impressionists and the other innovators who came after them, there was no one "correct" way to paint a meadow, a wood or, indeed, anything else. What they saw before them they painted with a fresh vision and sensibility. The great pioneers of Impressionism, Monet and Renoir, and their followers, noted the way light and shade were reflected in the moving waters of rivers, the way some tones and colours seemed to vibrate, how the outlines of solid objects seemed to lose their solidity under certain atmospheric conditions, and as they worked they evolved new techniques and ideas.

Such ideas were of little interest to the public. After Corot and the painters of the Barbizon group, landscapes were out of fashion in Paris. The public wanted a definite subject in a painting and they were not interested in any new way of representing a river, a meadow full of flowers or a clump of trees. Instead, they liked pictures which told a story or illustrated a moral, which appealed to their patriotism or their sentimentality. When a few fashionable artists did paint landscapes they did so in the manner of the highly successful Bastien-Lepage who used the countryside simply as a backdrop for scenes of idealised peasant life which continued to be a popular *genre* after his death in 1884. Such paintings were not inspired by any study of reality or any emotional response to nature. They were vehicles for story-telling and sentiment at its most superficial as in other "narrative" paintings. Had paintings like Courbet's *Stone Breakers* or Van Gogh's *Potato Eaters*, which express the essence of country life with uncomprising truthfulness, been hung in the Salon among Bastien-Lepage's insipid compositions, they would have been considered as ugly and repellent as were Zola's naturalistic novels which shocked so many people at the time.

The Impressionists' researches into form, colour and light were taken further by the artists known as the Neo-Impressionists who were exhibiting with the Impressionists and in the Salon des Indépendants in the second half of the 1880's. They were nearly all Parisian artists and their leader was Georges Seurat who lived quietly in a small studio near Clichy where he devoted himself to technical experiments in the representation of visual sensations, basing his methods on scientific observations and theories. He and his followers, notably Cross and Signac, were as interested in light as the Impressionists had been, but where the latter painted with dabs of colour which rendered the shimmering surfaces of objects, the Neo-Impressionists sought for new ways of depicting solid forms. Seurat and his friends were greatly interested by some recently published books which dealt with scientific colour theories, aesthetics, colour harmonies and the phenomena of visual sensations. The result of their studies and discussions was the short-lived movement called Divisionism or Pointillism. Its most immediately striking feature was the use of a multitude of small dots of colour applied with the tip of the brush and which blended together in the viewer's eye when seen from a certain distance.

The unprecedented ways in which both Impressionists and Neo-Impressionists represented visual reality completely baffled the public and the majority of the critics who accepted the picture-book techniques of the academics as the only way of painting and the only true kind of art. They could not understand artists who gave priority to purely pictorial values and who drastically diminished the importance of subject matter in a painting. "Working at things we do not understand" as Mirbeau had said, the new painters appeared to most of their contemporaries as eccentrics who were determined to commit professional suicide by ignoring or defying public taste and acknowledged standards. They seemed wilfully to be breaking the rules of art simply in order to please themselves. They were attacked as though they had failed in what was considered to be the artist's prime duty: to give society what it wanted and expected in the way of art.

Even worse shocks were in store for the traditionalists. By the end of the 1880's, a new kind of modern painting could be seen in Paris. In the entresol of the Goupil Gallery on the Boulevard Montmartre and in a café by the entrance to the 1889 Universal Exposition, a group of madmen were showing paintings which ignored even the conventions of perspective which the Impressionists and their followers had at least respected. The chief of these new revolutionaries was Paul Gauguin, and in his works the last links with naturalistic representation seemed to have been severed. Instead, the public were shown pictures in which shapes and human figures were made deliberately stiff and crude, in which colouring was applied in flat planes, heavily outlined, and in which perspective and tones had been banished. To make matters even worse, the perpetrators of these atrocities were claiming that they were expressing their souls and emotions in their works.

We shall not understand the extreme violence with which the revolutionary artists were attacked by the press and the public unless we bear in mind that the idea that a painter could or should use his medium for direct self-expression was alien to most people at the time. By their art, the Impressionists and those who succeeded them were all affirming their individuality and their artists' right to be independent of all systems, and it was this which particularly enraged the supporters of the Salon system and all those who profited by it. As the academics may well have asked themselves, what would happen to art as they understood it if painters were to make themselves sole judges of how they were to paint and of what they would offer to the public? The paintings of the revolutionaries made demands upon the viewer that few were prepared to meet. Salon art made no such demands since the message of every academic painting was: "This has been painted as you, the public, see it." The Impressionists and the Neo-Impressionists were saying in their works: "This is how I, the artist, *see* it." Now, at the end of the 1880's the revolution was being taken further by painters like Gauguin and Van Gogh who were proclaiming: "This is how I, the individual with a paint brush, *feel* it."

Seurat's Pointillist technique briefly interested the Impressionist Pissarro and two of the great lone wolves of modern painting, Gauguin and Van Gogh, but all three of them soon found the style too cramping for them to express themselves according to the flow of their inspiration. Seurat wanted to give his forms an architectural solidity and impose a tightly disciplined, carefully calculated and almost classical pattern on his compositions. The disadvantage of this type of painting—especially apparent in the less sensitive works of Seurat's followers—was that, by reducing the flickering, lively brush-strokes of the Impressionists to dots of different colours applied with mathematical precision within a rigid pattern, the picture was liable to become static and lifeless.

In 1891, Seurat died at the early age of thirty-two, and his followers seemed to be reaching a dead end. But already, before the beginning of the 1890's, an important and far-reaching reaction was in progress against the scientific attitude that underlay Impressionism and dominated Neo-Impressionism under Seurat's leadership. Van Gogh had broken away from Impressionism to follow his own path and use colour as a means of direct, highly emotional self-expression. He left Paris, worked in Provence and finally in the little village of Auvers-sur-Oise near Paris after suffering serious fits of insanity. On July 29, 1890, he died, two days after shooting himself. Another important individual artist who broke with Impressionism and Paris was Paul Cézanne who had been working since 1880 in seclusion in the south of France. A third great rebel against Impressionism was Paul Gauguin and of these three giants of modern art it was he alone who was involved to any extent in Paris's artistic life and society, and whose influence contributed to the formation of a new group of artists in the city during the late 1880's and 1890's.

Gauguin was a powerful and striking figure. He could be flamboyant, he was often arrogant and intolerant, but his devotion to art was absolute, and he was ready to sacrifice everything to it. He began his painting career in his spare time while working as a stockbroker's clerk in Paris after serving in the French navy previously. He was encouraged by his friend and office colleague Schuffenecker and, in 1883, he gave up his job and virtually abandoned his wife and children for his art. Shortly afterwards he rejected the Impressionist movement with which he had been associated and eventually he was to turn his back even on the civilisation in which he had lived.

Even though Gauguin had been interested for a time in Seurat's theories and had taken part in the eighth and last and now no longer meaningfully named Impressionist exhibition of 1886 in Paris, he rapidly moved away in a completely different direction. His objection to the Impressionists was that they had been obsessed with colour and that "they heed only the eye and not the mysterious centres of thought". Their attitude was too materialistic for him. They dwelt too much on surface appearances and in their own way they were as concerned as the academics with the depiction of visible reality. Instead of their own kind of naturalistic realism, Gauguin wanted to create a new, subjective art dominated by the artist's soul and which would express its stirrings and the innermost emotional reactions to the world of the unseen. What the eye did not see was to be as important as the object in front of it. In his own way, he wanted to bring back to art the sense of magic and mystery which was inherent in ancient, Oriental and so-called "primitive" art. As he made the attempt, he became increasingly fascinated by the countries of the tropics in which, he felt, art and life and the invisible universe became one.

In 1886, Gauguin moved to Brittany to live a simpler life, close to nature and away from city civilisation. He settled in Pont-Aven, a small resort which was becoming popular with artists. He soon began to attract a group of followers around him and, after returning to Paris for the winter, he sailed for Panama with a friend, the painter Charles Laval, in search of a truly primitive, unspoilt, exotic world. The climate in Panama proved disastrous to them and they moved to the French Caribbean island of Martinique where Gauguin began to evolve his new, individual style.

In February 1888, after his return to Paris for a while, Gauguin was back in Pont-Aven where he lived with his followers in a self-sufficing community, having little or nothing to do with the other artists in and near the village. In the summer, Gauguin won over another highly enthusiastic adherent to his theories —Paul Sérusier, an intelligent and articulate twenty-two-year-old painter who was working in the term time in a private art school in Paris called the Académie Jullian. A little while later, Gauguin was joined by Emile Bernard, another artist in his early twenties whom he had already met during his first stay at Pont-Aven. It was a historic encounter. Together, the two men were to elaborate theories of painting which were to have an important effect on the development of other innovating artists in Paris.

Emile Bernard was a brilliant theoretician of painting and he had already become known for his unconventional attitude towards art while working as a student under the academic Cormon in whose studio Lautrec also studied for a while. In Pont-Aven, Bernard not only discussed Gauguin's ideas but contributed his own. Out of this fruitful exchange the two artists elaborated a new artistic philosophy and a new pictorial technique. Bernard agreed with Gauguin that if an artist wanted to express his inner response and reactions to what he saw and felt in the world "instead of copying nature as he perceives it, he should *represent* it", and that what he put on his canvas would become symbols to suggest another kind of higher reality which lay outside the confines of the picture. Together the two artists worked for an art which could express not only the painter's visual impression of the model before him but also the emotions and the state of soul that it provoked within him. The idea suggested by the subject to be painted would become more important than the subject itself. As Bernard put it, the idea was "the form of things gathered by the imagination" and, to express it in forms and colours, the artist must "no longer paint by fixing his eyes on the subject". Instead, he must take his visual impression of the subject *into his imagination* and there transform it into "an idea of this visual apprehension". But how was the artist to represent this idea in painting?

The solution was, in the first place, to simplify forms on the canvas just as primitive and ancient artists had often used crude, simplified shapes in their art which contained the symbolic elements, magic and mystery which Gauguin and Bernard wished to put in their own art. As the artist's memory would not retain every detail of the subject seen but only its essential characteristics which had impressed themselves on his imagination, the result could only be that the subject's form and colours would undergo a simplification as they were translated into paint.

As Gauguin and Bernard discussed ways of expressing these pictorial equivalents for feelings and ideas, they evolved a technique which they called Cloisonnism and a style which they called Synthesism. Cloisonnism, as the term implies, was inspired by the technique of *cloisonné* enamelling in which bright, pure colours are kept separate from each other in heavily outlined compartments. It was part of the "synthetic" style by which form and colour jointly expressed an idea which could not be communicated by any conventional representation of visible reality. In Gauguin's work, such a synthesis was achieved by using crude shapes, sometimes simplified to the point of distortion, with strongly stressed outlines, and large, flat planes of glowing colours. It was the complete antithesis to Impressionism.

This new method of painting and approach to colour fascinated Sérusier. One day, he went to paint in a little wood near

Pont-Aven together with Bernard and Laval. He was using a small wood panel instead of a canvas and, as he was studying the effects made by the trees and their shadows, Gauguin came up to him to inspect his work. "How do you see those trees?" Gauguin asked Sérusier, after watching his progress. "You say they're yellow, do you? Well then, put in some yellow. That shadow's rather blue—paint it with pure ultramarine. As for those red leaves, paint them in vermilion." Such advice came as a revelation to Sérusier who called his little painting the *Talisman* and realised that it expressed a revolutionary approach to painting. At the end of his vacation, when he returned to Paris, he enthusiastically preached the new ideas to his fellow students in the Académie Jullian.

In October 1888, Gauguin went to Arles to join Van Gogh who had been writing to him and suggesting that together they should found a studio for the new painting. Although the two men worked amicably together for a while and Van Gogh gratefully absorbed Gauguin's ideas, the collaboration ended in disaster. After Van Gogh had quarrelled with Gauguin and tried to murder him in an insane rage and then later cut off his own ear, Gauguin hurriedly returned to Paris at the end of the year. The city was now in a state of great excitement over the forthcoming Universal Exposition. The official art section was to contain a centennial exhibition of French painting in which, thanks to a progressive critic, Roger Marx, the organisers agreed to include a few works by the controversial Manet, Monet and Pissarro. But the only way in which Gauguin and his friends from Pont-Aven could show their works to the public would have been by following the examples of Manet and Courbet in the past and setting up their own independent pavilion outside the exhibition. Gauguin, however, could not afford this. It was then that his friend Schuffenecker came to the rescue. Next to the official art section, he had seen a large, roomy café, called the Grand Café des Beaux Arts. Schuffenecker spoke to the owner, an Italian named Volpini, who was in a state of deep depression since the mirrors he had been expecting to decorate his walls would not be arriving in time for the opening of the Exposition. Schuffenecker and Bernard then persuaded Volpini that the way

out of his difficulty would be to cover his bare walls with red
material and hang works of art by Gauguin and his friends on
them.

When he heard the good news, Gauguin was delighted and
began to organise the show and decide which artists should
participate. Van Gogh was invited but his brother turned down
the invitation on his behalf; Toulouse-Lautrec was interested but
excluded. Eventually, Gauguin decided on a name for the exhibition: it would be held by the "Impressionist Synthetist
Group". Gauguin brought canvases to the café in a push-cart
and with his friends hung up about a hundred paintings, drawings and water colours, including seventeen of his own paintings
done in Martinique, Pont-Aven and Arles. Emile Bernard displayed twenty-three works and the rest were by painters who had
been at Pont-Aven, including Laval, and Schuffenecker. Posters
were printed in bold type to advertise the exhibition and a blue-
and-white banner was hung across the café. The café-exhibition
opened in May and, as an added public attraction, Volpini had
hired a pseudo-Russian all-women's group of violin players under
"Princess Dolgoronka".

The Paris press generally ignored the Impressionist-Synthetist
exhibition but it had a certain *succès de scandale*. As the public
came into the café to drink and hear the violin orchestra, they
were completely bewildered by the paintings they saw through
the thick haze of tobacco smoke. Although Gauguin had called
the exhibition "Impressionist" as well as Synthetist there was
nothing in common between the works on view and the few
Impressionist works inside the Exposition or, indeed, with any
other painting at all that was to be seen there. Instead of subtle
tones, the works were characterised by patches of strong, con-
trasting colours, crude, strong and often distorted shapes with
heavy outlines and a general lack of any kind of perspective.
While the public laughed or shrugged their shoulders, some of
the academic painters came and mocked and the critics indulged
in their usual abuse of *avant-garde* art. But three critics, Félix
Fénéon, Albert Aurier and Maurice Denis, were interested and
sympathetic. Writing in a small weekly paper called *La Cravache*,
Fénéon amusingly described the conditions under which the

works were displayed: "It is not easy to approach these canvases on account of the sideboards, the beer pumps, the tables, the bosom of Monsieur Volpini's cashier and an orchestra of young Muscovites whose bows unleash, in the large room, a music which bears no relation to the polychromatic works therein."

Albert Aurier reviewed the exhibition in a review called *Le Moderniste*. He was a highly perceptive writer, sympathetic to the new tendencies in art, and appreciated what Gauguin and his friends were trying to do. He perfectly understood that the Pont-Aven group were stressing that in art it is more creative to interpret then merely to copy, and pin-pointed the fact that the works showed "a marked tendency towards synthesis of drawing, composition and colour, as well as an effort to simplify these means of expression". But he did more than merely comment on the works: he linked them with Paris's foremost literary movement at the time by detecting in Gauguin's and Bernard's work and theories a trend which ran closely parallel to Symbolism in poetry and prose.

Many of Gauguin's and Bernard's aspirations were the same as those of the poets and writers who had rallied together in Paris under the name of Symbolism. Just as Impressionism and Synthesism represented revolt against past standards and conventions in painting, so Symbolism represented an attempt to shatter conventions in poetry and a determination to free poetic language from the mere task of conveying precise meanings.

Symbolism was a call for the liberation of the imagination and language. Its origins could be traced back to Baudelaire's poetic and literary theories, the narrative and descriptive techniques of Edgar Allan Poe whom Baudelaire had translated and made popular in France, Wagner's music and his endeavour to synthesise music, poetry and drama, and it had as its leading exponent in verse Stéphane Mallarmé who gathered other poets around him in Paris.

The Symbolist movement was officially defined and given its name by the Greek-born poet Jean Moréas in 1886. In its issue of September 18 of that year, the *Figaro* newspaper stated that after "the Parisian press has been greatly occupied with a school of poets and prose-writers known as 'decadents' for the past two years", it had asked Jean Moréas, "one of the best known of these literary revolutionaries", to formulate the "fundamental principles of the new artistic manifestation". It then printed Moréas's manifesto in which he declared that he and his friends had "proposed the denomination of symbolism as being the only one capable of reasonably designating the tendency of the creative spirit in art". Symbolism was "the enemy of teaching, of declamation, of false sensibility, of objective description". Its object was not to convey precise understanding but to suggest and to evoke feelings as music did. It was the suggestion and the symbol which counted, not the object itself.

With its rejection of everyday, prosaic reality and its call for the return of mystery, dreams and symbols to the art of poetry, the spirit of Symbolism ran close to that of Gauguin and Bernard. Mallarmé's objections to the descriptive, high-sounding declamations of the Parnassian school which had dominated French poetry previously were analogous to Gauguin's reactions against naturalistic art: "The Parnassians take the object in its entirety and show it; in this, they lack mystery; they deprive the spirit of the delicious joy of believing that it creates. To name an object is to suppress three-quarters of the enjoyment of a poem which consists of the happiness of gradually guessing; to suggest, that is to dream. It is the perfect use of this mystery which constitutes the symbol; to evoke an object little by little, to show a state of soul."

Symbolism was defended and preached in a number of little magazines, two of which, *La Plume* and the *Mercure de France*, were founded in 1889 and became extremely influential in artistic and literary circles in the 1890's. It became the best-known literary movement in Paris and grouped together Mallarmé, Moréas, Henri de Régnier, Stuart Merrill, René Ghil, Gustave Kahn and Vielé Griffin; and had close links with an important parallel Symbolist group in Brussels, where its most distinguished members were Emile Verhaeren and the poet-playwright Maurice Maeterlinck. It was one of the most brilliant galaxies of poetic talent ever assembled in literary history. Many critics and writers declared their sympathies with it while others dismissed it as something too high-flown and incomprehensible for the public.

But although it was often misunderstood, it was talked about by Parisians in their cafés, salons and clubs just as Existentialism was talked about so widely in the Paris of the late 1940's. Nowadays, it may seem strange that a poetry movement should have received such wide publicity, but poetry in late 19th-century Paris was taken very seriously indeed by a large public. Poetry magazines and reviews flourished, the newpapers commented on the latest sayings and doings of the Symbolists, influential and famous writers and members of the French Academy argued over the movement, it became connected in the public eye with the eccentric behaviour and rebellious attitudes of young Latin Quarter Bohemians, non-conformist artists, dilettanti, aesthetes and society poseurs. For a younger generation dissatisfied with middle-class values and traditions and angry with the complacency of their elders, Symbolism meant an affirmation of the individual, freedom of the imagination and unfettered self-expression. With its emphasis on the unseen, the mysterious and spiritual world of the soul and emotions, it united the poets with artists like Gauguin whom they regarded as a Symbolist in painting.

Once the Café Volpini exhibition was launched, Gauguin spent more time in the Exposition than the café. He was fascinated by a replica of a Javanese village that had been built inside the exhibition grounds and by groups of Indian and other eastern dancers who were performing there, and his interest in the Far East increased.

In April 1889, Gauguin went back to Pont-Aven, then, finding it too crowded, moved on to a little fishing village called Le Pouldu where he worked closely with Sérusier and was joined by a group including Laval and a very mystic and religious-minded young painter called Charles Filiger. In November 1890, he was back in Paris where he rented a studio after being rescued from destitution by Schuffenecker, and was soon frequently seen with the Symbolists.

Gauguin had already met one of the Symbolists' favourite artists, Odilon Redon, who expressed a private dream world of his own in etchings and lithographs; and Redon knew Mallarmé well and was able to introduce Gauguin into the poet's circle. While in Paris, Gauguin was a frequent visitor to the Goupil gallery where Van Gogh's brother Théo was the progressive manager. Théo Van Gogh had succeeded in showing works by Van Gogh, Gauguin and Impressionists in the entresol of the gallery which was open every afternoon, and it soon became a meeting place for poets and artists. In the Café des Variétés near the gallery, Gauguin met and became friendly with the journalist Charles Morice who was a spokesman for the Symbolist movement. In a short time, Gauguin met other poets, journalists and critics, heard Mallarmé speak to his followers in his famous Tuesday evening assemblies in his flat, and was attending the Monday night meetings in the Café Voltaire, opposite the Odéon theatre, which the Symbolists had chosen as their headquarters. There, Gauguin would join in the discussion over the Symbolist ideas which could be applied to every form of art, besides poetry. The theorists of the movement such as Albert Aurier and Morice spoke of Synthesism leading to Symbolism in painting, stating that works of art would become idealistic since they would be expressions of ideas represented by forms which were symbols. They acclaimed Gauguin because they saw his paintings as the pictorial demonstration of their ideas.

Gauguin now became a well-known figure in Paris's *avant-garde* artistic and literary circles. His admirers were impressed by his determination, his refusal to compromise and his frequently expressed intention to leave western civilisation for the tropics. Everything about Gauguin was unconventional, including the way he dressed with his Breton clogs, which he had carved and painted himself, his decorated seaman's jersey, his paint-splashed jacket, his cloak, tasselled beret, and his cane with the handle carved into the shapes of a couple making love. Although he admired many of the Symbolists, he grew increasingly impatient with the way they tried to put labels on him and his work. He would not be called a Symbolist. He was, as he called himself, "a child and a savage". While the poets and critics held forth in their cafés, he went instead to a brasserie in the Rue de la Gaîeté in Montparnasse where, amidst the noise of billiard players and the music of a steam organ, he would hold forth from time to time to his own followers. Théo Van Gogh's death early in 1891 came as a blow to Gauguin since the new manager of the Goupil gallery was hostile to his work. His determination to leave for the tropics grew day by day, and he decided to go to Tahiti after reading about the island for some time.

In February, Gauguin's friends organised a sale of his work at the Salle Drouot auction house to raise the money for his departure. Morice introduced Gauguin to Octave Mirbeau who admired his art and wrote an article which was reprinted as a preface to the sale catalogue. The article appeared in Mirbeau's paper, the *Echo de Paris*, on February 16, 1891, and was widely quoted by other papers including the *Figaro*. Mirbeau wrote that he had learned that Gauguin was about to leave Paris for Tahiti in order to flee from civilisation and to live alone for some years to seek "oblivion and silence", to gain greater self-knowledge, and the more clearly to hear the "inner voices which are drowned in the noise of our passions and disputes". As Mirbeau stated perceptively, Gauguin believed that it was in the lands of the exotic tropics that he could find "new, untouched elements in art conforming with his dreams". Of Gauguin's painting so far, Mirbeau wrote: "The splendour of barbarism, of the Catholic liturgy, of Hindu dreams, Gothic imagery, symbolism subtle and obscure—all are here in this absolutely personal and altogether new art which Gauguin has created." The article was widely read and, together with the fact that the Symbolist poets with whom Gauguin associated were often in the public eye, made him the most prominent revolutionary painter in Paris by the time he was preparing to go to the Pacific.

On March 23, 1891, a farewell banquet was given in Gauguin's honour at the Café Voltaire. On April 4, he departed for Tahiti, leaving behind him his ideas, which continued to exert their influence, his example, and a group of young painters who had been brought to his art by Sérusier and who were calling themselves by the unusual name of "the Nabis".

The artists who formed this group were students who worked in the Académie Jullian and several had been friends since their schooldays. Those who became best known later were Pierre Bonnard, Edouard Vuillard, Maurice Denis, Félix Vallotton, Arthur Ranson and Ker Xavier Roussel. Like Emile Bernard, whose revolutionary ideas reached them through Gauguin and

Sérusier, they were all extremely young. In 1889, Sérusier was twenty-six, Bonnard twenty-two, Vuillard twenty-one and Denis only nineteen. They were high-spirited, gregarious, passionately interested in art and ideas, intelligent and articulate.

There is something very appealing about these young painters and art theorists who were to play such a lively part in Paris's art life during the 1890's. They were enthusiastic and modern in their outlook and, unlike Van Gogh or Gauguin, seemed to have been born to be happy. From the beginning of their careers they showed themselves to be unacademic, innovating and original artists, who never had to make any painful transition from conventional to new styles. They revolted against academicism as though by instinct and followed their own paths with enthusiasm and idealism. Gauguin had said that "there are only two kinds of artists—the imitators and the revolutionaries". None of them were in any doubt about which kind they were to be.

Bonnard was to become the most famous of this group. He was the son of a senior official in the War Ministry and had been a schoolboy at the Lycée Condorcet in Paris where he became friendly with Roussel, Denis and Vuillard. Although his family made him study law he soon became bored with it for, like his friends, his first interest was art. He cut down his classes as much as possible, registered at the Académie Jullian; he also worked for a year in the Ecole des Beaux-Arts, but was unable to follow the academic training there with any success. At the Académie Jullian, where the atmosphere was far more conducive to innovation, he made new friends including Ranson and Vallotton. In 1889, after taking his law degree and failing the civil service examination, he was paid several hundred francs by the France-Champagne company for a poster he had submitted to them. His father was delighted and agreed that Bonnard should make art his career.

Later in life, Bonnard told how he had been working in the Académie Jullian in the autumn of 1888 when Sérusier returned from Pont-Aven in a state of great elation, saying: "I have met a genius. His name is Gauguin and he has revealed to me the true secret of painting: 'If you want to paint an apple, paint a circle!' " This may have been a pleasant myth or an exaggeration, but there is no doubt that Sérusier excited and intrigued his friends with his revelations of what Gauguin had been doing and preaching. Sérusier brought his *Talisman* painting with him and his fellow students studied it with interest. They noted the way its elements had been synthesised, the vivid use of colour and the way the forms had almost been reduced to abstraction; and they absorbed Gauguin's message that the artist had the right to express nature through his own personality, as he *felt* it.

The group eagerly discussed the new ideas and agreed that it was not necessary to represent nature by adhering to conventional formulas of perspective and colouring. They gave themselves the name of "Nabis", derived from the Hebrew word "nebiim" for prophets, which Sérusier had suggested to them. The choice of such a name showed that Bonnard and his friends were idealists. They were interested in philosophy and religion, dreams and mysticism, and followed Gauguin and Bernard by campaigning for the Idea and the Soul in art. After visiting the Café Volpini exhibition, they were completely converted to "Symbolism" and "Synthesism" in paintings which were meant to appeal to the viewer not through the choice of subject matter but through the suggestive power of lines and colours. Denis became the main theoretician of the Nabis, explaining how every human emotion and thought could be expressed through a pictorial equivalent. As Denis said later, every work of art the Nabis produced was to be "the passionate equivalent of some sensory experience", and in his article published in the magazine *Art et Critique* on August 23, 1890, he made the now famous statement that a painting is "essentially a flat surface covered with colours arranged in a certain order". For their idealistic art which, especially in the case of Denis and Sérusier, was often inspired by religion and medieval legends, they made use of the same kind of "synthetism" as that which Gauguin and Bernard had developed in Pont-Aven. It was a strongly linear style, used simplified forms and flat planes of pure colour, and was generally anti-naturalistic.

The Nabis continued to debate artistic ideas among themselves and with their friends outside their group. Once a month, they would meet at a small, cheap restaurant called the Os à Moelle in the Passage Brady, near the Académie Jullian, where they would elaborate their theories and expect each person present to contribute some idea or reveal some discovery which would enrich their art. Odilon Redon, whose sensitive, dream-like, mysterious prints and drawings were held in high esteem by the Symbolist poets, would join them and support their objections to naturalistic art with such remarks as that the trouble with the Impressionist painters was that "they have their ceiling too low". Maurice Denis became the chief spokesman for the group and put their theories into articles which he published, and Sérusier would be the most dogmatic member. In addition to their dinner discussions at the Os à Moelle, the Nabis also met on Saturday afternoons at Ranson's studio on the Boulevard du Montparnasse. There, they would indulge in a little gentle play-acting during their debates with each member holding a bishop's crozier as he solemnly held forth to the others. When they were not talking and working, the Nabis studied the works of other artists whose anti-naturalistic tendencies seemed to confirm their own ideas such as Van Gogh, Puvis de Chavannes and the Pre-Raphaelites; and in a small paint-shop-cum-gallery owned by a paint seller and friend of many new painters, Julien Tanguy, they came across the works of Paul Cézanne.

In 1890, Bonnard, Vuillard and Denis were sharing a tiny studio in the Rue Pigalle, and they were joined by another close friend, Aurélien Lugné-Poë, who had friends both among the Symbolist poets and in the theatre world. Gauguin was another visitor who also acted as a link between the Nabis and the poets, although he had now ceased to call himself a Symbolist artist. Although Gauguin had influenced the whole group, Bonnard and Vuillard were moving in an independent direction. While Sérusier and Denis became increasingly religious and mystical, Bonnard and Vuillard were beginning to show less interest in theories than in what they saw around them. As Vuillard studied his surroundings and painted interiors, expressing the poetry of humble, everyday objects, Bonnard observed Paris life in countless drawings and sketches. He also started to work in lithography which he found an ideal medium for his style. Toulouse-Lautrec, the other great observer of Parisian life, came to see Bonnard, who is said to have been personally responsible for attracting Lautrec to poster art.

In 1891, the Nabis held their first joint exhibition in the gallery of a dealer, Le Barc de Boutteville, who had come to their studio and expressed interest in their work. They also exhibited in the Salon des Indépendants and, through Lautrec, were brought into contact with the owners and editors of a newly launched literary and artistic periodical, *La Revue Blanche*, which not only gathered the Symbolists around it but started to play a vital rôle in promoting all new artistic tendencies in the decade. The Nabis became prominent members of Paris's most lively, forward-look-ing and creative artistic community which brought together poets, playwrights, sculptors, painters, draughtsmen, musicians and journalists, and led to a fruitful collaboration between the different arts. The artistic revolution was fast extending beyond painting and poetry. Lugné-Poë, leading the Nabis with him, and the Symbolists now entered the world of the Paris theatre where a revolution had already begun in the 1880's in the name of realism.

While the Salons gave Paris's upper classes and bourgeois the kind of art they liked in painting and sculpture, the theatres provided them with the only type of drama they appreciated and understood. With a few notable exceptions, the kind of theatre popular in Paris in the 1860's, 1870's and 1880's was that known as "boulevard theatre", the equivalent of our modern "drawing-room" plays. There was an apparently insatiable public appetite for comedies of middle-class manners, usually centering around the theme of infidelity and adultery, there were romantic dramas, and there were the classics. Scribe, Augier, Feydeau, Sardou and Alexandre Dumas the Younger were the leading playwrights of the time, Sarah Bernhardt, Mounet-Sully and Coquelin were the great names in acting, and the Comédie Française was to Paris drama what the Salon was to painting and sculpture.

The Comédie Française was an historical monument of the French theatre, with its imposing foyer, its galleries of busts of great French dramatists, its august traditions and sump-tuous decorations. With its noble Green Room, its luxuriously appointed dressing-rooms for the great artistes, it was a temple of dramatic art as it was then understood. There was no higher distinction for an actor than to play on the stage of the Comédie Française; nowhere else were the plays of Corneille, Molière and Racine played with more respect for traditional rules; and no playwright could have a greater success than to see his play accepted by the administration of the theatre.

Although it was such an old and revered state institution, the Comédie Française provided Paris with new plays as well as the old classics in its repertory. In principle, the system for selecting new works to be performed was quite fair: a writer need only send his play to the theatre, where it would be read by two specially appointed readers. A summary report would then be sent by the readers to a reading committee of twelve members of the company board who had been nominated by the Minister of Fine Arts upon the recommendations of the theatre's general administrator. If the reaction to the new play was favourable, the author would be invited to read his work before the committee, who would afterwards vote on its acceptance. If the playwright were fortunate, he was assured of his first night being a brilliant event. The President of the Republic would sometimes appear, the *tout-Paris* would go in all their finery, every important critic would be present, and during the six-month season, high society would have their boxes and stalls reserved by special subscription. Like the Salon, an evening at the Comédie Française was a social event. Unfortunately, the tastes of the selection committee were usually as conservative as those of the painting juries, and their ideas on production were almost non-existent.

The first demand of a play was that it be well constructed, like a painting by Meissonier or Gervex. A good plot was the prime essential. Interpretation was a matter of playing to the footlights, grandiloquent delivery, unnatural gestures and posing against vast backcloths. Most popular actors were public performers rather than artists and few of the rôles written allowed much subtle characterisation. With its repetitive society themes, the theatre that dominated Paris was the favourite literary genre of the middle classes and new plays were regularly published in a supplement to the very widely read magazine *l'Illustration*.

The leading representative of this Parisian taste for family dramas, melodrama and vaudeville entertainment was the newspaper critic, Francisque Sarcey. His influence in Paris was immense. For forty years he passed judgement on almost every play performed and his word was virtually law. In his long series of articles published every Monday in *Le Temps* he defended the traditions of French drama as he saw them and he measured the quality of every new play by the degree of its adherence to accepted rules. He was equally dogmatic in his view of acting, saying that "to recite Hugo well, you must have begun with Corneille and Racine . . . To play Dumas, Sardou and Augier well, it is indispensable to know one's *scales* and the scales are— Molière."

Sarcey made a religion of directness and simplicity. Everything in a play had to be immediately intelligible to every member of the audience and marked by that clarity and concision which were the great attributes of French thought and language. His theatrical culture was firmly based on Scribe, the author of dozens of mechanically plotted comedies of manners. He saw the play as an "essentially popular genre" and as a representation of continuous action. A well-made plot was what counted and all attempts at realism or psychology were irrelevant.

Sarcey literally lived for the theatre. He sacrificed all social life in the evenings to attend a play every night, whether it was at the Comédie Française, or in some small theatre in the outskirts of Paris, and he made it a point of honour to sit through every play no matter how much he might detest it. He saw himself as a public servant and his duty as being that of informing "the good people of Paris" who put their faith in his judgement.

In the course of his long career, from 1859 to 1899, he had won great prestige. No other critic was as powerful as Sarcey. He dictated theatrical taste to two generations of Parisians with his articles and he could make the reputation of an actor or playwright with his approval. Whenever he appeared at his usual seat at the Comédie Française, famous actors would anxiously look in his direction for encouraging signs or to see if he applauded when the curtain began to fall. Managers and playwrights would implore his presence at new plays and would

usually be gratified by his attendance. Despite his reactionary
views, he did at least have the great merit of being sincerely and
passionately dedicated in his search for new plays and authors to
bring to the attention of the public. Only illness could prevent
this most conscientious of critics from attending his beloved
theatre and no matter what theatrical innovations he witnessed
towards the end of his life, he remained faithful to his own ideas.
What he did not understand himself, so he believed, the public
would not understand. His influence on his readers and theatrical
managements did much to sustain the climate of controversy in
which creative, innovating producers and directors presented
new plays to the public.

Naturally such a man had his enemies. One of the bitterest was
Emile Zola who, not content with fighting on behalf of literary
realism, had been urging that there be a new movement of
realism in the theatre. He spoke for many when he said that
actors, writers, directors, theatre owners and even attendants
were in awe of Sarcey, and he attacked the way Sarcey ruled the
taste of audiences: "No sooner has a new work been performed
than the first question in the wings is this: did Sarcey laugh? Did
he cry? If he applauds, the fortune of the play is assured; if he
yawns, all is lost." "Sarcey," Zola continued, "goes to the theatre
as a bourgeois on an outing, intending to spend an amusing
evening. All he seems to ask of the theatre is that an evening
should be well spent. It follows from this down-to-earth idea that
the theatre is made for the public and that, logically, authors
should give the public what they desire. All his criterion lies
here. He is the apostle of success. Succeed and he will applaud."

In attacking conservatism in theatrical taste, Zola was also
taking part in a wider-ranging reaction against what many
artists, writers and poets considered to be the prevailing vulgarity and materialism of the time. The *café-concerts*, which had a turn-
over as great as that of the theatres in Paris, the operetta, the song
cabaret with its ditties about low life, the "boulevard theatre",
the can-can and popular entertainers—all those features of
Parisian night life which have nourished the legend of the Gay
Nineties—were seen as bourgeois entertainments for a philistine
public. All they cared for were songs about mothers-in-law and

cuckolds, or jingoistic numbers bellowed in cheap cafés, the glimpse of white thighs amid a swirl of petticoats and flounces at the Moulin Rouge, sentimental melodramas and bedroom farces. Paris was being kept in ignorance of true art, its tastes being bound by convention and kept low by a horde of reactionaries and greedy impresarios, academics and officials without the slightest interest in the new and creative. As early as 1879, Edmond de Goncourt had gloomily observed that "theatrical art has become a coarse distraction". A few years later, Zola noted that "actors play for the auditorium, for the gala; they are on the boards as on a pedestal; they wish to see and be seen. If they were to live the plays instead of playing them, things would be different. These artists do not possess the flame of the present literary movement. They are not suitable for the works that are coming."

To Zola, the typical kind of playwright who dominated French drama and stifled taste was Scribe, the leading author of superficial dramas. To bring the theatre up to date and make it a force in contemporary cultural life, the old conventions would have to go. There would have to be a new school of drama which mirrored real life and situations with scrupulous fidelity and which scientifically analysed human behaviour. Wings, backdrops and footlights would have to go; there was to be no more of the stereotyped acting that the Paris Conservatoire taught, and no more lavish display of expensive gowns by actresses who were more concerned with impressing the audience than with the truth of the part they were supposed to interpret. In other words, there had to be an end to "society" theatre.

Zola himself had written plays but without any great success. Other writers, Becque and Edmond de Goncourt, had shared his views and written realistic dramas but they were exceptions and until the late 1880's there was no single theatre where the principles could be consistently maintained.

The great innovator in Parisian theatre was not a playwright but an enthusiastic amateur producer, André Antoine. His appearance as a theatrical manager opened a new period in theatrical history. With his Théâtre Libre, the age of the experimental "little theatre" began.

Antoine had been attracted to the theatre from his early

youth, and he had been influenced by Zola's ideas. After being employed as a stage extra and as a member of the *claque*—an institution he detested—at the Comédie Française, and after being rejected as an actor student by the Conservatoire, he had become a clerk in the Paris Gas Company. To satisfy his passion for the theatre he had joined an amateur theatrical group in Montmartre, the Cercle Gaulois, and gained experience in production. It was while he was a member of this group that he had the idea of finding new plays and writers and of presenting them to the public.

The kind of freemasonry that existed in Paris among artists, journalists and writers helped him to find support and new plays. The first production was given on March 30, 1887, in a small hall hired from a *bistrot* owner, and had been attended by Zola and several critics. From the start, Antoine succeeded in drawing some of Paris's intellectual élite to his amateur theatre and in a short time he was proving himself more professional than many of the older established theatrical managers and producers. Seats were paid for by subscriptions, his company played on a number of stages in turn, Antoine left the Gas Company and devoted his whole time to his Thêâtre Libre which remained a private theatre club beyond the reach of the censor.

By the early 1890's, Antoine was one of the most famous producers in Paris and famous for his innovations on the stage. Even Sarcey helped him by consistently paying him attention in his column although he disapproved of most of the Théâtre Libre's productions. The theatre became a workshop and meeting place for serious-minded writers, actors and painters. The insularity of the Paris theatre was finally broken by the introduction of new plays from abroad in translation and notably works by writers like Ibsen, Hauptmann and Maeterlinck who had been attracting a great deal of attention in England and Germany.

The great period of the Théâtre Libre was from 1888 to 1893. Antoine not only gave Paris many new plays but presented a new, naturalistic style of décor and acting. Some of his innovations caused a sensation: when he acted himself, he would turn his back to the audience in some scenes, footlights would be extinguished, players no longer gravitated towards the front of the stage, furniture and props were as real as possible and every care was taken to ensure that foreign costumes were authentic. Even Sarcey approved of some of Antoine's methods, if not the plays, and Count Melchior de Vogüé, who did more than anyone else to bring the great Russian writers to the notice of French readers, praised the unprecedented naturalism with which a play like Tolstoy's *Power of Darkness* was performed, writing after the performance:

"It was the victory of Austerlitz. When the curtain fell on the last scene, to a storm of applause, the public was transported; I did not detect an instant of boredom or hesitation during these four hours . . . For the first time, we saw on a French stage décor and costumes taken from the daily routine of Russian life without any of the pretty-prettiness of comic opera, without that mania for the glittering and the false which seem inherent to the atmosphere of the theatre."

In an essay he published in 1890, Antoine explained his ideas on dramatic art and production. He made it clear that he was the enemy of all the conventions which had predominated on the Paris stage for so long. Every aspect of the theatre, from architectural design to acting methods, was discussed.

He began by criticising the way in which theatres were designed and urged that galleries and boxes in the wings should be abolished. The horseshoe shape of the auditorium was impracticable: people should only see the stage, not the audience opposite. Acoustics were generally bad in Paris theatres, many seats were badly placed, facilities for audiences and players were inadequate and it was outrageous that actresses were encouraged to ruin themselves by spending large sums on sumptuous gowns and dresses for their parts. Theatres were too big and their size encouraged over-acting and unnatural declamation as well as playing to the footlights. Current production techniques were almost non-existent. Teaching methods for actors at the Conservatoire were hopelessly old-fashioned. A "true play must be played truly". Characters in modern plays are people like everyone else, they have "voices like ours, their language is that of our daily life, with its elisions and familiar turns of phrase, not the rhetorical and noble style of the classics". Antoine recommended a "direct study of nature" adding that "the actor should no longer say his lines but talk them". Actors should lose their stage mannerisms and stage voices. Antoine observed from his experience that when most actors came on to the stage they substituted their own personality for that of the character they should be bringing to life: "Instead of entering into their character, it is their character which enters into them". Actors should learn to move naturally and stage sets should be realistic and represent an integral extension of the dramatic action. Feelings were not to be expressed by hammy gestures but by "familiar and real accessories; a pencil turned round, a cup overturned will be as significant and as intense to the mind of the spectator as the grandiloquent exaggerations of the romantic drama".

Antoine was unable to reform the whole of French theatre as he would have liked and never had his own ideal theatre, built to his specifications and as described in his essay. But what he did achieve was to create a closely knit ensemble of actors through which he could express his ideas. Unlike most other actors of the time, Antoine's team were all trained to obey the fundamental laws of the group, thus bringing greater truth and unity to each production.

As a producer, Antoine was a revolutionary and reformer, and his influence was to remain strong in the 20th century. But where he was less original was in his obsession with realism at all costs. The battle for a new naturalism in art and literature had already been fought and was no longer a great issue. Even as Antoine was illustrating his principles on the stage, a reaction against the realist movement was in progress. Many people had had a surfeit of what they were given to read or see in the name of realism. To many audiences, Antoine's dramatic "slices of life" were what we might call "kitchen sink" drama. Just as the singer Aristide Bruant had popularised songs of working-class and low life with themes of apaches, pimps and prostitutes, so it seemed to Antoine's opponents that he was concentrating overmuch on squalor and sensationalism in the name of art. Several of his productions aroused fierce controversy and as we may see from his programmes and reviews, some plays were quite as brutal as any produced today by *avant-guarde* companies. There was something of the "Grand Guignol" in Antoine's Théâtre Libre.

One such play which was widely regarded as evidence that this much talked about "realism" was only an excuse for shocking people was *La Fin de Lucie Pellegrin*. This was a one-act play about a dying prostitute which introduced such subjects as procuring and sodomy. Another, *Monsieur Bute*, was a study of a public executioner whose mind had become deranged after losing his job and who drank the blood of his maidservant after murdering her. Another even more sensational item was Auguste Linert's *Conte de Noël*, a semi-mystical play in which an adulteress's child is killed and its body thrown to hungry pigs to the accompaniment of Christmas carols sung offstage. Most controversial of all was *La Fille Elisa*, a dramatisation of Edmond de Goncourt's "realistic" novel of the same name.

La Fille Elisa was a stark story of a prostitute who falls in love and who then kills her man when he proves incapable of treating her as anything other than a whore. She ends up in prison, condemned to silence which was then a form of prison punishment much denounced by reformers. Although intended as a contemporary exposé of social evils, some of the more conservative critics violently attacked it as being immoral and obscene. In 1890, the Paris censor had forbidden it to be publicly presented at the Porte Saint Martin theatre whose manager had asked Antoine to put on some of his plays there.

There was a debate in the French Parliament. Several deputies were incensed by the fact that the government's Director of Fine Arts had officially encouraged the Théâtre Libre by paying a five hundred franc subscription for four seats and had praised Antoine's services to French drama. One play, *Les Chapons*, had caused angry scenes in the theatre and had been condemned as unpatriotic, and the grisly *Conte de Noël* had only made matters worse. Other ultra-realistic plays which turned some people against Antoine included Marcel Prévost's *Abbé Pierre*, in which an erring wife confesses her sins to a priest who is her own son. Ancey's *La Dupe* featured an anti-hero who squanders his wife's and mother's savings, brutally abuses the two women yet manages to win back his exasperated wife because of the overpowering sexual attraction which binds them together. The blunt and brutal language of the play and the explicit treatment of the theme upset the audience and together with a short-lived wave of imitations of such "realism" in other theatres helped to discredit the style of drama which seemed to be dominant at the Théâtre Libre.

But Antoine's successes more than compensated for his occasional exaggeration in the name of dramatic realism. Authors and actors who had made their débuts in his theatre became so highly regarded that other theatres lured them away. Foreign plays including Strindberg's *Miss Julie* and Gerhart Hauptmann's *Weavers* were brought to Paris for the first time, helping to make the city's theatrical life less insular and more open to outside influences. A period of crisis had started for many Paris theatres where too many unimaginative productions, routine comedies and poor acting had turned people away or brought them to the Théâtre Libre. Even while the value of some of the plays chosen by Antoine might be disputed, he was steadily increasing his influence and becoming known as a great director. Henceforth the theatre could no longer be the same in Paris. Antoine had too clearly shown up defects in acting and production for the older playwrights and managers to remain complacent and his fame abroad was spreading. But, in 1893, there came a decline in the fortunes of his theatre.

Expenses had become ruinous. Stage sets alone were costing Antoine a fortune. Lack of money forced him to postpone some of the plays he had announced to subscribers. By April 1893, a tired and discouraged Antoine, now convinced that realism as a movement was at an end in the theatre, had handed over his directorship to another manager whom he asked to complete the season's programme and left Paris to tour Europe with members of his company.

New dramatic endeavours and experiments were already being made but, unlike the Théâtre Libre, they were principally inspired by the idealistic, mystical, Symbolist movement in literature. An important part in the development of these tendencies was played by the music of Wagner, and a serious although short-lived attempt to create a "Wagnerian" theatre in Paris was made by one of the composer's greatest admirers there, Edouard Dujardin.

Dujardin was a romantic and flamboyant figure who came to Paris from the provinces in the 1880's. He studied music at the Paris Conservatoire where he became friendly with Debussy, distinguished himself by his dandyism, wrote free verse and used his private fortune to found a bookshop and a magazine, the *Revue Wagnérienne,* which first appeared in 1885. Dujardin's aim was to promote Wagner in France, not only as a great musician and poet but as an important thinker and the creator of a new art form. Although the *Revue Wagnérienne* only had a small circulation, it became influential among poets and writers and provided a rallying point for supporters of Dujardin's own theories on music and drama.

When Dujardin started his magazine, Wagnerism had already become fashionable among the Symbolists. Wagner's ideas that art was more important than everyday life, that instead of being merely an expression of society (mostly corrupt and coarsened by materialism) it was an expression of a higher reality of the spirit which should shape human life instead of being shaped by it, and that the true artist should aspire to an ideal world, had a great appeal for those who believed that the truly individual artist was at war against vulgarity and philistinism in a world dominated by sordid bourgeois values. By the mid-1880's, Wagner had won many converts among French intellectuals and artists but his Parisian admirers could only hear orchestral concerts of his music.

With the exception of *Tannhäuser,* which was performed in France in 1861, none of his operas had been staged. In 1886, the state-subsidised Opéra Comique had announced a forthcoming production of *Lohengrin* but there were some violent protests from anti-German chauvinists and the project was abandoned. It was performed privately in 1887, but even then protests among the audience were so violent that plans for a second performance were cancelled. Wagner's music-dramas were attacked as being too "un-French" and incomprehensible for the majority of music-lovers. But even though his operas remained unperformed in Paris, Wagner's theories on music as a language and a poetry more capable of expression than any words alone, and on the need to fuse all the arts together, attracted many Symbolists and encouraged them to experiment even more with verse and dramatic forms—sometimes with results that most people found either incomprehensible or just laughable.

Inspired by Wagner's mysticism and Mallarmé's theories of poetry, Dujardin wrote a trilogy of plays expressing universal emotions and the whole, eternal tragedy of mankind. This three-part play was called *The Legend of Antonia*, and insofar as it had a story it was that of a woman Antonia who falls in love, betrays her lover, returns to him as he dies, becomes a prostitute in the second play, *Le Chevalier du Passé*, and then repents. In the third play, *The End of Antonia*, she is finally unable to renounce the life of this world in her search for purity and the "ideal", and is brought back to earth by a shepherd who fathers her a son. The theme then is the eternal tragedy of mankind and its redemption by love. In order to stress that it was not the study of any particular individual but of all mankind, Dujardin made no attempt at characterisation, gave names only to Antonia and two or three other characters, the rest being called "the lover", the "young shepherd", etc., and produced each play as a kind of poetic dialogue with minimal action and rudimentary staging. All three plays, performed in Paris between April 1891, when Dujardin himself played the Lover, and June 1893, were extraordinary events and aroused mixed feelings with many spectators finding the proceedings either completely incomprehensible or boring to distraction. The actors' manner of delivery was artificial and monotonous, the scenery for the first play was non-existent, in the second it was a fanciful design of flowers and a few architectural features intended to suggest a palace. But the third play was highly successful and attended by nearly all of Paris's most fashionable society. This time the décor and the long flowing "Liberty style" costumes were outstandingly sumptuous, being the work of Maurice Denis whom Dujardin knew through Lugné-Poë. The audience were also particularly impressed by the then revolutionary device of plunging the whole auditorium in darkness while only the stage was illuminated. It was not a particularly successful event in terms of art but as a talking point for the *tout-Paris* and as a social event it was certainly a sensation. A friend of Dujardin's, the wealthy society painter Jacques-Emile Blanche, has left an amusing account of these performances:

"We used to invite everybody who was anybody to whatever theatre we happened to have, whether it was large or small—all the blue-stockings of Jewish finance and of the Faubourg Saint-Germain. The matinées attracted so many wealthy people with carriages that there was a traffic block on the boulevard when the performance was about to start. The uproar caused by the extravagance of the production of *Antonia* and the actors, by the protests and laughter of the public, who thought they were being made fools of, all led to scuffles. The police intervened. I, as one of the culprits, anticipating danger, used to take refuge in the Café Tortoni, so as to keep a watch on the street . . . One day I left my hiding place too early. Lord Lytton was getting into the Embassy carriage. When he saw me he said 'Are you *quite sure* Monsieur Dujardin has genius?'

"I answered that it needed talent, at least, to fill the Vaudeville Theatre and for a symbolist poet to have a hansom cab in which to drive to Longchamps."

Whereas Dujardin was essentially an amateur and a dilettante where the theatre was concerned, a more sustained effort to bring a new kind of poetic drama into Paris's theatre was made by the young poet Paul Fort while he was still in his teens. He had become friendly with another poet and playwright, Louis Germain, who had announced the foundation of an "Idealistic Theatre" in the magazine *Art et Critique*. While Germain went ahead with his plans, Fort had already started his own amateur company called the Théâtre Mixte which was to perform every kind of drama and represent every literary school. The Théâtre Mixte's first production was held in a hall in the Rue Condorcet in June 1890 and consisted of verse and lyrical plays. One of the critics who attended was the tireless Sarcey who afterwards wrote that the productions were marked "more by conscientiousness and gaiety than by talent". Later in the year, the Paris newspapers carried an announcement saying that Paul Fort's "mixed theatre"

was combining with Germain's "idealistic theatre". The new
company hired the stage at the Théâtre Beaumarchais and, in
October 1890, presented several short plays including a verse
drama by Germain and a one-act prose play by Fort. A month
later, Germain dropped out of the venture and Fort now called
his company the Théâtre d'Art. It became known as a stronghold
of Symbolism and although it provoked many controversies,
frequent ridicule and incomprehension, the so-called "symbolist" productions performed by the company wherever they
could find a stage were unlike any that had ever been seen before
in Paris.

Much later in his life, when he wrote his *Memoirs of a Poet*, Paul
Fort claimed that he had intended his theatre to represent the
Symbolists from the start. He described how every night, while
still a pupil at the Lycée Louis-le-Grand in the Latin Quarter, he
would go to the Café Voltaire where Gauguin and the Symbolist
poets gathered. He would sit in the café and listen for hours
while his idols and such literary and artistic celebrities as Mallarmé, Verlaine, Henri de Régnier, Moréas, Rachilde, Gauguin
and Rodin would meet and talk. It was a heady experience for
the young man for as he wrote "every night the Voltaire bubbled
like a crater".

One evening, according to Fort's *Memoirs*, he heard Vallette, the
founder of the *Mercure de France* magazine, say of the Symbolist
movement that "what this school lacks is a theatre". No sooner
did he hear this than Fort decided to give it one. He wrote a
manifesto and got the leading poets to sign it. An announcement
was made to the press. The Théâtre d'Art was founded on paper
while Fort skipped classes at the lycée to search for actors, plays,
decorators and subscribers. He enlisted out-of-work actors without much difficulty, met Sérusier and Vuillard who agreed to
help with sets and costumes, hired halls and stages and raised
money through subscriptions by going to the homes of wealthy
Parisians who were known to be interested in patronising new
artistic ventures. A few weeks later, said Fort, eminent members
of Paris's literary and artistic set were attending his productions.

Fort was exaggerating slightly and forgiveably. He did not begin
his theatre as a Symbolist establishment. He became caught up in

the movement later because some of his collaborators were in it and because it was the most influential and publicised of its time. In his first productions in a hired hall, the programme included such completely un-Symbolist offerings as poetic dramatic pieces by Victor Hugo and a one-act anti-bourgeois satire by the well-known lady novelist Rachilde, Vallette's wife. The Hugo playlets were greeted with laughter but the satire was well received.

So far, Paul Fort had done no more than any other enthusiastic amateur who had been able to bring together a small company and hire the occasional stage. But in the following year, his efforts attracted the attention of the Symbolists, who were then the most creative and original group of artists and poets in the city.

In January 1891, Fort presented his most ambitious production, Shelley's verse play *The Cenci*, which most critics considered to be quite unsuitable for staging. It was a brave attempt but the audience were cool and the critics severe in their opinions of the acting and rudimentary production techniques. But in the meantime, Fort's theatre had aroused the interest of an actor only a few years older than himself, Lugné-Poë, who had been working in Antoine's company, and was the friend of the Nabis. A few days after *The Cenci*, Fort made an ambitious announcement in the *Echo de Paris* newspaper, stating that as from the month of March the performances of his Théâtre d'Art would end with the display on the stage of a "painting unknown to the public or in progress by a painter of the new school". The curtains would be raised for three minutes and the display of the work would be accompanied by specially written music and the release of perfumes corresponding to the subject of the painting. This idea of combining arts and sensory effects was inspired originally by Richard Wagner and by Baudelaire who had declared that correspondences could be established between certain scents, colours and sounds—a theory taken up by Huysmans in his famous novel *A rebours* in which the aesthete-hero, Des Esseintes, experiments with drugs, strange materials, colours and perfumes.

In February, Fort announced his next performance and added that "the Théâtre d'Art will become resolutely symbolist after this performance. It is at present patronised by the masters of the new school, Stéphane Mallarmé, Paul Verlaine, Jean Moréas, Henri de Régnier, Charles Morice. At the end of the month of March there shall be given the first symbolist representation in benefit of Verlaine and the admirable symbolist painter Paul Gauguin."

The Théâtre d'Art's next programme was held on March 19 and 20, 1891, on the stage of the Théâtre Moderne. It was a strange and determinedly "arty" event. One of the plays was by Pierre Quillard, a poet who was one of Mallarmé's fervent disciples. It was called *La Fille aux mains coupées*. Nothing was further from the conventional theatre of the day or from Antoine's meticulously prepared realism. Advertised on the programme as a "mystery in two tableaux", the play which took place "anywhere or rather in the Middle Ages" showed a young girl praying to Jesus to help her keep her chastity, while a chorus of angels declaimed that her love of virginity was inspired by pride. Her father then "burns her hands with incestuous and brutal caresses" whereupon she has her hands cut off by a servant. In the second tableau, the father pushes the girl out to sea in a frail bark without oars or sails. The girl prays, sees her hands miraculously restored to her, and lands in a fairy island where a Poet-King is waiting for her to give herself up to him in love.

To interpret this peculiar piece, Fort made his actors recite in slow, monotonous voices, and move with studied gestures behind a muslin curtain, against a gold backcloth framed with red draperies and painted with angels by Sérusier, while an actress in a flowing blue tunic stood on the other side of the curtain and commented upon the action and feelings of the characters. It must have been a strange spectacle but the audience were kindly disposed and found it highly poetical. Unfortunately the evening ended in a tumult.

Fort had decided to put on a play which would ridicule the realist movement in drama and had found a one-act shocker by a writer of dubious talent named Chirac. It was called *The Prostitute* and was a crudely written story of a starving mother selling her body to feed her children. The audience reacted violently, some standing up in their seats and shouting "Vive Zola!", some crying "Vive Mallarmé!" and, while others booed and hissed, several came to blows. After this incident which could have been disastrous to Fort's theatrical prospects, Chirac went on to found his own brand of realistic theatre in Paris, staging similar plays with such names as *The Violated Corpse* and *The Abortion* until the police intervened and he was sentenced to fifteen months in gaol for outraging public decency.

One of Fort's few real successes was a play by the Belgian poet-dramatist Maurice Maeterlinck, one of whose plays had been put on by Antoine and whose talent had been warmly praised by Octave Mirbeau in an article that attracted a good deal of attention. The play that Fort obtained from Maeterlinck was *The Intruder*, and one of the actors taking part was Lugné-Poë.

The Intruder, a powerfully poetic study of a family visited by Death, was part of a programme presented on the stage of one of Paris's most fashionable theatres, the Vaudeville. The Paris newspapers had given advance publicity to the event and the audience was a brilliant one which included many men of letters and artists as well as members of smart society whose curiosity had been aroused by accounts of the strange, poetical new drama that the young Fort was presenting with his band of amateurs. Furthermore, the fact that the programme was being held for the benefit of Verlaine and Gauguin, both in urgent need of funds, ensured the attendance of many Symbolists. The rest of the plays were of unequal merit but *The Intruder* was a success and Lugné-Poë's acting was praised. Paul Fort's confidence now knew no bounds.

Even though the summer of 1891 saw Fort beset by money troubles, he made grandiose announcements of future programmes. He was going to stage Shelley's *Prometheus Unbound*, Oscar Wilde's *Salome* which was attracting attention in Parisian literary circles, Dante, Ovid, Schiller, Shakespeare, the Bible, Ibsen and Aristophanes. Fort had all the ambitions and dreams of a young man not yet twenty who had seen some of the leading members of Paris's cultural world come to see his productions. He also had a collaborator of talent in Lugné-Poë who was revealing himself as both an exceptionally good actor and producer.

The next programme was held at the Théâtre Moderne on December 11, 1891, and included something that was more in the nature of a psychedelic "happening" than a play. This was intended to be a music-cum-art-cum-poetry-cum-perfume spectacle which was an attempt at "total art", the *Cantique des Cantiques*, based on the Biblical Song of Songs. It was described as a "symphony of spiritual love in eight mystical emblems and three paraphrases with music" and had been written as a kind of dramatic love poem by a young and unknown poet called Paul-Napoléon Roinard. What Fort had once announced to the press was to be achieved at last: a complete fusion between poetry, colour, music, drama and perfumes. The personages were to recite their lines in the solemn, ritual manner thought suitable for this type of poetry, music was specially composed, and a commentator was to explain the mystic significance of each scene. It was to be a feast for all the senses.

As usual, the theatre was well attended by the Symbolists and their followers as well as society figures and critics, including Sarcey who was as ready as always to attend anything new that might be seen in a theatre. The first item, another short play by Maeterlinck, *The Blind*, went well enough and was thought "highly symbolist" by the *avant-garde* critics who saw meanings in it that were not to be detected by non-initiates in the audience. But the *Cantique des Cantiques*, which came at the end of the evening, provoked one of the most uproarious scenes ever to take place in a Paris theatre.

In his *Memoirs*, Paul Fort gave an amusing description of this odd evening, telling how he had installed projectors in the theatre so that "luminous projections changed colour with every sign, thus giving rhythm, one might say, to each greater or lesser surge of passion". The perfumes, chosen to create moods and to correspond to the music and the colours on the stage, were mostly taken from dressing tables belonging to wives of some of the company and were sprayed in the auditorium by Fort's fellow poets and stage hands, from the boxes and balcony. It must have been a hilarious sight as the enthusiastic young men leant forward with their sprays to splatter with scent one of the most brilliant audiences ever assembled for an amateur theatrical performance. Unfortunately for Fort's attempt at total art the sprays were not powerful enough to fill the whole auditorium

with odours and the efforts of the sprayers attracted more attention than the happenings on the stage. Several spectators began
to sniff noisily, either as a jest or because they were not quite sure
which of their senses they were supposed to be gratifying at
which time. The audience began to titter, to move restlessly but,
as Fort tells us, he had many distinguished allies present. There
were as well as the most important Symbolists, playwrights and
novelists, the musician Debussy, Edouard Dujardin, the eccentric
mystic poet Péladan, and Saint Pol de Roux, the flamboyant
exponent of a personal school of poetry he called *magnificisme*.
Thanks to this "sacred guard of poets" some sort of order was
temporarily restored but in the end what was happening in the
auditorium was more sensational than any of the peculiar
scenes on the stage. It was like something from a Marx Brothers
film:

"The auditorium was divided into two groups, the Symbolist-
ophiles and the Symbolistophobes. The performance was thus
livened up by disputes, fisticuffs, cane blows, whistling and enthusiastic applause. Two revolver shots were even heard near
the ticket desk ... One of the most important critics of the epoch,
Françisque Sarcey, long known as 'Our Uncle' and who had
succeeded—rightly or wrongly—in attracting the hatred of all
the young poets, spent a very uncomfortable quarter of an hour
among them, with great courage let it be added ... Some of the
younger symbolists had placed squibs under his seat. Who? No
one ever knew. In the middle of the performance, as old Sarcey
really was laughing too much. Saint-Pol de Roux became so
exasperated that he hung his hands from the balcony and cried:
'If you don't stop laughing, I'll let myself fall on your head!' "

Such fiascos did little to help the Théâtre d'Art or Symbolism
as a theatrical movement. Many Parisians who had visited the
theatre were inclined to share Sarcey's views on the kind of short
plays that typified Fort's programmes:

"It is night. To the right of the stage, a gentleman stands in a
doorway. To the left, a young man and a girl lean on a window
sill. In the centre, a man lies couched on the stage. All three
groups begin to dialogue. Are they speaking verse? It seems to
me that they are—an unending rattle of bizarre rhymes, like the

tinkling of half a dozen little bells all at once . . . Moreover it is impossible to understand a word. I cannot guess what is happening between the three groups. The curtain falls and people hiss."

This was his account of a short play based on a poem by Jules Laforgue, *The Fairy Council*.

Ridicule, lack of money, inexperience, public hilarity or incomprehension, and the disillusionment of the Symbolists who thought themselves being brought into disrepute, all combined to bring the Théâtre d'Art to an end, barely a year after it had started. The last performance on March 30, 1892, *Satan's Wedding*, an "esoteric drama" by Jules Bois, a writer on the occult, proved too esoteric and too absurd for the audience. Shortly afterwards, Paul Fort gave up his theatrical endeavour and continued his career as a poet with increasing success. His former colleague, Lugné-Poë, started his own theatre with the help of some members of the company and the Symbolist painters, and began to win fame with his more professional Théâtre de L'Oeuvre which was to play a brilliant part in Paris's theatrical life.

But although Fort's Théâtre d'Art ended in failure, his achievement had been a considerable one. He had brought Maeterlinck on to the French stage for the first time, he had shown that the theatre's range could be greatly extended, he had stimulated and provoked audiences and, like Antoine, used the theatre experimentally. Furthermore, he had shown that there was no reason why the other arts should not collaborate with the theatre instead of remaining in their own domains. It had been a noble attempt to create a new kind of theatre and, in spite of mistakes and absurdities, it was an enterprise on which Fort was to look back with affection.

The fact that such a very young man, barely out of school, could attract so much attention with his amateur productions was a sign of the times. It showed that behind the façade of established, officially patronised art and drama, there was an effervescence of innovating, creative talent in Paris and a new public to be won over.

Fort had the good fortune to be young, gifted and adventurous at a time when Paris was fast becoming the home of a new, comradely *avant-garde* community. It was because of this Bohemian artistic and literary society, which had rebelled against tradition, which stood outside the cultural world of its elders, whose members met constantly, who had friends and allies in some salons and in the press, who were interested in ideas from abroad and in new tendencies and who were ready to welcome any newcomer who showed signs of talent, that amateurs like Antoine and Fort were able to command interest and support among so many important personalities and make their own names known in the city.

In this Paris of the 1890's there seemed to be something in the air which stimulated adventure and experiment. There was a climate of curiosity and debate. The new society of the arts was rapidly expanding. One of the many foreigners who had been drawn to Paris at the time was a young Dutch writer, Willem Bijvanck. In 1891, he published his impressions of literary and artistic life in the city and recorded his sense of excitement as he moved among poets, sculptors, painters and writers in the cafés, cabarets, salons and studios. Like many other contemporaries, he found that something new always seemed to be happening or about to happen, remarking:

"The life of Paris is of such preponderant importance for all Europe that each trait of its physiognomy is heightened and observed, to be brought to the attention of the entire world. That which would pass unnoticed by the public in another city, or at the most only live as a curious memory in the minds of a few old bourgeois, at once becomes prominent and there acquires notoriety. In these same events there is to be seen a revelation of the spirit of the century; they are considered as phenomena which concern the history of every day until they vanish to make way for new phenomena."

The Paris that so excited Bijvanck was precisely this Paris of Paul Fort, of the new poets and painters, the students, the militant journalists, the eccentrics and dilettanti, the writers, musicians and humorists who kept the creative heart of the city beating at so intense a rate in the last decade of the century. It was not in the Academies and Salons that this heart beat, nor so much in the fashionable literary and artistic salons and drawing-rooms that still flourished in certain houses and brought together the more established celebrities. Instead it was in the many cafés, cellar-clubs, and offices of the little magazines that the creative life of the city was to be found at its most ebullient and picturesque.

The artists, poets and theoreticians of new movements were not living in ivory towers no matter what the general public, baffled or amused by their behaviour and ideas, might think. They were some of the most gregarious creative people who ever lived in a big city and they recognised few barriers between their different vocations. It was because they met so often and had so many places to meet that groups and new schools could be formed so quickly, and that the youthful attempts of Fort and the revolutionary ideas of Antoine could arouse so much quick support and interest. They formed a large and hospitable community which was open to all and which had its kingdom in the old Latin Quarter.

Ever since the early Middle Ages, poets had been living among the students on the left bank of the Seine, near Notre Dame. Victor Hugo, Théophile Gautier and Baudelaire had been there earlier in the 19th century. Baron Haussmann had driven the Boulevard Saint-Michel through the centre of the district, and many picturesque old streets and houses had been destroyed while the new blocks that had been opened up had become peopled with middle-class, conservative tenants. But, the spirit of the Latin Quarter was still the same: free, anti-authoritarian, rebellious, comradely and always lively. The area contained by the Seine, the Place Maubert and the Rue Monge, the Rue Tournon near the Odéon, formed a city within a city, with its own heroes, cults and traditions.

The Latin Quarter was the first, natural home for all the young provincials and foreigners who came to Paris to write poetry, paint masterpieces and generally revolutionise the world. Studios could be hired for as little as a hundred francs a month (twenty-five francs were then worth one pound sterling), there were many cheap eating places, feminine companionship was easily enough found and there were countless cafés where even the poorest and most unknown artist or writer had a chance of meeting some kindred soul or an ally.

Eccentricity, exaggeration and flamboyance were part of the normal pattern of life amid the Bohemians of the Latin Quarter. This life also had its darker side. Absinthe was cheap and dangerous; drug taking was already a problem and ether addiction, morphinomania and opium smoking made their ravages among many young men who sought for new sensations in the name of Art. The district claimed its toll of victims and more than one provincial family mourned a son who had succumbed to the lure of the quarter and there disappeared, after becoming a human wreck from drink and drugs, who would haunt the cafés and scrounge a miserable living until illness or suicide ended his life.

The Latin Quarter was also famous abroad and its foreign population increased rapidly in the last thirty years of the century. Every visitor who came there was struck by the number of languages that could be heard at every café terrace and by the noise and animation of the narrow streets until late at night. To many inhabitants, the district *was* Paris and the city across the Seine was alien territory.

One of the district's great meeting places for artists and poets was the Café Voltaire. Another was the basement of the Soleil d'Or café in the Place Saint-Michel. This was a café-cum-cabaret where songs and poems could be heard and had been started in 1889 by Léon Deschamps, a poet from the provinces. He had founded one of the many new magazines that appeared in the late 1880's, *La Plume*, an art and literary review which welcomed contributions by new writers. Whereas most other little magazines only represented a single tendency or school, *La Plume* was open to all. Some months after the foundation of the review, Deschamps had the idea of bringing his collaborators and artists together. At first they met at the Café de Fleurus, then, as the numbers grew, he hired the basement room of the Soleil d'Or. Its purpose was explained in *La Plume*:

"All artists meet there to hear verses, to make music or to devise art. Politics are excluded from these meetings, which are now attended by all the intellectual youth of Paris. No subscription is demanded since the establishment is public. Everyone

may come without an introduction, assured in advance of a
hearty welcome from all the comrades in general, and from the
president, Léon Deschamps, in particular."

The "*soirées* of *La Plume*" as they were known were held every
second Saturday and became famous, lasting until Deschamps
died in 1899. On those nights, groups of students, poets, artists
and singers, many wearing the capes and wide-brimmed felt
hats that were fashionable in the quarter, would make their way
to the café, passing through the largely deserted ground floor
where a few locals would play cards, and go down a narrow flight
of steps behind the bar to the basement. There, in a large, smoke-
filled room with walls decorated by rough sketches by Gauguin
and portraits of contributors to *La Plume*, songs and poems would
be given on a rough stage to the accompaniment of a tinny piano
while Deschamps benignly presided by the stage. As many as
two hundred would crowd into the room. All the various groups
and coteries, the Parnassians, Symbolists, "brutalists", "decadents", "instrumentists", "kabbalists" and anarchists would be
represented there. One of the virtues of the place was that everyone immediately felt at home. It was a democratic gathering and
the spirit which prevailed was far removed from that of the
Montmartre cabarets which had an increasing snob appeal for a
wordly clientèle who thought it smart to "go bohemian". There
was no admission fee and the visitor had simply to sign a book
before trying to find a place to sit and attract the attention of the
harassed waiter. Every now and again, a celebrity like Verlaine
would enter, causing a stir of excitement among the younger
habitués, and followed by his habitual train of disciples, friends
and hangers-on. At other times, a "master" like Jean Moréas
would step on to the tiny stage to recite his latest poems in a
vibrant, ringing voice which aroused intense admiration among
his younger emulators who hero-worshipped him.

Although these *soirées* were only held fortnightly, similar
gatherings were to be found almost every night at other cafés.
There was hardly a street in the Latin Quarter which did not
have its café where young men who saw themselves as the poets
and artists of the future would argue, read their works, show
their sketches, edit manifestoes or plan the launching of yet

another little magazine that probably would only last for two or three issues.

Pseudo-poets, poseurs of no talent, scroungers, adventurers and girls of easy virtue also crowded the cafés of the quarter and added to the atmosphere of good-natured rowdiness that either repelled or fascinated foreign observers. William Rothenstein was one of the many foreign artists who had succumbed to the enchantment of "that fascinating, overpowering siren Paris!" as he said in his memoirs, and found the noise and confusion of such popular cafés as the Harcourt on the Boulevard Saint-Michel a far cry from the staider meeting places of London: "Men and women passed constantly along the tables, already packed to overflowing, throughout the night. The atmosphere was stifling, and thick with tobacco smoke, with the strong perfumes of the *grisettes* and the fumes of alcohol, and the noise was deafening ... Far into the night this company would remain, tirelessly discussing theories of verse, reciting poems and execrating their successful contemporaries, while the *soucoupes* piled up before them upon the marble tables."

Certain cafés were headquarters for groups centred around a single personality. At the Taverne Panthéon, the youthful novelist, self-appointed expert on love, and dandy, Jean de Tinan, famous for his satin-lined cape, his velvet waistcoats with silver buttons, his paleness and melancholy smile, could be seen holding court among his even younger disciples when not feverishly scribbling on the café tables; Mallarmé would appear at the Voltaire, Moréas would swagger and hold forth at the Vachette, and at the Café François Ier, a whole generation of young writers could see Paul Verlaine, brooding over the inevitable glass of absinthe.

Verlaine had become a living legend in the Latin Quarter by the 1890's. With Mallarmé, he was the most widely revered poet in Paris and the personality who more than any other seemed to symbolise absolute dedication to art, uncompromising non-conformism, and the artist's scorn for society and the material things of the world. His life was pathetic: he had been in a prison hospital, he was ill and alcoholic, he had lost his wife and worn himself out in his ceaseless search for a few francs here and there from publishers and editors, and he lived in squalor. He was a familiar sight in the streets late at night as he would wander in a stupor in search of the last drink before returning to his miserable lodgings, often accompanied by Bibi-la-Purée, a repulsive and eccentric crone who would cadge at the cafés and run errands for him, mocked and egged on by a crowd of drunken good-for-nothings and local prostitutes.

And yet this 19th-century beatnik-poet who had suffered so terribly, who alternated between periods of uttermost self-degra-dation and bouts of religious piety, still wrote poetry and was admired by nearly every younger poet of importance. He was the prince of poets and the king of Bohemia, and the foremost per-sonality in the district. Until his death in 1896 he held a tragic fascination for every visitor to the Latin Quarter and no admirer of his poetry—some of the most beautiful and moving ever written in the entire 19th century—could fail to make his pilgrim-age to see him and pay his respects. Bijvanck was one of the many who drew his portrait for posterity:

"We found him at the Café François Ier at about ten in the morning, at the moment when the cafés still have their air of prosaic cleanliness. The soft light that came filtering through into the oblong room feebly lit the pale countenance of the poet who was waiting for me, his eyes fixed on the unseen.

"The face was worn and tired. His long coat gave him the appearance of a poor old street singer, exposed for years to the wind and the rain; a worn soft hat covered his bald head. All this apparel gave the impression of a bohemian who lives in his dreams without heeding what is happening outside himself. Only a yellow silk scarf broke the grey monotony of his sad exterior with its note of disturbing gaiety."

Bijvanck's literary snapshot of the solitary genius as he roamed the streets of the Latin Quarter was one familiar to thousands of its inhabitants:

"Verlaine was walking feebly on the asphalt of the road and the diffused light of evening threw his suffering face into sharp relief. He could be recognised from afar in the middle of the deserted boulevard. His eyes half-shut, his leg dragging, tapping his cane which he held in his trembling hand like a blind man searching for his way, he resembled one vanquished by life who pursues his solitary route, scorned by the world and scorning it in return."

Such was the best-known poet of the Left Bank. The other prince of the quarter was Jean Moréas, born Papadiamantopoulos, the son of a wealthy Greek magistrate. Whereas Verlaine starved, Moréas never had to worry about financial matters in his career. His hawk-like profile, his well-tended moustaches, his vanity and love of striking attitudes were well known, but his influence as a poet was great and he had many disciples who would follow him from café to café and even to the market area of Les Halles early in the morning, when the last café had closed on the Left Bank. He was one of the most famous of all the eminent *noctambules* who roamed Paris at night and was one of that company who were found present at every important manifestation of the new schools in art and poetry. After being a member of the Symbolist group, and indeed inventing the term, he had grown tired of the many fads it had encouraged, declaring that "everyone has been going to look for symbols which is a sure way of never finding any. The poet is a symbolist, but without ever telling himself so." The poet he most admired apart from himself was Verlaine and he would frequently go to the François Ier to pay him homage when not explaining his new "school" of poetry amid the noise and bustle of the boulevard cafés. To his admirers and young fellow poets, his enormous self-confidence, his scorn of what the public might think, and his heroic attitudes were all signs that the coming generation of artists would be a new, independent, defiant race outside existing society and transforming civilisation. His collection of poems, *Le Pèlerin passioné*, had been well received by the critics and his reputation was at its peak when a banquet was held in February 1891 to celebrate his success. It was one of those occasions dear to bohemian-artistic Paris. Moréas himself had the idea of a banquet and the project was welcomed by friends and supporters who saw it also as a way of announcing the triumph of the Symbolist school. The dinner was presided over by Mallarmé and held in the premises of the Sociétés Savantes in the Rue Danton.

Over two hundred guests were invited and the event proved

to be a spectacular demonstration of the solidarity existing between poets, artists and their defenders. Every representative of
the Symbolist movement who could attend was present and the
absent Verlaine, who was ill, was honoured by a toast. It was a
noisy, rather chaotic evening. Anatole France, considered an
opponent of the movement, had been invited and made a speech;
letters and telegrams of congratulation and good wishes were
read out and practical jokes were played by some of the painters,
including Gauguin. The dinner was typical of the kind of friendly
gathering that could be arranged at short notice by the Latin
Quarter and, like the banquet held in Gauguin's honour before
the painter left Paris for the South Seas, it demonstrated the new
alliance between the arts.

Inside and outside the quarter, new, independent talent had
its allies in many of the little magazines which were such a
feature of literary and artistic life in late 19th-century Paris. Just
as the painters who had been rejected by the official art world
had founded their own salons, so new magazines were founded
in profusion to publish the works of the poets and publicise the
art of the painters who were being ignored by most of the press
and the public. Every major poet, novelist, painter and critic
whose name has endured and become famous from that time
was represented in these magazines. Better than anything else,
they give an idea of the astonishing vitality and creativity of Paris
at the time. Most were created in a spirit of combativity and
violent dissatisfaction with the existing order of things in art
and society. Like *La Plume*, these magazines were open to the
young and hitherto unpublished and they numbered over a
hundred by the 1890's. They publicised the theatre of Antoine
and of Fort, they made propaganda for Symbolism and many
other "isms", they presented accounts of new movements in
painting, and some of the more prosperous owners gave receptions in their offices and homes, organised exhibitions and patronised talent wherever they saw it.

Such magazines, frequently created overnight in a rush of
enthusiasm, were often violently polemical, self-consciously
non-conformist and sometimes revolutionary, but even when
they were savagely satirical or wildly humorous they were in-

spired by an underlying seriousness of purpose and the determination of a new generation to establish itself in the face of ignorance, uninterest or opposition. There was a widespread feeling, strengthened by political movements of dissent and anarchism in particular, that there was a war in the arts. As Paul Fort wrote, Paris was split by the war "between the two banks" —Left Bank and Right Bank, the one representing youth and innovation, the other, age and conservatism. Another poet of the time, Ernest Raynaud, perfectly summed up the clash of attitudes that became marked in Paris's intellectual and artistic life:

"A new generation, having come to manhood, wished to take its place in the sun. It met with the opinionated hostility of its elders. All the newspapers, all the reviews were systematically closed to it. This was due to a disparity of mood and an extraordinary incompatibility of ideas. One would have said that the disasters of 1870 had dug a deep division between fathers and sons. The French soul had become transformed. The frivolous generations of the Empire, smitten with bawdy humour and fol-de-rols, were succeeded by a generation that was serious, concentrated and sad. Mallarmé commented on Wagner and aroused a new excitement. There was no possible compromise. The newcomers, too proud to buy the place which had been refused them with degradation and servility, too much in a hurry to take their place in a queue ... resolved to march into battle with their own arms, created willy-nilly. They opened fire. Too bad for those facing them!"

The battles were waged on several fronts. In 1892 the anarchists went to war with society by hurling the bombs that terrified Paris, but loud as these explosions were, their effects were not to be as long-lived as those being prepared in the arts.

IV

ANARCHISTS AND MAGICIANS

IN 1889, a politically restive Paris had been shaken by Boulangism and its threat to the parliamentary system of the Third
Republic. The years between 1892 and 1895 saw a new kind
of unrest, more alarming and more destructive than the first.
This time it was not only the political system but the edifice of
organised society itself that seemed threatened by enemies who
were even more to be feared since they were so often anonymous.

The threat was that of "anarchism". Unlike Boulangism it was
not specifically French in origin, but in the relatively short time
of its greatest activity in Paris, it was characterised by an epidemic
of bomb throwing and by its capacity to enlist the sympathies if
not the active participation of many of the city's leading intellectuals. In 1891, few members of the Parisian public knew exactly
what "anarchism" meant. Two years later, a new and semi-
legendary character had made its appearance and begun to
terrorise the capital which had already seen so much violence
in its recent past: the fanatical extremist determined on revenge
upon the society he hated, with a bomb in one hand and incendiary tracts in the other. He represented individualism taken to
excess, the complete outlaw and "outsider", a symptom of that
fin de siècle moral decay that some high-minded writers were
lamenting, as he exposed all the class tensions and the political
instability that simmered so dangerously in the country. To
many Parisians, the anarchist was as much a typical figure of the
1890's as the elegant dandy or dilettante, the *cocotte* and the
boulevardier. He was the antithesis of the comfortable middle-
class life reflected in the paintings of Renoir and Degas, and the
bawdy gaiety of the *belle époque* which Toulouse-Lautrec was busy
immortalising. He became a public figure and for three years he

cast his frightening shadow over the life of the city and focused attention on the remarkable popularity that certain revolutionary theories seemed to be enjoying among literary, intellectual and artistic coteries.

Anarchism and its advertisement by direct, violent action had already appeared in Europe in the 1880's. The idea of curing social iniquities and injustices by waging direct war on the state by striking at its heads or symbols had been accepted by many anarchists and their disciples who had despaired of obtaining reforms by peaceful means. By 1890, attempts had been made on the lives of the King of Italy, the German Emperor, the King of Spain and the Russian Tsar. Alexander II had been assassinated in 1881, although it was the Nihilists and not the anarchists who were responsible. Such terrorism was infectious. It was inevitable that the contagion should eventually spread to France where social unrest was increasing and the resentments of a fast-growing and underpaid proletariat were daily becoming more acute.

A congress, held in Paris in May 1881, had marked the decisive split between French anarchists and the socialist groups. Many anarchists now began to preach inevitable violent revolution and to advocate "propaganda by the deed". In January 1885, *Le Figaro* published an anonymous anarchist manifesto declaring that the anarchists had never been stronger in the capital and that they were constantly attracting new recruits, both from the provinces and from the city's working classes. In the years that followed, many small anarchist associations and militant working men's clubs were formed throughout the Paris suburbs and the eastern working-class districts, where memories of the Commune were very much alive, and the traditions of social revolution had been maintained since 1789. Such clubs were usually under close police supervision and often had to dissolve only to reappear in another district a few weeks later. By the end of the century it was estimated that there were no less than one hundred such organisations, nearly all committed to the idea of revolution. Their names were as picturesque and violent as the image they left in the public mind: Le Drapeau noir, La Jeunesse antipatriotique de Belleville, La Révolte des travailleurs, La Dynamite, Les Coeurs de chêne, etc. At the same time, clandestine or semi-clandestine printing presses were constantly turning out floods of incendiary pamphlets and ephemeral broadsheets with such titles as *L'Attaque, La Lutte sociale, l'Affamé, Le Drapeau noir*, which urged their readers to overthrow the social and political system by armed action and told them how to make bombs at home. The revolutions and street fighting of 1830, 1848 and 1871 had left a heritage of revolutionary and anti-bourgeois songs which were often more popular than the ill-printed broadsheets and theoretical pamphlets of the time. Most famous of all such songs was the *Internationale,* composed by Eugène Pottier who died in 1887 after a turbulent life of revolutionary activity. Other songs of anarchy and revolution, protest against authority, and vilification of the middle classes were sold on the Paris streets together with ballads, sentimental ditties and topical songs composed at a moment's notice by itinerant musicians and vendors. They were sung in the little wineshops and cabarets of the *faubourgs* which carried on the traditions of the historic *goguettes* where singers had been berating the governments of the day and the bourgeoisie ever since the days of Charles X and Louis-Philippe. These songs were an important and popular medium for disseminating ideas of protest and social discontent. Even the most serious-minded anarchist theoreticians of the working-class suburbs regarded them as one of the most effective means of spreading their doctrines to the ordinary working man who lacked the patience or inclination to plough through long theoretical articles. Some singers became celebrities and, besides the more fiery blood-and-thunder compositions of unknown song writers who sold their products for a few centimes in the streets, they brought the songs of Aristide Bruant and Xanrof to the less sophisticated and fashionable public of the bistros and working men's clubs.

The most famous, the most violent and the best written of all the anarchist papers published in Paris was *Le Père Peinard* which lasted from 1889 to 1894. Unlike many others which glorified "the knife that purifies" and "the bomb that cleanses", *Le Père Peinard* was written entirely in the racy, colourful slang of the Parisian working class. It was almost completely the work of its editor, Emile Pouget, a dedicated revolutionary and embittered ex-clerk who had been forced out of his job after he had tried to

organise a union among his fellow employees. He brought to his
subversive paper something that was lacking in most others—
talent. He played upon the resentments and prejudices of the
working man with unerring accuracy in a style that was both
jovial and grim, satirical and witty, ribald and deadly earnest.
Every anti-social activity was encouraged in the name of the
coming revolution. Its readers were urged to commit theft and
arson, to counterfeit bank notes, to destroy the houses of the
rich, to desert if they were conscripts, to pillage the middle
classes and to kill the enemies of the working people. If a workman was unemployed, wrote Pouget, all he need do was to steal
food for himself and his family; if he wanted to work, then he
should take over the factories with his comrades. As for the
upholders of the reactionary capitalist system such as deputies in
the parliament, senators, judges, priests or army officers—they
were to be immediately assassinated by any means at hand. Its
impassioned flowing style, the quality of its cartoons which were
often drawn by well-known and gifted caricaturists, and its
relentless emphasis on violence and subversion soon made it the
most celebrated revolutionary paper in Paris. It became known
to the bourgeois, many of whom bought it out of curiosity, and
it reached the considerable circulation of 15,000 at its peak. Because of the liberal press laws of 1881, it never had to close down
or change its name since only the editor at the time of prosecution could be held responsible for incitement to violence and
defamation. In three years, ten successive editors—all unpaid—
appeared before the courts but Le Père Peinard continued its career
triumphantly, as aggressive and defiant as ever, until forced to
close in 1894 because of emergency legislation rushed through
by a panic-stricken government. But despite the violent tone of
anarchist propaganda with its repeated summons to the working
people to rise against their masters and exploiters and to destroy
the social system by violent means, and the publication of such
famous pamphlets as the "Manual of the Perfect Dynamiter"
which circulated throughout Paris for several years, there was
little violence at first. In 1881, there had been the curious affair
of the statue of Thiers which was the object of an attempted destruction by a "revolutionary committee", which many believed

to have been stage-managed by the police themselves, and in 1886 a young fanatic had thrown vitriol in the Paris Stock Exchange and fired three revolver shots which harmed nobody. But, until 1892, anarchist violence remained confined to the printed word and the song. Instead of sacking the homes of the rich and stabbing judges and priests, the anarchist clubs contented themselves with group discussions, preaching, and with occasional attempts at setting up local communes where workers could meet after work, attend lectures, provide help for their more needy and unemployed comrades and be given free scholastic instruction.

Fears that anarchists were seriously planning physical violence in France seemed confirmed in 1890 when a group of Russian *émigré* Nihilists were discovered by the police to be making explosives in the suburb of Le Raincy and were arrested. In November that year, a former Russian Minister of Police was assassinated in Paris by a Pole whose subsequent escape was aided by some French revolutionary friends. Neither case could be interpreted as a direct threat to the French social system and there was still no reason for the public to suspect that for some years Paris had become a centre for determined agitators who hated the middle-class complacency and ideals of a parliamentary Republic. It was not until 1891 that two separate but related incidents precipitated the epidemic of anarchist activity that culminated with the assassination of a French President in 1894.

On May 1, 1891, there had been much industrial unrest in the small mining town of Fourmies in northern France. A large crowd had gathered in the streets, police and troops were called in to keep order and at a certain moment both the sub-prefect of the district and the officer commanding troops had lost their heads and given orders to open fire on the demonstrators. Ten people were killed, including two children in their early teens. Some forty other demonstrators were wounded. The tragedy immediately had repercussions throughout France. That same day, as soon as they had learned the news, a local party of some twenty anarchists from the northern Paris suburbs decided to demonstrate at once. They had reached Clichy and were parading through the streets behind a woman holding a red flag when they were pursued by the police. There was a scuffle and several shots were fired, both by the police and the marchers, some of whom had come armed with revolvers. Three men were arrested after a struggle and were taken to the local police station, where they were so brutally beaten up that they had to have medical treatment before facing a court. Although the jury pleaded extenuating circumstances, the judge inflicted severe penalties of imprisonment as an example to all other subversionists.

In the summer of 1891, a seedy character, with a past that included robbery from a grave and murder, came to the working-class suburb of Saint-Denis and took lodgings under the name of François Léger. His real name was François Koenigstein but he became known under his mother's name of Ravachol. The man in whose house he had rented a room had a wife who had been on friendly terms with one of the anarchists who had been sent to prison for his part in the Clichy demonstration. In a short time Ravachol had become a member of the local anarchist group and was sharing their determination to exact vengeance for the imprisonment and ill-treatment of their comrades. It was decided that the time had come for direct action. Nevertheless it was not until March the following year that they were ready to begin the offensive. At first, they decided to blow up the Clichy police station and prepared a bomb consisting of some fifty sticks of dynamite and iron scraps packed in an iron casserole, but the police station was so well guarded that they had to give up their attempt. A few days later, they had singled out the lawyer who had presided over the assize court of 1891, Benoît, who lived in a block of flats on the Boulevard Saint-Germain. After a preliminary reconnoitring expedition had failed to discover on which floor Benoît lived, it was decided that Ravachol should go with the bomb and place it on one of the upper landings so that it would explode from the centre of the building. On March 11, armed with two pistols, Ravachol slipped unseen into the house with his bomb and placed it on the first-floor landing. He lit the fuse and made his successful escape from the house a few moments before it was shaken by a terrifying explosion which, fortunately for the tenants, only caused one slight casualty despite considerable material destruction.

In the next few days, Ravachol and his accomplices decided to blow up another of the judges who had been at the trial of the Clichy anarchists, but a police informer brought about the speedy arrest of two of the band. Ravachol had managed to escape in time, and undeterred, went by bus to the Rue de Clichy where his victim lived and succeeded in setting off a second bomb which did more damage than the first and wounded seven people. After the bombing, he went to the Restaurant Véry on the Boulevard Magenta. There he met a waiter who began to grumble about military conscription, in the course of a conversation. Encouraged by the prospect of recruiting a new member to the anarchist cause, Ravachol began to expound anarchist doctrine to him. Three days later he returned to the same restaurant but this time the waiter had become thoroughly suspicious of his customer and had recognised his identity thanks to a scar on his left hand and to newspaper descriptions. He called the police and Ravachol was arrested after a fierce struggle.

The night before his trial at the assize court of the Seine in the Palais de Justice, the Restaurant Véry was wrecked and two men were killed by a terrible explosion. The anarchist "terror" had begun in earnest. The following day the trial opened in an atmosphere of fear and foreboding. But despite outraged public feeling and the Restaurant Véry explosion, Ravachol and his accomplice who appeared with him escaped the death penalty, being sentenced to forced labour for life. Two months afterwards, Ravachol appeared at a provincial court to answer to the murder charges relating to his earlier life. He was condemned to death. He was executed on July 11, 1892, after refusing a priest, and singing as he went to the guillotine. In a short time he had become a hero in revolutionary circles. His unsavoury past and his murders were forgotten. His proud, fearless bearing at his two trials, his defiant attitude and his defence of anarchist principles made him the first great martyr of the French anarchist cause. Broadsheets and songs in his memory were published and he bequeathed his name to the most famous of all the anarchist songs, based on the *Carmagnole* and the *Ça Ira* of the French Revolution:

Dansons la Ravachole,
Vive le son, vive le son,
Dansons la Ravachole,
Vive le son
De l'explosion.

The sound of the next explosion to reverberate throughout Paris was heard in November that year. On the morning of November 8, some employees of the offices belonging to the Carmaux coal mine company, where a strike had been roughly suppressed three months before, noticed a bulky package wrapped in newspaper on a landing in the building. After tearing off the wrapping, they found a heavy cast-iron pot with the lid fastened firmly. The concierge and the office boy carefully took the mysterious object down to the pavement outside where a curious crowd gathered while the police were summoned. A few moments after the object had been taken into the offices of the nearest police station, in the Rue des Bons Enfants, there was a terrible explosion killing four policemen and the unfortunate office boy who had gone with them.

Although anarchy was now very much in the air and anarchist theories were widely discussed and publicised in the Paris press, the next spectacular display of revolutionary activity did not take place until December 9, 1893. This time it was the French Parliament which was the target. A number of deputies were engaged in debate at four o'clock in the afternoon when a bomb was thrown from one of the public galleries, exploding in mid-air in a deadly shower of metal nails. When the smoke cleared, several deputies and members of the public were found to be wounded by inch-long nails but no one was killed. The sitting was resumed twenty minutes later, when the wounded were being treated, order had been restored and the police had surrounded the building and were checking the identity of each public visitor as he came out. A few hours later, one of the injured who had been taken to the Hôtel Dieu hospital was freely talking to the policeman by his bedside about anarchist ideas and admitting that he had thrown the bomb. The bomb-thrower was Auguste Vaillant, a young man whose life had mostly been one of unrelieved

misery and disillusion. He had been abandoned by his parents
when a child, had moved from one ill-paid job to another,
joined various revolutionary groups in France and spent two
miserable years in the Argentine before returning to France where
he endeavoured to support his ten-year-old daughter and his
mistress. He was no more successful than before in his attempt to
earn a decent living and decided to end his own life although not
before punishing the politicians he held responsible for all the
corruption and social injustice in his country. He had borrowed
the money to make his bomb and filled it with nails rather than
iron scraps, since, he declared, his aim had only been to wound,
and to impress public opinion. There was no sign of remorse
when he appeared on trial in the heavily guarded law courts.
He calmly admitted that he had wanted to strike at the
ministers' bench in the Chamber of Deputies since he held all
members of the government to be those primarily responsible for
all the social miseries of his country. His explosion, he said, was
"not only the cry of a Vaillant in revolt but the cry of a class
which demands its rights and which will soon match deeds to
words".

Although Vaillant was represented by a brilliant left-wing
lawyer who had already defended the Clichy anarchists in 1891,
and although he had not killed anyone, he was condemned to
death. The sentence aroused much public indignation and there
was even a petition in the Chamber of Deputies to have the
sentence commuted. Intellectuals and artists demonstrated in
his favour and his daughter wrote to the President's wife in a
despairing plea for her father's life. But all was in vain. The President and his advisers were determined that an example should
be made of Vaillant and the ghastly ritual of a public execution
was performed in the first light of dawn before a large crowd of
spectators, five hundred policemen, four companies of infantry
and a squad of cavalry in the square outside the prison of La
Roquette near the Bastille, on February 5, 1894. Vaillant died
bravely, shouting "death to bourgeois society and long live
anarchy!" as he was led out to the guillotine. The fact that
he was executed without having committed murder and that he
had maintained his resolute bearing to the end impressed many

Parisians. Like Ravachol, Vaillant also became a martyr of the class war.

Astonishing scenes took place by Vaillant's grave in a public cemetery. His death was widely deplored in literary and artistic circles and even in the bourgeois press. Poems were composed and printed in his honour and a public pilgrimage to his grave was so spontaneous that the authorities were unable to prevent it in time. A headstone was placed by sympathisers, bouquets of fresh flowers and even a crown of thorns were laid on the grave, and poets stepped forward to recite their impromptu odes. After the wicker basket used by the executioner to hold the decapitated head had been found, thrown in some bushes near by, men, women and even children were seen to knot lumps of blood-stained sawdust in handkerchiefs and carry them away as precious relics.

A week later, another bomb explosion inaugurated the final, climactic period of anarchist terrorism in Paris. On the evening of February 12, a bomb was hurled in the Café Terminus near the Saint-Lazare station. The café was crowded with working people taking their aperitifs and the orchestra was playing. Twenty people were wounded, one fatally. After the explosion, a young man had been seen to run away and had been pursued. After shooting a policeman, the terrorist was overcome with the help of passers-by. His name was Emile Henry and he claimed that it was he who made the bomb that had killed five men in the police station in the Rue des Bons Enfants.

Emile Henry was the perfect example of the cold-blooded, ruthlessly determined anarchist who, by the most direct means possible, wages war on a society he hates. He had chosen the Café Terminus after inspecting the elegant cafés on the Avenue de l'Opéra and deciding that they were not full enough for his purpose. He had ordered a drink and waited for half an hour until the café was crowded, for, as he admitted, he wanted to kill as many as possible. When asked in court whether he had realised that many innocent people would suffer as a a result of his action, he answered that all bourgeois and those who allowed themselves to endure bourgeois society were equally guilty. If the public supported or endured the actual state of society, then they must suffer for it. He had no respect for human life since the bourgeois themselves did not respect it. As he said in his final declaration to the judges:

"We wish neither to show mercy nor to stumble, and we shall always march onwards until the revolution, the final aim of our efforts, shall have come at last to crown our work by freeing the world.

"In this war without pity which we have declared on the bourgeoisie, we ask for no pity.

"We ask for no pity.

"We bring death; we shall know how to suffer it."

He was only twenty-two but to the public and the press he was the perfect embodiment of the anarchist as the public had imagined him, with his ruthless fanaticism, his iron determination, his courage and absolute contempt for the life of others or his own. He was guillotined on May 21 before a huge crowd of spectators which included the writer Maurice Barrès and the politician-journalist Georges Clemenceau. When he died the anarchist terror was at its height in the city. In March 1894, there were bomb explosions in the Rue Saint-Jacques and the Faubourg Saint-Martin. An anarchist named Pauwels blew himself up while attempting to take his bomb into the church of the Madeleine. In April, there was an explosion in the Restaurant Foyot. Quite as terrifying as the real bombs were the hundreds of imaginary bombs that were rumoured to have been placed all over Paris. There were bogus plots to blow up the Paris Opéra, the Palais de Justice and the Presidential box at the Longchamps racecourse. A bomb was found on the window-sill of a house near the Parc Monceau and exploded when thrown into the street. A package bomb sent to Baron Alphonse de Rothschild badly injured his secretary while he was opening it. Another bomb was flung into the doorway of the Rothschild offices in the Rue Laffitte but failed to explode. For months on end the Paris press published reports of anarchist activities, their presumed projects and aims, thus creating a psychosis of terror in the city. Popular singers composed songs about dynamite and there were wild rumours that anarchists were plotting to introduce deadly microbes into Paris's water supply and to blow up the sewers. The police built specially equipped laboratories with reinforced walls in the suburbs for the analysis of all suspicious objects that were found. Innumerable scares were started when nervous Parisians discovered odd boxes and tins in dustbins or the streets, and many landlords of apartments were frankly terrified, even going to the lengths in some cases of advertising the fact that no lawyer or policeman lived on their premises. Some intellectuals known to be sympathetic to anarchist theories were eagerly sought after as customers by café and restaurant owners who thought by this means to guarantee the immunity of their premises from attacks. The police and government became increasingly edgy and everywhere saw evidence of a vast nationwide revolutionary conspiracy. After Vaillant's bomb attempt in the Parliament, the government hastily passed laws restricting press freedom and the right to form associations. Anarchist theorists, who were often the first to deplore violent action, had a hard time as police raids and government repression increased. Many anarchist papers were forced to close and clubs were constantly being raided.

Anarchism expressed by violence ended in France with the sensational assassination of the President of the Republic, Sadi Carnot, in Lyons by the Italian Saverio on June 24, 1894. The outrage shocked all France but it was the last of its kind for the period. One of its results was that both the government and the police in Paris decided to put the best known of the anarchist theorists on trial and prove that they were directly responsible for all the outrages. Houses of suspects were searched, a number of arrests were made and finally, in August, a number of petty criminals and famous anarchist journalists such as Sébastien Faure and Jean Grave appeared in court together with the writer and critic Félix Fénéon who had written for many anarchist papers, and the artist Maximilien Luce whose radical political views were well known. The trial became known as the "Trial of the Thirty", aroused intense public interest and ended in complete fiasco. The main charge of the prosecution was that the accused had combined together to form "an association of malefactors" but the witty replies in court of Fénéon and the dignified statements of Jean Grave and Sébastien Faure soon convinced the jury that there was little substance in the accusations

made against the writers and intellectuals in the dock and certainly nothing to implicate them in the recent bomb explosions.
Most of the accused were acquitted with the exception of a few
petty criminals and no more bombs exploded in the city. The
"terror" was over.

Eleven major bomb explosions had occurred in Paris between
March 1892 and the summer of 1894. In view of the extremely
violent tone of the anarchist broadsheets and reviews which
called for class war and the overthrow of established society, it
was perhaps surprising that there were no more acts of violence.
Only one of the known bomb throwers bore any real resemblance
to the ruthless, anarchist terrorist of popular legend and that
was Emile Henry. Ravachol had come to anarchism as a conclusion to a life of larceny, robbery and murder; Vaillant was a
poor wretch whom poverty had inspired to make his protest
but who had not intended to take human lives. But none of the
philosophers and theoreticians of the movement had ever been
involved in direct action. What the bombs did do, apart from
their immediate effects, was to show how widespread was the
sympathy for the ideas expressed by the leaders of the movement,
especially among Paris's intellectuals and artists. The popularity
enjoyed by anarchism was symptomatic of something more than
political disillusion and proletarian discontent; it was also one
aspect of that manifestation of extreme individualism which
became increasingly marked in the arts and literature as the
century drew to its close.

That anarchy should have become intellectually fashionable
among so many of Paris's intelligentsia and artists in the 1890's
was partly due to the immense influence and prestige of its
leading philosopher, Jean Grave, and also to many artists' and
writers' bitter resentment against a complacent middle-class
society whose reactionary views and conservatism prevented
public and official recognition of all that was new and most
creative in *avant-garde* art and literature.

When Ravachol's first bomb exploded on the Boulevard Saint-
Germain, the great leader of anarchist thought in France was
Jean Grave. He was a self-educated man who had first been a

leather worker and then a printer and he had been engaged in anarchist journalism ever since the early 1880's when he had founded a paper called *Le Droit Social* in Lyons in 1882. He had collaborated with Kropotkin—the immensely influential Russian anarchist—and in 1885 he came to Paris where he continued to publish a weekly paper *Le Révolté* under the new title of *La Révolte*. By 1889 it was already the best-known anarchist organ in Paris. Like another great French anarchist thinker, Elisée Reclus, a scholarly geographer, Grave's anarchism tended towards idealistic communism. Everything was to be owned in common; everything needed for human life should be distributed according to each individual's needs and each man should be free to àct and speak as he liked within the limits laid down by his own natural respect for others; state interference was wicked and should be abolished. No matter what form it might take, any form of control by a single, strong state was inimical to independent thought and action and thus prevented man from living the full and good life. But although he was a kind and gentle man, with a sincere and optimistic belief that men were naturally good if so allowed to be, Grave eventually conceded that violent revolution must inevitably come before any of his aims could be achieved.

Grave was especially successful in enlisting the sympathy and aid of writers and artists in Paris. He showed a constant interest in all the more advanced tendencies in literature, poetry and painting and by the mid-Nineties was on friendly, often close, terms with practically every important member of the *avant-garde*. In his paper *La Révolte*, he dealt with the modern movement in the arts, violently attacked the prevalent ugliness and bad taste of the time, and supported the neo-Impressionists and other painters in their struggle against conventions and tradition. He showed a keen interest in the relationships between art and society, translated excerpts from the writings of William Morris and his followers, and ceaselessly proclaimed the rôle that art could play in shaping a new and better world and defended the artist's right to express himself with limitless freedom. Such ideas were in perfect harmony with those held by many of the more progressive artists and poets of the period and Grave was soon corresponding on the most cordial terms with a large number of artists and writers who readily collaborated on his paper. During the "black year" of anarchism in Paris—1894—after the police had seized subscription lists for *La Révolte* from his offices, they found to their surprise that the subscribers included such eminent personalities as Alphonse Daudet, Anatole France, Huysmans, Leconte de Lisle, Mallarmé, Pierre Loti, André Antoine, Lugné-Poë, Rémy de Gourmont, Paul Signac, Camille Pissarro and Jean Richepin. Half intellectual and artistic Paris seemed to be on Grave's side, and the journalist-novelist Octave Mirbeau even wrote an enthusiastic preface to Grave's book, *La Société Mourante et l'Anarchie* for which the author was prosecuted and sentenced to two years' imprisonment in 1894, on the charge of incitement to murder, arson and pillage. Mirbeau and another writer, Paul Adam, testified on behalf of Grave, and after the trial, an interview with Mirbeau made it plain why many artists had found anarchist doctrines so seductive:

"The state exerts its detestable influence everywhere . . . crushing, oppressing the individual . . . Look, let us take art in which its influence appears so harmful—it creates a school in which it tries to destroy all kinds of tendencies. After this, there are juries, exhibitions and rewards for only those who come closest to the administrative ideal."

Mirbeau was echoing what many artists and writers had been saying in Paris for the last few years.

In literature, most of the members of the Symbolist group were sympathetic to anarchist ideas. When the weekly anarchist publication, *L'En Dehors*, edited by a revolutionary and ex-deserter who called himself Zo d'Axa, was founded, its contributors included the poets Roinard, Pierre Quillard, René Ghil, Saint-Pol de Roux, Emile Verhaeren, Henri de Régnier and François Vielé-Griffin, and a distinguished band of writers and critics including Félix Fénéon, Mirbeau, Lucian Muhlfeld, Tristan Bernard and Paul Adam. The first number appeared in May 1891, a few days after the tragic shooting of demonstrators at Fourmies. In 1892, the staff of the paper defended and even glorified Ravachol after his execution, with Mirbeau contributing a magnificently polemical apologia for the anarchist's actions, and not surprisingly it was later said of the paper that "it raised more passions in Paris than a street riot".

The *avant-garde* review edited by Félix Fénéon, *La Revue Indépendante*, published articles on modern painting and political pieces which were almost entirely pro-anarchist; the Symbolist poet Stuart Merrill sent subsidies to Jean Grave's *La Révolte*, and the extremely influential *Revue Blanche* which did so much to publicise every new movement in art and literature throughout the Nineties was a centre and meeting place for many pro-anarchist intellectuals. Many of the Symbolist poets who wrote for such publications combined advocacy of free verse in poetry with radical political sentiments and calls for a new society. To such poets as Quillard, Gustave Kahn and Henri de Régnier, to be a revolutionary in politics was the necessary corollary to being a revolutionary in poetry. Freedom in verse meant freedom of thought and expression which in turn implied a maximum of political and social freedom for the individual which could only be achieved by the transformation of existing society, the overthrow of the capitalist, bourgeois-dominated social structure and the abolition of restricting conventions. Jean Richepin, who had composed songs and poems dealing with society's outcasts, was for a long time a regular contributor to radical magazines and the lyric poet Laurent Tailhade made himself famous to the public by such spectacular declarations of support for violent revolutionary action as his "what matters the death of a few vague humanities as long as the gesture is beautiful and if the individual affirms himself by it?" upon hearing of Vaillant's bomb-throwing in Parliament. Tailhade was not only a gifted poet but a dandy and one of the best-known habitués of the poets' cafés in the Latin Quarter. Although he had a fondness for making grand gestures and spectacular pronouncements (for which he got into trouble with the press and the authorities more than once), many other poets agreed with the impassioned way he championed the assertion of the individual against society. What young, struggling poet determined to smash conventions, defy existing rules and impose himself as an individual in his art could resist calling himself an anarchist and an enemy of the bourgeois? Naturally, there were many hangers-on and poseurs in anarchist circles, but the fact remains that nearly every poet and literary innovator of consequence inclined towards anarchism in the last decade of the 19th century.

Revolutionary sympathies were also evident in the progressive art world. While the neo-Impressionists were defended and supported in the left-wing press, some of the most talented draughtsmen and illustrators of the time, including Ibels, Willette and Maximilien Luce, designed covers for *Le Père Peinard* and other anarchist organs. The review *La Plume* published a special number devoted to anarchy on May 1, 1893, with illustrations drawn by Willette and the brothers Camille and Lucien Pissarro. The painters Signac, Camille Pissarro and Félix Vallotton, the *dessinateurs* and caricaturists Forain, Caran d'Ache, Léandre, Steinlen, Hermann-Paul and Abel Faivre who used their art in the service of radical journalism were all anarchists by sympathy, on friendly terms with Jean Grave and in touch with the anarchising members of the Symbolist school.

Such a political ferment among the most creative members of artistic and intellectual society indicated a new political and social awareness, and a widely held conviction that society was hostile to the truly original mind. The artist was becoming alienated from society to an extent unprecedented in the past. The change in his social position became increasingly pronounced in the late 19th century. In the old days, the painter or sculptor was integrated in the social structure and could rely on patronage. There was a constant demand for his work and his place in the world was both defined and secure.

Now only the most sterile and conformist artist could be sure of patronage and official approval in a state dominated by middle-class materialistic values and in which the general public's idea of beauty was represented by the trite, academic painting and sculpture of the Salons. The situation of the true independent artist was worsening. Each successive creative innovation could be sure of encountering resistance and incomprehension from the majority of the press, the public and those in official positions of authority. Artistic non-conformism acquired political significance. In poetry, the campaign for free verse came under attack from conservatives in literature who took the attitude that such an untraditional poetic form was somehow unpatriotic, and "un-French".

The popularity of anarchist ideas among artists and writers and their idealisation of such sworn enemies of society as Vaillant, Ravachol and Henry did not mean that they themselves were in favour of blowing innocent people to bits or of involving themselves in violent physical action. They were idealists and not political agitators although the police and members of a nervous government were often inclined to think otherwise. Many painters who had fought desperately to make a living, and who had to contend with the philistinism and hostility of the leaders of officially-favoured art, saw themselves as victims of an unjust social order that was blind to truth and beauty and hostile to progress in any sphere of life.

Parisian writers and intellectuals found a great deal in the anarchist ideas of Kropotkin, Grave and Reclus that corresponded to their own ideals: the exaltation of the individual, his right to freedom, a new society without inherited prejudices and in which the creative mind would have every opportunity and encouragement. To call oneself an anarchist meant to insist on maintaining one's individuality as a creator, to reject outdated rules, and passionately to affirm the validity of the artist's own judgment and sole authority as far as his work was concerned. But to many contemporary observers, this militant attitude simply meant chaos and an irresponsible conspiracy to alienate the public. There seemed to be a parallel between the terrorist outrages of a man like Emile Henry and the apparent wilful determination of a group of poets, painters and writers to reject every noble tradition in French civilisation and to scorn the prevailing taste of the majority. When the poet Stuart Merrill asserted that "the Symbolist is the anarchist in literature" and Vielé Griffin wrote of "the literary anarchy for which we have battled", every worst fear of the conservative supporter of cultural tradition seemed confirmed.

Naturally, the word "anarchy" was often indiscriminately applied to anything new or esoteric, not immediately comprehensible or likely to appeal to a large public. It was seen by some critics and social writers as a sign of the times, and as a symptom of a crisis of civilisation. It meant the end of art and literature since it seemed to imply chaos and destruction beyond which lay—nothing. A French writer and historian, Fierens-Gevaert, perfectly summed up the traditionalist attitude to radical movements in art and literature in *La Tristesse Contemporaine,* "an essay on the great moral and intellectual currents of the XIXth century" which was published in Paris in 1899.

To Fierens-Gevaert, the curse of mankind was "modernity" which equalled decadence, and the triumph of soul-destroying materialism. There was a lack of "love" and of time for "spiritual contemplation". The great scientific advances which were gathering momentum in the last two decades of the century were "precipitating our moral agony". Looking at politics, art and society in general, he could see corruption everywhere: people were losing respect for institutions; sceptics were mocking at tradition and the heritage of the past; literature was in a state of anxiety and "dramatists consider with melancholy our social decadence". The whole of contemporary France was infected with "anarchy": "Every philosopher, writer, poet, dramatist, artist is today a latent anarchist. And very often they boast of being one. Anarchy is even fashionable in the salons where it should terrify the most. *Avant-garde* authors have adopted the theories of Kropotkin and Jean Grave."

Art, especially, was in danger: "The art of today in its highest, or at least, its most original expressions, is essentially anarchist. It ceases to address the crowd." Certainly, Gevaert conceded, a great artist may be permitted to isolate himself in his dreams, but now lesser artists were losing all their talent and their inspiration by wilfully cultivating their individual esotericism. The present conditions in art and literature no longer allowed the creator to feel in constant communion with his public and, isolated in his ivory tower, he had become "a victim of our social anarchy".

The connection in such critics' minds as Gevaert's between anarchy in politics and experiment in art and literature was also made by members of the Paris theatre-going public. To the fashionable young Parisian intellectuals of the 1890's, no theatre breathed a greater spirit of revolt against the existing social order than the Théâtre de l'Oeuvre, founded by the twenty-four-year-old actor-manager and former colleague of Paul Fort's, Aurélien Lugné-Poë. The company he founded in 1893 was the heir to Fort's short-lived Théâtre d'Art and it did more than any other theatre in Paris to bring the best new foreign plays to the attention of the public. In 1896, it won spectacular notoriety from its production of a play which seemed to represent the apotheosis of defiant anarchy in the arts—*Ubu Roi*, a savage farce hurled at the public like a stick of dynamite.

At the beginning, the Théâtre de l'Oeuvre was intended to continue Paul Fort's and Dujardin's endeavours to provide a stage for Symbolism and poetry in drama. After the Théâtre d'Art had run out of funds, Lugné-Poë had agreed to Fort's request to stage the first performance of a new mystico-poetical play by Maeterlinck, *Pelléas et Mélisande*. While Fort rapidly lost interest in the project and soon abandoned the theatre to devote himself entirely to poetry, Lugné-Poë gathered some of their young painter friends, the "Nabis", Vuillard, Bonnard and Sérusier to help him with stage sets, costumes and programmes, scraped some money together and hired the stage of a music hall, the Théâtre des Bouffes Parisiens. The performance took place on May 17, 1893, won some praise and completely enchanted the young composer Claude Debussy who, a decade later, was to become famous for his opera inspired by the play. Towards the end of 1893, Lugné-Poë was able to establish his company in the Bouffes du Nord, a dingy and uncomfortable theatre near the working-class district of the Boulevard de la Chapelle before moving a year later to the Nouveau Théâtre in Pigalle, an annexe to the Casino de Paris *café-concert*.

The first production at the Bouffes du Nord was Ibsen's *Rosmersholm*. In a short time it became clear that Lugné-Poë had given up any attempt to specialise in "mystical" or "symbolist" plays and had simply decided to present the best foreign plays he could find, notably those by the Scandinavian playwrights Ibsen, Bjornson and Strindberg who were becoming well known in northern Europe and England. His first season coincided with the outbreak of anarchist violence that began with Vaillant's bomb in the

Chamber of Deputies, and from the start his theatre became a place of pilgrimage for young people with anarchist ideas, and was seen as a "cradle of subversion" by the police and the government authorities. Four days after Vaillant's bomb, the Paris Prefect of Police forbade a production of Gerhart Hauptmann's German play *Solitary Souls* even though it was impossible to find the slightest hint of revolutionary provocation in the text. But one of the anarchists who had been arrested in Paris after the bomb-throwing was a Dutchman, Alexander Cohen, who was found to have anarchist sympathies and to have collaborated with Lugné-Poë by translating Hauptmann's play. He was expelled from France but in the meantime it became known to the police that several supporters and friends of the theatre such as the critic Félix Fénéon, the poets and writers Tristan Bernard, Henri de Régnier and Saint-Pol de Roux, all had anarchist sympathies. A petition was sent to the government and Lugné-Poë argued with the authorities who eventually permitted a dress rehearsal which took place before a large audience who had waited patiently for hours in the rain. But soon there were other troubles. Police continued to keep a close watch on the theatre, fights broke out among the audience during the more controversial productions, and there was no denying that a sizeable proportion of the public was sympathetic towards left-wing radicalism and inclined to make noisy demonstrations.

The type of audience at the Théâtre de l'Oeuvre became notorious. It was usually a mixture of wealthy and worldly society dilettanti who could be relied upon to patronise anything unusual, young poets who claimed allegiance to Symbolism or any of the other "isms" in vogue at the time, "aesthetes" and dandies, critics and writers for the many small artistic and literary reviews, students and painters. Several newspapers made fun of the public by stressing the determinedly "arty" garb of the spectators, the prevalence of the long-haired young men in their trailing capes and long velvet coats with silver clasps, and the pretty girls with flowing neo-medieval robes and "Botticelli-esque" hairstyles. Every evening, Lugné-Poë could count on some thousand spectators. As the Théâtre de l'Oeuvre was nominally a theatre club, seats had to be booked by subscription, but hun-

dreds were often given away free—especially in the gallery, which
became one of the noisiest in Paris. Many notabilities were among
the subscribers: the playwright Sardou, Emile Zola, Pierre and
Marie Curie, the painters Jean-Paul Laurens and Puvis de
Chavannes. Every literary and artistic tendency of the time was
represented and most of the plays performed had never been
seen in France before.

To many of the younger people who flocked to the theatre,
the plays of Ibsen and Bjornson reflected their own views—
especially Ibsen's. They were seen as dramatic exaltations of individuality and as violent criticisms of society, social conventions
and taboos. As they were plays of ideas, they appealed to the intelligentsia, and were regarded as vehicles for fashionable radical
ideas on emancipation from authority, and as embodying the
anarchist spirit of revolt. The character of Hilda in *The Master
Builder* was seen as the incarnation of youth in revolt against its
egotistical elders. A play like *The Enemy of the People* aroused the
Paris Prefect's suspicions when he learned that it had as its theme
the loneliness of the strong-willed individual, and that the
anarchist-minded poet Laurent Tailhade had given a lecture
before its performance to a large and excited audience. *Pillars of
Society* could equally be considered "subversive" since it satirised
the ruling classes. Bjornson's play, *Beyond Our Powers*, dealt with
social conflicts between workers and employers, and when, in
the third act, a bomb was thrown in the play, the scene was
applauded by members of the audience, and cries of "Long live
Anarchy!" were heard.

Another playwright, Edouard Schuré, gave a lecture on Ibsen
and extolled him as the "playwright of individualism" whose
dramas stressed the conflict between the individual sensibility
and will and restricting social and collective conventions. Other
plays seemed to continue the "arty", "for-initiates-only" line for
which Fort had been reproached in his day—such as *La Gardienne*
by Henri de Régnier, which seemed to prove that anarchist ideas
led to incomprehensibility in art.

La Gardienne was really a poem in dialogue form played to music,
with actors reciting from the orchestra while others mimed on
the stage, and showed the "Master" returning to his ruined home

to lament the death of his young love whose phantom reappears to him. The poets in the audience were delighted; the others became increasingly restive and the evening ended amid laughter, jeers and slow handclapping. Certainly not all Lugné-Poë's productions were of such esoteric or "subversive" a nature, but the Théâtre de l'Oeuvre's reputation as an anarchists' rendezvous was soon secure. But no single play ever caused a greater scandal than *Ubu Roi* and no one seemed better fitted to typify the popular image of the wild anarchist individualist in art than its eccentric author, Alfred Jarry.

Jarry is one of the most curious characters in French literature. He made non-conformism the chief aim of his short life, and as such he was ideally suited to write the play which, more than any other, was seen by the public and most critics as the highest expression of the anarchist rejection of society and scorn for every established convention.

He was born in the small town of Laval in 1873. His father was a travelling salesman in the wool business, and his mother a romantic-minded daughter of a judge, with artistic inclinations. By the age of fifteen, Jarry was already showing signs of literary talent and eccentric behaviour while a schoolboy at the *lycée* in Rennes where he had moved with his mother. One of the school staff, a physics master named Hébert, was a fat and incompetent teacher who became the perpetual butt of the pupils' cruel humour. A few months after his arrival at the school, Jarry was engaged in writing satirical farces based on the character of Hébert, and producing plays in a friend's house. In 1891, he came to Paris to finish his studies after gaining experience in amateur theatre, puppet and marionette shows, and in writing. Like many young men of that time he found the intellectual and artistic climate of Paris a heady one, with Nietzsche, the Russian novel, Anarchism, Symbolism and Wagnerism all very much in the air. He gave up his studies for literature, soon made friends among the young poets, met a publisher of a small literary review who introduced him to other writers and journalists, and in a short time became a member of a group that included most of the literary *avant-garde*, well-known journalists like Mirbeau and Fénéon, and the lively circle of writers and artists who gathered every week at the home of the owner of the influential magazine *Mercure de France*, where Jarry become particularly friendly with Vallette's wife, the lady novelist Rachilde.

Jarry became a well-known figure because of his literary talent, his strange manner of speech, his delight in practical jokes, bicycling and pistol shooting, his unusual attire and his determinedly eccentric behaviour. But even while he was deliberately playing the fool and cultivating his reputation as an eccentric, he was busily writing and involved in magazine publishing, in which he spent most of the money left him by his parents who had recently died. He had become a co-director of a beautifully produced art and literary magazine, *L'Ymagier*, and then director of another review called *Perhinderion*, and he had some poems published in the *Mercure de France*. Like other young *avant-garde* writers, he had taken a keen interest in Lugné-Poë's theatre and announced his support for the endeavour. After one of his colleagues had left him, Lugné-Poë asked Jarry whether he would help him and he eagerly accepted, assisting with the administration of the theatre, subscriptions and advertising, and the planning of future productions.

By now Jarry had written a play which was loosely based on the schoolboy farces he had written when at the Rennes *lycée*. It was published in two parts as *Ubu Roi or the Poles*, "a drama in five acts", in the *Livre d'art*, an artistic and literary review directed by Paul Fort and a colleague. The play was mentioned in the *Revue Blanche* and reviewed by the poet Verhaeren in *L'Art Moderne* as "a curious and droll little book appearing from the first lines to be mystifying and mad . . . not giving a damn for the reader"; while Vielé-Griffin in the *Mercure de France* found it impossible to read without exploding into " a great burst of approving laughter". Once he began work at the Théâtre de l'Oeuvre, Jarry persuaded Lugné-Poë to stage *Ubu Roi* after the first-ever production in France of *Peer Gynt*, designed the posters, invited all the most important critics, and hired an excellent actor from the Odéon to play the part of Ubu: Firmin Gémier.

The first night at the Nouveau Théâtre, on December 10, 1896, made theatrical history. The audience was both distinguished and restive. As Laurent Tailhade wrote later:

"On the evening of this *première* . . . the audience was as stormy as during the great days of Romanticism. It was, without exaggeration, a battle of *Hernani* between the young, decadent, and symbolist schools, and the bourgeois critics . . . hairy poets, unwashed and grandiloquent aesthetes, supporters and retainers of the new literature were arguing, gesticulating, exchanging slander and doorkeepers' gossip. The entire editorial staff of the *Mercure de France* brought a note of elegance and discretion into this din."

Before the performance, Jarry came on to the stage to talk about the play for ten minutes. With his short legs, his baggy and ill-fitting suit, his pale and intense face in which his great sombre eyes glowed like coals, and his monotonous delivery, he made a strange impression. Even stranger was his speech in which he thanked the people who had helped to make the production possible, said that the actors would be wearing masks, and that the audience were quite free to see any allusion they liked in the play, and ended by stating that the action was set in Poland which was to say "nowhere". The curtain went up and showed a rudimentary set with trees, a painted bed and a door opening against the sky with a dangling skeleton beside it. It had been designed and painted by Jarry himself in collaboration with Bonnard, Vuillard, Toulouse-Lautrec and Sérusier who were, as always, faithful friends of the theatre and ever willing to collaborate. Changes of scene were indicated by cardboard notices hung on a nail by an old man who came on stage.

One word sufficed to make *Ubu Roi* famous. Firmin Gémier costumed as the obese, evil-minded, foul-mouthed tyrant of the play stepped forward and bellowed "Merdre!" ("shit"), the best-known expletive in the French language, to which Jarry had added an "r" to make it more resonant, and one which no one at that time would have dreamed of uttering before a mixed public. There was such a tumult in the auditorium that the play could not continue for a full fifteen minutes. Spectators rose scandalised from their seats, others clapped or booed, and slogans were shouted such as "It's Shakespeare" or "It's Lugné *Pot-de-chambre!*"

The story of the play was of little importance: Ubu murders

his way to the throne of Poland, pillages the country, is chased by the dead king's son and comes to France where he promises the population that he will commit new atrocities. It was the personality of Ubu, the monstrous, swollen-bellied, cruel, greedy, hypocritical and obscene usurper, that mattered and nothing else. Every time that Gémier repeated *"merdre!"* during the performance (it recurred frequently) there was another near-riot in the theatre. The evening ended with frenzied applause by the Pro-Ubuists and hissing and jeers from the anti-Ubuists, and there were the by now traditional fisticuffs between quarrelling spectators. There had never been anything like this première in the entire history of the French stage. *Ubu Roi*'s shock value was immense.

Most of the hostile critics saw *Ubu Roi* as an affront to the public, to their profession and to French literature. It was more than a mere practical joke perpetrated by a literary lunatic, it went further than any previously imaginable provocation of the *avant-garde*, it was worse than bad taste, worse than sacrilege—they had difficulty in finding words strong enough to condemn it. But some critics, including Henri Bauer of the *Echo de Paris*, the critic of the *Mercure de France*, Jean Lorrain the columnist, and Catulle Mendès the poet, praised it. The most eminent of the play's defenders was Bauer who asked why some spectators had refused to understand that Jarry had been making fun of them all. He saw that *Ubu Roi* was essentially an anti-bourgeois, anarchist attack on conventional hypocrisies. It was a "barefaced philosophico-political pamphlet which spits in the faces of the chimerae of tradition and the masters created by people's servility". Like Mendès, Bauer considered that Ubu was the creation of a universal, eternal type of being, and that "from this enormous and strangely suggestive figure of Ubu there blows the wind of destruction, the inspiration of contemporary youth which overthrows traditional respect and centuries-old prejudices". Mendès hailed Ubu as an immortal character and declared that no matter how many spectators shouted or jeered or tried to fling their seats at the stage, the fact remained that *Ubu Roi* was an attack on human imbecility, lust and cruelty. In the *Revue Blanche*, Romain Coolus observed: "Ah! a fine and historic evening, that of the première of *Ubu Roi*! Ever since, literature, art and politics are impregnated with Ubu; from every side you can smell Ubu; people fight for Ubu and for Ubu people disembowel each other . . . "

Old Sarcey dismissed it briefly in his column, leaving it to the last after discussing two other plays: "Shall I speak of *Ubu Roi* which L'Oeuvre gave us with an incredible fanfare of publicity? It is a filthy practical joke which only deserves the silence of contempt. I saw with pleasure that the public (even that very special public of the Oeuvre) revolted against this excess of ineptitude and coarseness. Despite its usual sceptical indulgence towards these performances, it booed openly. It is the beginning of the end. These jokers have been making fun of us too long now. The limit has been reached."

Other newspaper critics agreed with Sarcey that *Ubu* was scatological, incomprehensible nonsense. To *Le Paris*, it was "a mystification in very bad taste. There is no other word to describe the performance." The large-circulation *Petit Parisien* thought that the Théâtre de L'Oeuvre "decidedly prefers to give asylum to turpitudes which seem to have been written by the inmates of a lunatic asylum", and added that "not for a long time have we ever heard such a din in a Parisian theatre. The public protested with uncommon violence while listening to this succession of phrases in which coarseness was only rivalled by incoherence".

More significant than these attacks was the way in which two other critics immediately linked *Ubu* with the Symbolist movement and the popularity of anarchist doctrines among young writers. In the magazine *La Critique*, the writer declared that there was no doubt that *Ubu Roi* was a historic date in the history of the theatre and for that reason, and that reason only, he would deal with the play since "Stupidity has its limits; the indecency of practical jokes has its bounds, and a whole period of more or less Ibsenian symbols has ended in this coarse and scatological allusion against which the public has opposed the rampart of common sense . . . We must go backwards. We must renounce this symbolism which is not in the French genius." He held the young generation of writers responsible for such a play which could only have been written because of the present decadent trend in literature and because "lulled by the idealised sensuality of Péladan, enfevered by the blood of anarchy, these spoilt children and sullen butchers, their brains either empty or filled with nightmares, exalted by hypocritical and cowardly double meanings, have nothing in their innards except what Oscar Wilde might have left there. This mystico-symbolist onrush has as its conclusion the most shameful chapter in the annals of our literature."

What was so interesting in this attack was the way the critic unhesitatingly judged *Ubu* to be part of a general process of decadence in literature and drama, and to have been a by-product of the Symbolist movement. Jarry was not an exception or merely an eccentric outsider: he had been inspired by the climate of anarchy and was as much a protagonist of "immoral decadence" as Oscar Wilde, whose play *Salome* had been performed at the same theatre, and Péladan, the mystic semi-occult writer. The most influential critic in the controversy was Henri Fouquier who wrote for the *Figaro* and eventually defeated Henri Bauer and caused him to lose his post after a duel fought in the newspaper columns. Fouquier had no doubt in his mind about the significance of *Ubu*: it was an anarchist attempt to tyrannise art and literature as part of a general attack on the state.

In his long, carefully reasoned articles, Fouquier said that the play was a sign of the public appearance of certain revolutionaries in literature, theatre and art. Some of these revolutionaries, he admitted, might be honest and sincere men but others were "simply furious madmen". They were "Anarchists of art", for just as politics had its anarchists, so did music, painting, sculpture and even architecture. Like the terrorists of the Paris Commune, their aim was simply that of destruction. They were few but they were prominent and their influence was dangerous. Summing up, Fouquier declared that they were "united in their efforts despite their private hatreds and jealousies. Distinguishing and recognising themselves by means of uniforms and slogans that are sometimes picturesque and funny, audacious and noisy, and sometimes not fearing to astonish by their singular appearances, these men who seem incoherent but who play politics so skilfully are playing the game—so often won—of a minority oppressing a majority. Some, directly, by their threatening enthusiasms in theatres, others, indirectly, by their articles in newspapers and reviews, are exercising a veritable terror over the public. And it is the imposition of this special, wholly literary terror that public opinion is permitting."

Jarry seemed ideally suited to represent the popular idea of the literary terrorist. He had all the characteristics of the *avant-garde* anarchist. He was eccentric, he scorned society's conventions, he would deliberately behave like a madman, he would be rude and threatening, he drank to excess and in every way seemed determined to become Ubu himself, a complete outsider with no need for society and no other aim than to play his own part. As far as the Paris public was concerned, he retired into oblivion after the two performances of *Ubu Roi* but he had left the impression of one who had been bent on bringing down the whole structure of civilised culture to the accompaniment of a gigantic, savage cry of *"merdre!"* Behind his picturesque figure there seemed to lurk a whole gang of anti-painters, anti-poets, anti-writers and anti-dramatists, all sympathetic to a political doctrine which implied destruction and chaos and an excessive cult of individualism which would only lead to suicide, both physical and mental.

Jarry died, an alcoholic in abject poverty, in 1907. The year of *Ubu* also saw the death in the most wretched circumstances of another literary outlaw, the poet Verlaine. Although he became a legendary personage in the cafés and cabarets of the Latin Quarter and was widely recognised as one of France's finest lyric poets, he lived little better than a tramp, with a total and monumental disregard for society's conventions. He died a physical wreck, in the Rue Descartes, near the Boulevard Saint-Michel, in January 1896 but his death was the occasion for the most spectacular funeral procession a poet had been given in Paris since Victor Hugo's state funeral in 1885.

The pall bearers included François Coppée, Catulle Mendès, and the dandyish dilettante Count Robert de Montesquiou. Nearly all of literary Paris turned out to pay him homage. After a mass had been said at the church of Saint-Etienne-du-Mont, the coffin was accompanied by a crowd of the poet's friends and intimates who represented every tendency in French poetry. Followed by painters, bohemians and habitués of the Latin Quarter cafés and a crowd of curious hangers-on, the procession slowly made its way in the bright winter sunlight through the centre of Paris, across the Seine, and all the way up the Avenue de l'Opéra, across the Grands Boulevards, finally to reach its destination in the Montmartre cemetery where a distinguished band of poets led by Mallarmé, Jean Moréas and Gustave Kahn made speeches over the grave. It must have seemed to the many spectators who watched the cortège pass as if the whole of the Latin Quarter and most of Paris's literary world had assembled to pay homage to this man who had spurned society, whose life had been one long scandal and yet who had written some of the most beautiful verses in the whole of French poetry. In its way, Verlaine's funeral represented a homage paid by many artists and writers to an idea that some people might call individualism taken to extremes, and others define as the artist's complete fidelity to himself and his art alone. It was both a challenge and a triumph.

If anarchy was one of the predominant tendencies attributed to the art and literature of the *avant-garde* in the Paris of the 1890's, the other was an idealistic mysticism which tended towards the occult.

The anarchists were involved in the life and society of their time, no matter how much they wanted to change it. They were very much a part of the material world. The tendency towards mysticism, other-worldliness, dreams and visions which was apparent in Symbolist art and poetry also led to the formation of esoteric cults, to involvement in magic and even to Satanism.

One of the most flamboyant and eccentric figures who trod this dangerous path—without, however, meeting with disaster —was the novelist and art critic Joseph Péladan. He was inspired by the same urge as the Symbolists had been to escape from the realities of everyday existence to another spiritual realm of dreams, lofty ideas and noble emotions, and although he was often derided for his strange behaviour and poses, he became a prominent figure in Paris's non-conformist art world.

Péladan was born in Lyons in 1859. His father was an old man who worked in journalism, had written a book on prophecies, was obsessed by a kind of philosophic-occult version of Catholicism, who was in close touch with the city's leading intellectual circles and who held learned discussions in his home with his friends. It was in this earnest, erudite atmosphere, impregnated with religion and mysticism, that Péladan grew up. His eldest brother Adrien was deeply interested in alchemy and occultism and it was not long before these subjects became Joseph's main preoccupations, together with art—not modern art but the art of medieval Europe which went hand in hand with religion.

When Joseph Péladan was twenty-one, he went to Italy for a year and the country's wealth of artistic treasures of the Middle Ages and Renaissance was a revelation to him. In 1882 he came to Paris where the prominent art journalist Arsène Houssaye gave him a job on his review, *L'Artiste*. In a series of brilliant and polemical articles, Joseph expressed his hostility towards both the art of the academics in the Salons and to the new developments in painting pioneered by Courbet and Manet and continued by the Impressionists. What he wanted was a revival of the artistic canons of Italian art and a return of the religious element. Like some other writers, he was convinced that he was living in a period of decadence and that the true values of civilisation were being lost and submerged by a flood of base vulgarity and commercialism. Only art, so Péladan argued, could offer mankind salvation from the corrupting materialism of the times. Being, by its very essence, divine, art brought man closer to God and enhanced the spiritual quality of existence.

In 1884, Péladan published his first novel, *Le Vice Suprême*, a strange, mystic-erotic work filled with a parade of monstrous vices and villains and a spirit of tormented sensuality, but which recommended the salvation of the West through the adoption of the occult magic of the ancient East. The book was the first of a long series called *La Décadence Latine*, was an immediate success, ran into twenty editions and launched Péladan as a literary figure of some importance. In 1888, a visit to Bayreuth where he saw Wagner's music-drama *Parsifal* performed three times was the second decisive experience of his life. The mystical, solemn

atmosphere which attended the performances, the lofty idealism of the work, its fusion of poetry, drama and music and its
idealistic conception all aroused Péladan's passionate admiration
and made him into one of Wagner's most enthusiastic followers.

Back in Paris, *Le Vice Suprême* had been discovered by a young
poet, the Marquis Stanislas de Guaita, who had come to Paris to
make his name in poetry and who was studying mysticism and
magic. Guaita and Péladan met, exchanged ideas, agreed that the
world needed saving from banal materialism, and together with
a few friends who held similar views founded a "Kabbalistic Order
of the Rosy Cross" which they claimed to be a revival of the
medieval Rosicrucian sect and which combined visionary mysticism, Kabbalistic mysteries and freemasonry at its most esoteric.
Soon afterwards, serious differences arose between Guaita and
Péladan, who insisted on regarding Rosicrucianism as an essentially Catholic type of philosophy and occultism. In addition,
Péladan's behaviour was becoming increasingly peculiar and the
way he tried to monopolise the order upset Guaita and his
friends.

In May 1890, Péladan grandly issued what he called "episcopal
decrees" or commands, called *mandements*. There were three such
decrees, each of which could with some justice be regarded as
the ravings of a madman. Péladan addressed the first to all prac-
titioners of the "art of drawing", ordering them to combine
together and to submit to his sole aesthetic authority and direction. The second was addressed to the Cardinal-Archbishop of
Paris, and concerned a proposal to organise a Spanish bull-fight
in a ring to be set up in the Rue Pergolèse near the Champs-
Elysées. Péladan attacked the project, stressed the mystical symbolic significance of the bull and solemnly warned the eminent
churchman of the moral dangers of such a spectacle, insisting
that the sight of a *corrida* would only arouse lubricious feelings in
the feminine spectators. The third missive was even more eccentric for in it he angrily reproached Madame Rothschild for having
destroyed a chapel in a château she had bought and also for
having demolished a house in which Balzac had lived. For these
crimes of "iconoclasty and sacrilege", Péladan "excommuni-
cated" Madame Rothschild. He told her that henceforth men of

letters and artists were no longer permitted to greet her, and that anyone finding her setting foot in a church, a library, a museum, concert hall or art gallery had the right to expel her from the premises forthwith.

This was too much for the other Rosicrucians and the group split up. Péladan's attitudes and the strange airs he gave himself were an embarrassment to the others. After changing his name Joseph to Joséphin, he decided he was a "Chaldean" by "spiritual adoption". While reading the Bible he had come across the name of an ancient Babylonian king, Merodach Baladan. The similarity between the monarch's name and that of Péladan struck him and in the course of his imaginative reveries he seemed to discover a relationship between himself and the long-dead king. In the Louvre, he had studied the casts of the gigantic figures of ancient Assyrian kings on bas-reliefs from Nineveh. There he found similarities between their features and his own, and accordingly had his beard trimmed in an "Assyrian" style. The fact that the figures who impressed him were priest-kings led him to see himself as a "Priest and King" in art, and as a descendant of the ancient Magi in occult and philosophical matters.

Péladan now gave himself the royal Assyrian title of *Sar*, adopted the name Merodach, wore strange, flowing costumes and maintained that he was the direct descendant of the biblical Magi and the heir to the mystic doctrines of Zoroaster, Pythagoras and Orpheus, as well as of those of the Knights Templar and the Rosicrucians. In all this play-acting he took himself very seriously and founded his own Rosicrucian order, calling himself the Grand Master of the Supreme Hierarch of the Third Order of the Catholic Rosy Cross. He dressed himself in archaic costumes of his own making, designed his own coat of arms, appointed "commanders" and "dignitaries" of his Order with such titles as "archons", "aesthetes" and "grand priors", called his letters "commands" or *mandements*, addressed people as *magnieques*, "adelphs" or "peers", grandly christened his novels *fithopées*, published books such as *How one becomes a Magus* which were adorned with mystic symbols, rose-crosses and winged Assyrian bulls, and became notorious as one of the most picturesque and eccentric Parisian personalities of the time. But his aims were quite serious. In the first place he intended to give back to the Catholic church the hidden wisdom he was sure it had lost, and secondly he wanted to found a new artistic and literary movement. He explained the aims of his "Catholic", "orthodox" and "aesthetic" society in the *Figaro* after announcing that he was to hold a salon of his own to exhibit "idealistic" works. He intended to form a new brotherhood of artists, and to oppose the trend of naturalism since "realism has fallen into the same mud it used for its models". Wagner's works and ideas were the only panacea for the ills afflicting art. He invited all sculptors, painters, musicians and men of letters who shared his views to follow him as their leader. His proposed Salon would only contain works of art that were idealistic, noble, thought-filled and thought-provoking. The Salon of the Rosy Cross would be a "temple dedicated to the Art God with masterpieces for dogma and geniuses for saints".

At the same time, he was writing plays inspired by Wagner and his own Babylonian obsessions. Like those of Dujardin and Paul Fort's theatre they were intensely unrealistic and "spiritual". The first of these "inner dramas of the human soul" which he called *Wagnéries* was *Le Fils des Etoiles*, a "Chaldean Wagnery". It was rejected by both the Comédie Française and the Odéon but was eventually performed at his own theatre of the Rose Croix on a hired stage in March 1892 and repeated a year later when he managed to hire a hall in the Palais du Champ de Mars which had been built for the 1889 exhibition. The *Fils des Etoiles* was a long poetic, declamatory drama of the triumph of love in some strange pseudo-Assyrian country, with a minimum of action, lengthy dialogues and no attempt at individual characterisation. It attracted considerable attention and was followed a year later by another play, *Babylone*. This was the story of Merodach, the "Sar" of ancient Babylon who, after showing himself pitiless as a conqueror in war, is converted to sentiments of love and pity in defeat and who sacrifices his pride in order to redeem defeated Babylon, thus showing that love and compassion can triumph over brutality and crass materialism.

It was as an impresario of art exhibitions that Péladan was most successful. The first Rosy Cross exhibition was held in the well-known Durand-Ruel gallery. How the paintings were selected could be seen by the rules of the Salon which Péladan published in 1891. The first aim of the Salon was to "restore the cult of the IDEAL in all its splendour, with TRADITION as its base and BEAUTY as its means". It was to "ruin realism, reform Latin taste and create a school of idealist art". There were to be neither jury nor entrance fees for artists sending in their works. Many subjects were expressly forbidden. They included: all paintings of historical or military scenes, representations of contemporary life, rustic scenes, still-lives, animals, humorous subjects and all landscapes except "those composed in the manner of Poussin". Paintings expressing Catholic dogma, "Oriental theogonies except those of the yellow races", allegories and "the nude made sublime" were especially welcome. French or foreign artists could take part for the word "foreign" was meaningless to the Salon, but "following Magical law, no work by a woman will ever be exhibited or executed by the order". Furthermore, the exhibition would be preceded by a Solemn Mass of the Holy Ghost to be celebrated at the church of Saint-Germain-l'Auxerrois, and music by the "superhuman" Wagner would be played as well as a fanfare for harp and trumpet composed by a young musician Péladan had found called Erik Satie.

The first Salon went more or less as planned and was a huge success. It opened after a preliminary mass had been said at Notre Dame on March 10, 1892, and drew as many as 11,000 visitors, according to the *Figaro*. The event had been made possible by the financial generosity of a young nobleman, Count Antoine de la Rochefoucauld, who had joined Péladan's circle of followers. The presentation of the exhibition was inspired by the elaborate ceremonial that Péladan had seen in Bayreuth. Flowers were strewn everywhere, incense was sprayed throughout the gallery, invisible organs played and there had been opening fanfares composed by Satie and the prelude to *Parsifal*, played on trumpets. The ambassadors of Sweden and the United States came and traffic outside was brought to a halt by the crowds. Péladan himself, sumptuously attired in a black doublet with lace cuffs and ruff, presided over the exhibition like the Priest-King of Art that he thought himself to be.

The actual works were somewhat disappointing, especially for those who had hoped to see evidence of a revolutionary new movement in painting or the representation of sensational occult themes. The two hundred paintings on view were by sixty-nine artists of widely differing tendencies. Subject matter had been of more importance to Péladan, when making his final selection, than painterly technique, and the general level of execution was not outstanding. Péladan was a great admirer of the painters favoured by the Symbolists but three of the most important, Puvis de Chavannes, Gustave Moreau and Burne-Jones, all refused to participate. Even so, some highly individual works came to the notice of the Paris public for the first time. Emile Bernard, who had been working with Gauguin, exhibited; the sculptor Bourdelle sent in drawings on religious themes, and Eugène Grasset, who was to play an important part in the movement that raised poster design to a fine art in the Nineties, also took part in the first Salon. The type of spiritual, mystical art preached by Péladan was particularly evident in the paintings of Charles Filiger who had been exhibiting with the Independent group and had worked with Gauguin in Brittany, and in those of Charles Osbert for whom painting was a kind of religious ritual, a way of evoking the mysteries of the spirit and the harmonies of nature, and who expressed his ideas in delicately coloured paintings of saints and visions.

The Rosy Cross Salon also gave some extremely interesting and unusual foreign painters a chance to make themselves known in Paris. The Belgian Jean Delville was a disciple of Gustave Moreau and showed the same gift for composing fantastic, surreal images with jewel-like detail. He became an ardent follower of Péladan in Brussels where he broke away from the young and lively *avant-garde* group in painting who called themselves the "Twenty" and even began his own Salon of "idealistic" art in 1894. Two other artists from the Low Countries were to become linked with the *Art Nouveau* movement which developed in western Europe in the last five years of the century. The first, the Dutch painter Jan Toorop, composed strange, symbolical paintings, with weirdly elongated, sinuous figures which seemed to writhe like snakes, in works with such titles as *The Sphynx, Faith*

Giving Way, and *The Three Brides*, the last being one of the sensations of the Rose Cross Salon. The Belgian Fernand Khnopff also showed a predilection for mysterious, allusive subjects and elongated figures with slender, "spiritual" females reclining or standing languorously like lilies or entwining exotic plants, and was especially admired for his "idealism" by Péladan. The third, also a Belgian, Carlos Schwabe, not only sent in his paintings but designed the poster for the first Salon, expressing its lofty conception of art with the allegorical picture of a naked lady sinking into the mire of the everyday world while two slender females ascend a flower-strewn staircase towards the light. He also was to exert his influence in poster design and impressed Alphonse Mucha whose theatrical posters were to become some of the most famous examples of the "new art" in France. Another foreign painter whose linear style lent itself so well to poster design and book illustration was the Swiss Félix Vallotton who not only was a well-known member of the Nabis but specialised in the revival of the woodcut.

The 1892 Salon was followed by five others. They varied in quality and in their success but they became an established feature of the Paris art calendar and aroused the interest of a growing number of dealers. Péladan quarrelled with his wealthy friend Antoine de la Rochefoucauld but managed to hold his second Salon in part of the official Salon building in the Champ de Mars Palace. In 1894 and 1895, two more Salons of Rosicrucian art were held in a small gallery in the Rue de la Paix. The fifth was a comparative failure and was held while Péladan was away on honeymoon in Venice but the sixth and last in 1897 was a triumph. The most fashionable art gallery in Paris, the Galerie Georges Petit, agreed to display over two hundred works and attracted a great crowd of journalists and some 15,000 spectators. The great discovery of the exhibition was the young painter and disciple of Gustave Moreau, Georges Rouault.

In the meantime, Péladan had given up his crusade for spiritual art in Paris. Instead he went to the Middle East and only returned at the end of the century to continue his career as a writer although he gave several more performances of his plays, mostly in the South of France. Apart from financial troubles, one reason he may have left Paris was because he had become a figure of fun to many critics. His strange airs, his extraordinary costumes and poses made him a butt for the humour of the critics like Mirbeau who saw him and his artists as so many effete poseurs, just as the English aesthetes of the 1880's had been caricatured as languid fops holding lilies by *Punch* and by Gilbert and Sullivan.

The art dealer Ambroise Vollard described in his *Souvenirs* how he had once paid a visit to Péladan in his home, finding him dressed in a "red sort of dressing gown with disciples, all very young and equally dressed" in a room turned into a kind of shrine with candles burning in front of a painting of a black lily with a woman's head emerging out of it and one disciple busily tearing pictures of subjects forbidden to the Rosicrucian painters out of art magazines. Such an impression was typical. The painters whom Péladan had assembled together could be taken seriously, but he himself remained an eccentric or a charlatan to many of his contemporaries. But one achievement of his could not be denied: he had helped to make the Paris art world more cosmopolitan and he had given added encouragement to the new painters to move even further away from the almost photographic imitation of reality which remained the paramount preoccupation of the academic artists.

Péladan had been involved to some extent in occult circles. Symbolism and the "idealist" tendency in art coincided in France with a tremendous upsurge in the popularity of magic and the supernatural. The renewed interest in the occult was by no means confined to a few eccentrics and scholars and it was inevitable that artists and poets who had turned from naturalism to the world of dreams and the mysteries of the spirit should include magic in their sphere of interests. A wider public which avidly read accounts of new scientic marvels was also becoming fascinated again by supernatural subjects.

In the second half of the 19th century in France there was a boom in the publishing of books on magic, beginning with the monumental studies of occult lore and tradition by Eliphas Levi whose real name was Alphonse Louis Constant. More than any other writer of the time, it was Levi who made occultism fashionable again with his famous *History of Magic* and the *Dogma and Ritual of High Magic* which he published in the 1860's after leaving the Church in which he had taken deacon's orders. His two successful books were followed by many others, some of which were serious attempts to analyse supernatural phenomena in the light of contemporary scientific discoveries, while others simply vulgarised Levi's writings and exploited public gullibility. By the late 1880's, several Paris publishing firms were specialising in books upon such subjects as the Kabbala, alchemy, clairvoyance and sorcery. The popularity of such subjects was also linked with the growth in the practice of spiritualism which had become extremely popular in England and the United States at that time, with the activities of the Theosophical Society which had been founded in 1875, and, in Paris, Doctor Charcot's famous experiments in hypnosis at the Salpêtrière Hospital.

Many Church authorities and scholars were worried by this vogue of the supernatural at a time when anti-clericalism was widespread in France. To some observers it seemed that it was a sign of an epidemic of anti-rationalism, to others it was a symptom of the growing irreligiosity of the age. To the politically minded, it could also be considered part of a general reaction against bourgeois values, materialism and the coming machine age and therefore part of a wider trend embracing anarchism, anti-semitism, artistic idealism and Symbolism, and utopianism. With the rise of the Symbolist movement as a reaction against emphasis on everyday reality and, particularly, its more sordid aspects in literature, strange and exotic subjects became very fashionable among many writers, poets, and painters. Des Esseintes, the hero of *À Rebours*, had popularised the notion of the aesthete who seeks new sensations, turns his back on the ordinary world to plunge into new realms of sensory experience, and surround himself with exotic, artificial, bizarre objects and works of art. Partly because of *À Rebours* and partly because of the Symbolists' passion for the exotic, magic and the occult appealed to many young men of artistic inclinations, who sought to attain their own, refined brand of individualism. Magic and sorcery were the most exotic subjects of all. The great imaginative artists of the age whom Huysmans had done much to publicise in his sensational book—Gustave Moreau, Odilon Redon and Félicien Rops—specialised in supernatural and visionary subjects, and the great novelists who so influenced the Symbolists, Barbey d'Aurevilly and Villiers de L'Isle Adam among others, dwelt on "decadent" themes that included sexual perversion, sadism and the Devil. For the general public, the many popular books being published on the scientific marvels of the age made the occult seem more credible, with their revelations about animal magnetism, electricity, hypnosis and spiritualism.

One consequence of this craze for the occult was that Paris acquired a sinister reputation as a centre for black magic in the Nineties. Foreign visitors such as the poet Yeats were impressed by the way so many young men of letters were talking of magic. But after a while, something even more lurid was being mentioned in connection with Paris, and that was Satanism. In 1891, another book by Huysmans, *Là-Bas*, suggested the existence of widespread satanical cults in France with its sensational description of a black mass being celebrated in Paris and such statements as "many people, not in the least crazy, whom you meet in the street and who are similar to everybody else, are linking themselves or attempting to link themselves with the spirits of darkness in order to do evil". Even though the book was a novel, its extraordinary descriptions and the fame of its author convinced many people that it was based on true events. From the time of its publication until the end of the 1890's, the Paris press regularly published stories of sorcery, black masses and mysterious cults in the city, and in 1899 even the conservative *Le Matin* appeared with a story by one of its leading journalists, describing how he had been taken blindfolded to a house in Paris where he witnessed a Satanic ritual followed by an orgy.

A few literary personalities were certainly engaged in occult practices. One of the best known was Stanislas de Guaita, the poet who had turned to magic after reading Eliphas Levi's books, and founded the Kabbalistic Order of the Rose Cross with Péladan. After breaking with Péladan, Guaita and a circle of intimate friends retired from the public eye to study the secrets of alchemy, the prolongation of life, the conjuring of spirits and other occult sciences. Strange séances were held in his Paris flat; his friends spoke of a familiar spirit which he kept in his cupboard (although this was certainly a hoax); and Guaita eventually undermined his health and probably his reason with his prolonged nightly vigils as he surrounded himself with old spell books, magic manuscripts and occult apparatus. His friends included the anarchist poet Tailhade, Paul Adam and another young poet, Dubus. Both Guaita and Dubus took drugs; Dubus became subject to hallucinations and died half-mad in a Paris urinal after injecting himself with an overdose of morphine; Guaita practised astral projection of the body, believed himself haunted by *larvae* (imperfect apparitions of souls), experimented with chemicals and kept himself awake for night after night with morphine and hashish. He too became half-crazed and even when he left Paris for his country home, he was said by his old friend Maurice Barrès to have fired revolver shots at supposed apparitions. He died at the age of thirty-six after having written three volumes of a monumental study, *Essay on the accursed sciences*.

In 1893, a famous quarrel between Huysmans, another writer on the occult, Jules Bois, and Guaita and his group, drew public attention to a kind of "gang warfare" being waged in French occultist circles. While preparing *Là-Bas*, Huysmans, who seems to have been very credulous as far as the occult was concerned, had been gathering information from various occultist and spiritualist circles in Paris and the provinces and in particular from a defrocked priest, the Abbé Boullan, living in Lyons.

Huysmans had corresponded at length with Boullan and asked him to help him provide proof of Satan worship in France. Boullan was a shady character who had trained as a priest and doctor in theology. He had been condemned for fraud after a case involving a girl supposed to have visions and the gift of prophecy, and who had won a local reputation for being able to perform exorcisms and miraculous cures. At Lyons he had met another strange character, a local prophet and mystic called Vintras who had founded a sect and a Temple, and he had succeeded him after the latter's death in 1875. Huysmans went to Lyons to visit Boullan who claimed he was fighting back against maleficent spells being cast upon him by his enemies in Paris:

Stanislas de Guaita, Péladan and an associate occultist, Oswald Wirth. Boullan explained to Huysmans that the Paris occultists were jealous of his power and wanted to wrest it from him. By means of their spells, he would suddenly be struck physical blows and receive shocks from what he called "occult fluids" but he managed to fend off some of these attacks and, through his own magic, return them against the sender.

Huysmans was deeply impressed by what Boullan told him and shortly afterwards experienced similar attacks himself. He said to his friends that he had been struck on several occasions and that he would even have died without Boullan's help. After the publication of *Là-Bas*, he was convinced that Guaita and Péladan were trying to attack him. For his protection, he had been given some "miraculous hosts" by Boullan who told him that they had appeared with blood upon them upon the altar in Vintras's temple, and he would brandish them at his invisible enemies although even then he would receive "fluidic blows" on his head and face when going to bed. Sometimes, sudden shocks like those of static electricity would prevent him from sleeping and, once, while he was at home after having obeyed an urgent message from Boullan not to go to the Ministry of the Interior where he worked, a heavy mirror which hung behind his chair in the office suddenly fell on his desk for no apparent reason. Then, on the eve of a projected visit to Paris where he had been invited to give a series of lectures on the Kabbala, Boullan mysteriously died after a collapse, in January 1893.

The affair now came out in public. Huysmans was convinced that Boullan had been murdered by Guaita and his fellow Rosicrucians and he was supported in his belief by Jules Bois. In a sensational article in the daily newspaper *Gil Blas* (issue of January 9, 1893), Bois repeated the charges against Guaita and added: "I have been assured that M. the Marquis de Guaita lives alone and wildly; that he handles poisons with great skill and with the most marvellous assurance; that he volatilises them and sends them through space; that he even has . . . a familiar spirit in his home which he shuts in a closet and which makes its visible appearance on his orders."

The following day, an interview with Huysmans was published

in the *Figaro*. Huysmans agreed with Bois's accusations and stated
that there was no doubt that both Péladan and Guaita had been
practising black magic. The next day, Bois returned to the attack
in *Gil Blas* and said that Huysmans had been hit by the magic
"fluids". Guaita denied the accusations in the *Figaro*. Then, in
Gil Blas, Bois claimed that Guaita and his colleagues had already
condemned Boullan to death some years previously. The press
battle in *Gil Blas* went on with a long denial of the charges and
the assertion that Boullan was a fraud who had been suffering
from heart and liver trouble. Bois counter-attacked again and the
dispute reached a climax with Guaita challenging both Huysmans and Bois to duels. Huysmans declined and made a statement saying that he had never intended to disparage Guaita's
character but Bois agreed to fight, first with Guaita and then
with another writer on the occult who called himself Papus.
Both duels took place in a strange atmosphere of sorcery. One
of the horses drawing Bois's carriage to the site near Paris stopped
suddenly and trembled with fright for twenty minutes before
proceeding. The duel was to be fought with pistols, with Laurent
Tailhade seconding Guaita. No one was hurt but it was later
stated that Guaita's bullet had never left his pistol—perhaps
through magical intercession by Bois's supporters. Three days
later, on his way to fight a sword duel with Papus in the Bois de
Boulogne, Bois's carriage overturned. He took another carriage
and that too fell over. Happily neither side inflicted more than a
scratch and occult honour was safe all round.

These extraordinary duels and the newspaper accounts of
long-distance battles fought between magicians did much to
increase public belief in black magical practices in France. In
1895, Jules Bois's own book *Satanism and Magic* appeared and sold
in large numbers. It contained a preface by Huysmans who stated
that there was an epidemic of stealing consecrated Hosts from
churches for the purpose of black mass rituals. Accounts appeared
abroad of devilish rituals being conducted in Paris. It seemed
that there were two main sects: one was called the Palladists, said
to worship Lucifer, the fallen angel, as the one true God; the
other was that of the Satanists who believed in the Christian
divinity but turned the church ritual upside down by trans-

ferring their allegiance to God's evil opposite, Satan. Stories of blasphemous rituals found a public eager to accept them and reinforced the "decadent" and "perverse" reputations of some of the leading *avant-garde* poets and writers in Paris.

An even greater sensation was the hoax perpetrated from Paris by a resourceful and unscrupulous journalist-publisher, Gabriel-Antoine Jogand-Pagès, who became one of the best-known "exposers" of occultism in France, and who wrote under the name of Léo Taxil. The enormous popularity of his scurrilous publications throws interesting light on the social psychology of the late 19th century in France with its craze for the strange and supernatural and is a part of the religious and political history of the period.

Léo Taxil's great achievement was to convince a large part of the public and many church officials, both in France and abroad, that black magic and freemasonry were inseparable. He did this at a time when many Frenchmen were deeply disturbed by the growth of free-thinking, militant socialism and by the long, bitter quarrel in progress between the French church and the Republican government. The feverish political atmosphere in which the left-wing radicals and the conservative Catholics were conducting their disputes and violent Catholic prejudices against freemasonry in France were favourable to his disreputable enterprise. The fact that so many people believed that the age was corrupt, that morals were in decline, that literature was being invaded by pornography and the arts falling into chaos, that science was trying to destroy religion, and that bomb-throwing terrorists and scheming Jews were plotting against France's social order made them ready to believe almost any sensational "revelation" if it were well enough presented. Taxil had a genius for spreading the most preposterous scares, as he worked on the principle that the bigger the lie the more readily will people swallow it.

He was born in Marseilles in 1854 and became a free-thinker and socialist radical when he was a young man. He worked as a reporter, mostly for some of the many anti-clerical papers then circulating. After various scandals and trouble with the law, he fled to Geneva and then returned to France after an amnesty was proclaimed in 1878. He became a freemason, stood unsuccessfully as an anti-clerical candidate for parliament, and began to publish a series of violently scurrilous anti-Catholic books under the imprint of his own "anti-clerical" library. Thanks to a distribution arrangement with a large-circulation Paris newspaper, he was soon able to flood France with a succession of books and pamphlets with such lurid titles as *The Pope's Mistresses*, *The Crimes of the Clergy*, *Leo XII the Poisoner* and *The Jesuit's Son*. At the same time, as he confessed later, he had begun to indulge his lifelong passion for practical jokes and hoaxes. Once, he sent a radical socialist Paris newspaper a series of "revelations" by a "private secretary of the Cardinal-Archbishop of Paris", including an account of how the canons of Notre Dame were constructing torture chambers in the cellars underneath the cathedral in preparation for an imminent restoration of the monarchy and the arrest of republican leaders. Such wild stories were eagerly accepted for as Taxil later said "the slightest lie, sparked off in a corner of the most obscure paper, immediately blazes into flame throughout France like a powder train catching fire".

Taxil was soon involved in a series of lawsuits. The more serious anti-clericals suspected him to be little better than a venal, pornographic charlatan. He was expelled from his masonic association and went bankrupt. In 1885, he suddenly announced his repentance, abjured his past errors and was received back into the Catholic fold. The return to the Church of France's leading anti-Catholic writer caused a sensation. Many Catholics remained sceptical about Taxil's sincerity but others saw his conversion as a sign of divine grace, or, at least, as a much needed victory for the embattled French church. He continued his career as a publisher and writer—this time on the Catholic side—and suddenly discovered a wonderful way to profit from the Church's obsession with freemasonry and the public's fascination with occultism.

For several years, Catholic hostility to freemasonry had been reaching an unprecedented pitch, ever since an encyclical by Pope Pius IX in 1873 had stated that freemasons throughout the world were working on Satan's behalf. In 1884, another encyclical by Leo XIII said that freemasons were Satanists aiming to overthrow the Church and to restore paganism. The encyclical made a great impression among believers and did much to encourage a belief that freemasonry and devil-worship were inextricably linked, and connected with anarchist subversion in Europe. Many books were published to tell "the truth" about free-masonry. There were stories of secret orgies in masonic lodges, child-sacrifices, black masses and sinister plots. The Pope issued two more terrifying encyclicals and in 1888 the writer Paul Rosen published *Satan and Company*, a book which claimed to prove that freemasonry was a gigantic plot on behalf of the Devil, and aimed at social chaos.

After writing a study of contemporary prostitution and another called *La Corruption fin de siècle* on the widely popular theme of the decline of morality as the century drew to its end, Taxil started to publish a highly successful series of pseudo-revelations on freemasonry. In 1891, he published *Are there Women in Freemasonry?* in which he mentioned the existence of a mysterious order of masonic "Palladists" who worshipped Lucifer, and boasted that he had received the congratulations of seventeen cardinals, archbishops and bishops. A number of similar publications, some by Taxil and his collaborators under various pseudonyms, followed, but the most sensational and successful of all was a periodical publication written by Taxil and a colleague named as Doctor Bataille, called *The Devil in the 19th century*. It appeared monthly for more than two years and was sold all over France. It was written in a simple and vivid style, and included fanciful illustrations of black masses, conjurations of devils and blasph-emous masonic rites. The writer was said to be a doctor from the merchant navy who had decided to tell the world of the machinations and Satanic rites of freemasonry which he had himself seen in the guise of a freemason in his travels around the world, and who had to adopt a pseudonym for reasons of safety.

One of the chief villains in the book was said to be a real mason, Albert Pike, who had been the Grand Master of the Scottish Rite in South Carolina. According to Bataille, Pike was the supreme head of freemasonry throughout the world and had created a Lucifer-worshipping "Palladic" movement in 1870, in order to prepare the world for the reign of Anti-Christ. Devilish rites were held in the Temple and he even had Lucifer in person appear regularly every Friday afternoon for a private chat. There were descriptions of a secret laboratory near Naples where deadly poisons were prepared for use by freemasons against their enemies, and of vast workshops under the Rock of Gibraltar where the sons of "Perfidious Albion" (freemasons and heretics to a man!) were preparing deadly microbes and fiendish idols and instruments for use in their unholy rituals. A female arch-fiend, Sophie Walder, was introduced and also a girl called Diana Vaughan. She was said to be the half-American, half-French descendant of a celebrated English mystic of the 17th century, Thomas Vaughan, and to have been initiated into Pike's order by her father, who was also a member. By 1889, she had made such progress that she had become a leading mason, learned how to conjure up Lucifer, and divided her time between America and Paris where she organised masonic, devil-worshipping sessions. Later, after Pike had died, readers were told that she had rebelled against an Italian mason and "Palladist", Adriano Lemmi, who had unlawfully taken Pike's place. She later began to have doubts and to break away from her Satanic colleagues.

At this point, many Catholic reviews which had been following the story with great interest began to urge their readers to pray for Diana Vaughan's repentance and conversion. Letters from her and even an interview with her were published. In 1895, Taxil suddenly informed the press that Miss Vaughan had been con-verted. The news was welcomed joyfully by the French Catholic press and also in Rome. Letters were sent from Miss Vaughan to high-ranking Papal dignitaries and the Pope himself was said to be overjoyed by the news. A month after the conversion was announced, Taxil started to publish Diana Vaughan's memoirs under the title of *Memoirs of an ex-Palladist*. They told how she had been beset by doubts and remorse and had been converted by a statuette of Joan of Arc to whom she had been praying when she was suddenly attacked by demons, and of the fearful things she had seen in the American masonic headquarters. Another book under her name telling of masonic conspiracies in Italy appeared in 1896. The Pope's Vicar and even his private secretary wrote to her to express Papal thanks for her revelations. But one thing was missing and that was her physical appearance before the Church and the public.

A controversy over her supposed existence broke out in the French press and in religious periodicals. Some Catholic personalities claimed that they had met her, others said that she was a mythical figure. Diana Vaughan continued to deny all the rumours concerning her in her memoirs and finally, in April 1897, the leading French Catholic newspaper *L'Univers*, announced that she would appear with Léo Taxil who would deliver a lecture on the theme of "twelve years under the Church's banner" and that she would speak on the overthrow of Palladism to the accompaniment of magic-lantern projections. The occasion was announced for April 19, and was to be held in the lecture theatre of the Paris Geographical Society. It was well attended by churchmen and journalists who, on entering the premises, were politely asked to leave their canes and umbrellas in the foyer. To the audience's disappointment only Léo Taxil appeared before them. Of Miss Vaughan there was no sign. But it was still a memorable event.

After thanking the Catholic press, Taxil said that from his early youth he had been a hoaxer. But to prepare "the most grandiose hoax of my existence" he had first undergone a false conversion to the Catholic faith. He decided to create and spread the myth of devil-worshipping to exploit the credulity of both Church and public. With the help of a colleague, an old friend who had been a sea doctor, he had launched the *Devil in the 19th century*, to prepare the public for the appearance, conversion and confession of Diana Vaughan. To condition his readers into accepting the idea of female masons, he had also created the character of the irredeemably evil Sophie Walder. For Diana, he needed an accomplice who could correspond with important Church dignitaries and religious magazines and arrange for letters to be sent from various addresses in order to lend conviction to the story. This colleague he found in the shape of an obliging young American lady who was a skilled typist and the representative of an American typewriter company. Her real name in fact was Diana Vaughan.

Taxil proudly declared that the story of Miss Vaughan's conversion had created a magnificent sensation. The Papal delegate to the central committee of one of the many anti-masonic leagues which had been formed, partly by Taxil's own efforts, had celebrated a service of thanksgiving in a Rome church, and a"hymn to Joan of Arc", supposedly composed by Diana Vaughan herself and "lifted" by Taxil from a popular tune, had also been played in the city. Even the official Jesuit organ in Rome, *Civilità Cattolica*, had praised her as a valorous champion of the Church in the battle against its enemies. But as the controversy grew over her existence, Taxil had felt obliged to organise the meeting. He ended by saying, "Palladism is now dead, well and truly dead. Its father has just murdered it." As the press reported, "an indescribable tumult" broke out in the hall. Taxil prudently slipped away to the accompaniment of jeers, laughter and abuse. The incident both crowned and ended his career as a hoaxer.

It might have been expected that ridicule would kill the vogue that occultism had been enjoying in France. But even after Taxil's confession that there had been no satanic conspiracy by freemasons, rumours of devil worship, black masses and plots continued to circulate in Paris and the provinces and to appear in newspapers. When the Dreyfus controversy exploded in 1898, there were widespread fears in France that sinister attempts were being made in secret to destroy the nation's social order and even its civilisation. For some years, a number of writers had expressed fears that France was fast declining as a great power. An atmosphere of political turbulence and uncertainty, envenomed by outbreaks of hysterical anti-semitism and anti-clericalism, did much to encourage pessimism. While many writers, artists and intellectuals sympathised with anarchism, the alleged corruption of French society became a favourite theme for some novelists. As early as the first half of the 1880's, the fashionable Parisian society novelist Paul Bourget had said that the growth of individualism was a forerunner to society's eventual disintegration, and was it not precisely this mania for individual self-expression that was leading to such dangerous dabblings in black magic and such strange new art forms?

The occult craze that Taxil had so brilliantly exploited in his country was seen by his more gloomy-minded contemporaries as yet another sign of national degeneration. Magic and spiritualism, the fight between freemasonry and the Church, the rebellious and anti-conformist attitudes assumed by members of Paris's *avant-garde* groups, the poses and exaggerations of some poets and dilettanti, accounts of drug addiction and alcoholism in Paris's Bohemia, the flight from reality towards the mystical and fantastic in certain schools of painting, and the popularity of anarchist ideas among intellectuals all combined in the eyes of hostile critics to produce an alarming picture of French decadence.

While the majority of the French people ignored the new tendencies and remained firmly confident in progress and their nation's future, pessimism was becoming an intellectual fashion, both in France and in northern Europe. There was much talk of the *fin de siècle* and of "decadence" as though the waning of the 19th century was bringing with it the end of a way of life which many had come to consider as civilisation at its highest. The 1890's might be a *belle époque* for some, but to the more pessimistic, they were a *fin de siècle* which also meant *fin de civilisation*.

V

FIN DE SIÈCLE

IN THE 1890's, the expression *fin de siècle* became widely popular in France and was frequently applied to a number of artistic and literary tendencies. Writers, critics and journalists used the words as an adjective for anything strange, exotic and artificial. Simultaneously, the term was often associated with the idea of "decadence". Uneasy or reactionary observers of French life and cultural activities linked the two notions together with a frequency which suggested that, to their minds, the outstanding characteristic of the last few years of the century was that of a widespread decay—even an illness— which afflicted the arts as much as national manners and morality.

Writers on both sides of the English Channel made the term even more fashionable and it was picked up by the public. *Fin de siècle* pessimism and "decadence" often became poses—especially among young men who wished to shock their elders and the middle classes—but to reactionaries and traditionalists it seemed clear that the first was thoroughly justified and the second everywhere apparent. Their gloomy outlook appeared even more justified and their prejudices were strengthened by the publication of a book which made a long, violent, detailed attack on all forms of modern culture to which the epithet *fin de siècle* seemed most appropriate. The author of this book was a German amateur sociologist called Max Nordau, who had lived in Paris throughout the 1880's. In 1893 he published the results of his studies under the title of *Degeneration*. The book was a sensational best-seller and convinced many readers that their civilisation had indeed become worn out and was fast sinking into a mire of corruption.

Degeneration was soon translated into French and provided fresh ammunition for all the enemies of "modernity". Nordau's opinions and judgements must have gladdened every reactionary critic for whom the officially approved art of the Salons was the last word in artistic creation and for whom free verse, Scandinavian and mystical drama, Zola's naturalistic novels and Wagner's music were so many affronts to glorious tradition. The methods Nordau employed as he dealt with his wide-ranging subject were modelled upon those of the Italian criminologist, Cesare Lombroso, who had stated that criminals belong to a special human type differing both anatomically and psychologically from the rest of the race. Nordau applied the same theories and diagnoses to the makers of contemporary culture which he saw as being in an alarming state of anarchy and decay—above all in Paris which he accused of being the centre from which the gangrene in civilisation was spreading.

Nordau's theories have long since been dismissed but it is still worth exhuming his book from the disrepute and oblivion into which it later fell because it tells us a great deal about how *avantgarde* movements appeared to many people at the time and how Paris seemed to have become the European capital of "decadence".

As Nordau stated at the beginning of his work, he intended to deal with all "these degenerates in literature, music and painting" who had "in recent years come into extraordinary prominence, and are revered by numerous admirers as creators of a new art and heralds of the coming century". From what he had himself seen, he continued, he could only conclude that what so many "progressive" critics, fashionable art lovers and snobbish intellectuals were praising as creative innovation were merely examples of "mental decay". His approach as he studied the allegedly sick body of contemporary culture would, he threatened, be that of a doctor:

"The physician, especially if he has devoted himself to the special study of nervous and physical diseases, recognises at a glance, in the *fin de siècle* disposition, in the tendencies of contemporary art and poetry, in the life and conduct of the men who write mystic, symbolic and 'decadent' works, and the attitude taken by their admirers in the tastes and aesthetic instincts of fashionable society, the confluence of two well-defined conditions of disease, with which he is quite familiar, viz. degeneration (degeneracy) and hysteria, of which the minor stages are designated as neurasthenia . . . ''

According to Nordau, this pathological *fin de siècle* state of mind could be seen everywhere, but of all places Paris was "the right place in which to observe its manifold expressions". His reason for selecting Paris as his special field for study was simple: France was in the worst state of all. It was the country with "the craziest fashions in art and literature . . . the country where hysteria and neurasthenia are much more frequent than elsewhere" and it was the "cradle" of the *fin de siècle* mentality. He noticed how popular the expression had become in recent years with journalists, the public and artists alike, and he proceeded to define it with a wealth of examples. To his mind, it implied: contempt for the traditional views of custom and morality and "a practical emancipation from traditional discipline . . . to the voluptuary this means unbridled lewdness, the unchaining of the beast in man . . . to the believer it means the repudiation of dogma, the negation of a super-sensuous world . . . to the sensitive nature yearning for aesthetic thrills, it means the vanishing of ideals in art, and no more power in its accepted forms to arouse emotion. And to all, it means the end of an established order, which for thousands of years has satisfied logic, fettered depravity, and in every art matured something of beauty".

Nordau repeated the accusation that this spreading degeneration was the work of a few who were trying (apparently with success) to impose their corrupt tastes on the mass of ordinary humanity. In words of which a Sarcey or a Chauchard might be proud, Nordau wrote that most men preferred the old forms of art and poetry, "Mascagni's *Cavalleria* to Wagner, farces and music-hall melodies to Ibsen, chromo prints of Munich beer houses to open-air painters". Such "healthy" tastes were being spurned by the new dictators of culture. The truth was that "it is only a very small minority who honestly find pleasure in the new tendencies . . . but this minority has the gift of covering the whole visible surface of society, as a little oil extends over a large area of the surface of the sea".

Nordau then went on to describe the symptoms of degeneration he had observed during his years in Paris. He had seen it in male and female eccentricities in fashion and in the taste for interior decoration and the collection of unusual and exotic objects. He had been to the art galleries only to emerge profoundly depressed by what he had seen there. Snobs and fashionable society seemed only to "worship Besnard's women in painting and Puvis de Chavannes, Carrière, Roll and Manet" while "only honest ordinary folk like seamstresses still linger over the story and subject of a painting". Obviously, aesthetic appreciation of painting in Paris had become a matter of social class to Nordau whose querulous remarks echoed the resentment of the dull but honest, hard-working middle-class family man at seeing the antics of the frivolous rich aristocracy: "steering in the wake of 'society' through a picture gallery, one will be unalterably convinced that they turn up their eyes and fold their hands before pictures at which the commoner sort burst out laughing ... they shrug their shoulders and hasten with scornful exchange of looks past such as the latter pause at in grateful enjoyment". Nordau moved on from painting to music but alas!—"at the opera and concert the rounded forms of ancient melody are coldly listened to ... Applause and wreaths are reserved for Wagner's *Tristan and Isolde* ... " In French literature, the situation was even worse. Admittedly, "the filth of Zola's art and his disciples in literary canal-dredging has been got over" but now there was worse. Literature had gone beyond the stage of what we would now call "permissive". As Nordau saw it "mere sensuality passes as commonplace, and only finds admission when disguised as something unnatural and degenerate. Books treating of the relations between the sexes, with no matter how little reserve, seem too dully moral. Elegant titillation only begins where normal sexual relations leave off. Priapus has become the symbol of virtue. Vice looks to Sodom and Lesbos ... "

Two of the chief characteristics of modern poetry and drama were obscurity and a self-indulgent striving after sensational novelty: "the book that would be fashionable must, above all, be obscure ... Readers intoxicate themselves in the hazy word sequences of symbolic poetry. Ibsen dethrones Goethe; Maeterlinck ranks with Shakespeare ... But art exhibitions, concerts, plays and books, however extraordinary, do not suffice for the aesthetic needs of elegant society. Novel sensations alone can justify it. It demands more intense stimulus and hopes for it in spectacles, where different arts strive in new combinations to affect all the senses at once. Poets and artists strain every nerve incessantly to satisfy this craving."

After having described the sickness, Nordau went on for hundreds of pages to analyse the writers, musicians and artists he held responsible for its cause and diffusion. Relentlessly and humourlessly, he studied the Symbolists, Mallarmé, the Pre-Raphaelites, Tolstoy, Wagner, mysticism, the Parnassian poets, the Decadents, Verlaine, Ibsen, Nietzsche, Zola and modern painters. They were all found to be sick and everything they produced, with a few exceptions, was the product of their disordered minds, their unhealthy and perverted instincts and their morbid complexes. In short, what Nordau was saying was very much the same as the Nazis said forty years later as they endeavoured to purify the Third Reich of "degenerate" art and literature. Every new cultural movement and innovation was anathema to Nordau. He was one of the greatest reactionaries and philistines ever to have put his ideas into print. Even Sarcey and the Salon juries appear progressive and enlightened in comparison. Certainly, they could be more tolerant on occasion.

We need only glance at the book to see how thoroughly Nordau had listed the artistic and literary tendencies and fashions of *fin de siècle* Paris. He must have cut a curious figure in the city as he ploddingly hunted down every new sign of the cultural degeneration he saw around him. Adolphe Retté, a poet and chronicler of the Symbolist school, wrote an amusing account of how the "degenerates" saw Nordau as he looked for material for his book among the cafés and cellars of the Latin Quarter. In order to observe the poets of the district, he would assiduously frequent one of their most popular meeting-places, the Café François Ier on the Boulevard Saint-Michel. It was there, wrote Retté, that "he would sit as close as possible to the table we were occupying (while talking of art and literature), and note down our remarks while ingurgitating much absinthe.

"We would end by taking notice of this hirsute listener who

would cast sly glances at us while pricking up his ears, when he was not muttering Teutonic oracles into his beard.

"One of us went to gather information and he learned that Monsieur Nordau was gathering material so that he might lump us together under the heading of 'Neuropathology' for one of the chapters of the book he was preparing.

"From that time onwards, we were careful to provide him with the most amazing details of our personalities. One of us credited himself with unnatural tastes and would celebrate the beauties of unisexual love. Another would pretend to be a votary of 'artificial paradises' and would ostentatiously swallow bread pellets which he pretended were pills of opium or hashish. All of us made the weirdest speeches on religion, sociology or morality.

"Nordau rejoiced. He noted down everything with the most delightful avidity. And this is how he composed that part of *Degeneration* which deals with the Symbolists."

In spite of his shrill and often hysterical tone, his absurd theories and methods, and his insistence that "decadence" was not the monopoly of any one coterie but the predominant characteristic of contemporary life and culture, Nordau did at least record the aspects of art, literature, music and drama which were becoming or had become fashionable with an influential number of Parisians and which were attracting a good deal of attention in the press. But he was quite indiscriminate in his attacks and he wildly lumped the most diverse tendencies, artists and writers together in the same categories, branding such disparate geniuses as Van Gogh, Ibsen, Tolstoy and Mallarmé as pathological degenerates. Yet, in its way, his long diatribe was a kind of involuntary, unconscious homage to the vivacity and richness of Paris's cultural life and its increasing cosmopolitanism.

Nordau's Paris was one far different from that so often evoked by sentimental memoir writers for whom the city seems mainly to have been characterised by Toulouse-Lautrec and Chéret posters, ladies bicycling in the Bois, café-concerts, and can-cans, glittering high life and a scattering of picturesque eccentrics and alcoholic geniuses moving against a background of popping

champagne corks and cabaret ditties. Paris life certainly did have
its glamorous aspect in the Nineties with its society beauties and
witty hostesses, its lavish fêtes and banquets, its elegant *salons*,
boulevards, night-life and wealth of opportunities for worldly
dissipation, but so did Vienna, London and other capitals. But
Paris was also becoming Europe's most cosmopolitan intellectual
centre and a cultural magnet.

The cultural consumption of prosperous middle-class Parisians may have been largely confined to amusing Montmartre
cabarets, farces and comedies by Feydeau and Courteline, dramas
by Sardou and Rostand, salon painting, and novels by Gyp, Paul
Bourget and Marcel Prévost, but there was steadily growing
another public, ready to welcome and debate the culture which
Nordau thought so pernicious. Its tastes and judgements were
becoming more influential and, as they did so, Nordau and the
many whose views he represented complained that public taste
was being dictated by a tight-knit group of snobs and poseurs.

This new, *fin de siècle* culture which so alarmed Nordau as he
studied it in Paris was often cosmopolitan and had political
undertones. It had been nourished since the 1880's by the philosophy of Schopenhauer and Nietzsche, the poetry and aesthetic
theories of Baudelaire, Gautier and Mallarmé, the novels of
Dostoievsky and Tolstoy, the music and ideas of Wagner, the
English arts and crafts movement, the paintings of the Pre-
Raphaelites and their followers, the revival of interest in mysticism and the occult, the art and decoration of the Orient and
Japan in particular, the revival of handicrafts and design, the
Scandinavian drama, socialism and anarchism. With it there came
a reaction against cultural complacency and insularity, materialism and vulgarity. It was animated by the desire to return to
the individual, the exceptional, the hand-made instead of the
machine-manufactured. It was idealistic and tinged with the
spirit of revolt.

The vehemence of Nordau's attacks and the popularity of his
book were signs of how prominent the new cultural manifestations had become. New theories, experiments and tendencies
were immediately publicised and diffused by the many artistic
and literary magazines that had been recently founded. Printing

was cheap and the press was flourishing as never before. Lugné-Poë's Théâtre de l'Oeuvre became a Paris landmark, attracted large audiences, drew important newspaper critics, caused noisy controversies and gained added publicity from its occasional brushes with the suspicious authorities. Péladan's Rose-Croix Salons were visited by huge crowds at first—and later his own eccentric behaviour was widely reported. Parisian journalists devoted much space in their chronicles to the activities of *avant-garde* groups while humorous and satiric periodicals made fun of them, thereby helping to bring the "aesthetes" and "decadents" to the notice of a large public. But what neither they nor Nordau understood was that even the more eccentric manifestations of the *fin de siècle avant-garde* were often inspired by a genuinely creative, forward-looking spirit which was anything but decadent.

Although Nordau went wildly astray in his survey, there were certain elements in late 19th-century art and taste in France which did present characteristics against which the charge of "decadence" could be made with some justification. Together, they form a curious chapter in the history of cultural fashions in Paris—a city which has long been extremely fashion-conscious in ideas as well as in art and dress. But the great difficulty in picking out and defining the decadence of the 1890's lies in the fact that what many people called decadent because it appeared perverse, precious, unnatural and over-elaborate could also have a serious purpose behind it. It could be a creative innovation and provide an impetus for greater artistic freedom.

The word "decadence" was often misinterpreted ever since it became fashionable. After being at first used as a term for a specific artistic or literary style or attitude, it was given moral connotations with the result that eventually not only the content but the style of a work of art could become considered from a moral point of view. The poet of the late Romantics, Théophile Gautier, who influenced the Symbolists, made resounding use of the word in his preface to an edition of Baudelaire's *Fleurs du Mal* in order to define and extol the beauties of a style peculiar to past, exotic civilisations in their decline. Subsequently, "decadent" came to be applied to any aesthetic taste for the artificial, the esoteric, the extraordinary and highly refined, in art as in

literature. A number of poets and writers in Paris in the 1880's
had called themselves Decadents and associated themselves in
the short-lived movement called *Décadentisme* or *Décadisme* with
Paul Verlaine as their chief sponsor. Verlaine, in his turn, had
helped to make the word "decadence" *à la mode* with his poetry
in which he declared

Je suis l'Empire à la fin de la Décadence

and with such statements as: "I like the word decadence, all
shimmering with purple and gold . . . It suggests the refined
thoughts of extreme civilisation, a high literary culture, a soul
capable of intense pleasures . . . It is composed of a blend of carnal
spirit and sad flesh and all the violent splendours of the late
Empire . . . "

The Decadents and the Symbolists who succeeded them and
shared many of their aspirations were self-declared revolutionaries in poetry and enemies of the modern world which they felt
was being shaped by the bourgeois spirit and soulless science.
They were ill at ease in a society which they were sure was moving
inexorably in the direction of greater materialism, vulgarity and
mass conformism to standards only acceptable to the herd
mentality. But they were not puritans: they demanded more of
life than it seemed to offer them in the modern age, they revolted
against the mediocre, and they sought more refined pleasures
such as those, they thought, which had been lost with the coming
of the industrial age of the common man who was being forced
into a mould of banal mediocrity. As they found little to satisfy
their aspirations and their aesthetic demands in the world around
them, they sought escape through art and the imagination.
In their revolt and their dissatisfaction, they looked towards
the unseen mysteries they sensed in the universe and to the past
and especially to certain historical periods when art and civilisation were at their most sumptuous and exotic.

The "empire" to which Verlaine referred was the late Roman
Empire of the East—Byzantium. Just as previous artistic and
literary movements had looked back to classical Greece and
Rome or the European Middle Ages for their inspiration, so did
the exponents of "decadent" taste find a major source of inspira-

tion in the hedonistic, elaborate, overladen, highly artificial "violent splendours" of the centuries-long Byzantine Empire in which originally Roman and Greek civilisation had been smothered and fossilised in the heavy, gorgeous raiment of the Orient. Admiration of this colourful past civilisation was expressed by many of Verlaine's admirers, but the writer who not only did the most to publicise such escapism and decadence in aesthetic tastes but who gave the public the impression that those holding them were tainted with moral degeneracy was Joris Karl Huysmans.

Huysmans' astonishing novel *À Rebours*, which the English poet and critic Arthur Symons called the "breviary of decadence", was first published in 1884, and created one of the greatest literary sensations in France for many years. With its peculiar hero, Des Esseintes, who has a mania for collecting strange objects and experiencing every kind of aesthetic sensation, it did much to foster the image of the ultra-refined, *fin de siècle*, ivory-tower dilettante divorced from ordinary society and who only lives to satisfy his cravings for the odd, the unnatural and the artificial, and to indulge every whim of his overheated imagination. Also, because of Des Esseintes' amorality and exploration of the stranger paths of eroticism, it encouraged many members of the public to think of the "modern" poet or artist as a social eccentric with deplorable morals.

Fantastic as it was, *À Rebours* was rooted in reality. It publicised certain aesthetic tendencies and tastes which existed in both France and England in the 1880's and which became widely publicised in the '90's. To the anti-"decadent" critics and a largely hostile public, the emphasis on the extraordinary and anti-natural shown by aesthetes and dilettanti under the influence of Baudelaire, Swinburne, Gautier and Verlaine was predominantly that of an affected, snobbish clique which tended towards aesthetic and moral depravity. Just as the bomb-throwing anarchist became one of the symbolic figures of the 1890's so did the figure of the decadent aesthete emerge before the public as another kind of anti-social, non-conforming individualist in revolt. Without the *fin de siècle* and the reaction against conventions in art, literature and decoration, there would have been no aesthete. He was not only an art patron who supported and encouraged new tendencies but an amateur who himself dabbled in artistic creation while inspiring and bringing together various branches of all the arts to create an overall "decadent" style amid which he and his like would live far removed from the vulgar everyday world and its people.

The direct, living model for Des Esseintes was an elegant young nobleman, Count Robert de Montesquiou-Fézensac. No one could have been better fitted to play the part of the semi-legendary *fin de siècle* aesthete in Paris.

Robert de Montesquiou belonged to one of France's oldest and most illustrious families. He had grown up in a rather dull and conventional country atmosphere before entering high society to which he belonged by right of birth and where he had the good fortune to have relatives and friends such as the beautiful Comtesse de Greffulhe who, unlike most of their peers in the stuffy Faubourg Saint-Germain, were highly cultured art-lovers.

As a youth, Robert had begun to discover the poetry of Baudelaire and Mallarmé, to write his own verses and educate himself in art. He soon became a dandy and a connoisseur and started to move in the freer, more cultivated society of the new rich, the *salons* and the eminent Parisian Jews who were among the city's most important art patrons. He succumbed to Symbolist poetry, Wagner's music and Japanese art like other imaginative young men of artistic tendencies of the time, and established himself as an aesthete with bold and unusual tastes by the way he furnished his apartment on the top floor of his father's mansion on the Quai d'Orsay. He was still a very young man, barely thirty, when he became famous in Paris society and art circles and Huysmans used him as his model for Des Esseintes. But he was very far from being an ivory-tower recluse dwelling in his own private and artificial universe.

Robert de Montesquiou kept his position as a leading figure in fashionable and cultured Paris until the First World War. He was famous for his dandyism, his light blue or almond green suits with white velvet waistcoats, his sophistication as a man-about-town, his wit and humour which could often be cruel, and his talents as a raconteur. He was one of those people who are seen "everywhere" and who know "everyone" and he was a centre of attention at tea parties and soirées where elegant *Parisiennes* would excitedly gather around him and beg his advice in matters of taste and decoration. He was to be seen at every Salon, major exhibition, concert and theatrical performance—especially of the *avant-garde*—and reigned as a prince of the society *salons*. He became a friend of the painter Gustave Moreau, whom he passionately admired, in the artist's last years, and with Edmond de Goncourt who shared so many of his aesthetic preferences; he introduced the young artist Helleu to Parisian society, thus launching him on his career as a fashionable portraitist of pretty women, was on close terms with the talented bourgeois painter Jacques-Emile Blanche and met Whistler frequently; he attended Mallarmé's Tuesday evening sessions in the Rue de Rome, was an ardent admirer of Japanese art, an early appreciator of Debussy and was an invaluable patron to the talented glass artist from Nancy, Gallé, whose vases became so famous in the French *art nouveau* period; he admired and helped Verlaine during the poet's last wretched years and in 1898 he met and befriended the young Marcel Proust and guided him in society, thus making a precious contribution to world literature and providing the model for Baron Charlus.

Like some other Parisian art-lovers, he was interested in English art and decorative movements which he helped to publicise in France. He admired the Pre-Raphaelites, William Morris and Celtic art which was then arousing great interest among decorative artists, explored London and met Oscar Wilde. Back in France, he gave lavish parties in Paris and Versailles, helped to organise exhibitions, wrote art criticism and promoted artists. He also wrote poetry very seriously, if without great talent, and would give his friends slim, beautifully bound and printed volumes with such "aesthetic" titles as *Les Hortensias Bleus, Les Chauves-Souris* and *Le Chef des Odeurs Suaves* and he knew almost every Symbolist poet, writer and dramatist in Paris.

Robert de Montesquiou is now mostly remembered as a dandy and society exquisite and as the author of a few preciously wrought and mannered poems which rarely appear in anthologies. More substantial figures with longer-lasting achievements have eclipsed him in the artistic and literary history of the period, reducing his image to that of one of the gaudier social butterflies who fluttered over the stage of Parisian society of the *belle époque*. He was certainly a snob, he was often preposterously affected and vain, the great number of portraits of himself that he commissioned suggest a high degree of narcissism and he posed as much for his own pleasure as for that of others. But in addition to having been a poseur and dilettante, he may now be seen as one of the most typically *fin de siècle* figures in Paris and as a conspicuous representative of the particular aspect of French cultural life of the '90's to which the term of decadence was often applied at the time.

Montesquiou's famous apartment which had inspired Huysmans after he had first heard about it from Mallarmé was a veritable museum of artistic and literary tastes which grew fashionable and notorious for more than a decade afterwards. In his father's house, Montesquiou had created a kind of fairy-tale, poet's palace and what an English visitor, Graham Robertson, called "a vague dream of Arabian nights translated into Japanese". He had used old tapestries with leaf patterns and green carpets to create the illusion of a garden in his hall; he covered the walls of his library with green and gold leather stamped with peacock feather patterns and kept the manuscripts of his poems in a green leather chest he had specially designed for him. Another room was decorated with gold spider's web patterns on a red background; three walls in his dining-room were in different shades of gold, the fourth being wine red and the ceiling the colour of amaranth. People talked of his extraordinary bedroom, his exotic bathroom, his elaborate lighting effects, his coloured windows and a room in which everything from the walls to the smallest object it contained was grey. The entire apartment was filled with an assortment of ecclesiastical furnishings and objects, Oriental knick-knacks and furniture, Japanese prints and fans, antique musical instruments, framed poems by Baudelaire, strange old prints and paintings, rare books and manuscripts, peacock feathers, mounted butterflies, delicately shaped vases and glassware, fancifully designed decorations and mirrors with variations on floral themes.

Among these many examples of Montesquiou's tastes which spread during the 1890's were some paintings and prints which were particularly important both because of their influence on other *fin de siècle* artists and because they showed some of the prime characteristics of the so-called "decadence". A type of painting which became very popular with the aesthetes and the Symbolists was one inspired by legends, exotic past civilisations and the supernatural. The Symbolists, as already mentioned, had admired Gaughin and were friendly with members of the Pont-Aven group and the Nabis, but they also favoured painters whose techniques were far less revolutionary but whose visions were more deliberately surreal. Such artists might even paint in a conventional academic style but if their subject-matter were fantastic enough and corresponded to the vogue for occultism and "out of this world" escapism, they were sure of a welcome from the Decadents. The art they sought was one which rejected all reality and everyday life in favour of dreams and carefully constructed fantasies which suggested the existence of an alternative world of the imagination.

A great master of this fanciful, obsessive style of painting was Gustave Moreau. Appreciation of his sumptuous, brilliantly coloured compositions with their teeming, hard, gem-like detail painted with the precision of a miniaturist became almost an obligation for any self-respecting aesthete or "decadent" of the '80's and '90's. Moreau stood completely apart from any of the established schools of painting. He was one of the most individual artists of the second half of the 19th century in France. Like the self-taught Douanier Rousseau, he painted a world of his own visions, nourished by oriental art, ancient architecture and mythology and, again like Rousseau, he came to win the admiration of a number of important writers and poets. He was a literary artist and with his strange, oriental palaces, his flying horses, weird monsters, sphynxes, chimerae and statuesque, heavily adorned princesses and god-like apparitions, he produced a pictorial equivalent to the poems of Baudelaire and Gautier and the rich descriptions of ancient Carthage in Flaubert's historical novel *Salammbô*.

In the course of his long career, which had begun in the 1860's,

Moreau had been frequently criticised and derided. He had never been a success in the Salons but he had come to have a great fascination for the Symbolists and he taught for some years at Paris's School of Fine Arts until his death in 1898. Fourteen years earlier, Huysmans had introduced him to the public.

As in academic painting, the subject was all-important in Moreau's paintings but there the comparison ends. He showed that there could be another kind of picture-illustration painting from that of sentimental domestic scenes, historical incidents and battles in his fairy-tale compositions which he produced so painstakingly and with an abundance of high coloured detail as though he were faithfully reproducing a vision in its entirety.

Another artist admired greatly by both Montesquiou and Huysmans was Odilon Redon. He, too, became a favourite with the Symbolists and their followers and, as already mentioned, was a friend of the Nabis. He was born in 1840 but it was only in the second half of the '90's that he began to paint on any scale after having devoted most of his career previously to drawings and lithographs. He was a poet in art and the circles in which he moved were far more literary than artistic. He was a friend of Mallarmé and many other poets and shared their enthusiasm for Wagner. When Dujardin published his *Revue Wagnérienne*, Redon contributed a magnificent series of lithographs inspired by *Parsifal* to the magazine. Like Moreau, he was neither a Salon artist nor a disciple of the Impressionists. He went his own way.

Redon's main interest lay in expressing ideas with pictorial shapes and in exploring his own inner world of visions and dreams. He laid great emphasis on the images and emotions which came to him from his subconscious and for this reason, among others, he had a strong appeal for the Symbolists in his own time and the Surrealists after it. Both in his graphic work and his paintings he created his own private world as Montesquiou had done with his apartment and Moreau with his harder, more precise fantasies. In the 1890's, Redon's colours would glow no less strongly than Moreau's but his forms were vaguer and, being less rigorously defined, hinted more strongly at the supernatural, the half-glimpsed "other world". His exquisite paintings and pastels of the late '90's were as mysterious and haunting as opium dreams and, again like Moreau's, contained enough monsters, strange figures and apparitions to satisfy any devotee of fantastic art. With Moreau, he became part of *fin de siècle* taste and it was no coincidence that both artists should have been two of the three French artists who Péladan admired above all others—the third being another great individual in late 19th-century French art, Puvis de Chavannes. After being a cult figure among a small circle of connoisseurs for years, Redon's art was finally brought before the Paris public in 1894 when the enterprising Durand-Ruel gallery held an exhibition of his works.

Both Moreau and Redon had their followers and their influence was felt abroad, where other artists contributed to the short-lived but intense flowering of fantastic art in Belgium and Holland, Scandinavia and the German-speaking countries in the 1890's. The same mysterious and imaginative qualities are to be found in the works of Toorop, Munch, Ensor, Delville, Lhévy-Dhurmer and Aman-Jean who also became fashionable in Paris. Their enigmatic female figures, their obsession with death and phantasms, their dream-like landscapes and scenes and their total withdrawal from reality laid them also open to charges that they were "decadent" and they make a strange contrast to the art of the post-Impressionists and the revolutionaries in pictorial technique. In their refinement, strangeness and exaggerations, their exaltation of the abnormal and visionary, they perfectly corresponded to the *fin de siècle* taste made notorious by Oscar Wilde in England and Montesquiou in France. If the Impressionists and their successors may be said to have painted with their eyes, the Academics with technique, Moreau, Redon and others who fitted into the "decadent" pattern of the 1890's may be said to have painted with their imaginations.

Montesquiou's passion for novelty and exotic colour also extended to the applied arts. His mania for the most exquisitely refined workmanship and virtuoso objects was another characteristic of the time. It could be taken (and it was) as a sign of an esoteric taste of an élite which could easily degenerate into mere snobbery and affectation. For the aesthete-snob, nothing could be too artificial; the ordinary and simple were despised while anything extravagant and bizarre was eagerly sought after. The long passages in Oscar Wilde's *Picture of Dorian Gray* in which he describes his hero's collecting obsessions were inspired by *À Rebours* and although some of the descriptions read almost like caricatures of *fin de siècle* fashions, the book still illustrated tastes in France for some years after its publication in 1890 and reinforced Anglo-Saxon suspicions of Gallic decadence. Montesquiou's extravagant preferences and aesthetic inclinations influenced many young would-be Dorian Grays in Paris who pretended to lead aesthetes' lives in accordance with a belief that true beauty had to be elaborate and reserved for an élite divorced from the common public.

But for all its exaggerations, this taste for a new type of beauty stimulated a revival of the applied and minor arts and handicrafts. It encouraged the making of high-quality small objects, higher standards of book-binding and printing, the design of ceramics and glassware which all culminated in the dazzling creations of the jeweller Lalique, Gallé's vases, the beautifully produced art reviews of the decade, new achievements in graphic art and, particularly, in poster design.

Another factor which brought *fin de siècle* taste and art into disrepute was the suspicion, loudly voiced by some critics and satirists, that it was all a sign of sexual effeteness and degeneracy. There were two kinds of eroticism typical of the *fin de siècle*. One was that represented by the can-can, the *cocottes*, and the good-humoured libertinism to be found in Feydeau's farces and the bawdier side of Paris's night life; the other was one associated with "decadence" and the perverted obsessions of its literary representatives. With their pale, muted colours, their fondness for mauves, pinks, anaemic shades of blue and red, and their unusal themes, the painters of "mystical" and idealistic painting fell under the suspicion of being sexually unhealthy. Critics stressed the languidness or lifelessness of female figures in *fin de siècle* painting —and what strange heroines they were who appealed to the painters of the Nineties whose works could be seen in Paris and provoked charges of decadence! Whether they were the misty, "spiritual" figures in meditative or trance-like attitudes of Charles Osbert, the idealised, angelic creations of Carlos Schwabe, Walter Crane's drooping ladies with their air of English genteelness, the weird and statuesque feminine enigmas that Khnopff depicted with obsessive repetitiveness, Toorop's elongated witches with flowing tresses or the soulful maidens of Lhévy-Dhurmer and Jean Delville, they all suggested bloodless eroticism, physical languour and an unhealthy spirituality. Like the heroines of Burne-Jones who could be seen as caricatures of Botticelli's women and who became so fashionable, they might hint at mysterious sensuality or an intense inner eroticism, but they were all too pallid, too drooping and withdrawn ever to translate their innermost urges and obsessions into physical activity. Mythical women and legendary figures of antiquity became favourites with painters and poets. There was a great fashion for Salomes, Ophelias, Sapphos and Sphynxes, often depicted in marble poses as though they were more than half way to death, and in some paintings the suggestion of necrophilia was strong.

The feminine type created by the English Pre-Raphaelite painters had led to a minor fashion for an archaic type of female beauty and dress in England where elegant young ladies would don medieval-style gowns and Liberty prints and would do their best to look "soulful" and resemble a Botticelli, a Rossetti or a Burne-Jones heroine. In Paris, women's fashions remained generally unaffected by the craze that had afflicted some of their English sisters, although, as mentioned, some journalists did remark on the "Botticelliesque" attire and hairdress of many young people who frequented the Théâtre de l'Oeuvre. Nonetheless, partly under English influences, partly under the influence of Byzantium and the Slav countries which so fascinated the decadent writers, painters and authors together established a *fin de siècle* style of female beauty that reappeared in countless paintings and novels. This mythical woman was a combination of a *femme fatale*, Oriental Princess and Madonna. She was incarnated by Sarah Bernhardt in such plays as *Fedora, Tosca, Theodora* and *Gismonda*, but Bernhardt had a more robust, direct appeal for the public than the de-sexed creations of a few bizarre artists.

The ideal woman of the *fin de siècle* artists was also closely linked with the lily—the symbol of purity and the soul—whose gracefully flowing lines echoed the willowy attitudes which were among the attributes most frequently given by the painters to their figures. There was a mania for lilies in poetry, art and decoration. Together with such other items as peacocks' feathers and precious stones, they were an essential part of the outward stage trappings of the Decadence. The poems of Samain, Verhaeren, Lorrain, Verlaine and Vielé Griffin were all liberally strewn with lilies. Ever since Swinburne had associated lilies with virginal purity in his line "the lilies and languors of virtue", artists and writers had used the flower as a symbol which made a perfect foil for images of decadence and perversion. Their ideal woman had the lines of the lily, she had its pallor and, to hostile critics, no more sex appeal than the flower. In France, as in England, the lily came to be the symbol of *fin de siècle* preciosity.

The lily-like ladies of the Pre-Raphaelites who had played their part in the evolution of fashions and taste in Paris appealed to decorative artists and writers as well as to painters. Although the first Pre-Raphaelite paintings had been seen in Paris at the 1855 Exposition Universelle, they had attracted little attention in France until the '80's when Rossetti's and Burne-Jones's reputations were steadily growing abroad and influencing a number of French writers and poets who had seen their work in England. In the early '80's, Georges Petit's fashionable gallery had exhibited works by Watts, Millais and Burne-Jones. The visitors had included Robert de Montesquiou and Huysmans and they both placed Burne-Jones in the artistic category most favoured by "decadent" taste. In 1887, the *Revue Indépendente* published an article on the English aesthetic movement and, by the 1890's, Burne-Jones had become one of the best-known English painters in Paris and was much publicised by Jean Lorrain in his newspaper column. At the same time, Botticelli, the great inspirer of the Pre-Raphaelites, was also growing fashionable in Parisian aesthetes' circles. At the 1889 Exposition, Burne-Jones's *King Cophetua and the Beggar Maid* aroused enormous interest in the pavilion of English art and it was not long before the artist became acclaimed in Paris as a kind of up-to-date Botticelli, one of his chief admirers being Péladan.

Burne-Jones exhibited in the Paris Salon almost every year

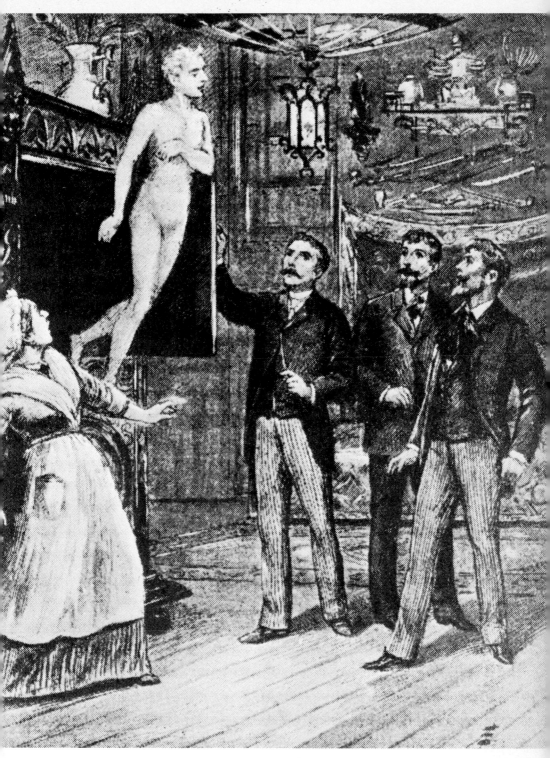

Stanilas de Guaita's Familiar Spirit

Robert de Montesquiou

Jean Lorrain

Le vin Mariani
Effroi de la Neurasthen
c, au poète rajeuni
Fournit la rime à l'inf

Jean Lorra

Homage to Cézanne by Maurice Denis

Sappho by Gustave Moreau

The Offering by Sérusier

Light by Redon

Winter by Puvis de Chavannes
Parc Montsouris by Henri Rousseau

Bonnard Poster
for *La Revue Blanche*

Place du Havre
by Camille Pissarro

La Comtesse de Greffulhe

Liane de Pougy

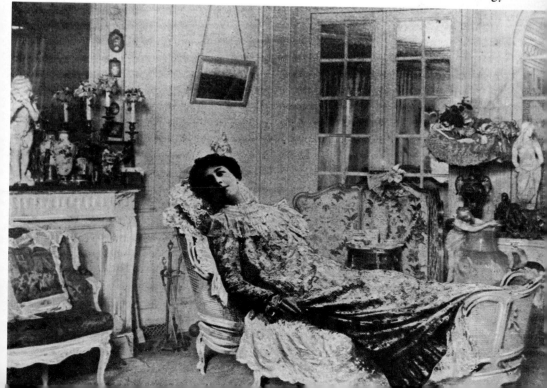

A Maquette for Rodin's *Balzac*

from 1890 to 1896. He became popular with the Symbolists and studies of his work were published in French magazines and art reviews. In the 1893 Salon, his *Perseus* was a sensation but it was not long before there was a reaction against his work and the "Botticelliesque" type of woman in general. After having at first admired him, Jean Lorrain began to attack him as did other critics and journalists who had become tired of lilies and wilting, desexed females in art. Snobs and poseurs were ridiculed for their unmanly tastes, their exaggerated enthusiasms for such effete representations of feminity, and the two painters, Burne-Jones and Botticelli, rapidly waned in popularity. The mode for their art was savagely and wittily attacked by Octave Mirbeau in a resounding newspaper article in *Le Journal* with the punning title of *Des lys! Des lys!* and again in another article entitled *Encore des lys!* in which, as so many others had done, he used the lily as the symbol for aesthetic affectation. In the same year, 1895, Lorrain wrote that after the "crash of Burne-Jones" there had come "the "crash of Botticelli" and when Burne-Jones exhibited his controversial portrait of the Parisian patroness of the aesthetic movement, the Baronne Deslandes, in 1896, attacks multiplied until ridicule finally killed the craze. Even Montesquiou tired of it, wittily remarking that Burne-Jones's ladies showed that "Botticelli's Primavera has ended by becoming a shopgirl in Liberty's."

The 1890's were not only a period of preciosity in art and literature, but also of sexual abnormality. Much of the *fin de siècle* art and poetry of these "mauve Nineties" as they were called held hints of sexual ambiguity if not of frank homosexuality. The disquieting sensuality that underlay certain pictures and poems expressed a vague, ambiguous, indecisive eroticism which also became a literary fashion among the "decadent" writers and which had been well expressed in a famous verse by Théophile Gautier years before:

> Est-ce un jeune homme? Est-ce une femme?
> Une déesse ou bien un dieu?
> L'amour ayant peur d'être infame
> Hésite et suspend son aveu.

(Is it a young man? Is it a woman?
A goddess or indeed, a god?
Love, fearing to be infamous
Hesitates and defers its confession.)

There were thinly veiled and even open statements of homosexual themes in the engravings and illustrations of Félicien Rops,
a graphic artist of overrated talent who enjoyed huge popularity
as a book illustrator in France for the last forty years of the century, and who specialised in titillating vulgarisations of erotic
themes; and Verlaine's poems were often homosexual. But Oscar
Wilde's condemnation in England, which virtually killed off the
aesthetic movement there, was also taken as a warning by many
people in Paris that "decadence" could go too far. The influence
of Baudelaire's poetry of eroticism and perversity upon the
Symbolists and their young disciples was well known and the
scandals of Verlaine's life were notorious. To suspicious observers, it seemed inevitable that the *fin de siècle* search after new
forms, sensations and experiences should lead to sexual devia-
tion. In addition, there was much in the poetry and novels of the
time that seemed to confirm that themes of sexual corruption
and unnatural practices had become high fashion, symbolising
the general decline of civilisation that Nordau and others had
lamented as the century drew to its end.

Sexual perversity was widely alleged to be one of the most
characteristic traits of those who had *fin de siècle* tastes. The proclamation or affectation of ambiguous sexual inclinations and a
keen interest in erotic aberrations were present among many
writers and aesthetes and did much to strengthen prejudices
against their artistic and literary movement. Surprisingly, Robert
de Montesquiou escaped allegations of sexual degeneracy. One
of the most typical representatives of this kind of sexual non-
conformism was Jean Lorrain, the critic and journalist who became Montesquiou's bitter enemy.

Lorrain was a curious figure, although one with undoubted
literary talent, and in spite of all his poses he was widely liked
and popular because of his brilliant reportages of Paris life and
because his robust Norman looks were in such comical contrast

to the monster of decadence that he would pretend to be. A French writer has called him a "poor man's Oscar Wilde" and the label suits him well. His real name was Paul Duval and he was the strapping son of a business man and insurance company owner in Normandy. Like so many other ambitious young men with literary aspirations and a budding talent, he determined to conquer Paris after first writing some poetry and he had eventually succeeded to a large extent, becoming a well-known figure in society and famous for his "Pall Mall" column in the *Echo de Paris*. Once established in Paris, he did his best to assume the more extravagant attitudes of the *fin de siècle* and to imitate Oscar Wilde's ambiguities and poses. But no matter what his sexual inclinations might have been, many people found it hard to take Lorrain too seriously as a sexual rebel. He had to work hard at his pose. He did everything to be as provocative as possible, dressing up in strange costumes, dying his hair red, wearing make-up, loading his fingers with rings and signing his articles with such absurdly feminine pseudonyms as "Mimosa", "Salterella" and "Sentillama", while trying at the same time to assume a ferocious and sinister aspect. When he was not play-acting in this way or working hard (he was a very conscientious journalist), he would haunt cheap dance-halls and night-clubs, cabarets, fairs, slaughter houses, boxing booths and all the Parisian world of Aristide Bruant's songs, making friends with jockeys, professional wrestlers and grooms.

Many stories were told of Lorrain which is probably exactly what he wanted. He fought duels as did most journalists of the time, he would stalk out of a fashionable bar, shouting to the head waiter: "Tell the page-boy I've had enough of him!" and even had the fanciful idea of becoming engaged to the famous *cocotte* Liane de Pougy, a piece of news soon picked up by the Paris press and which brought forth a witty, mordant piece by Laurent Tailhade. Lorrain also had a public quarrel with the lady journalist Séverine who replied to him in the press and made Paris laugh by beginning her letter "Ma bonne Lorrain". To Albert Keim, one of the many writers who knew him, Lorrain was one of the most disturbing personalities in Paris "with his obsessions and the vices which he displayed so cynically as though cynicism should be the supreme form of virtue", and to another, the lady novelist Rachilde, he was simply "a braggart of all the vices". His excessive homosexual affectations had been too much for Montesquiou who had declined Lorrain's offer to dedicate to him a collection of highly suggestive poems in 1882 and the antipathy between the two men, both so representative of the *fin de siècle* in many ways, became public knowledge in Paris.

In 1897, the then fashionable portraitist Boldini had painted a portrait of Montesquiou holding one of his favourite canes and it had been exhibited in the 1897 Salon. Lorrain wrote sneeringly of the portrait and with a minimum of subtlety had accused Montesquiou of effeminate habits. Shortly afterwards, there had occurred the terrible catastrophe of the fire at Paris's annual Charity Bazaar when many of high society's and the French nobility's leading ladies had perished in the flames. Lorrain again mentioned Montesquiou and his cane, linking him with a totally false rumour that he had been one of the cowards who had used their canes to beat a way to safety through the throng of women-folk inside the blazing bazaar hall, and reporting that morbid curiosity had brought Montesquiou to examine the charred bodies of the victims, using the same cane to lift aside the remnants of their clothing. The distasteful incident caused a stir in Paris society and led to a duel between Montesquiou and the poet Henri de Régnier, who had believed Lorrain's accusations.

Four years after such a vicious—and dangerous—attack on Montesquiou, Lorrain again showed his interest in the dilettante professor of Beauty by using him, as Huysmans did earlier, as the model for a character in a novel, the Duc de Fréneuse in *Monsieur de Phocas* which again took up the theme of the decadent aesthete. Lorrain's other novels, like his poems, are now forgotten and unread, but in their themes of sexual decadence and obsessions they represented that peculiar *fin de siècle* literary school whose manifestations and sadistic inspirations have been traced so thoroughly by Mario Praz in his famous study of literary decadence, *The Romantic Agony*.

The most famous feminine exponent of decadent eroticism in literature at the time was Rachilde. She not only became notorious for her "scandalous" fiction but was one of the most popular figures in Paris's literary and artistic world. She was also a warm-hearted, much adored hostess after she married the founder of the *Mercure de France* magazine which did so much for poetry in the '90's.

Rachilde's real name was Marguerite Eymery and she was born in 1860. She was the daughter of an authoritarian army officer and grew up deep in the countryside of France where she became an avid reader early in her youth and an amateur poet, besides the author of short stories, some of which she succeeded in having published by local newspapers. After escaping an arranged marriage and reaching her majority, she left home for Paris where she was lucky enough to have a cousin who directed a woman's magazine, *L'Ecole des Femmes*. Very few women worked in journalism at that time but her female cousin not only gave Rachilde a job but published one of her first novels in the magazine. Rachilde then became a latter-day George Sand, dressed as a man, cut her hair short, took her pseudonym and called herself on her visiting cards an *homme de lettres*. In 1884, a Belgian publisher brought out the novel which made her instantly famous. It was called *Monsieur Vénus* and may have been inspired by a passage in Huysman's *À Rebours*. It was a sensation, newspapers called it obscene, there was a prosecution in Brussels where a court sentenced Rachilde to a large fine and two years' imprisonment which she escaped by living in Paris.

The theme of *Monsieur Vénus* was one taken up with variations by other writers of the "decadent movement" and concerned the inversion of sexual roles. A young lady, Raoule de Vénérande, takes a fancy to a young workman and installs him in her luxurious and lengthily described apartment where she reverses the rôles of lover and mistress, keeping him as though he were the woman and enjoying the situation cerebrally rather than physically. The novel attracted great interest in Paris, it was admired by Verlaine, and the Paris police took such an interest in it that eventually Jean Moréas agreed to conceal copies in his own apartment after having also succumbed to Rachilde's charm and persuasiveness. She was thoroughly launched and famous, and became friends with almost every member of the Symbolist group and a patroness to young artists and writers, while continuing to write novels with such titles as *The Marquise de Sade*. She was a controversial figure for a while in staider literary circles and even the *salons* where, shortly before his death, another "scandalous" author, Barbey d'Aurévilly, had defended her against the charge of writing pornographic books by saying: "Pornographer—so be it then! But such a distinguished one!" But by the end of the century, it was plain that her charm and generous capacity for encouraging and helping talent would outlive her "decadent" period as a writer, even though she continued to produce novels for the next thirty years.

A similar fanciful *fin de siècle* eroticism could be found in the novels of her friends such as Catulle Mendès and Maurice Barrès whose works teemed with themes of death, sadism, exaggerated voluptuousness and *femmes fatales*. Barrès particularly showed his fondness for erotic themes including that of incest in such books as *Le Jardin de Bérénice* (1891), *Du Sang, De la Volupté, De la Mort*, all published in the 1890's and as crammed with exotic detail and sensations as the earlier novels of Péladan. Together with some other writers, they were responsible for a minor literary school in which they expressed the manias of the aesthetes and dilettanti, borrowed their exoticism from Moreau's paintings and Gautier's poetry, their sadism from Baudelaire and Barbey d'Aurévilly, and shocked people by seeming to suggest that sex could not be interesting unless it was as bizarre and unnatural as possible. The effect of such works, often imitative and derivative, was to strengthen the myth of the moral depravity of the aesthetes and Symbolists of the '90's.

The fashions of the *fin de siècle* did not survive the decade in which they reached their climax. Ridicule and reactions against influences from abroad helped to kill them. The public's image of the *avant-garde* crusader as an effete young man with a craze for lilies and mauve colours, who swooned before esoteric paintings, who was homosexual if not impotent, and who could appreciate nothing unless it was abnormal and *outré*, was hard to destroy and often seemed confirmed by reality. Cultural dandyism and snobbery was fiercely satirised in humorous magazines and in novels, as well as in jingoistic newspapers which urged their readers, in a time of acute nationalism, to sweep away such unhealthy, foreign-inspired pseudo-art and return to what was French and sane.

But the tendencies of the *fin de siècle* were not all affected and artificial. The individual was being encouraged to express himself freely in art and literature and to be ready to experiment. Even though many absurdities flourished for a while in the hothouse flower bed of Decadence and Symbolism, it was from that same soil that important innovations in art and design were to blossom. On one hand, *fin de siècle* tastes and creations provided ammunition for those who attacked all modern art and literature as something degenerate, thereby encouraging public hostility to modernism; on the other hand, they encouraged some artists to make the great break between the past and the new which became so evident in the early 20th century. Moreau and Redon, who despite themselves became associated with the idea of decadence, created a new kind of beauty and both, in their unassuming ways, were revolutionaries. It is worth remembering, in this respect, that two of Moreau's pupils in the Ecole des Beaux-Arts were Rouault and Matisse, and that Montesquiou was not only a snob-aesthete but a perceptive connoisseur and patron who had been one of the first to appreciate Debussy and Fauré, who had helped Proust and welcomed the Russian Ballet to Paris in the new century.

Decadence and preciosity are only two aspects of artistic tastes and tendencies in *fin de siècle* Paris. While a society figure like Montesquiou used his wealth and social position to patronise an art which, in many cases, was too *recherché* and sterile to survive for long, other well-known Parisian personalities were using their pens to champion more vital artistic movements which bore great fruit in the 20th century.

One of the most influential supporters of the pioneers of modern art in France was the journalist Félix Fénéon. He was undoubtedly one of the most intelligent, lucid and far-seeing art critics who has ever written. He ignored the stranger paths that were being taken by some of the artists who so fascinated Montesquiou and concentrated on what we may now see to have been the mainstream of artistic development at the close of the century.

He seemed to have an unerring instinct for picking out the artists who eventually became world famous and recognised as great innovators. Fénéon's role in Paris's cultural life was a long and important one and deserves greater recognition than it has often had. In his lifetime, he was an almost legendary figure. He was the friend of nearly every important painter, poet and writer of the 1890's and he was a brilliant publicist as well as a noted wit.

Félix Fénéon was born in 1861 and his father was an employee of the Bank of France. In 1881, Félix came to Paris and passed his examinations for the post of clerk in the War Ministry. He was an able civil servant who seemed destined for a long and secure career in the service of the nation but his real interests lay elsewhere, especially in poetry and painting. In 1884, he founded with a friend one of the many new literary magazines that were beginning to appear with such astonishing rapidity, the *Revue Indépendante*, which collected contributors from among the members of the declining Naturalist group and the rising Symbolists. Fénéon was therefore associated with the Symbolist movement from the very beginning and became one of its main propagandists, as well as a friend of Mallarmé, Verlaine, Moréas, de Régnier and other poets of the first rank. He published contributions by Mallarmé and Huysmans and tirelessly searched for new talent.

At the same time, Fénéon had become greatly interested in the new movements in painting. In the same year that saw the foundation of the *Revue Indépendante*, he discovered the painting of Seurat who was exhibiting his first works in the newly founded Salon des Indépendents. The press was fiercely hostile to the exhibition as was most of the public who saw it, but Fénéon was deeply impressed by Seurat's work and his technical experiments. In 1886, Fénéon met Seurat when the latter was exhibiting his painting *La Grande Jatte* at the controversial eighth (and last) exhibition of the Impressionists. A short time afterwards, Fénéon became a close friend of Seurat, Signac and the ageing Pissarro and did everything to make sure that they were known by his colleagues on the *Revue Indépendante*.

Seurat's *La Grande Jatte* is now recognised as one of the most important works in the history of modern painting and Fénéon has the distinction of being one of the first who realised that in some way it marked a turning-point in the road that painting had been taking for so long in Europe. *La Grande Jatte* was derided and misunderstood and this became a challenge to Fénéon who decided to champion Seurat and his theories by writing on his behalf. He was also a contributor to another recently founded little magazine, the *Vogue,* and in it he published a series of articles on current art exhibitions in which he persistently emphasised Seurat's importance and talent and gave forceful expression to his own views on contemporary art. He became a spokesman for the Neo-Impressionists, as he called them, and everything he wrote was based on the most thorough and detailed discussions with the artists involved. Fénéon then assembled his articles in a small book which he had published, and which was called *Les Impressionistes en 1886.* It was the first book in the history of art criticism to have acknowledged that the Impressionist movement was no longer the *avant-garde* but had been overtaken by new developments—and this at a time when only a tiny minority would even consider Impressionism as a serious form of art!

Fénéon continued to write articles and reviews for a number of magazines. Because of his intelligence and his friendships with the artists he supported in Paris, he knew what they were trying to do and was able to explain it in lucid terms free from any pedantry or pretentiousness. He was one of the first writers to make art criticism sensible and although his articles were often strongly polemical it was only because the new artist so badly needed allies against reaction and philistinism that aggression seemed often the only answer.

By the 1890's, Fénéon was one of Paris's most distinguished critics even though he was still only read by a small minority. He followed and supported Antoine's Théâtre Libre, he defended Wagner, Ibsen, Jarry and Dostoievsky and still managed to fulfil his duties at the War Ministry. With his piercing intelligence, his wit and understanding, his polished manners and elegant appearance, his long, grave face with its Mephistophelean pointed beard, his clear, sceptical eyes, his wide and somewhat sardonic mouth, the beautiful manner in which he expressed his ideas, underlining them with grave, solemn gestures, and his occasional air of refined eccentricity, he fascinated the many writers and artists who came into contact with him. At times they might be disconcerted and puzzled by his initial reserve and his irony but it was not long before his talented contemporaries discovered his enormous capacity for friendship and loyalty and realised that true creative genius could wish for no better champion.

After Seurat died in 1891, Fénéon did his utmost to make his paintings known to as many people as possible and to insist on the significance of his work. At the same time, Fénéon's warm heart led him towards support for the ideals of the anarchists. He knew that the really individual artist was in danger of being an outcast and a misfit in society and consequently he supported protests against a social order which seemed to crush creative self-expression. He wrote for some allegedly "subversive" magazines such as *L'En Dehors*, *La Cravache* and the *Revue Libertaire* which were frequently banned or raided by the police, and his contributions generally took the form of art reviews which he left unsigned to avoid compromising his position as a civil servant. In April 1894, when the government was taking harsh repressive measures and Paris was terrified of dynamiters, Fénéon became a suspect. His political sympathies were no secret. His home was searched and a suspicious-looking metal flask was found which might have been used in the preparation of a bomb and which seemed to provide evidence of a link with the bomb-thrower Emile Henry. Fénéon was arrested and confined in the Parisian prison of Mazas together with the artist Maximilien Luce, some other writers and an assortment of petty criminals. Although the newspapers *L'Echo de Paris* and *Le Journal* courageously protested at the government's action in imprisoning him, Fénéon was dismissed from the War Ministry even though no formal charges had yet been brought against him. His witty replies in court at the "Trial of the Thirty" made him famous and Mallarmé testified in his favour. After his triumphal acquittal, he went straight to his friend Thadée Natanson whose magazine *Le Revue Blanche* had been appearing in Paris since 1891, and joined the editorial staff. Natanson could have gained no more valuable collaborator and, for the rest of the decade, Fénéon did much to make it the most brilliant and influential of all the city's many artistic and literary reviews and also a meeting place for the *avant-garde*. It also had the advantage for Fénéon of providing him with a livelihood since it was one of the few magazines which could pay its staff and contributors.

The *Revue Blanche* started its life in Belgium in December 1889 as a little literary magazine started by a group of French and Belgian writers and intellectuals as an outlet for all the new tendencies in art and literature. One of its collaborators was Louis-Alfred Natanson, the youngest of three rich brothers who lived in Paris. Early in 1891, the three brothers Natanson took over the magazine by an amicable arrangement and began to publish it in the capital where it became famous. The Natansons were the sons of a Polish-Jewish businessman who had emigrated to Paris and made his fortune there. The eldest son was Alexandre, a lawyer at the Paris bar and an excellent businessman. Thadée, who became the most famous brother, was Fénéon's friend and had arranged a Seurat exhibition with him in 1892, holding it in the magazine's premises. Louis-Alfred was a poet, critic and playwright, a close friend of the painter Vuillard, and he had bought the Durand-Ruel gallery in the Rue Royale. Although they were primarily businessmen by profession, the brothers were great art lovers with many connections in the press and in Paris society. Louis-Alfred died tragically early, but Thadée and Alexandre were closely involved in the artistic and literary life of the capital throughout the '90's and into the early years of the new century.

One of the reasons for the *Revue Blanche*'s success was that, unlike other magazines, it was never tied to one particular movement or "ism". In a rich and complex period of France's literary and artistic history, the *Revue Blanche* was always open to every different tendency, welcoming contributors irrespective of their special allegiance, and it thus came to reflect the whole cultural spectrum of its day. It also owed a great deal to the business acumen of its owners and to the brilliance of its editorial staff, especially its clever and perceptive editorial secretary, Lucien Muhlfeld, who was literary critic from 1891 to 1895.

In 1893, the *Revue Blanche* acquired and incorporated another little magazine *Le Banquet* which had been founded by Fernand Gregh and some friends including the young Marcel Proust who was beginning to make a name for himself with his articles on Paris's society life and personalities. This was the beginning of the magazine's greatest period. After Louis-Alfred's death, the driving force behind the *Revue Blanche* was Thadée, a huge, black-bearded, jovial man whose main aim was to attract the attention of the public to the works of the writers, poets, painters and *dessinateurs* in Paris and abroad whom he and his colleagues considered to be the most talented, and in this he was highly successful. Thadée wrote articles on painters and exhibitions and, in May 1893, he performed another great service for the arts by announcing that, from its July issue, the *Revue Blanche* would publish original prints by artists. One of the first artists to have his work publicised in this manner was Vuillard; he was soon followed by a brilliant band which included Bonnard, Denis, Ibels, Ranson, Redon, Sérusier, Vallotton, Signac, Van Dongen and, in particular, Toulouse-Lautrec who worked very closely with the magazine until 1899.

Fénéon was an invaluable colleague for the Natansons. Not only was the magazine publishing important articles on such painters as Cézanne, Gauguin, Monet and Renoir, but Fénéon helped it attract such literary figures as Tristan Bernard, André Gide, Rémy de Gourmont, Jarry, Gustave Kahn, Pierre Louÿs, Maeterlinck, Mirbeau, Proust, Marcel Schwob, Jules Renard, Emile Verhaeren, Maxim Gorki, Henry James and Strindberg. It published the manuscript of Gauguin's *Noa Noa*, written in Tahiti, and held many small but enterprising exhibitions, the first being one of Vuillard's work. It also became a meeting-place for artists and writers who would come with their work, exchange ideas and then get Fénéon and the Natansons to put them into print, or simply to gossip and make new friends. It soon became considered as an anarchist-leaning organ because of the political views of many of its contributors but it never fell into the trap of being the mouthpiece of any one clique.

In 1893, the *Revue Blanche* moved its offices to the Rue Laffitte by the *grands boulevards*, in the most lively centre of Paris near the newspaper offices, the theatres and the great fashionable cafés. Visitors were no longer only poets, painters or novelists but *boulevardiers*, men-about-town, wits and actors who would come to chat and swap gossip and bring a breath of the life of the boulevard and the café with them as they kept the editorial staff up to date with the latest doings of fashionable society and other events in the capital. At first, visitors were only supposed to come on Thursday afternoons, but soon they arrived every day and could always expect to be welcomed by Fénéon, Thadée and his charming, intelligent wife Misia who also gave parties in her flat and country house near Paris. The *Revue Blanche* consequently became a kind of club. Under the leadership of Fénéon, who became editor-in-chief in 1896, the magazine helped to elaborate new ideas, to develop movements and build reputations, and could always be relied upon to take an interest in everything vital and original in art and literature.

Late in his life, André Gide said that there was no painter or writer of worth and who had won fame in the 20th century who did not owe a great debt to the Natansons and to Félix Fénéon. He was right. Had there been no other magazine, newspaper or review in Paris during the 1890's, the *Revue Blanche* alone would have sufficed to give a clear and comprehensive picture of all that was most important and significant in Paris's cultural life.

Another great habitué of the *Revue Blanche* and crusader on behalf of writers and artists was Octave Mirbeau, the big, life-loving, warm-hearted columnist and critic. He relished nothing better than a good fight and he epitomised the brilliant, polemical spirit that was so prominent in the Paris press during the various artistic and literary controversies which exploded so frequently. There was no greater enemy of the philistine and reactionary either in the arts or in politics. Mirbeau was always one of the first to throw himself heart and soul into the fray and to champion a new cause. His enthusiasm was tremendous, his indignation when aroused was explosive and devastating, and although he was less intellectual than Fénéon, and sometimes less intelligent, he was a sensitive and discerning critic and publicist. He played a vital part in the endeavour to bring recognition to new artists and dramatists in Paris and to educate public taste when he was not castigating it for its conservatism.

Octave Mirbeau was not only a great crusader and journalist

but a novelist and dramatist of no mean stature. He was one of that rarest of species—a critic and supporter of the *avant-garde* whose articles, books, pamphlets and criticisms could be and were read and appreciated by both an intellectual élite and the general public. By 1900, he was one of the best-known writers in France and still a rebel. He had been one since his youth.

Mirbeau was the son of a country doctor and was born in Normandy in 1848. He had spent four years in a Jesuit school and his wretched life there left him with a lifelong hatred of priests, conventional religion, hypocrisy and puritanism as well as a spirit of rebelliousness. He went to Paris on the pretext of studying law, led a dissolute life for a while and then fought for his country in the Franco-Prussian war of 1870. Again, his experiences encouraged his spirit of revolt and non-conformity and gave him an enduring hatred of war, militarism and chauvinism.

After the war, Mirbeau began his career as a journalist and writer and caused his first sensation. He had been put in charge of the art section of a magazine called *L'Ordre* and in his first article he launched a violent attack on academic painting while praising Monet and Cézanne. After an interlude in which he worked as a political journalist in the remote south-western department of the Ariège, as an employee of the Stock Exchange, and among the fishermen of Brittany, he returned to journalism in Paris and wrote for the conservative *Le Gaulois* and some other newspapers. He also expressed his radical opinions in his early novels, the first being *Le Calvaire*, published in 1887. Its main theme was that of revolt against blind and uncomprehending authority and against the kind of ultra-patriotism which was being whipped up by the bellicose nationalists who supported Boulanger. This novel was followed by his anti-clerical *L'Abbé Jules* in which he showed how normal sexual instincts can be repressed by religious dogma and authoritarianism with dangerous consequences. His writing was praised by Edmond de Goncort who became his friend, he was soon in close touch with Huysmans and Maupassant, and became a well-known literary figure while his wife started a small *salon* to welcome and encourage the artists and writers her husband felt worth helping. Naturally, Mirbeau became an anarchist sympathiser and his reputation as a firebrand increased when he agreed to write a preface to Jean Grave's book *La Société Mourante et l'Anarchie* in 1893.

Apart from his political polemics and his novels, it was on account of his writings on art and literature that Mirbeau became especially influential in the 1890's. He denounced conventional art and fashions with relentless zeal, discovered such talents as Maeterlinck whose fame he did much to establish in Paris by a famous article in the *Figaro*, and campaigned ardently on behalf of Rodin, Monet, Cézanne, Van Gogh, Gauguin, Renoir and Pissarro. He was one of those critics who are incapable of indifference and who can only proclaim their passionate enthusiasms or complete detestations. He loved art when he felt that it was true to life and nature in its essence and inspiration and he loathed anything that he suspected of being affected, esoteric or insincere. He flayed the artists of the Salon and the *fin de siècle* "aesthetes" with equal venom, which he also exercised in his articles on the Pre-Raphaelite craze which repelled him as a snobbish affectation. Above all, he could neither understand nor forgive when others refused to recognise what he had praised and publicised as genius.

In spite of his tempestuous approach towards art and literature, Mirbeau rarely made a mistake in picking out what he believed to be the best and the most likely to endure. Like Fénéon, he ignored many of the by-paths of art and concentrated on the mainstream of modern artistic development. Today, it is easy enough for us to see the most significant milestones in the history of modern art in France, but it is all too easy for us to forget the problems of seeing them at the time they were created. It must again be emphasised how rigidly banal and conventional was the overwhelming majority of painting and sculpture on view to the public of the '90's. "Modern" art was only to be found in the pages of some art magazines, in a small number of enterprising and progressive galleries, or in the Salon des Indépendents, apart from the homes of a few discerning patrons and collectors. Mirbeau was a man ahead of his time and many of his judgements have been vindicated by posterity. It is still very worth while reading his articles and essays, for they record the climate in which the great innovators worked and struggled for acceptance.

With Fénéon, Mirbeau was wholeheartedly on the side of progress and creation.

Octave Mirbeau was also one of those Parisian personalities of the 1890's who moved both in the world of journalism and society, and who stood half-way between art and literature in the making and the world of the cultured *salons*. It was in this peculiarly Parisian institution of the *salon* that successful writers and painters and musicians would be lionised, and where new talent, if it were fortunate, might be encouraged by a few sympathetic and cultured ladies of means who did much to give artistic and intellectual achievement an elegant social accolade.

The atmosphere in which established artists and writers moved in Parisian high society was a well-bred, worldly one and, unlike the boulevard and Latin Quarter cafés, the focal figures who brought them together were women. Among these cultured hostesses, a leading figure in the *belle époque* was the Comtesse de Greffulhe. She was a famous beauty and Robert de Montesquiou's cousin, five years younger than he. She was born a Caraman-Chimay and had married the Comte de Greffulhe, a man of vast wealth, a friend of the Prince of Wales, a collector of race-horses and beautiful mistresses, who gave his wife *carte blanche* to entertain on a sumptuous scale in his mansion on the Rue d'Astorg. Her *salon* became one of the most elegant in Paris and, although she was not very intelligent, she fascinated men with her slightly enigmatic charm and what Proust called "all the mystery of her beauty in the enigma of her eyes". This "last queen of France", as she was called, was equally at home in the highest reaches of Parisian society and in the princely courts of Europe. Kings, grand-dukes and ministers would mingle in her drawing-room with scientists, scholars, poets and musicians. Throughout her long reign, which extended well into the 20th century, she helped to introduce the Russian Ballet in Paris, welcomed Diaghilev, Chaliapin, Caruso and Debussy, modern painters and sculptors, and went to England to promote Rodin, Manet, Renoir and Picasso.

Paris's veteran hostess was Princess Mathilde Bonaparte who was a very old lady in the '90's. By then her *salon* was legendary and she had been meeting France's creative and intellectual élite for half a century. In her last *salon* in the Rue de Berri where she lived after the Commune until her death in 1898, she gave literary dinners for such eminent and diverse personalities as Anatole France, Paul Bourget, Henri de Régnier, Pierre Loti and Edmond Rostand, and kept up with new trends. Unfortunately, she was less progressive and aware in her artistic tastes. She was equally unappreciative of the romantic painting of Delacroix, the realism of Courbet and the new vision of the Impressionists, and her salon became virtually a temple of academic art.

A far more progressive hostess who entertained equally brilliant guests, although on a much more modest scale, was Misia Sert, who had married Thadée Natanson when she was only fifteen. Youth was especially favoured in her gatherings and her apartment became a meeting place for the colleagues of the *Revue Blanche* and many of the Symbolists. Frequent guests included Mallarmé, the young Gide, Bonnard, Lautrec, Vuillard and Jarry. Misia endeared herself to many young and unknown painters by posing for them to paint her portrait and by her delightful informality.

Another equally open-minded hostess was Madame Geneviève Strauss. She was one of a number of cultivated Jewish ladies who played an important part in the cultural life of the *fin de siècle* in Paris and who, together with their wealthy husbands, represented the growing social importance of a large section of Jewish high society. They assiduously patronised the arts and their guests tended to be more varied and met in a more easy-going atmosphere than in the older-established, more conventional *salons*. It was in such a *salon* as that of Madame Strauss that a new kind of *tout-Paris* was formed. She mingled society wits and dandies, businessmen and financiers, artists of all genres, writers and journalists, while her husband contributed to the gatherings by bringing ministers, politicians and members of the exclusive Jockey Club. Her home in the Rue Miromesnil became a popular meeting-place on Sundays for many of Paris's most brilliant conversationalists and literary figures including Jules Lemaître, Anatole France, Victorien Sardou, Paul Bourget, and the socially ambitious, clever and opportunist journalist Arthur Meyer.

Two other Jewish ladies who became prominent members of

Paris's cultured society were Ernesta Stern and the Baronne Deslandes. Madame Stern's great Gothic-style *salon* in the Rue du Faubourg Saint-Honoré was the more old-fashioned of the two with its collection of tapestries, portraits by old masters, marble statues and faiences, silver ware and its famous antique organ. Rodin became a frequent guest, but her "stars" were mostly the more established and conventional writers and painters such as Carolus Duran, Bonnat, Rostand and Hérédia.

The Baronne Deslandes was a somewhat eccentric and enthusiastic adherent to the *fin de siècle* fashions which Mirbeau had ridiculed. Her first husband had been Count Fleury and when she was forty she married the handsome young Prince de Broglie who was only twenty and adored her. She was beautiful, bosomy and emotional and although she could draw and wrote some highly sentimental and flowery novels, her main talents lay in attracting flattery and in interior decoration. After falling madly in love with the "aesthetic" movement she made great efforts to live in as Pre-Raphaelite and Huysmanesque atmosphere as possible. Her home, which she called her "fairyland", became famous for its bedroom with rose-pattern decorations woven in imitation of Botticelli's flowers in the *Birth of Venus*, her large drawing-room with its white furs, black marble fauns, carved wooden unicorn from a Neapolitan merry-go-round, her portrait by Burne-Jones which she always kept on an easel, her Luca della Robbia ceramic angel on the wall, her stained glass and the large bronze toad which she liked to say she "fed with jewels". Such exotic tastes and her striking looks brought her many admirers. Aesthete poets read their works to her, she posed for paintings, she was flattered to the point of adulation by Oscar Wilde and Jean Lorrain. Maurice Barrès fell deeply in love with her for a time and she lavishly subsidised parties given by Paris's foremost dandy and playboy, Boni de Castellane. But essentially she was a picturesque oddity and a kind of society aesthete whose passions outstripped her judgement rather than a genuine patroness of creative art—a social product of the "decadent" *fin de siècle* with all its poses and exaggerations. Sadly, she outlived her period, became penniless and nearly blind, and then as a final consolation, turned to lesbianism, as did some other literary ladies of the early 20th century.

The great *salons* of the 1890's generally represented the social rewards which Paris's richest and most cultured families could offer success in literature and the arts. Some certainly did encourage genius and give young talent the opportunity to win allies and make its way in the world, but mainly the *salons* gave writers, painters and musicians the pleasant opportunity to meet in elegant surroundings as though in a club. Some hostesses merely seemed to gather as many celebrities as possible while others played an important part in the political as well as the artistic life of the capital. Two *salons* of the latter kind were ruled by the Comtesse de Loynes and Madame Arman de Caillavet.

The Comtesse de Loynes had been a great beauty and society figure in Paris since the early 1870's but she reached the height of her glory in the 1890's when all the most brilliant and successful in the intellectual and artistic élite came to her dinners and receptions. She had had a remarkable and adventurous early life. She was born the daughter of a textile worker, the father being unknown, during the Second Empire she was a discreet *demi-mondaine*, met Alexandre Dumas the Younger, lived with the critic Sainte–Beuve and the director of the Porte Saint-Martin theatre. She had also been the mistress of Prince Jérôme Napoléon who encouraged her to organise a *salon*, and she had a genius for turning past lovers into devoted friends. After inheriting a fortune from one lover who died in the Franco-Prussian war, she married the Comte de Loynes and although she later separated from him she kept her Countess's title. Her dinner table was known as one of the best in Paris and, after having attracted the celebrities of the Second Empire, she continued to charm an intellectual and literary élite with her grace, her sweet nature and finesse until the end of the century when she became politically active and her *salon* more conformist and conservative. As a patroness of the arts, her great achievement was to give confidence and security to the theatre critic Jules Lemaître, and she was to bring him into the political battles provoked by the Dreyfus affair.

Madame Arman de Caillavet was another famous hostess of Jewish origin. One of her greatest claims to fame was that she became Anatole France's friend, guide, inspirer, collaborator, adviser and protector and provided a centre for literary and political intellectuals as well as successful artists. She had trained as a hostess under Madame Aubernon de Nerville whose own *salon* has become one of the legends of the *belle époque* and whose tyrannical manner and eccentricities such as dictating subjects for dinner-table conversation and ringing a bell to change subjects or speakers have been described in many memoirs, and whose snobbery and flamboyance either irritated or intrigued her guests.

Madame Caillavet broke away from her mentor, who died in 1897, and set up her own more relaxed *salon* in the 1880's. The greatest event in her life was when she met Anatole France, then a shy and socially awkward man. She discerned his true talent, completely succumbed to his intelligence and erudition and made it her life's mission to give him encouragement and discipline as well as the comforts he needed to become a truly great writer. Her guests included many important theatrical figures including Sarah Bernhardt, Réjane and Sardou, and her Sunday evening in the Avenue Hoche provided yet another great attraction and rendezvous for Paris's intelligentsia. She too was to play an important part in the political battles of the end of the century.

All these *salons* helped to give Paris its incomparable brilliance as an artistic and literary capital for all Europe by the end of the century. They were an aspect of society life at its most cultured and sophisticated and also at its most broadminded and receptive in contrast to the massive conservatism of the middle classes who dominated general public tastes. They were also a sign of another great tendency in the artistic and literary life of late 19th-century Paris: the urge to meet, to form groups, to debate, to exchange ideas and recruit followers, and to spread influences. This was such a prominent characteristic of the time that it was to be found at all levels, from Mallarmé's famous Tuesday evening conversations when all his visitors were offered was ideas and tobacco, to sumptuous parties in aristocratic mansions, from noisy poetical-musical evenings in café cellars to impromptu banquets. They appealed to the extreme sociability of artists and writers who had never been more gregarious and brought them into society and new social circles. They also helped to create a new society of the talents in which the painter, the scientist, the philosopher, the politician, the novelist and the musician could meet on equal terms in a sympathetic atmosphere and into which newcomers might make their way, not for reasons of social ambition but because they were made to feel that it was *their* society. As much as public indifference and philistinism, the hostility of a large part of the press, and the conservative prejudices of academic artists and officials, the *salons* were an important and integral part of the Parisian background against which new art movements emerged and must be seen. In a politically unsettled and often stormy period, they also helped to bring the nation's creative élite into the great controversies and struggles which became so acute in the second half of the '90's.

THE ARTISTIC REVOLUTION
PART II

A FTER THE Nabis, no other group of artists bound together by any new "ism" appears in Paris's art history
until the early years of the new century. Instead, the main
characteristics of the 1890's decade were a steadily growing public
acceptance of the Impressionists; a limited vogue for "idealistic",
mystical, symbolist and "Rosicrucian" art; a number of important and often controversial exhibitions held by the city's few
modern-minded art galleries; the way in which a few great
individual artists followed their own path to evolve personal
styles owing nothing to any special theories; the democratisation
of art through the medium of the poster; a frequent stress on
linearism in painting and decoration; a flowering of the graphic
arts in general; and some noisy, bitter clashes as the old guard in
the arts fought their last-ditch battles.

Although its supporters failed to realise the fact, the importance of the official Salon was steadily declining. Despite the
continuing hostility of the public and the academics, perceptive
critics realised that it was in the progressive galleries and independent exhibitions that the main tendencies in new painting could
be studied. The branch of Goupil's gallery where Théo van Gogh
had worked had been one of the first to show the new artists. The
Durand–Ruel gallery had championed the Impressionists ever
since the 1870's, although it continued to sell academic works, on
which its finances mainly depended. But in the 1890's, it held a
number of especially important exhibitions: Monet in 1891, 1892
and 1895; Renoir in 1892, 1896 and 1899; Camille Pissarro in 1892
and 1898; Degas in 1893. Among the post-Impressionists, it displayed works by Gauguin in 1893, paintings, drawings and prints

by Bonnard in 1896, and a joint show of works by Bernard, Signac, Sérusier, Denis, Vuillard and Vallotton held as a "homage" to Odilon Redon in 1899. Another gallery which helped to present the new trends to the public was that of the dealer Le Barc de Boutteville who really preferred Salon painting but allowed himself to be persuaded to make his gallery a meeting place for the Nabis whose works he exhibited annually from 1891 to 1894, without, however, any great financial rewards.

The gallery which did the most to attract Paris's fashionable clientèle to exhibitions of modern art was that of Georges Petit who had first opened his luxurious showrooms in 1882. In the 1890's, it was the city's most socially eminent gallery, renowned for its soirées, concerts and previews, its rich clients and such distinguished habitués as the Comtesse de Greffulhe and Robert de Montesquiou. After he had made a considerable profit in his early days by hunting down Corots and by selling and later reselling Millet's *Angelus*, Petit realised the commercial possibilities of the Impressionists. He became Durand-Ruel's rival and began to show works by Monet and also sculptures by Rodin. A newcomer who greatly helped to publicise the revolutionaries, and Cézanne in particular, was Ambroise Vollard, a Creole who gave up law for picture collecting and dealing. He opened his gallery in the Rue Laffitte, among the older, conservative dealers, in 1893. He remained in close touch with the artistic *avant-garde* for the rest of his life, and recorded his experiences—not always reliably—in his *Recollections of a Picture Dealer* published in the 1930's.

Such galleries helped to educate public taste and make people aware that there was much more to painting than subject matter and photographic naturalism. Even so, as far as most people were concerned the most daringly "modern" painting they were prepared to accept remained that of the earlier Impressionists and artists like Degas and Toulouse-Lautrec whose style might be completely new but who still gave them recognisable pictures of Paris life and amusements. Otherwise, works by the great independent artists, such as those to be seen in the annual Salon des Indépendants, continued to be misunderstood or to provoke angry reactions. Meanwhile, and unknown to the public and critics, some young artists who were to carry the painting revolution further in the first years of the coming century—Matisse, Marquet, Rouault—were quietly feeling their way forward, making contact between themselves and absorbing the lessons of the older pioneers.

Early in August 1893, a sick and discouraged Gauguin returned to France from Tahiti. He landed at Marseilles, with works painted in Tahiti, and after borrowing from friends made his way back to Paris, where he was determined to exhibit the artistic results of his self-imposed exile. After a disappointing response from the new manager at Goupil's, Gauguin enlisted the aid of Degas who, impressed by the Tahiti paintings, persuaded a hesitant Durand-Ruel to hold a one-man show for one month. The exhibition opened on November 4, 1893, and the preface to the catalogue was written by Gauguin's old ally among the Symbolists, Charles Morice.

The exhibition was controversial and disappointing. The majority of the works—thirty-eight of them—were those brought back from Tahiti. Only eleven were sold. The Impressionists, including the ageing Pissarro, were shocked and distressed, the Symbolists, Nabis and their friends were generally enthusiastic but the public were also shocked. Many of the Tahiti paintings were serene and radiant but they were too strange, too exotic, too "un-French" for most of the spectators. They were paintings from another world, painted with unconventional, "un-European" colour schemes and compositions. Gauguin's flat simplified shapes, mystical allusions and audacious juxtapositions of colours were too much for most people. A visiting Englishman's shocked cry of protest because a dog had been painted red in one picture was symptomatic of the general reaction and confirmed the popular belief that most modern artists were madmen.

Although the exhibition brought him little financial gain, Gaugin inherited some money from an uncle, hired a studio and resumed his place in Paris's poetic and artistic circles. He made generous loans to his needy friends, flamboyantly decorated his studio in the Rue Vercingétorix in Montparnasse, held soirées attended by Rodin and Maillol, Mallarmé, Strindberg (then living in Paris), Verlaine, Morice and the Nabis among others, picked up a half-Javanese model, Anna, and installed her as his mistress; and then, tired with city life and parties, went back to Brittany in the spring of 1894. He quarrelled with his former devoted friend Sérusier, was beaten up and broke a leg in a fight with local fishermen who were resentful at Anna's insolent and provocative behaviour, and returned to Paris after convalescing only to find that Anna, who had gone ahead of him, had ransacked his studio and run away. It was the last straw: tired of endless arguments and discussions with other painters and dealings with dealers and critics, Gauguin decided to return to the South Seas for good. Forty-nine of Gauguin's paintings were again put on sale at the Salle Drouot in February 1895 but his profit was just under 500 francs. After trying in vain to obtain the official patronage of the Director of Fine Arts and an official administrative post in the Pacific, and after contracting the syphilis which was to prove fatal to his health from a Paris prostitute, Gauguin returned to Tahiti, never to see France again.

After Gauguin's final departure, and for the rest of the decade, the great individual painters in Paris were Puvis de Chavannes, Henri Rousseau, Bonnard and Vuillard, Degas and Toulouse-Lautrec. Although Bonnard and Vuillard had been founder members of the Nabis, and orientated in the direction of Symbolism, and although Degas had associated with the Impressionists, they worked along their own lines afterwards. One thing was common to them all: a search for complete autonomy in pictorial expression.

The only one of these unique artists who won official approval and recognition was Puvis de Chavannes. By 1890, he was nearly seventy years old and without doubt one of the most famous painters in France. But he was still largely an odd-man-out in the Salons and in official art circles. In the course of his long career, which had started in the 1850's, he had never been a success in the Paris Salons although he continued to exhibit in them. He was never appreciated or understood by the academic artists or by the Impressionists and yet his tenacity and refusal to conform won him official recognition and honours towards the end of his life. He was the only officially commissioned painter of real new talent to be employed by civil servants whose idea of art ordinarily was that it should be big, rhetorical and uplifting, and preferably used in the decoration of the huge interiors of public buildings. In his own way he painted the neo-classic semi-nude females, landscapes, and allegorical figures that officials wanted for the grandiose allegorical wall and ceiling paintings in town halls and university buildings in which Science, Art, Literature and Justice would customarily be represented by goddess-like female figures striking "classical" poses. In 1876, Puvis was commissioned to decorate the inner walls of the Panthéon with allegorical and historical paintings of the history of Paris. In 1889, the President of the Republic decorated Puvis with the Legion of Honour after he had painted the great amphitheatre of the Sorbonne with a huge painting of the university represented by a dignified if somewhat stiff maiden standing in a sacred grove surrounded by nudes symbolising the various branches of culture.

Puvis was the last of the great fresco painters of the 19th century and he was certainly the most talented. All his life, he had remained faithful to a kind of calm, dignified beauty which had been inspired by the fresco art of 14th-century Italy and he had succeeded in becoming a favourite with the Parisian dilettanti who liked his predilection for the pale, faded colours which were so fashionable in "decadent" or "aesthetic" art. Unlike the aesthetes and the pompous academics, Puvis was neither precious nor pretentious.

At a time when history and allegorical painting were prized by conservative art pundits, Puvis was far more interested in the rhythms and lines of his compositions, in harmony of colours and poses, than in telling a story in two dimensions. He was not an exciting painter, he was often dull, his colours and compositions have a cold, frozen quality which fails to excite or to move the emotions, and for this reason he is largely forgotten, but by the 1890's his stature as an artist was a great one. His paintings with their statuesque female figures, their dreamy, muted landscapes and classical temples amid sacred groves, had a noble simplicity and a dignity which greatly impressed several of the newer artists and notably Gauguin, Seurat and then the Nabis. He was a friend of Gustave Moreau, he had encouraged Degas, who had studied with him, he was one of the most jovial, popular and sympathetic teachers at the School of Fine Arts in

Paris, and he was admired by several of the Symbolist poets through Mallarmé. He even had some influence on the young and unknown painters who were to become the "wild beasts", the *Fauves*, in the early 20th century, and he thus played his part in fostering a spectacular revolutionary movement. He was as unmovable in his artistic convictions as the rock-like figures in his allegorical compositions and he always preserved his style and individuality as did Moreau and Redon. Faithful and hard-working to the end, when he learned from his doctor in 1898 that he had only a few days to live, he employed them in finishing his last great decorative painting in the Panthéon, *Saint Genevieve watching over the sleeping city of Paris*, before returning to his home to die.

While Puvis's fame reached its height, another great artistic outsider was hard at work in Paris and expressing his own vision of the world in works which were ridiculed for years and which are now world-famous and loved. He was Henri Rousseau, nick-named *Le Douanier*.

His life as an artist had begun in 1885, at the age of forty-one, after he had been a soldier and then an employee of the Paris municipal toll service. He had no formal training although he said that he had received advice from the two ultra-academic painters, Gérôme and Clément, and in 1885 he had exhibited two works in the official Salon. It had been a catastrophic ex-perience. His canvases were reviled as an outrage against public taste and had been slashed by irate spectators amid abuse and ridicule which were to accompany his career for many years. Despite this setback, he exhibited his works at the newly formed Salon des Indépendents every year, with the exception of 1899 and 1900, in the company of such geniuses as Seurat and Redon.

At first some critics commented favourably on Rousseau's work but from 1894 the majority turned against him and hence-forth he was regarded as the yearly joke of the Independents' Salon and as an eccentric who could be depended on to make the public laugh. His stiff, wooden portraits, his "naïve" and appar-ently childlike views of Paris, his exotic landscapes and forest scenes with wild animals which were probably inspired by his visits to the Paris zoo and botanical gardens at the Jardin des

Plantes, and his apparently deliberate "childishness" all marked him out as a curiosity. To some conservative critics, his primitive qualities and his crudeness simply meant that he could not paint at all, and to others it seemed another sign of the depressing tendency to ignore the techniques of "well-rendered" academic art and to defy public taste.

But after a while, a number of artists and writers came to recognise the individuality of Rousseau's vision and the original way in which he expressed it and they spread the word that here was a truly unique talent. He was befriended by Jarry, noticed favourably by that other painter of visions and dreams, Redon, and by Toulouse-Lautrec, and was soon on close terms with Gauguin and Degas. By the end of the century, he had painted three pictures which are among the most famous of his career— the *Carnival Evening* of 1886, the *War* of 1894 and the magnificent *Sleeping Gypsy* of 1896.

At a time when other new artists were so receptive to the influence and theories of previous innovators and cross-fertilising each other's art, Rousseau had the distinction of being the only great painter to have declared himself inspired by such reactionary academics as Gérôme and Bouguereau. It is one of the oddities of the history of modern art that had it not been for the dull and unimaginative art of the Paris Salons which he wished to reproduce in his own works, Rousseau might never have become what he did. It was also his great fortune to have been working in a city where a spirit of revolt, innovation and insistence on the artists' individual vision, and contacts between the *avant-garde* in art and literature brought him friends and influential supporters when otherwise he might have been condemned to lasting obscurity.

The tendency to move away from all schools and theories of painting in favour of self-expression became marked in the works of Bonnard and Vuillard. After their early, idealistic phase, they broke free in their art from the literary and intellectual atmosphere fostered by the Symbolists who gathered around the *Revue Blanche*. The Nabis were no longer a group bound together by a commonly held ideology but an association of friends who continued to exhibit together and often collaborate—as in work for

Lugné-Poë's Théâtre de l'Oeuvre. While Denis and Sérusier followed a religious path in art, Bonnard and Vuillard went on to paint domestic and outdoor scenes of everyday life and to experiment with colours and compositions, making less use of the strong outlines and flat, pure colour planes inspired by Gauguin.

By the end of the 1890's, Vuillard was painting some of the finest works of his career and exemplifying a trend towards absolute simplification and concentration on a few basic essentials which became conspicuous in *avant-garde* painting. At the same time, Bonnard's paintings exploded into a riot of colours in some of the most joyful, warmest, most spontaneous painting of the whole period. He was a great free artist who expressed his love of life and his visual sensations with intensity and refinement and a feeling for colour and pattern which marked a vital step forward in the emancipation of painting at the turn of the century.

While Vuillard composed pictorial poems with the humble interiors he loved to paint, Bonnard was a delighted observer of everything he saw around him and especially in his beloved city. Throughout the 1890's, he celebrated the colours, life, bustle and landscape of Paris as did a number of other artists, some minor and forgotten, others world-famous, like Pissarro and Toulouse-Lautrec.

The depiction of Paris's life, entertainments, streets and boulevards, suburbs and slums, theatres, racecourses and the river Seine was one of the most conspicuous features of the decade's art although such themes had already been treated years before by Monet, Renoir, Manet and Degas. In the second half of the 19th century, Paris itself became the hero of many painters. Not since the great Dutch schools of the 17th century and the Venetian art of Canaletto and Guardi in the 18th century, had there been such a rich and fruitful concentration of painters on urban themes. The academics had used ancient Greece and Rome and history as some of their main sources of inspiration; the Symbolists and *fin de siècle* mystics had turned to religion, legend and exotic past civilisations; the Impressionists had been mainly interested in catching varying moods of nature in the countryside of northern France, but Lautrec, Bonnard and Pissarro all found a rich source of material in contemporary urban civilisation.

For such artists, the gaiety, the colours, the bustle of crowds and traffic in the streets and wide avenues of Paris seemed to cry out to be interpreted and recorded in paint. Even the scientific-minded Seurat and Signac used such Parisian themes as the can-can, the banks of the Seine and the Eiffel Tower for their compositions. Now, the visual attractions of the streets and broad avenues around the Place Clichy led Bonnard to forget high ideals and theories and simply to paint his own response to what he saw around him.

In 1896, Bonnard held his first one-man show in Vollard's gallery. His paintings were witty, human and spontaneous without a hint of the gravity and soulfulness which had been the aim of the Nabis when they first banded together. They were both decorative and naturalistic. Bonnard had achieved a happy harmony between his observation and his technique. One of the most balanced and sensitive critics of the day, Gustave Geffroy, drew attention to the peculiarly Parisian qualities of Bonnard's art, praising him as a painter with a singularly acute eye for the incidents of Paris life, the everyday and the unusual and "the ever-changing panorama of the streets". Not only the people of Paris and their activities were attracting attention but the visual qualities of houses and the street themselves became a theme for painters. Interest in such urban landscapes was well represented and expounded by the poet and critic Gustave Kahn when he published his *Aesthétique de la Rue* in 1899. Between 1897 and 1899, the elderly Camille Pissarro painted a series of bird's-eye views of Paris boulevards and main thoroughfares with rich dashes of colour and flickering brushstrokes that perfectly caught the vivacity of the city with its surging crowds, it strollers and traffic, its bright new shop fronts and street lighting. In 1898, he was commissioned by Durand-Ruel for further Parisian landscapes, a series of studies of the Avenue de l'Opéra, before he moved towards the Tuileries to study the urban landscapes by the Seine.

Minor artists who also showed their fascination with Paris in their works included the Italian Boldini, Raffaelli and Jean Béraud. All of them have left us a vivid picture of the *belle époque* and the life of the city. Boldini, who was to become one of the most famous society portrait painters of the entire pre-war period from the 1880's to 1914 and even until the 1920's, had begun to paint Parisian landscapes in Montmartre and Clichy in a nervous, vivacious style which won him much admiration after he had settled in Paris in 1872. Jean Béraud, who was born in 1856, painted gentler scenes of everyday life, from fashionable weddings in the great society churches to racecourse meetings at Longchamps, together with scenes in Paris shops, post offices, schools, the Folies Bergère and the Moulin Rouge. Raffaelli, who became a member of the Salon, showed the same interest in Paris slums, suburbs and *la zone*, the melancholy no-man's-land by the fortifications, which had contributed so much to the new folklore sung by Aristide Bruant and which had inspired Steinlen's drawings of Paris's low life and the working classes.

The two great artists of the period whom we now associate indissolubly with the Paris of the theatre and ballet, Montmartre and its can-can and cabarets, the Paris of pleasure and dissipation, are Toulouse-Lautrec and Degas. Both were the most thoroughly *Parisian* of the great independent artists, both were outstanding draughtsmen as well as colourists and both had been deeply influenced by the compositional techniques of the Japanese print artists, Degas having been one of the first painters to see them in Paris in the late 1850's. Degas, who was a worldly and snobbish man, had acquired great prestige among the younger artists in the 1890's and was still urging that subjects should be drawn from everyday life although he had stopped painting genre scenes in his earlier realistic style and was concentrating above all on form and movement, as in his scenes of women at their toilet or the ballet.

Toulouse-Lautrec was the more gregarious artist. Whether he was portraying scenes in the Moulin Rouge or the Paris brothels he did so as a man completely at home in a great city and as one for whom life was to be lived amid crowds, noise, colour and activity. He was a wholly urban artist, an inquisitive and sophisticated explorer of Paris life and pleasure. Even more than of

Paris, he was a citizen of Montmartre. It was there that he found
his *milieu* among the artists and pleasure seekers, the popular
entertainers and personalities who had made this part of Paris
so fascinating since the flourishing of its night life. His art was
never sentimental or mannered, it could be realistic to the point
of brutality but it had a spontaneity, a liveliness and a truth
which made it immediately accessible. It was a firmly contemporary art. It required acute observation and the ability to catch a
scene with immediacy. Neither Degas's nor Toulouse-Lautrec's
style was the result of any long theorising. It was essentially
practical in spirit and arose out of their need to find the best,
most direct and simple way of expressing the essential of what
they had seen and decided to reproduce. Both were great
sketchers and draughtsmen: one of the essential qualities needed
by a good draughtsman is the ability to *select* and this the two painters possessed to a high degree. In this respect, their works are
outstanding examples of the triumph of draughtsmanship in
a decade when the graphic arts reached great heights.

Whereas the most talented painters of the time—Cézanne, the
post-Impressionists, Gauguin, Rousseau—had to overcome public incomprehension, the most gifted, "modern" *dessinateurs*,
whose simplifications and compositions might be as revolutionary
as those of the painters, were enjoying a great success and popularity. The proliferation of newspapers and magazines, many of
them humorous and satirical, provided enormous opportunities
for graphic artists. The list of genuine artists who drew for them
from the '90's to 1914 is an impressive one and includes Lautrec,
Forain, Steinlen, Van Dongen, Kupka, Caran d'Ache and Juan
Gris. In the new century, Guillaume Apollinaire was to claim
quite seriously—and with justification—that they had contributed to the evolution of modern art. What the painters could
not do without shocking the majority of the public, the *dessinateurs* could do with the certainty of instant appreciation. They
evolved an expressive, simplified style with a minimum of lines
and pencil strokes which became a kind of visual shorthand for
the telling of a story or the making of their point. In their wit,
their sophistication and even in their cruelty, they were essentially an urban, artistic phenomenon—a new popular art born of

A Chéret Poster

Connoisseurs of the Poster

Anti-Dreyfus Cartoon

The Duel Between Déroulède and Clemenceau

The Siege of Guérin's *Grand Occident* Headquarters

After the Charity Bazaar Fire

From Meliès' Film *Journey to the Moon*

Vase by Gallé

Loie Fuller

A Cartoonist's View of
Sarah Bernhardt

Edmond Rostand

The Paris Exhibition of 1900

life in a great city—as modern and as immediate in its visual impact as the posters that were now adding to the colour of the Paris streets.

With the flowering of draughtsmanship and caricature there was a revival of interest in printing and lithography which reached its climax by the mid-1890's. Bonnard was typical of a number of painters who showed their desire to reach a larger public through the medium of the print and he had lithographed a series called *Some aspects of the Life of Paris* in 1895, while Vuillard, Vallotton and Lautrec were often showing more interest in making prints and drawings than in painting and were collecting many of the drawings that appeared in the periodicals. The Japanese print, with its flat colour planes and dramatic linear composition, had already influenced painters; now, its influence became apparent in the medium best suited to receive it—the poster. Such gifted painters and graphic artists as Bonnard and Lautrec were not content with merely recording the Paris they loved on canvases and in prints for collectors but took a direct part in brightening the city landscape through the medium of the advertising poster. As a result, poster design was raised to the level of a fine art in the decade and did much to accustom the public to a new kind of artistic vision.

Of all the visual arts which flourished in Paris at the time, that of the poster was the most immediately successful with both the general public and the collectors. Innovations in the colouring and composition of paintings might cause a furore in official art circles but the boldest and most resolutely "modern" poster designs became suddenly popular and brought art into the streets to an unprecedented extent. We now take illustrated street posters for granted and tend to forget what a recent innovation they are, but, at the time, the coloured picture poster did more to change the appearance of the streets than any other single factor. From the start, many critics and journalists were quick to see poster design as a new, mass art with enormous possibilities, and publishers brought out books of poster reproductions just as they had albums of engravings of Salon paintings. As one poster collector and critic, Maurice Maindron, noted, since the advent of the modern poster it had become possible for Parisians to see new works of art every day in the streets. To another poster connoisseur, the critic Roger Marx, it was a new kind of "fresco art" and one which was "understood by all ages, loved by the people". As he went on to write in his book, *Les Maîtres de l'Affiche*, " . . . the poster addresses itself to the universal soul. It has come to satisfy new aspirations and that love of beauty which the education of taste spreads and develops ceaselessly; both outside and in the home it has replaced the paintings which were formerly visible on the walls of palaces, under the vaults of cloisters and churches. It is the ephemeral moving picture which has been demanded by an epoch enamoured of vulgarisation and avid for change". Like society itself, Marx continued, the city street had changed and acquired a new picturesque quality which was essentially a modern one and in which the poster was the essential element. In his *Aesthétique de la Rue*, Gustave Kahn described the poster as "the mobile decoration of the street" and also drew attention to the way it had been transforming the urban scene. So seriously did he regard the poster as an art form of the first importance that he suggested that there should be critics for this "art of the street" who would write reviews of each new poster as it appeared on walls and hoardings just as they wrote articles on paintings in galleries and Salons.

The man who did more than anyone else to inspire poster art and make Paris its centre was Jules Chéret. The son of a typographer, he had been apprenticed to a lithographer and in his youth had managed to find the time to visit the Louvre and attend art classes. He then lived and worked in London from 1859 to 1866 where he had perfected his knowledge and techniques of colour lithography before returning to Paris where he began to produce his first posters on a commercial scale and opened his own printing works. Nothing like Chéret's posters had been seen before. Previous posters were mainly black and white printed advertisements displayed in the windows of bookshops to draw the attention of passers-by to new publications or else the printed notice covered with a jumble of typography that was common to all countries. Now, the progress made in printing techniques, the rise of great department stores and other commercial enterprises who needed to bring their mass-produced wares to the attention of as large a public as possible, and the French press law of 1881 which ordered and regulated bill-sticking, gave Chéret his opportunity. He had soon realised that the best way to impress the eye of the casual passer-by was to use a simple, striking design based on a few pictorial elements and as little typography as possible. He received a flood of commissions, especially from theatres, music halls and other places of popular entertainment, and as the 1880's progressed, his designs grew increasingly colourful and radiant. By the 1890's, Chéret had become famous for his explosive colours and striking designs and his laughing, swirling figures of the gay *Parisienne* who seemed to embody all the good cheer and humour of Paris's brilliant night life and entertainments. In 1889, he had done so much for poster art that he was awarded the Legion of Honour which previously had been an honour reserved in the arts for only the most academic and officially approved painters. In 1890, he became art director of the Paris printing firm of Chaix which specialised in posters and, by 1891, had produced over a thousand designs and was the dominant figure in both French and foreign poster art.

With Chéret's success and the emergence of other graphic artists, poster collecting suddenly became extremely popular. Books were written about them, printers increased their editions of posters in order to sell copies to collectors and, by 1891, the business of dealing in posters and selling them to foreign connoisseurs and dealers was well established. Less scrupulous collectors would even bribe bill-stickers to let them have new posters the night they were put up and others would steal from the hoardings by the comparatively simple method of dampening them with a sponge and then removing the posters at night, as soon as the bill-sticker had moved on.

After Chéret, artists like Steinlen, Lautrec, Bonnard and Grasset continued to clothe the Paris walls and hoardings with a mass of bright colours and striking designs. As mentioned, Bonnard had designed a successful poster for the France-Champagne company early in his career, and magazines like the *Revue Blanche* had so encouraged him and his fellow artists to design posters that after a while Paris became a kind of open-air museum of modern art, with Toulouse-Lautrec as the leading and most powerful figure in the field. His first poster had been commissioned by Zidler, the owner of the Moulin Rouge, and was said to have been made with the help of Bonnard. In any event it was an immediate success with its unusual brilliant design, its unprecedented composition in three planes with the dramatic dark silhouette of Valentin-le-Desossé in the foreground. It showed the influence of the Japanese print, and heralded three years of even more brilliant posters, nearly all related to Montmartre and its entertainments. Not all poster artists were as talented as Lautrec, Bonnard and Steinlen, but henceforth poster design spread and developed abroad with great rapidity, and was taken seriously by other artists as they showed increasing interest in the applied arts. The poster gave them the opportunity to communicate their art directly to the largest possible public and even to educate its eye. Modern art was beginning to emerge from studios and galleries and become a part of everyday life and surroundings.

Both the poster and the magazine or book illustration were signs of a tendency that became increasingly noticeable in the 1890's: the interpenetration of the arts and the discovery that even the most humble, mundane object could be made into an art object. Bonnard and Lautrec were only two of many painters who drew for magazines and made prints for them. There was a great revival of book binding and illustration. Vollard promoted prints and commissioned Bonnard to illustrate a volume of Verlaine's poems which he published. Lautrec and the Nabis made original lithographs and drawings for the *Revue Blanche* as well as for humorous magazines. Artists not only keenly collaborated with the theatre but turned to other applied arts. Gauguin made wood-carvings and ceramics and Degas sculpted models. At the 1895 Salon, the American jeweller Tiffany displayed stained-glass windows made from designs by Bonnard, Lautrec, Roussel, Vuillard, Ibels, Denis and Sérusier. Such artists were attempting to restore art to its globality, to free it from being merely a museum piece or something put on a stand or isolated on a wall in a frame, unrelated to its surroundings.

But while even more audacious developments were being

prepared in the visual arts in the 1890's, a series of bitter controversies exploded in Paris's art world. Although the Impressionists no longer seemed revolutionary to many art collectors and members of the public, they again came under vicious attack from a number of officials and academics in high places in 1894 and 1895. After having survived ridicule by the critics, rejection by the Salons and public indifference, Impressionism still had to win its place in the state museums, and particularly in the Orangery Museum in the gardens of the Luxembourg Palace where works by still living artists were acquired and displayed, unlike the Louvre where artists had to be dead for at least ten years before their paintings would be bought.

A battle against reactionary officials had been fought already over Manet's great painting, *Olympia*. Monet, who was always a rebel against official art tastes, had suggested that the painting be bought by public subscription and given to the nation. The amount needed to meet the price, asked by Manet's widow, was 20,000 francs. More than 19,000 was raised, not only by other "moderns" such as Degas, Pissarro, Lautrec, Renoir and Rodin, but even by some influential Salon artists including Béraud, Carolus Duran, Boldini, Helleu and Tissot, as well as by writers and poets led by Mallarmé, Huysmans and Mirbeau. After much argument, the painting was eventually hung in the Luxembourg where more enlightened officials had realised the absurdity of continuing the pretence of ignoring Impressionism, some agreeing that it deserved its place in the museum, even if a small one. Then, in 1894, a crisis arose over a bequest of paintings by Gustave Caillebotte.

Caillebotte was a painter and friend of the Impressionists who had collected works by Renoir, Degas, Monet and Pissarro as well as by Cézanne whom he had also known. In his two testaments, he had stipulated that his collection should not remain hidden in "some attic or provincial museum" but go to the nation. His bequest was considered by an embarrassed special committee while a dispute raged in the newspapers. After complicated and lengthy negotiations, thirty-nine of the sixty-seven works in the bequest were accepted. In February 1896, the paintings were displayed to the public in the Luxembourg gallery but the controversy continued. A number of prominent academicians threatened to resign their posts in the official art world and, by a vote of eighteen to ten, the Academy of Fine Arts decided to send a letter of protest to the official responsible for the decision, the Minister of Education, calling the collection "an insult to our school". In the Senate, some members made harsh attacks on the government but, fortunately, the politicians—probably tired of being pestered by the academics whom they had honoured so often in the past—decided to stand firm.

This half-victory over the reactionaries helped to establish the reputations and respectability of the Impressionist artists by the close of the century. It also showed that old-fashioned painters like Gérôme would no longer have the final say in art matters. But even while Impressionism was beginning to become acceptable to a wide public in Paris and losing its image as a violently anarchistic movement, the art of one of the world's greatest revolutionaries was suddenly brought out of obscurity by the art dealer Vollard.

In December 1895, an exhibition of Cézanne's paintings was held in Vollard's gallery in the Rue Laffitte. It was one of the most important events in the history of modern painting and came both as a revelation and a scandal to the public. The discovery of Cézanne by a number of young artists also had a decisive effect on the course of modern art in France and led directly to some of the great art movements of the 20th century.

Cézanne has a claim to be the greatest of all the lone wolves in French 19th-century painting. In his youth, he had been associated with the Impressionists and had exhibited with them in 1874 when his works were among those most ridiculed by the public. He then broke away from the group and left Paris to follow his own path in isolation, divorced from the artistic world of the capital, in the south of France near Aix-en-Provence. The work and innovations of his talented contemporaries meant little or nothing to him. Instead of joining in their attacks on the Salon, he hoped for years to win recognition in it. He felt no need to spend further time in studying past masters in the museums, nor to join in the debates and exchanges of ideas of the post-Impressionists. Neither the theories of his contemporaries nor the paintings of Van Gogh or Gauguin meant anything to him. For the rest of his life, he struggled and experimented to develop the pictorial techniques which were so greatly to excite and influence new, younger artists.

One of the main reasons why Cézanne became so influential was that he demonstrated that the painting of a picture need not simply be a process of translation, an attempt to imitate the visual reality of a subject with colours and shapes on a piece of canvas. It could also be the creation of a language of its own owing little to the rules of classical perspective and other traditional devices. If an artist had the integrity, the talent and something deep within him to express, then he must search for his own pictorial language and create his own, individual pictorial reality. His art was one of a personal response to nature and the world. He was not only interested in surface appearances but in what he felt both with his emotions and his eyes to be the deeper, underlying basic reality of his subjects. As he strove to express it, he evolved certain techniques which were to be taken up again later by other painters, such as how to model forms and suggest volume, space and perspective by colour alone. By experimenting with basic geometrical shapes, the cube, the cylinder, the cone and the sphere, he sought for the overall rhythm, pattern and structure of nature. Naturally enough, such a way of working was incomprehensible to most people in his day who could only see his art, as it had Gauguin's or Van Gogh's, as a wilful distortion of reality for its own sake. But a few highly perceptive and gifted painters who wanted art to be more than something that was technically accomplished in the traditional sense, and aesthetically pleasing or picturesque, found valuable lessons in Cézanne's approach and a new source of inspiration in his works no matter how imperfect he might find them himself.

Although Cézanne had cut himself off from Paris after breaking away from Impressionism, some of his works were slowly beginning to attract the attention of one or two critics by the end of the 1880's. In 1888 Huysmans had written of him and he devoted a whole chapter of his book *Certains* to his art. In 1889, a painting by Cézanne was included in the Paris Exposition at the insistence of the artist's friend Choquet, the critic; three other works were shown in an exhibition in Brussels held by the group who called themselves "the XX". Emile Bernard and a few other writers wrote about him but by the mid-Nineties he was still almost completely unknown in Paris. Yet his influence was already beginning to be felt by a small number of artists in the city.

At the 1892 Salon, Maurice Denis had stated that some younger artists were especially indebted to Monet, Degas, Pissarro, Renoir and—Cézanne. As some artists talked about this hermit-like painter who was working along such different lines from anyone else, others became interested in what they heard and naturally asked where they could see his work. The one place in Paris where they could see it until the Vollard exhibition was not a gallery, not a studio, but a dark little shop that smelt of paint kept by an eccentric generous-hearted man called Julien Tanguy, better known as *le père Tanguy*, who had become a picture dealer on a modest scale and a well-known figure to the new artists. Julien Tanguy, who was a friend to some of the best-known painters of modern times, was a Breton. He had come to Paris with his wife in the 1860's when he was about thirty-five years old and worked as a grinder of colours for the Maison Edouard in the Rue Clauzel—a famous firm which provided colours for Paris's leading artists. After a time, he grew tired of working as an employee and decided to make his own colours and sell them while his wife kept house as a concierge. Now that he had his freedom again, Tanguy fell into the world of art by becoming a regular supplier of colours to the painters who frequented places near Paris like Barbizon and Argenteuil, and in a short time he met and became friendly with such clients as Pissarro, Monet, Renoir and Cézanne. After the Commune, in which he had taken part as a *Fédéré*, he spent two years on a prison hulk at Brest but was released after a friend helped him obtain a pardon. After another two hard years, during which he was forbidden to return to Paris by the police and lost contact with most of his former customers, he returned to the Rue Clauzel where he had worked for the Maison Edouard, which had now moved, and he opened his own little shop. Two of his first regular customers were Vignon and Cézanne, both so poor that he often gave them credit.

Tanguy soon became a friend of Van Gogh whom he met in 1886 and whose idealistic, socialist views he shared. Both men were extremely poor and, according to Emile Bernard, Van Gogh practically lived in the shop for a time, exchanging many of his canvases for Tanguy's colours, while others were sold for a few francs to itinerant junk collectors and occasional clients. It was in this period that Van Gogh showed his work to Cézanne who made the famous remark: "Sincerely, you paint like a madman!" Meanwhile, Tanguy's list of regular customers was growing, with Pissarro, Guillaumin, Renoir, Gauguin, Anquetin, Signac, Denis and Lautrec all being frequent visitors to his shop, often leaving some of their work in it for Tanguy to sell if he could.

Tanguy gradually acquired the reputation of a near-saint, someone always ready to offer hospitality and to befriend poor and struggling young artists. After his harrowing experiences in the Commune and as an ex-prisoner, Tanguy had become a gentle humanitarian philosopher, and contact with the new artists led him instinctively to appreciate the brightness and light of the Impressionists and creative non-conformity in painting. Many touching stories were told of Tanguy in his last years: of how he had gone out once in despair with a Cézanne under his arm to sell it for 200 francs; of how, when news of Van Gogh's suicide at Auvers-sur-Oise reached him he had gone there at once to lay recent pictures by the artist around his bier. According to Emile Bernard, who knew him so well, Tanguy was an inseparable friend of the Symbolist painters and the Pont-Aven school and, by being the only dealer in Paris to have works by Cézanne, this monopoly gave him a kind of glory among the younger artists who came to see his treasures.

Well-known critics and even members of the Institute eventually made the pilgrimage to his shop where they would be shown works that were either controversial or the kind dismissed as "horrors" by the academicians. Artists who were intrigued by what they had heard would use Tanguy's shop as a museum in which they could study the few canvases left by Cézanne. What particularly interested the young painters, according to Maurice Denis, was the way in which Cézanne reduced nature to pictorial elements, eliminating all others. Emile Bernard has left an eye-witness description of one of these momentous occasions when Tanguy was asked to display a Cézanne:

"He would disappear into a dark room, behind a brick partition, to return an instant later, carrying a carefully tied packet of restricted dimensions; on his thick lips there would play a mysterious smile, his eyes would shine moist with emotion. He would feverishly untie the strings, after using the back of a chair as an easel, and he would then exhibit the works, one after the other, in a religious silence. His visitors would linger behind, making remarks, pointing at sections with their fingers, waxing ecstatic about tones, the matter, the style and then, when they had finished, Tanguy would pick up the conversation again and speak of the artist.

" 'Papa Cézanne,' he said, 'is never content with what he's done. He always gives up before finishing . . . Cézanne works very slowly, the slightest thing costs him a great deal of effort. . . . ' "

Vollard had been to the Rue Clauzel and seen Cézanne's works there in 1892. Other places where a few friends and acquaintances could see them were the homes of the painter Caillebotte and of Zola, who had been inspired by Cézanne for his fictional character, the painter Claude Lantier in one of his novels. But for the majority of art lovers and fellow painters, there was only Tanguy's shop which could reveal Cézanne's work to them. It became so well known that the critic of the *Mercure de France*, Albert Aurier, made a point of mentioning any new Cézanne that was to be seen there.

In 1894, the gentle, humble old dealer died and tribute was paid to him by famous personalities in society, literature and the arts who went to his funeral. As generous as ever, Octave Mirbeau devoted a fine article to Tanguy in *Le Journal* and then helped his widow by launching an appeal for paintings for a charity sale which was answered by Gyp, Rochegrosse and Détaille, Puvis de Chavannes, Helleu and Rodin among others, while some of the Cézannes in the shop went for as little as ninety or a hundred francs.

Vollard's interest in Cézanne was aroused again by the affair of the Caillebotte bequest which contained some Cézannes, including the now famous *Bathers*. The controversy had encouraged Vollard to fulfil a project he had been nurturing for some time: to hold his own exhibition of Cézanne's works. He knew that Pissarro had several works and was willing to lend them for this purpose if Cézanne agreed, but the difficulty was in finding the painter. Hunting for him in vain after hearing that he had been painting in the Forest of Fontainebleau and had returned to Paris, Vollard eventually managed to contact Cézanne's son who brought back his father's written consent from the south of France. Pissarro then suddenly changed his mind and decided that he could not let his own collection go to the exhibition. In spite of everything, Vollard managed to get a hundred and fifty canvases, all unframed, from Cézanne's own studio. After framing them, he announced the show in a few newspapers and in December 1895 they were ready for display.

The show was neither a total failure nor a total success. Many amusing stories have been told about the reactions of visitors— especially by Vollard himself in his *Recollections*. Naturally, the people who passed Vollard's gallery on the way to the others in the same street, which dealt mainly in such popular masters as Henner, Ziem and Détaille, were scandalised as they looked at his window. The *Bathers* from the Caillebotte collection had been given the place of honour, together with another nude study and *Leda and the Swan*. Inside, the passers-by who had been attracted by the novelty of the works would stare uncomprehendingly at the paintings and then leave silently or with loud protests. Charges were made that the exhibition was an affront to public morality as well as to art. Vollard tells how he saw one woman struggling in the grip of her husband in front of the *Bathers*, saying, "Making me go to the trouble to see this—I who once had a prize for drawing!" with her husband replying, "That'll teach you to be nicer to me!"; and of how the ex-king of Serbia had been persuaded by a Paris connoisseur to buy some of the pictures and then asked, "Why don't you advise your Cézanne to paint pretty young women instead?"

The academic-minded *Journal des Artistes* violently attacked the whole exhibition, as was to be expected; other critics varied in their reactions from comparatively restrained criticism to sincere interest, one of the most enthusiastic being Gustave Geffroy. The *Figaro* writer mentioned that Zola's fictional painter was inspired by Cézanne and added that one of the most interesting things about the artist was his influence on others who had recently become well known to the public. Cézanne was now "launched" in Paris by Vollard and henceforth his reputation was to grow steadily, both in France and abroad. Five years later, Maurice Denis exhibited a painting, *Homage to Cézanne*, showing himself, Bonnard, Redon, Sérusier, Vuillard and Roussel grouped around the "Master of Aix", and there was little doubt that he was the greatest single influence on modern painting in Paris.

Whereas Cézanne was only partly attacked by critics in 1895, the treatment meted out to France's greatest sculptor in 1898 was vicious. Unlike Cézanne, Auguste Rodin was already famous by the 1890's but, even after he had received important state commissions and won praise in many quarters, his struggles were far from over.

From the time that Rodin had first shocked conservative sculptors with his astonishing statue of a naked youth, the *Age of Iron*, in 1876, he had been recognised as a threat to all the officials and sculptors who had a vested interest in keeping sculpture dull, conventional and academic. His genius alone endangered their reputations and even though he was obtaining important commissions in the 1880's and being praised by enlightened critics and fellow-artists, spiteful accusations were still being made against his working methods and even his private life. After his successful joint exhibition with Monet at the Georges Petit gallery in 1889, and the unveiling in 1895 of his *Burghers of Calais* group, commissioned by the city of Calais, when the Minister of Fine Arts had publicly acclaimed him as France's greatest living sculptor, it seemed as if he was finally unassailable and that his genius was now beyond dispute. But he still had one last great battle to fight, and as it raged, the strength of reactionary opposition to his art was to be spectacularly displayed.

The pretext for the clash came when Rodin was commissioned to sculpt a monument to Balzac. The proposal that a statue of the writer should be set up in the heart of Paris had already been made by the Society of Men of Letters in France in 1883. In 1885, the Society raised a subscription fund and the commission went to a sculptor named Chapu, a member of the Institute of France. In 1891, Chapu had died, leaving a model for his statue which was found satisfactory by three artistic advisers to the Society, including the sculptor Falguière who was highly regarded in academic art circles. At this point, a special Committee appointed by the Society rejected his model. The name of Rodin was put forward by some of his most fervent admirers. A report was sent to the Society's president, Zola, another great supporter of the sculptor, and in the end Rodin was awarded the commission by a majority of the votes cast. Now carried away by his enthusiasm for the task, Rodin promised to deliver the statue within eighteen months. Paris would be honoured by a statue of one of France's greatest writers, made by France's greatest sculptor.

But the choice of Rodin angered several other sculptors and art officials and the fact that eighteen months passed with no statue forthcoming encouraged them in their determination to deprive Rodin of the commission. The great problem facing Rodin was how to represent Balzac's genius and personality while overcoming the difficulty arising from his physical defects. Balzac had a magnificent head but a short, stout body deformed from years of spending as much as sixteen hours a day at his writing desk. Rodin's problem was to reconcile the two, and by 1893 he had made a rough model. By then, several subscribers were worried by the delay and wrote to the Society where a deeply divided Committee met to discuss the problems and speculate on what Rodin had been doing since he had neglected to invite any of their members to his studio to see the work in progress. In July that year, some of them did visit Rodin, only to be dismayed by the design which showed a rough model of a naked Balzac with no attempt made to disguise the ungainliness of his short, squat body. After they had urged Rodin to change the model, Zola defended him to the Society and it was agreed that he should be granted a new deadline of spring 1895.

In April 1894, the Society had a new president who was also a friend of Rodin, the poet and novelist Jean Aicard. Despite his support, several members were becoming increasingly impatient and worried. After another visit to the studio, they declared that the work was a formless mass and "artistically insufficient". To make matters even worse, Rodin was in poor health at the time and some pessimists began gloomily to wonder whether the statue would even be ready for the Balzac centenary in 1899.

Half the Committee were now split and in October a proposal was passed that Rodin should deliver the statue completed within twenty-four hours otherwise the contract would be considered as having been broken and the advance as repayable. Again Aicard defended Rodin and managed to obtain yet another respite. Then Rodin wrote a letter saying that all he needed was time and peace in order to complete the great task which he found so inspiring, and offering to repay the advance, or put it in a savings bank to earn interest for them until the work was completed. Most important of all, he asked for another full year's delay. The controversy now began in earnest. Although the Committee accepted the proposal, several members withdrew after angry arguments which were reported in the Paris press. The unfinished statue was soon talked about in the *salons*, with Rodin's partisans arguing with others who wanted their own candidates to make the statue. While a depressed Rodin was obliged by poor health to leave Paris for the country for a while, it became an open secret that a number of jealous sculptors were plotting to deprive him of the commission.

An academic sculptor of no talent but with influential friends, Marquet de Vasselot, had already made a bust of Balzac for the Théâtre Français twenty years previously and now offered to do a new statue in a very short time. He exhibited a model at the 1896 Salon and invited the entire Committee to see it. Its design —an absurdly small head perched on a supposedly leonine body in a sphinx-like position—was received with ridicule.

Then, the first of many unfair, wounding and even libellous attacks was made upon Rodin in the Paris press. In its issue of September 30, 1896, the newspaper *Gil Blas* carried an article called "A failure of genius" by a former admirer of the sculptor, Félicien Champsaur, a part-time critic and an author of popular novels. He now tried to demolish Rodin's reputation by alleging that he only owed it to "the snobs of literature, journalism, the salons and the boulevard". He praised the earlier bust of Balzac by Vasselot, took a cruel delight in detailing Rodin's physical infirmities and accused him of only being a dreamer, incapable of ever completing a task. The article ran to three columns, was largely inspired by malicious gossip which the author had picked up in the academies and was so outrageous and spiteful that even Rodin's rivals were shocked by it. Then, in 1897, as there was still no sign of a finished statue, fresh attacks were made by members of the Committee. In March, one member saw the maquette and was assured by Rodin that the statue would be ready for its inauguration in October. In May, Rodin asked for another short delay and it was not until March 1898 that the completion of the statue was announced.

The Committee agreed that the work would be exhibited at the forthcoming Salon. Rodin delivered the statue together with his marble *The Kiss* which he had completed fifteen years earlier, to the Salon Nationale des Beaux-Arts to which he had adhered since 1890 when the old Société des Artistes Français had split into two groups and in which he had been president of the sculpture section since 1893. The exhibition was held in the Champ de Mars in the great Gallery of Machines built for the 1889 Exposition and promised to be sensational as it included some other controversial works including a great painting by Puvis de Chavannes. But the main attraction for the public was undoubtedly the statue. The question being asked all over Paris was: what had Rodin been doing all those years since he had been commissioned? A masterpiece? Surely something extraordinary?

It *was* extraordinary. Some hint of how the statue was to be received by officials was given by the attitude of the President of the Republic, Félix Faure, as he arrived for his private visit to the Salon the day before it was opened to the public. After Rodin had greeted the President on behalf of all his fellow sculptors, Faure had inspected *The Kiss*, complimented Rodin upon it, and then walked straight past the plaster model of the *Balzac*, turning his back on it to look at a collection of busts lined up on the far side of the corridor. Unperturbed, Rodin calmly took up his stand in the hall near *The Kiss* and waited for the first public reactions to his statue. He did not have to wait for long. The first response generally was one of dumbfounded silence. Nothing like this statue had been seen before. Rodin had solved the aesthetic problem of Balzac's physical disproportions brilliantly and with an audacity that seemed to violate every accepted canon of sculpture at the time. Balzac had been one of nature's geniuses: Rodin showed him as a great elemental force, a rock or a tree of a man, surging out of the ground. The statue resembled a thick upright column, a rock with a human face, in which the body was treated like a giant root or stem culminating in the powerful, tragic head of the novelist which irresistibly drew the eye of the spectator. It was an expression of the triumph of the human mind over a body which Rodin had reduced almost to abstraction. With its rugged simplicity and monolithic power the work was a thundering, categorical statement of genius.

A crowd soon grew around the statue. While some visitors remained silent, trying to work out in their minds what Rodin had meant by his design, others either laughed or grew angry. Some even lost their tempers and began to insult the statue. Rodin himself was soon lost in the crowd, but remained calm and chatted with a group of friends as more and more people came swarming into the sculpture gallery. By the middle of the afternoon, an estimated two thousand people had crowded in front of the statue, with many French and foreign artists admiring it despite the loud jeers and murmur of shocked disapproval all around them.

The next day, the Paris press was filled with controversial and, often, savagely violent articles. Not since the première of Victor Hugo's *Hernani* or the scandal of Manet's *Olympia* had there been such a furore and a pretext for reactionaries in art to launch yet another full-scale campaign against the *avant-garde* and all its eloquent supporters, the "snobs of literature, journalism, the salons and the boulevard". Newspapers again berated all those "intellectuals who believe they know about art" and in a fit of patriotism complained that "all the *avant-garde* critics launched the assault, all with equal ardour, against that old fortress of French commonsense". The *Figaro* admired *The Kiss* which had been generally well received, but expressed its sadness about the Balzac statue, saying it was "painful to see". In the conservative

Gaulois, the writer suggested that "the statue should be cast in bronze and set up high so that future centuries will know to what degree of mental aberration we have come at the end of this century. I only ask that the foot of this statue should be engraved with the names of the eminent sculptors who commissioned and praised it. This would be their punishment and our vengeance."

Naturally, all Rodin's supporters took up their pens as well. Battle was joined. The affair degenerated into a public scandal.

There were deplorable scenes of vulgarity and abuse as groups of visitors came with the premeditated aim of insulting the statue and its maker as loudly and as violently as possible. Caricatures of both the statue and Rodin were published in newspapers and satirical magazines; street vendors appeared on the boulevard near by offering small white figurines that looked like penguins or seals and shouted "Ask for Rodin's *Balzac*!"; one Paris art dealer even gave a fancy dress ball in which he costumed himself with a papier-mâché caricature of the statue.

The Society of Men of Letters was dismayed by the whole affair. In view of the general public reaction, they proposed that Rodin should be forbidden to make the bronze cast of the statue on the grounds that what they had received "was not a statue", but they agreed that he was still free to make another Balzac if he chose. After several heated meetings in the Committee, a resolution was passed and communicated to the press, stating: "The Committee of the Society of Men of Letters has the duty and regret of protesting against the rough sketch which Monsieur Rodin is exhibiting in the Salon and in which it refuses to recognise the statue of Balzac."

The resolution further inflamed the controversy. There was stupefaction in many artistic and literary circles where France's foremost writers and artists were mainly in favour of the statue, while strong approval of the Committee's action came from the Paris Municipal Council and members of other municipal commissions on art. But the *comitards*, as the Committee members were labelled, were also attacked in the press. Friends begged Rodin to stand firm, to insist on his rights as an artist and on the purchase and erection of the statue in public. A declaration of support for Rodin and protest against the infamous attacks made on him was signed by a prodigious list of writers, critics and artists, including Gustave Geffroy, Mirbeau, Toulouse-Lautrec, Vincent d'Indy, Signac, Catulle Mendès, Courteline, Paul Fort, Maillol and Bourdelle, Clemenceau, Debussy, Monet, Lugné-Poë, Moréas, Henri de Régnier and Anatole France.

A subscription was opened for the statue to be set up after casting, and contributions came in from newspapers, reviews and publishers; the most touching sign of support being the five francs sent by a dying and desperately poor Alfred Sisley. Rodin was deeply moved by this tremendous support he had been given by France's creative élite but he refused to be drawn into the controversy. With great dignity, he finally decided to remain the sole owner of his work. The letter was published in the press, but even this did not prevent more ugly scenes taking place in the Salon where a succession of spectators seemed to have come with no other purpose than to compete with each other in vilification of the great sculptor's supreme artistic effort.

Finally, Rodin withdrew the statue from the Salon, handed back the advance he had received together with the interest it had earned, and carried the statue off to his country house at Meudon where he set it up in the open. The sculptor Falguière, who had once been a warm supporter of Rodin and was deeply saddened by the affair, agreed to accept the commission for the 1899 Salon but, when it was displayed, the public were mainly indifferent to it. Rodin emerged out of the storm with his reputation enhanced rather than diminished. The very violence with which he had been attacked brought him world-wide publicity and aroused great interest in his work. Foreign journalists and writers came to visit him as did collectors, and when he held the great retrospective exhibition of his work at the 1900 Paris Exposition, visitors came to admire, not to mock. Similarly, the Paris public, which had given such an ugly display of philistinism, made amends to him. Falguière, who had movingly admitted to his pupils that he was wrong about Rodin's statue, had died before his own statue could be set up by the municipality at the intersection of the Rue Balzac and the Avenue de Friedland. Rodin had come to the unveiling ceremony to pay homage to his old friend and was listening to the official speeches when the crowd suddenly recognised him and gave him a long, enthusiastic ovation.

It was not until the summer of 1939, twenty-two years after Rodin's death, that his Balzac was set up at the point where the Boulevard Raspail cuts across the Boulevard Montparnasse. It is now as familiar a part of the boulevard as the plane trees which line it. But years earlier, before the century had ended, Rodin was already vindicated. Rodin's *Balzac* created a spectacular controversy, but after the statue had been withdrawn from the Salon, the nation returned to a far more dangerous dispute.

For some months, it seemed that the whole of France was angrily arguing over the guilt or innocence of the Jewish army officer Dreyfus who had been condemned for treason. It was the greatest and bitterest debate of the century. In a decade of controversies, it was the one which threatened to end in a civil war, and it brought violence back on to the streets of Paris. For two years, it overshadowed the social, political, artistic, literary and intellectual life of the capital. Paris became a battleground where the survival of the Third Republic and twenty years of democratic government were threatened.

VII

THE DREYFUS PERIOD

THE STORY of the arrest, trial, imprisonment, re-trial, pardon and final rehabilitation of Captain Alfred Dreyfus is so well known and has been told so many times that only the outlines of the affair need to be mentioned here. In October 1894, Dreyfus was a staff captain attached to the General Staff intelligence section known as the Deuxième Bureau, and was arrested on the charge of passing on documents to the German Intelligence in Paris. A document alleged to be in his writing was produced as evidence against him. He was found guilty by a military court, and on January 5, 1895, he was publicly degraded in a humiliating ceremony before being sent to the penal colony at Devil's Island, Cayenne.

A year later, another army officer, Commandant Picquart, had begun to suspect that Dreyfus was innocent and that the evidence against him had been fabricated. A number of prominent personalities expressed their doubts about the case, contradictory "revelations" were published in the press and another officer, Esterhazy, was accused of having forged a document which had incriminated Dreyfus. Esterhazy was court martialled, acquitted and, a few days later, the newspaper *L'Aurore* published a sensational letter by Zola who accused ministers and high-ranking officers of concealing the truth, thus inaugurating the bitterest phase of the controversy. Esterhazy and a colleague, Colonel Henry, were arrested for forgery. In 1899 Dreyfus was brought back to France, re-tried, found guilty again, there was a fresh uproar, and he was pardoned. Calm returned to France and Parisians were able to celebrate the dawn of a new century in a comparatively peaceful atmosphere enlivened by the 1900 Exposition.

The fact that the affair had so greatly divided the nation showed that the main issue was not merely that of the guilt or innocence of one army officer whom many believed to have been wrongly condemned. Dreyfus himself became only the pretext for the quarrel. The question of his guilt was a political weapon used by both sides, and the reason the affair blew up to such a huge extent was because it occurred at a time in France when passions were being stirred by violent anti-semitism, militarism and anti-militarism, delirious chauvinism, anti-republican plotting and social agitation. Nothing else could have explained the remarkable displays of hatred that France witnessed; it was a time when politicians and journalists fought duels regularly, when an archbishop of Paris patronised an anti-semitic league of army officers, when writers and artists who had formerly assumed attitudes of detachment from life and world-weariness suddenly engaged themselves in political argument and propaganda, when mobs reappeared in the streets of Paris, and when society *salons* split into opposing factions and raucous ultra-patriots called for a *coup d'état*.

Anti-semitism in France did not begin with the Dreyfus affair. It had already been a factor in French life for some years and it became especially prominent after the publication in 1886 of a violent and inflammatory book, *La France Juive*, by the journalist Edouard Drumont. The main theme of the book was that the Jews had been responsible for France's misfortunes and failures ever since 1870 and that they were menacing the livelihood and fortunes of honest Frenchmen. The book became a best-seller almost overnight and led to a spate of others in the same vein. In 1889, a French National Anti-Semitic League had been founded but it soon collapsed, although not because of any great waning of anti-semitism in the country. Paris became the centre of organised racism and several publishers could be relied upon to print anti-semitic books. Wealthy Jews in banking, business and society were arousing resentment among the more conservative middle classes—especially after the scandalous revelations of the Panama canal affair. In 1891, in the French Parliament, the fire-eating, ultra-right-wing nationalist, Paul Déroulède, who had been baying for years for a war "of revenge" against Germany, accused the Jews of wanting to "de-christianise France", and a month later another deputy demanded the expulsion of the Rothschilds from the nation's soil. In 1892, prejudices were stirred up still more strongly by a newspaper *La Libre Parole*, which Drumont founded, and which became the most prominent of several openly racist sheets. A number of ugly scenes occurred in the capital. In 1894, a group of law students founded the Paris Students' Anti-Semitic League which held public meetings, broke up gatherings of Jews and Socialists, noisily demonstrated and generally encouraged mob violence and anti-Jewish feelings. In June 1895, it paraded through the streets, although only some hundred members took part. In 1896 there were several more public meetings, an attempt to stone the home of the Rothschilds, and to disrupt lectures by Jews or pro-Jews.

La Libre Parole soon became the most influential paper of its kind. In May 1892, it began to publish a series of articles under the heading *The Jews in the Army* in which the growing number of Jewish officers was denounced as a danger to national security. Naturally, when names were mentioned, challenges to duels tended to ensue and were regarded as the normal outcome. Drumont himself fought a Jewish army officer, Crémieux-Foa, and then, in another duel, the rabidly anti-semitic Marquis de Morès, a leading patron of *La Libre Parole*, killed a Jewish army officer, Captain Armand Mayer. The affair was a public scandal: in a statement to the press, the Marquis declared that he regretted the death of Mayer but added, "We are at the beginning of a civil war"; and his words were echoed by many other papers in the city, most of which denounced the killing of a French officer. There was a sudden revulsion against the excesses of the anti-semites, and thousands of sympathisers followed the captain's funeral procession. But in 1893, when prominent politicians and financiers were involved in a scandal arising out of revelations of corruption in the dealings of the Panama Canal Company, the Jews were again accused of being responsible for the spread of corruption in high places, while wild rumours circulated in the corridors of Parliament, the newspaper offices, clubs and the Stock Exchange. The *Libre Parole*, thanks to its influential connections, was one of the best-informed papers and it became one of the most widely read and feared in Paris, with a circulation of

more than 200,000. But Drumont got into trouble, mainly because
he had defended the anarchists, and he fled to Belgium. The
Dreyfus case then gave him a splendid opportunity, when he
returned, for renewing his anti-Jewish campaigning in the name
of patriotism.

In October 1894, the *Libre Parole* published a brief account of the
arrest of a Jewish staff officer accused of passing secrets to the
Germans and began asking questions about the case. On November 1, 1894, it appeared with a huge headline: "HIGH TREASON
—ARREST OF THE JEWISH OFFICER A. DREYFUS". A month
later, as the trial was about to take place before a military tribunal, Drumont's paper was claiming that Dreyfus—whose
guilt was taken for granted—was probably only a tool of the
Jewish financiers in France and part of a vast, nation-wide Jewish
plot to betray the French people and deliver them unarmed and
unprepared into the hands of the enemy—Germany. There
followed stories of conspiracies in Paris's Jewish high society, of
secret meetings with foreign agents in the homes of prominent
Jewish ladies, and many similar rumours; but the majority of the
French people remained uninterested in Dreyfus's fate. He was
found guilty and condemned by the tribunal and although
several thousand Parisians did queue for hours in the bitter cold
to see the ceremony of Dreyfus's degradation by his fellow officers
and men in the courtyard of the Ecole Militaire, it seemed that
the case was closed. The fact that Dreyfus had shown so much
calm and dignity in enduring his humiliating ordeal, and had protested his innocence, incensed the anti-semitic and conservative
press and was taken to be another sign of typically Jewish duplicity.
To the royalist son of Alphonse Daudet, Léon, who reported the
event for the *Figaro*, "the wretch was not a Frenchman. We all
understood it from his deed, his demeanour, and from his face";
and some other papers gleefully exulted over the degradation,
publishing cartoons and drawings showing a triumphant, venge-
ful Marianne punishing the semitic traitor.

If the *Libre Parole* played a leading part in publicising Dreyfus's
arrest and condemnation and exploited it to whip up further
anti-semitism, the Paris press as a whole played a leading part in
the great controversy which exploded. All that Frenchmen knew

about the affair they had learned from the newspapers. When Zola and a few others including the Jewish newspaper publisher Bernard Lazare and the politician Joseph Reinach had doubts about Dreyfus's guilt and began to make investigations, each fresh piece of evidence or document that appeared to throw light on the case was given to the press to publish and it was upon this that the public was urged by powerful columnists to make up its mind in one direction or the other. Public fears that a monstrous conspiracy had been hatched, by the Right or Left depending on their sympathies, were also encouraged by the press. Official opinions on the rights or wrongs of Dreyfus's condemnation were not forthcoming. When the Prime Minister Méline declared in 1897 that "there is no Dreyfus case" he was correct from the government's point of view. It was agitation— for justice and against the army and anti-republicans by some, against the Jews in particular and the Republican régime in general by others—which made the affair assume the proportions of a national crisis and suggest that there was a very real possibility of a civil war in which the Republic's existence would be at stake. But apart from acquainting the public with each new move being made to establish Dreyfus's innocence or to prove his guilt again, the most influential newspapers were used as much, if not more, to alter the opinions of their public as to inform them. Newspapers were as violently partisan as their readers. Some of the Paris papers had played an important part in the battle to have innovations in art and literature accepted and recognised, but in the controversy which overshadowed all others in a decade of violent polemics, the press displayed its power to an unprecedented degree.

By the mid-Nineties, the Paris press was one of the richest, most varied, influential and uninhibited in the world. It was the golden age of the newspaper since the liberalisation and simplification of the press laws in 1881. Henceforth, any offences a paper might commit were related to the common law and were brought before a jury in the courts. Comment could be free, outspoken and even savage, for the laws of libel and defamation were often vague and uncertain, although the right to reply of persons attacked in the press was legally established. Newsprint was cheap, production costs were low and a comparatively small amount of capital was enough for anyone who wished to start a newspaper, with the result that an astonishing number of news-papers appeared in the last two decades of the century. In 1889, Paris alone had some seventy political weeklies and dailies reflect-ing every viewpoint and no less than thirteen evening papers. There were many technical improvements, newspapers published supplements and employed increasing numbers of artists and cartoonists, and the interview became an established part of daily journalism.

But if Paris was the richest city in the world for newspapers, its press was also widely reputed to be one of the most corrupt. It was notorious for the way it accepted subsidies from various quarters, for its openness to bribery, its use as a political weapon and its ferocity in attacking individuals. One of the distinguishing characteristics of the Paris press was that it was far more *Parisian* than national.

Few newspapers spent much money on foreign news coverage or correspondents abroad. They had an enormous influence on society, their offices and waiting rooms would constantly be crowded with elegant ladies, politicians, writers and theatrical personalities. It was assumed that the first interest of the readers lay in events in fashionable society, in the theatre, the arts and the literary world, and in the corridors of parliament and the Stock Exchange. Large sums were paid to popular authors to have their novels and stories serialised, as Maupassant's were in *Gil Blas*, for example.

The newspaper world was one of opportunism, scandal, in-trigue, self-seeking and campaigning, in which a clever journalist might make a name in society and wield great personal power. Maupassant's novel *Bel Ami*, although published in the 1880's, gives a brilliant picture of this excitable, feverish, intriguing atmosphere which reigned in the great newspaper offices. The profession of journalism was highly regarded although generally poorly paid, many writers being paid by the line. Editors and top-ranking journalists like Arthur Meyer had their entrée into high society—something unthinkable in Britain or the United States. Prominent writers and politicians such as Zola and Clemenceau willingly and frequently contributed articles to newspapers. Another dominant characteristic of the press was the social importance and forceful personalities of editors, chroniclers and leader writers. In contrast to the English press, anonymity was more often the exception than the rule, with well-known journalists signing articles every day and paying great attention to style as they endeavoured to give each article a worldly, literary tone. Little quarter was given or expected whenever there was some scandal to be exposed or when a controversy exploded, as in the newspaper duel between Fouquier of the *Figaro* and Bauer of the *Echo de Paris* over *Ubu Roi*, when Bauer was eventually forced to resign. A Parisian columnist or gazetteer could often command consideration and respect; to be attached to a certain newspaper could greatly enhance his social standing but he also had to be prepared to fight and defend himself with other means than the written word.

The whole decade was marked by a vogue for duelling that sometimes reached the proportions of a mania. To have fought at least one duel at some time in his career became practically obligatory for any self-respecting journalist and politician. They often fought as much to attract personal notoriety or make an impact on public opinion as to avenge any affront they might have received. Some of the duels were public sensations, for instance when Drumont taunted Meyer of the *Gaulois* into fighting him and Meyer seized his opponent's sword with his left hand while striking him with his right. Occasionally, they ended in a death as in the Marquis de Morès's duel with Captain Armand Mayer. Codes of etiquette for duellists such as the Comte de Châteauvillard's *Essai sur le Duel* or the later work by the Comte du Verger de Saint-Thomas lay ready for reference in newspaper offices. Earlier in the century, duellists from Paris would go to the French frontier to fight but by the 1890's official tolerance of non-fatal duels was so great that they would usually fight just outside Paris in the woods of Vincennes or else behind the grand stand at the racecourses of Auteuil or Longchamps. Most duels were fought with the rapier rather than the pistol, or the sabre if the duellists were army officers. According to the French writer and historian of the period, André Billy, between 1885 and

1895 at least one hundred and fifty duels were fought. They became part of the social-literary scene with men like Mirbeau, Catulle Mendès, Drumont, Rochefort, René Maizeroy, Moréas, Déroulède and Stanislas de Guaita all involved in fights. The number of duels went up sharply in the last five years of the century, as the Dreyfus affair reached its climax and when to be a journalist on a paper like *La Libre Parole* made it advisable to be something of a swordsman as well.

The great newspapers of the 1890's in Paris besides the virulent *Libre Parole*, were *Le Temps*, *Le Gaulois*, *Le Figaro*, *Gil Blas*, *Le Journal*, *L'Echo de Paris*, *Le Matin*, *Le Siècle*, *L'Aurore* and *L'Intransigeant*. The newspaper with one of the best claims to be the most serious-minded was *Le Temps*. In addition to having the best foreign news coverage, it employed Sarcey as its dramatic critic until his death in 1899 and Anatole France was another of its regular contributors. The *Figaro* was the first French newspaper to give its readers six pages with its issue of December, 1 1895; it was both authoritative and conservative although it supported the demand for a revision of Dreyfus's trial, thereby losing thousands of subscribers and having to change its editor. The next most influential newspaper was probably *Le Gaulois*, under its monarchist, socially-minded editor Arthur Meyer who had many useful connections in the highest reaches of society and in politics and whose Jewish birth did not deter him from ardently supporting the anti-Dreyfus side. The wittiest and most sophisticatedly Parisian paper of the time was *Gil Blas* which was famous for its illustrated supplement, featuring Bruant's songs and Steinlen's drawings, and for its list of literary contributors which included Maurice Barrès, Marcel Prévost and Jules Bois.

The most recently founded Paris daily newspaper was the highly popular *Le Journal*. It was started in 1892 by a reporter, Fernand Xau, who had been encouraged by the success of many literary journals and decided to launch his own paper which would be free from any political allegiance and cater for intelligent readers among the lower and middle class and artisans. It did a great deal to publicise cultural events in Paris and among its many gifted collaborators were Catulle Mendès, the left-wing woman journalist Sévérine, Mirbeau, François Coppée and

Barrés, and Jean Lorrain. Two papers which clashed bitterly over the Dreyfus issue were *L'Intransigeant* edited by the veteran pamphleteer and socialist Henri Rochefort who had become an anti-semite, and *L'Aurore* to which Clemenceau contributed daily. It was around such papers that the intellectual and artistic élite of Paris gathered and it was in their columns that they fought each other when the Dreyfus affair reached its most dangerous and bitter stage.

Various contradictory articles and pieces of "evidence" had been published for some time in the press after Dreyfus's imprisonment on Devil's Island but, by 1898, most people seemed inclined to forget or ignore the case. According to the future Prime Minister, Léon Blum, who was a journalist at the time, Jewish society in Paris was not in the least interested in Dreyfus after his condemnation. It was only after Picquart, an army officer in the French military intelligence service, had become convinced of Dreyfus's innocence, and a number of Dreyfus's friends and such important public figures as the vice-president of the Senate, Scheurer-Kestner, the historian Joseph Reinach, and the journalist Bernard Lazare had begun to call for a retrial, that public interest in the case was revived. A series of revelations in the newspapers, and Picquart's own suspicions, led to another officer, Commandant Esterhazy, being suspected of having forged the documents used to convict Dreyfus. Accusations were made against army officers, high-placed members of the general staff and War Ministry officials. Naturally they provoked violent reactions in France from all who believed that the army represented the nation's honour and that the Jews were trying to demoralise and then destroy the nation. But it was not until the publication of Emile Zola's letter *J'accuse* that France really plunged into a civil-war atmosphere.

After studying the case deeply, Zola had become convinced not only of Dreyfus's innocence but of complicity between ministers and generals in the "burying" of the affair. He decided to bring the matter out into the open and make a direct appeal to public opinion by means of an open letter to the President of the French Republic in which he levelled accusations at government officials and army officers even though he risked imprisonment for defamation. On January 13, 1898, three days after a court martial which had exonerated Commandant Esterhazy of the charge of forgery, to the great joy of the French Right, France's most controversial writer had his letter published across the front page of *L'Aurore* under the banner headline J'ACCUSE, which had been Clemenceau's own inspiration. According to eye-witnesses, Paris was stunned by Zola's audacity. The unprecedented number of 300,000 copies of *L'Aurore* were sold in the streets. War had been declared between the two Frances and as another journalist and writer, Urbain Gohier, wrote in the newspaper *Le Soleil*, the cause of Dreyfus had served as the pretext which caused "all the political, social and religious hatreds to enter into a war which may still be confused but which is certainly a reasonable one".

With Zola's letter, and his trial for defamation in February 1898, there came a sharp increase in political extremist activities, outbreaks or threats of violence in the Paris streets, a violent anti-semitic campaign in the Catholic press, and much-publicised splits in social and cultural life; while Zola's attack on the military establishment quickly won him the support of many writers and intellectuals. A fierce press battle raged while a number of new periodicals and broadsheets appeared on the newspaper stands. Famous caricaturists supported one side or the other with equal vigour, and newspaper editors soon became aware that a clever drawing with a sharp, short caption could have a much more immediate impact on public opinion than a long article. Each side in the press battle had its favourite targets: for the pro-Dreyfus and pro-Zola press, the leading villains who were caricatured countless times were Commandant Esterhazy, Henri Rochefort of *L'Intransigeant* and Drumont, besides military men, priests and judges in general. For the anti-Dreyfusard, the main enemies to be vilified were Zola and Joseph Reinach. Zola provided a favourite target, especially as his books had been so often attacked for obscenity and as he personified that arch-enemy of the chauvinistic Right—the intellectual. Dreyfus himself was rarely featured, as cartoonists preferred the archetypal racist image of the Jew with big nose and blubbering lips. Some papers were specially created for this war of cartoons, the two most famous being the curiously named *Psst!* and *Le Sifflet*. The first appeared on February 5, 1898, three weeks after Zola's letter and two days before his trial began. It consisted of four full-page cartoons drawn by the talented Forain and Caran d'Ache who had decided to use their pens to crusade for the "truth" which, for them, was the honour of the army. The first page was always drawn by Forain and had the most incisive captions. Despite all the ugly passion they inflamed, these papers were masterpieces of their kind and became famous all over France with drawings such as one of a Jewish judge breaking the French flag-staff over his knees or another of a German officer putting Zola's mask over a Jew's face. The pro-Dreyfusards replied to *Psst!* twelve days later by bringing out *Le Sifflet* for which the two main artists were Ibels and Hermann Paul who expressed their message with such drawings as that of a French officer kicking the scales of justice in the air. Meanwhile the anarchist press had revived in Paris and supported the "Dreyfusards" since the affair gave it a magnificent opportunity to press home its attacks on the state, the army, the church and the judiciary. Zo d'Axa brought out a series of *Feuilles* which created a sensation and Sébastien Faure, the theoretician of the movement, founded *Le Journal du Peuple*, which combined anarchist preachings with a spirited defence of Dreyfus; while Jean Grave continued to solicit the support of Paris's intelligentsia with his *Temps Nouveaux*.

Violence soon spread from the printed word in the press to the Paris streets. Anti-semitic and ultra-nationalistic organisations were either founded or given new impetus. Men who were anti-Jewish to the point of insanity such as Jules Guérin and his League demonstrated in the streets and formed their own strong-arm groups. There were violent, threatening scenes around the Law Courts as Zola stood trial, while rival squads of supporters patrolled the streets and sometimes came to blows. Some Jewish shop windows were broken; stones were thrown at the windows of *L'Aurore*; some policemen sent to stand guard in front of Zola's house in the Rue de Bruxelles were seen to join in with the crowds who had assembled to cry *"A mort!"* The scenes in the Law Courts scandalised many foreign observers. Although severe restrictions had been placed on the admittance of the public to the courtroom, there was little attempt to preserve order outside the building. At the end of each day of the trial, Zola had to be protected from a screaming, surging mob as he came out on to the Quai des Orfèvres and he was in real danger of being thrown into the Seine when fights with fists and canes broke out around his carriage. Officers testifying against Dreyfus had to struggle through hostile pro-Zola crowds, or else were cheered and greeted with cries of "Death to the Jews! Long live the army!", and some bystanders were jostled and assaulted for refusing to remove their hats whenever a general or a staff officer passed by. The situation grew worse with each new day of the trial. Jules Guérin would appear surrounded by an escort of muscular thugs with orders to strike down anyone who would not leave the pavements free to them. Several times the police had to intervene to prevent people from being thrown in the river. Dreyfusard newspapers were burned on the quaysides and anti-Zola songs were improvised. It was an astonishing, and frightening, display of hatred and civil discord in which Zola and his friends showed great personal courage. One witness to the hatred whipped up against Zola at the time was Raphael Viau, a journalist on the *Libre Parole*, whose book, *Twenty Years of Anti-semitism* gives a striking account of the atmosphere of perpetual ferment and frenzied excitement in which the anti-semites and ultra-nationalists in Paris campaigned during two long years of pamphleteering, lobbying, meetings, processions, demonstrations, duels and street fights:

"When, at about half past seven . . . Emile Zola, condemned to a year in prison, went down the steps of the palace facing the boulevard on the arm of his friend and defender Maître Labori, it was a sight of an unforgettable, tragic grandeur.

"On these wide steps, in the midst of this swarming, screaming crowd which overflowed past the railings, this short-sighted, stumpy, greying-haired, timid-looking man looked indeed as if he was being dragged away to some ignominious execution . . . As the day darkened, he went forward slowly amid a circle of clenched fists and mouths twisted by insults. Admittedly he was struck by no one, but there was no doubt that had but one hand touched him, a hundred canes would have fallen on him at once and a hundred pairs of hands would have torn him away from the arms of his friends. I have seen men who, in ordinary life, were incapable of cowardice, call this unarmed weakling, protected by a bare dozen friends, a *coward* to his face, and be ready to spit upon him, in hatred of Dreyfus. The least excited— and I was among them—were bellowing 'Down with Zola!' 'Down with the Jews!' like dogs howling at the moon. If the journey from the staircase to the railings where his carriage was waiting had taken a few minutes longer, it would not have been certain that Emile Zola would have returned home alive that evening."

After Zola's trial and sentence to one year's imprisonment and a 3,000-franc fine, the literary, artistic and intellectual world was deeply divided. The upper middle classes in the city, the monarchists, the royalists, most of the French Academy, the official painters and the Salon juries were all against Zola and Dreyfus. Practically every writer of consequence joined in the controversy. The signatories to a collective protest in favour of a retrial of Dreyfus published in *L'Aurore* included Zola, Anatole France, Jehan Rictus, Lugné-Poë, Daniel Halévy, Pierre Quillard, Félix Fénéon and Proust. When Zola was condemned, his supporters who demanded a retrial for him included Mirbeau, France, Marcel Prévost, Gustave Kahn, Courteline, Monet, Tristan Bernard, Laurent Tailhade, the actress Réjane and Edmond Rostand; while Arthur Meyer, Pierre Louÿs, Willy, Jean Lorrain, François Coppée, Gyp, Paul Valéry and Paul Léautaud were all against Dreyfus. The younger literary sets were markedly pro-Dreyfus and their headquarters were in the Latin Quarter, in the Librairie Bellais bookshop in the Rue Cujas, while the more famous intellectuals and artists, contemptuously known to their opponents as "the syndicate" or "*les intellectuels*", met in the offices of the *Revue Blanche*. There were a number of spectacular conversions, breaks between friends and a shifting of loyalties in the world of the Paris *salons*, as habitués would leave one drawing-room for another according to their political loyalties. The young André Gide, who had founded a poetry review, *La Conque*, with his friend Pierre Louÿs, was pro-Dreyfus, while Louÿs joined the ranks of Rochefort, Gyp and Drumont. Madame Strauss's *salon* naturally became a centre for pro-Dreyfus supporters (she had even worn mourning for Dreyfus's conviction), but although she made it into a centre for propaganda on his behalf, her charm and good nature kept her the friendship of even such passionate anti-Dreyfusards as Forain, Barrès and Jules Lemaître. Madame de Caillavet's sympathies forced Maurras to leave her for ever and drew her great protégé Anatole France into the crusade, while Poincaré, the Socialist leader Jaurès and Clemenceau became frequent visitors to her *salon* and discussed their strategy together with her. Other important centres for nationalism and anti-semitism were to be found in the *salons* of Gyp and the Comtesse de Loynes, the latter being by far the more important, and it was there that the poet François Coppée became an ardent pro-army man while the gentle and politically naïve Jules Lemaître was converted into a raving nationalist almost overnight.

But even when nearly every French family group, *salon*, artistic or intellectual circle became split over the question of Dreyfus's guilt or innocence, the passions aroused by the affair transformed the controversy into a spectacular dispute about the political future of the régime as a whole. From the time of Zola's conviction, the great issue for many Frenchmen was: would the Republican régime survive or would the army take power? Anti-semitism reached a paroxysm among the right-wing extremists but, even while they continued to cry "Death to the Jews" in their noisy meetings and processions, the cry of "The army to power!" became increasingly frequent, and fears grew in Paris that some general might stage a *coup*. While a feverishly patriotic, pro-army "League of the French Fatherland" was founded in the salon of the Comtesse de Loynes, with Coppée as its honorary president and Lemaître as its nominal leader, and the young writers Charles Maurras and Léon Daudet were preparing to found the monarchist Action Française group, other extremists were resorting to more direct and violent measures. By 1899, it seemed perfectly feasible that an attempt would be made to seize power in the name of the army and it was estimated that the League of Patriots founded some years earlier by the fire-eating super-patriot Paul Déroulède now numbered some 100,000 members, while the Ligue de la Patrie Française could count on some 15,000 enthusiastic and sometimes influential adherents.

The situation in the capital became even tenser in September 1898 when serious labour troubles broke out, and a strike was started by the men employed in preparatory work for the buildings of the planned Universal Exposition of 1900 (a series of other important public work projects such as extensions to the stations and the building of Paris's first underground railway were also in progress). After the workers had realised that they were being paid rates below the minimum set by the Paris municipality, they quarrelled with their contractors and struck. The strike soon assumed a sinister aspect for pessimistic Parisians. Strikers formed bands and went all over the city to urge other workers to join them and in a short time the Paris building trade had come to a standstill. On the morning of October 8, Parisians awoke to find troops patrolling the boulevards and quaysides of the Seine and large police detachments massed at important points: an army corps had in fact been secretly mobilised in the near-by provinces and silently brought into the city at night. But even though the strike soon ended, with the employers conceding the workers' demands, general unrest and the threat of a railway strike led to more troops on duty at the stations and junctions. The presence of so great a military force at a time of acute political unrest encouraged rumours of military plots and an imminent *coup d'etat* by army officers and royalists.

To many French and foreign observers it looked as if 1899 would see the end of the Republic with the army rising against a government which seemed incapable of keeping order. As the English *Annual Register* for the year put it: "In Paris, the violent ruled in the streets and the cynics in the press."

A leading figure in the extremist camp was Paul Déroulède, now a parliamentary deputy and one of Clemenceau's bitterest enemies. After years of preaching a war against Germany and leading his vociferous Ligue des Patriotes, he was returned at the 1898 elections and became at once involved in the Dreyfus affair. Although he said that he was not himself an anti-semite, he saw pro-Dreyfusism as a huge plot against his beloved country and was resolved to exploit it to the full in his long fight against the Republic. He began another hysterical campaign on behalf of the French army and against the régime which, he said, "had allowed the most abominable anti-national campaign of all this century to be born and to grow". On September 23, 1898, he organised a public meeting in support of the flag. Speaking before an audience of several thousand Parisians, in a riding school, with thousands more on the boulevard outside, he declared that the army was under attack but that it would be their ally and, when the time came, as it surely must, it would march with the patriots as they went down into the streets to save their country. Later, Déroulède admitted that it had been his firm intention at the time to make both the army and the people of Paris march together against the government and that he had begun to prepare a *coup d'état*.

With the re-formation of Déroulède's Ligue des Patriotes, and the growing strength of Guérin's band of bullies, scuffles and beatings-up became frequent in the Paris streets. Rallies and counter-rallies were held, the police were often reluctant to intervene, and rival sides protected themselves with their own vigilantes and armed guards. Duels were fought between the leaders of the opposing factions, raids were made against each side's headquarters and meeting-places. Sometimes there was vicious violence, at other times the clashes were characterised by a certain quixotism and panache. A typical incident occurred in December 1898, when Déroulède (who with his great, long face and straggling, pointed beard looked himself like a Don Quixote—to the delight of hostile cartoonists) decided to intervene in a big pro-Dreyfus meeting being held, with speakers including Mirbeau, Sébastien Faure and a number of eminent scholars and intellectuals. Déroulède's League sent circulars to its members calling them to assemble outside the hall but stating that the intention was not to break up the meeting inside but only to "assure the liberty and safety of our patriotic orators". By the time Déroulède arrived with some five hundred of his *ligueurs*, one such patriot had entered the hall to cry "Long live the army!" and had been beaten up and expelled. After arguing with the police inspectors, in charge of a protective cordon outside the building, Déroulède was allowed to enter the hall with a friend. They then astonished the speakers and audience by crying "Long live the army!" at the tops of their voices before beating a hasty retreat to hostile cries of "Down with the Fatherland!" while the Dreyfusards reached for their canes.

Déroulède made his next important move against the Republic in February 1899 after the sudden death of the President, Félix Faure, who, so Parisians said, had died in the arms of his mistress, Madame Steinheil. Loubet, a gentle but staunch upholder of parliamentary government against the army, was called upon to succeed Faure, to the great anger of the anti-Dreyfusards and the Right. Excitement in Paris reached a new pitch. Loubet was insulted in the streets and Jules Lemaître wrote to the newspapers to say that he and his newly founded party would not accept the election. Déroulède promptly returned from the country to Paris and was widely acclaimed by a huge crowd at the Gare Saint-Lazare. Not since Boulanger's popularity had been at its height had there been such scenes of enthusiasm in the streets. Déroulède went to the Military Club in the Place de l'Opéra where crowds shouted "Down with Loubet!" and then spoke to his followers in front of Joan of Arc's statue near the Tuileries. As Loubet came back to Paris from Versailles, all the extremist organisations were mobilised in the city. Déroulède, Guérin and Coppée paraded the streets reviewing their partisans, and although several arrests were made by the police, bands of rioters openly defied the government and shouted seditious slogans. Lectures and meetings were held at Guérin's headquarters. They were attended by members of the monarchist group, "L'Œillet blanc", so called because its members wore a white carnation in their button-holes, the dandy Boni de Castellane came to speak, concerts and dances were held for the cause, the singer Eugénie Buffet sang newly composed anti-Jewish ditties and Jules Guérin recounted his violent exploits to mixed audiences of former anarchists, society ladies, royalists and anti-semitic allies from Algeria, where there had been recent disturbances.

Although there was a certain rivalry between Déroulède, Guérin, Drumont and the monarchists, they all united under the banner of anti-semitism and agreed that the time had come to stage a *coup*. After trying in vain to persuade General Pellieux to support him, Déroulède manoeuvred to get the military governor of Paris, General Zurlinden, who was daily being attacked in the Republican press, to agree to accept a post in his "shadow cabinet". Although he was now supported by a mixed crowd of Bonapartists and royalists, Déroulède made it clear that what he wanted was not a restoration of the monarchy but a new kind of authoritarian Republic based on a popular referendum.

It was openly claimed in Paris that the rising that seemed inevitable would take place on the day of President Faure's funeral. The government ministers decided as a precaution that there should be no official procession but only a religious ceremony in Notre-Dame. After loud protests by parliamentary deputies, the government then changed its mind and agreed that there would be a procession from the Elysée Palace to the cathedral, and the municipal council urged Parisians to keep calm. Loubet, who had the advantage of possessing something of the "common touch", made himself popular with many Parisians by announcing that after the service he would go on foot to the Père Lachaise cemetery. The League of Patriots were told that they would have no place in the procession and the Prefect of Police was ordered to place his men on the alert.

On the decisive day, February 23, Loubet showed that his confidence in the public had not been misplaced as the procession went to the cathedral and then to the cemetery. Meanwhile, after the Duc d'Orléans, the pretender to the throne, had come to Paris incognito, Déroulède was preparing his grandest, most quixotic gesture. He had told his *ligueurs* not to ask what he proposed to do but simply to trust him and meet him that afternoon at the Place de la Bastille. He had learned that General Zurlinden's troops would be returning from the cemetery past the Place, and believed that they could be persuaded to join his League, march to the Elysée Palace and depose Loubet. The whole affair was a fiasco from the beginning. Police informers had discovered the plan, orders to the *Ligueurs* were intercepted and even faked so that many plotters were directed to the Place de la République instead; and when the troops passed Déroulède's temporary headquarters, he saw they were headed not by Zurlinden but another general, Rôget. Déroulède rushed forward, seized the general's horse by the bridle and urged him to march on the Elysée, but Rôget rode impassively on. Then, while the main body of troops were sent back to their quarters via the outer boulevards, thus avoiding contact with the now confused and misdirected plotters, Déroulède followed Rôget and his men into their barracks at Reuilly and proceeded to harangue the officers. He refused to leave the premises, was arrested by the police and taken into custody. The next day, the Chamber of Deputies voted to lift his parliamentary immunity, but he was tried on a minor charge only, acquitted, and carried by his supporters back to his headquarters in triumph.

The extremists combined again to make a violent demonstration against the President in June, for the news that the government had decided to bring Dreyfus back for a retrial had sent them into a new fury. On June 4, as Loubet took his seat in the presidential box at Auteuil racecourse, the young Baron Christiani struck at him with a cane, fortunately only knocking his hat off. Christiani was arrested, there were more noisy demonstrations, and tensions rose again in Paris as fresh anti-government agitation increased daily. There were appeals to the army to save the nation and when General Marchand—famous for the Fashoda confrontation with the English—arrived at the Gare de Lyon, he was wildly cheered and called upon to march to the Elysée. Almost every day there was news of a riot, scuffle or demonstration somewhere in the streets of Paris. On the night of August 26 to 27, there was a serious clash between right-wing demonstrators and the police, and the Prefect realised that he was dealing with powerful, organised forces. The government took swift, decisive action against the ultra-nationalistic and royalist organisations; Déroulède was arrested again, together with other agitators.

The news that the retrial of Dreyfus at Rennes (the decision not to hold it in Paris for security reasons was obvious) had ended in another conviction was celebrated as a great triumph by the extremists. Processions of anti-Dreyfusards clashed on the boulevards with the pro-Dreyfus groups. Jules Guérin, who had given his league the masonic title of "Grand Occident—Anti-Jewish Rite", went with his thugs to set up a temporary rallying-point on the Boulevard Montmartre in front of the editorial offices of Drumont's *Libre Parole* where the Dreyfusards had threatened to demonstrate. For two evenings there were brawls, Guérin sent his men armed with lead-tipped canes among the enemy demonstrators, and the offices were crowded with his followers who drafted proclamations and harangued the crowd. But after arrests were made among members of the various leagues and the monarchists, Guérin went into hiding in his headquarters. Parisians were then treated to the curious spectacle of a non-violent siege which lasted for forty days and ended amid ridicule, with a consequent lowering of the political temperature in Paris.

The headquarters of Guérin's Grand Occident was a curiously converted house at number 45, Rue Chabrol, near the Gare de l'Est. It had been transformed into a virtual fortress, its windows were protected by sheet-iron shutters, it had its own electrical warning system and telephone communication from the attic to the cellar. The main entrance had been strengthened with an iron grille, two printing presses were installed and manned by some twenty mechanics and compositors, the main door was guarded by men recruited from the slaughter-houses at La Villette, and it was rumoured that a large stock of arms had been built up. On the third day of the "siege", the Paris press published a proclamation to the Paris Prefect in which Guérin announced that he was ready to resist and defend his fortress by armed force. The government was unmoved. On August 14, the newspapers published another manifesto under the heading "Call to the patriots", which said that a handful of resolute men were determined to make liberty respected by a "government capable of every infamy" and asked whether the people of Paris would make common cause with the patriots or let them fight alone against a government which executed the orders of "cosmopolitan Jewry". Whatever happened, promised Guérin, he and his men would fight to the death. The real siege only began on August 15 after people had been freely entering and leaving the house. At dawn, a police inspector came to the house with a warrant for Guérin's arrest and spoke to him through a window.

After Guérin refused to let him in, the warrant was pushed under the door. In the next few days, there were renewed parleys while the Minister of the Interior allowed typographers and other employees of the Grand Occident to leave the house without fear of arrest. The government announced that no force would be used and contented itself with placing a military cordon outside the entrance.

For the next two weeks, morale seemed to be high among the besieged. Guérin and his men had ample supplies of food and drink, they composed and sang patriotic songs and, at night, their neighbours could hear them playing a phonograph. Supporters would find ingenious ways of throwing food parcels through the windows from neighbouring houses and even from passing omnibuses. The Paris public was kept up to date with every detail, real or imaginary, of what was happening in the house; hot-air balloons carrying defiant messages were seen drifting out of the windows and across the roof-tops. But there was no sign that the people of Paris were in a hurry to deliver the "patriots". Instead, they amused themselves at Guérin's expense. A visit to the Rue Chabrol became a popular after-dinner excursion for many families. After a month had passed, Cook's travel agency organised special parties for curious tourists. To make matters worse for the besieged, they had become a joke in the press and were providing copy for advertisers who told newspaper readers that the beleaguered men were using Congo soap and Pouges Saint-Léger mineral waters which "quench the thirst, sharpen the appetite and develop the necessary strength with which to resist both the police and the great heat". Finally, on September 21, Guérin and his band agreed to leave the building and were promptly arrested.

With the arrest of Guérin and Déroulède, and the announcement of a presidential pardon for Dreyfus, the crisis suddenly ended. Although Dreyfus was not to be fully exonerated and reinstated in the Army until 1906, the extremists had been defeated and the Dreyfusards were now content that they had won their fight for justice. There were still fears of an army *coup*, however, and it was announced that the President would not attend the annual review of troops at Longchamps. The last great demonstration in the city that year occurred when Dalou's sculpture, the *Triumph of the Republic*, was unveiled in the Place de la Nation in the presence of Loubet, the prime minister and the municipal authorities. During a march past of various union groups and workmen, some red flags were carried in defiance of police prohibition. The President and his ministers left their stand but there was no violence. In the following year, there was a new propaganda campaign by the Right, and at the municipal elections in Paris the Nationalists won over half the seats in the council; but in the rest of the country the overwhelming majority of seats went to the Republicans and the Socialists. The army was under control, a staunchly Republican general was put in charge of the Paris division, and a new War Minister removed monarchist and anti-republican officers from the capital. For Parisians the excitement of the Dreyfus affair was succeeded by that of the Boer War, which stimulated much anti-British and pro-Boer feeling, and the great 1900 Exposition. As the century lived its last months, the streets and boulevards of Paris were no longer the scenes of demonstrations and violent clashes but were thronged with peaceful provincial visitors and foreign tourists. There would be no revolution or *coup d'état* in Paris.

Although social, artistic and intellectual life had been over-shadowed and at times dramatically affected by the Dreyfus crisis, and had become politicised to an unprecedented degree as friends, colleagues and acquaintances took up opposing positions, signed petitions, organised or joined rallies and con-tributed to fighting funds, there were still topics of conversation other than those of Dreyfus, the army and Zola. Much of Paris's everyday life continued as before. There were other subjects to be argued over and disputed—Rodin's *Balzac* statue, *avant-garde* painting, *art nouveau*, new books, and plays and such political questions as the Franco-Russian alliance which was condemned by the intellectuals of the Left and the Socialists. People still went to the theatre, enjoyed themselves in Montmartre and gave parties or made excursions with their families to the coun-tryside near Paris.

For many people, Paris had never seemed a lovelier or more

progressive city. At last, Paris was building its underground railway system, long after London, Berlin, Vienna and New York
had their metropolitan railways. The use of electric lighting and
the telephone was increasing, the first motor cars had made their
appearance and there was a craze for bicycling in the Bois de
Boulogne. Another huge international exhibition in the city's
centre was being prepared for 1900. The physical aspect of the
city was brightened not only by posters but by the new, English-
style shops known as the *boutiques anglaises* with their illuminated
window displays at night. Although the Anglo-Boer war excited
most Frenchmen's sympathies for the Boers, Anglomania reached
a new peak in Paris as far as many fashions went. As Georges
Montorgueil, the chronicler of Paris's boulevards and night life,
wrote in 1896 about such new shops as the Old England on the
Boulevard des Capucines, "people sang hosannas to the products
of the other side of the Channel, and the Parisian who never
ceases to rail at the perfidy of Albion and its trading posts will go
there straight away to have himself shod, braced, belted and
swathed". Fashionable ladies would drive in their carriages to see
the great couture shops in the Rue de la Paix, the territory of
Worth and Doucet, between four and five in the afternoon before
taking the English-inspired "five o'clock" tea, and admire the
new-style shops with their thin colonnades, wide fronts and open
display. "Like Macbeth," wrote Montorgueil, "the English shop
has killed sleep. It never sleeps. It never closes its shutters—the
eyelids of its façade. It remains awake the whole night long, only
closed by a grille in front of the door. It is a disadvantage for
thieves and a distraction for night-watchmen."

Paris had been supreme in women's fashion for decades and,
as the year 1900 drew nearer, the Parisienne became the world's
great sex-symbol. She was extolled and made legendary in books,
plays, posters and magazines. The eroticism of the *belle époque* was
at its height. Paris was the international capital of Woman.
To another chronicler of the *fin de siècle*, Octave Uzanne, the
right bank of Paris was more feminine and erotic than the
left:

"In the sense of fantasy, noise, movement, lightness, exterior-
isation of pleasure, the right bank, situated to the north, frankly

belies its topography . . . There, woman blossoms with greater elegance and gives out, to a greater degree, that perfume of Parisianity which is in her. The Right Banker exactly reflects the tone, the spirit, the *chic*, the general aspect of the region she inhabits. The most flourishing districts of gracefulness, richness and distinction spread towards the west where every day they gain ground."

As for the left bank with its Latin Quarter, its Bohemian and intellectual centres, "it presents an overall physiognomy which is infinitely colder and more peaceful. It is the province of the metropolis, a province full of charm . . . The Left Banker *Parisienne* differs essentially from the Right Banker. She is generally more reserved, more profoundly imbued with respectability; her bourgeoise allure is moderated but already outlined . . . "

Paris had also acquired a vast and ever-increasing army of working girls and secretaries as well as maids. The great department stores were full of shop girls at their counters and the profession of model had become respectable although it was mostly confined to the great couturiers' shops in the Rue de Rivoli, Rue de la Paix and the Chaussée d'Antin. The city also had a growing horde of prostitutes and working girls from the provinces who were often only too willing to dispense their favours to a "protector". The last of the great legendary *cocottes* could be seen in all their finery at Paris's newest, most modern, most daringly designed restaurant which became famous—Maxim's. The *cocottes* were still famous public figures. They provided gossip for the cafés and clubs, they could be seen riding in their carriages in the Bois de Boulogne, and they had collected a large variety of popular appellations, including those of *horizontales*, *belles-petites*, *tendresses*, *agenouillées* and *dégrafées*. Some became world-famous performers, like the temperamental Belle Otéro who toured Europe, was said to be the mistress of kings and who danced a fandango on the tables at Maxim's, now rapidly becoming Paris's headquarters for the *demi-monde*; and Liane de Pougy, who became a great friend of Jean Lorrain after having once whipped him in public for a hostile article he had written, and who then performed at the Folies-Bergère in a short scene he had written especially for her.

But, according to Uzanne, who had spent a great deal of time studying the subject, the *cocotte* had declined since her great days of the Second Empire. She had become an institution and a tourist attraction, she was more calculating, less witty, less fresh in her beauty and less spontaneous in her manner—even less interesting in her general character than the lower ranks of prostitutes. The *cocotte* became an artificial creation, a deliberately manufactured article rather than a natural phenomenon. It was hard work being one of those dazzling creatures who could drive a prince to bankruptcy or a luckless suitor to suicide, and whose presence at a première at the theatre or opera caused a sensation: "The high-flying *horizontale* of today more than ever before needs a sleeping partner [Uzanne's pun was unintentional] who will launch and furnish her with the initial starting funds so that she may be classified, catalogued at the top, and seriously tariffed. For her to be out of the ordinary, she must run to Nice in the winter, show herself on the Promenade des Anglais in great fur-belows, draw the looks and homage of men of the world who never consent to frequent any but a certain category of *demi-mondaines* well in the limelight and with some distinguished pseudonym. She must go to the tables at Monte Carlo, and, like an actress, constantly stimulate public attention by always astonishing others with her manners, hairdress, jewels, robes, hats, coats, laces etc., and it is only when honest and indignant women cry out that only such 'creatures' can display such scandalous luxury, that they will have arrived." As if all this was not enough, she must also "submit her body to all the exigencies of elegant life, conform to all the rules of snobbery, study the code of contemporary worldly laws, learn to ride, learn about sports, speak a few 'in' words and English expressions, learn the great families in the Almanach de Gotha, etc., etc."

By a cruel irony of fate, Paris's most virtuous and aristocratic family society was decimated by a terrible disaster while immorality continued to flourish at both the most elegant and the lowest levels. On May 4, 1897, a charity bazaar was being held on a vacant site in the Rue Jean-Goujon, near the Avenue Montaigne. It was an important event in the Paris social calendar and took place annually, with leading ladies of the French aristocracy and upper classes coming together to raise funds for the relief of the poor. A large wooden hall had been specially built for the occasion and was decorated with flags, bunting and painted scenery around the booths. On the afternoon of the sale, some twelve hundred people were inside the hall when a fire broke out and rapidly spread. There was only one exit—a dreadful negligence on the part of the builders—which became blocked by panic-stricken men, women and children. There were 125 victims, including the first lady of France, the Duchesse d'Alençon, and of these only five were men—a circumstance which did not escape notice by the Paris press which echoed accusations that many of the gentlemen present had behaved with abominable cowardice and used their canes to beat down women in their path as they made for the exit. The whole of high society went into mourning, and for weeks it seemed as if its only activity was that of attending funerals and memorial services.

As far as could be discovered, the cause of the fire was a device which had recently added to Paris's many entertainments—the cinematograph. A motion-picture projector had been installed in a curtained-off booth to give shows for children and the source of light was a pressurised ether lamp which seemed to have exploded when the operator tried to relight it after it had gone out. The immediate result of the catastrophe was a public prejudice for some time against motion-picture shows and the introduction of strict safety regulations. But, even despite the fire at the charity bazaar, Paris was on its way to becoming Europe's centre of the newest art—the film—and in the coming century it was for some years to rival the United States as a film-producing and -exporting country. Paris already had the honour of being the city where the first successful public film showing had taken place.

In 1895, the Lumière brothers, Auguste and Louis, owners of a photographic equipment firm in Lyons, had become interested in the idea of motion picture photography and projection which was very much in the air at the time and already the subject of experiments in the United States, England and Germany. After perfecting their own device and demonstrating it successfully in Paris at a private lecture meeting, they decided to show it to the public. The première on December 28, 1895, was a famous occasion. The basement of the Grand Café in the Boulevard des Capucines was hired, posters for the *Cinématographe Lumière* were printed and barkers were engaged to bring in the public. At first only a few customers could be persuaded to pay their one-franc admission fee in order to go down into the uninviting cellar, but they were not disappointed. The show began with a still of the Place Bellecour in Lyons and then an astonished audience saw the screen come to life as a horse pulling a cart flickered into motion, and was followed by another and yet another. They saw a street seething with carriages and pedestrians, a train pulling into a station, a wall falling down, workers leaving the Lumière factory in Lyons, and a baby girl—Auguste's daughter— eating her soup. No painting in any Salon had ever caused such a sensation. Paris already had several magic lantern entertainments. There had been the shadow shows of the Chat Noir and, in the 1880's, Emile Reynaud had made a reasonably successful attempt to project moving cartoon strips on a screen, using the principle of the optical toys popular with children at the time; but the "living photograph" was an unprecedented attraction. The first day's showing only brought in a total receipt of thirty-five francs but its success was assured as the world's first cinema audience told their sceptical friends of the miracle and Parisians began to form long queues in the street outside as they waited for seats. Profits reached more than two thousand francs a day and the Lumières were famous.

By the time of the charity bazaar fire, the *cinématographe* had been shown all over the world and several foreign firms were already in competition; but the film still had to become a creative as well as a recording medium.

It was in Paris that the film first began to become an art form due to the imaginative talent of Georges Meliès, an illusionist and director of a small theatre, the Théâtre Robert Houdin, where he gave magic shows. He had made Auguste Lumière an offer for his invention but it was politely declined and he was assured that there was no commercial future in the *cinématographe*. He then succeeded in making his own camera and in obtaining film. After taking a series of views in the manner of Lumière, he discovered the camera's ability to create illusions on the screen. Trick photography was born and Meliès began to make films in a studio he had built in the garden of his house at Montreuil near Paris early in 1897. For several years afterwards, he delighted and astounded French and foreign audiences with such novelty films as his *Disappearing Woman, Journey to the Moon* and other fanciful, fairy-tale films in which, by using a few mechanical contrivances, fantastic backdrops and papier-mâché props, he gave expression to his ideas and creative genius. He even exploited the Dreyfus affair in 1899. He read press accounts of the case and the retrial at Rennes, and then studied newspaper photographs and drawings before reconstructing the main events in his own studio. The "seventh art" had been born and Meliès's talent and popularity, followed by the commercial flair of Charles Pathé and Gaumont, made the French film industry one of the most important in the world in the first decade of the 20th century.

Cultural life in Paris during the Dreyfus affair remained rich and vital. Whistler, then an influential figure among young painters, was teaching there. Matisse, Vlaminck, Derain, Marquet and Rouault were all feeling their way in painting, taking lessons and making contacts in preparation for the time when they would astonish the art world with the Fauve movement. Sarah Bernhardt, the elder Coquelin, Jean Guitry, Réjane, Mounet-Sully, and Porto-Riche reigned over the fashionable Paris theatre; literature was as rich as ever, and in poetry the reaction against Symbolism had led to the rise of the new school, the Ecole Romane, which not only signified a return to what was held to be a French, classically-inspired, traditional culture stemming from ancient Greece and Rome rather than from Nordic and "un-French" sources, but showed the influence of nationalism and the growth of a chauvinistic spirit that influenced new cultural tastes. Writers and poets had been drawn as never before into politics by the Dreyfus affair, and it was no coincidence that some of the leading members of the Ecole Romane were vociferous nationalists who attacked French culture for being in a state of decline and excessively influenced by foreign cultural importations and theories that were destroying its basic French character. Bourget, Barrès and Léon Daudet all assumed aggressively patriotic attitudes in their writing.

As in England, after the Oscar Wilde trial, there was a public reaction against the esoteric manifestations of the *fin de siècle* trend and a return to a less intellectual, less spiritually disturbing, "healthier" and jingoistic spirit in poetry and drama. Maurras, together with Léon Daudet and others, became a violent ultra-nationalist and founded the monarchist Action Française movement in 1899. He went even further than other cultural nationalists in his denunciations of foreign culture in France. His nationalism, which became so infectious to a number of writers, had begun partly as an aesthetic theory before being inflamed by the Dreyfus affair which so many Frenchmen had seen as part of a foreign-inspired anti-French conspiracy. Maurras put himself forward as the defender of the French literary tradition by supporting the Ecole Romane, which had been founded as early as 1891. These cultural patriots, who were joined by Maurice Barrès, considered their task as that of fighting the cosmopolitan spirit of all foreign influences. Instead of Germanic romanticism, Slav soul-searching and Nordic mysticism, there would be a return to the traditional French virtues of reason, order, discipline and clarity. This nationalistic tendency in attitudes towards the arts could also be observed in the reception which in many quarters greeted exhibitions of the international *art nouveau* movement when they came to Paris.

Although *art nouveau*, the "Liberty style", or the "modern style", as it was variously called in France, left its mark on interior decoration and the applied arts and has become a fashionable subject for reappraisal in the last few years, it did not dominate French arts and crafts in the 1890's. It was not even a French creation and its popularity never spread very far beyond a small minority of art lovers, collectors and dilettanti although some *art nouveau* objects became very fashionable with elegant society.

It began as part of a revolt instigated by a number of European art schools, designers and architects against both academic art and naturalism. Their expressed aim was to create a new style owing nothing to the past, which would be in harmony with the spirit of a world being transformed by the industrial machine age, and which would provide a new environment for everyday living. It was a reaction against the most noticeable trend in French, and indeed, most European architecture, interior decorations and design: an obsession with past styles of certain historical periods in western art, and unimaginative attempts to reproduce them. *Art nouveau* came to France when a wealthy and fashionable household might, for example, have a living-room in the Louis XVI style, a pseudo-Italian Renaissance dining-room, a medieval library, and a mass of *bric à brac* and furniture ranging from pseudo-Moorish to neo-Gothic, and when architecture was the most fossilised and pseudo-historical in Europe. *Art nouveau* called for the abolition of distinctions between the fine arts and the crafts and for a revival of good craftsmanship. In the ideal *art nouveau* home, not only the outer aspect of the house but the entire interior and all its contents would harmonise in their lines and style, from the windows and façade to the door-knobs and sideboard. This implied collaboration between artists working in different media. In a way this had already occurred among the artists and poets of the *avant-garde* in Paris, where Gauguin made pottery and sculptures, Toulouse-Lautrec designed posters and book-bindings, where the sculptor Maillol and the Nabi painters designed tapestries and stage scenery, and Carlos Schwabe turned his attention to typography.

The most conspicuous and recognisable characteristic of the *art nouveau* style in France as in other countries was the use it made of long, flowing, interlacing linear patterns. It came to France at a time when the line was already triumphant, when the graphic arts in Paris had reached a very high level of accomplishment and the linear qualities of Japanese art and pictorial composition were influencing many of the new painters such as Gauguin and Toulouse-Lautrec. This use of lines in *art nouveau* had been inspired by a study of natural shapes, particularly of plants. Theories and books on the subject of "natural movements" in line and form were encouraged in a number of progressive art schools and these influenced some talented architects, particularly in the Netherlands.

The danger inherent in the style was that the use of linear patterns and decorations could degenerate into eccentricity and confusion. Its emphasis on floral and plant shapes, its convoluted, intertwining, drooping lines and arabesques in bookbindings, architecture, pottery, glassware, interior decoration and furniture were taken by hostile critics as signs of the degenerate eroticism and spiritual decadence of which they had already accused the Symbolists and Decadents. *Art nouveau* in Paris became notorious for its use of languid creeping plants and flower motifs—like the lily so beloved of the *fin de siècle* aesthetes—whose lines lent themselves so well to fantastic and exaggerated refinements and which seemed to spread like serpentine, parasitical growths over furniture, façades, vases and lamps. Its pale, pastel shades and refined tones also seemed to echo the preciosity of *fin de siècle* poetry and it could therefore be attacked as "unmanly". But although it did often lapse into facile mannerisms and imitations, it was an important attempt to give all the arts a genuinely modern style and a new unity, and to confer high aesthetic qualities on machine-made and functional objects.

The man who did more than anyone else to bring *art nouveau* to Paris and make it fashionable to a limited extent in France was the German dealer Siegfried Bing who became a central figure in the movement. He was born in Hamburg in 1838 and had worked in the ceramic industry in that city. In 1871, he came to Paris, was naturalised a French citizen, and opened a shop in which he sold objects from the Far East. In 1875, he travelled to China and Japan, and on his return to Paris he opened a second shop, specialising in Oriental art. After attracting the attention of the art world in the 1878 Exposition, Bing became Paris's most important dealer in Japanese art which was becoming increasingly popular. His customers included Edmond de Goncourt who was among the first to collect Japanese prints, and he became friendly with Van Gogh, who in turn introduced other artists, including the painters Anquetin and Emile Bernard, to Japanese art.

In 1888, after opening a branch of his shop in New York, Bing published a finely produced magazine, *Le Japon Artistique*, each issue of which contained ten beautifully printed colour plates. Only thirty-six issues were published but its influence on Paris's younger artists was considerable. In 1892, Bing was chosen by the

Ministry of Fine Arts for a mission to the United States where he was to investigate the level and achievements of American decorative and industrial art which had begun to arouse widespread interest in Europe. Bing had become particularly interested in the question of art and design in an age increasingly dominated by the machine, in techniques of mass manufacture and in the problem of reconciling art and industry in order to create a genuinely modern and original style. He returned from America greatly stimulated by what he had seen, especially the work of the New York firm of Tiffany, and he became convinced that instead of escaping the machine age by taking refuge in past styles, art must now come to terms with it. He rejected the idea that "the machine is a predestined enemy of art" and claimed that "the machine could become an important factor in the raising of public taste and . . . popularise infinitely the joy of pure forms". In order to put his ideas into practice and to achieve that union between all the arts which was being advocated in various countries, he transformed his Oriental art shop on the corner of the Rue de Provence and the Rue Chauchat into a "House of New Art" which, he said, would be a "palace of new ideas". The building was a late-18th-century house of two storeys. He commissioned a forward-looking architect, Louis Bonnier, to alter the house and design ironwork for it, and a large number of young artists to make stained glass, pottery, furniture, tapestries, sculptures and glassware. By the time it was finished and ready for the public it was the most original building in Paris. The outer walls were painted in brown with olive-green bands against a yellow ochre background, the frieze of the cornice was painted by the British artist Frank Brangwyn, there were plaster sunflowers by the front door, the inside vault of the entrance hall was made with hexagonal glass bricks, and the interior was a mass of pottery, glass, paintings, drawings, etchings, beaten metal decorative plaques, ironwork, stained-glass and electric lights. Besides having enlisted the collaboration of Ranson, Vuillard, Bonnard, Grasset, Vallotton, Lautrec, Sérusier, Ibels and Roussel—much of Paris's artistic *avant-garde* in fact—Bing stressed the international character of "modern art" by showing paintings, prints and objects by Beardsley, Brangwyn, Khnopff,

Walter Crane, Tiffany and Van de Velde. The purpose of the building, as Bing declared, was to be "an establishment opened as a meeting ground for all ardent young spirits anxious to manifest the modernness of their tendencies".

Bing's *art nouveau* collection was the most comprehensive and international ever seen in Paris. No other single exhibition of the 1890's could rival it for its cosmopolitanism and it gave many Parisians their first opportunity to study achievements in modern design and art abroad. The exhibition opened in December 1895. It was soon attacked by conservatives and nationalists and provoked outbreaks of a cultural xenophobia which, unhappily, became more frequent as the Dreyfus affair reached its climax three years later. It seemed as if most Frenchmen did not want anything new—copies of old French styles sufficed for them—and were deeply suspicious of what they believed to be an attempt to foist the styles of other countries upon them. Edmond de Goncourt's reaction in his journal to this attempt to present new international art to Parisians was typical of many critics. After his visit, the one-time friend of Bing's had written:

"What! This country which had the coquettish, well-rounded, coddling furniture of the 18th century is now menaced by this hard, angular furniture which seems made for the rough humanity of cavemen and lake-dwellers! France would then be condemned to forms that might have been crowned in a competition of ugliness." The critic of the *Figaro*, Arsène Alexandre, echoed accusations that the whole show had been a gigantic, snobbish confidence trick. The day after the opening, he wrote that "the *Tout-Paris* of those who swallow anything has been making its way to the Rue Chauchat since yesterday evening", after announcing that he would judge Bing's attempt with "a sympathy totally deprived of good-will". He had emerged from the house with his "nerves on edge" and "his head filled with nightmares" and he ended his diatribe with a racist comment that became famous: "All of this smells of the vice-loving Englishman, the Jewish morphine addict or the wily Belgian, or else of a pleasant salad of all three poisons."

But Bing was undeterred by hostile comments and aroused enough interest and support to be able to announce the following spring in an architectural review that "*Art Nouveau* calls upon all master craftsmen of furniture to send in projects exempt from all past styles. The best designs will be executed at the expense of *Art Nouveau* and exhibited in its galleries, 22 Rue de Provence." He was also anxious to save the movement he had started in Paris from any kind of disorder and confusion. Henceforth he only exhibited articles made under his personal direction with carefully chosen collaborators including Georges de Feure, who combined the talents of a painter and sculptor with those of a jeweller, furniture-maker, ceramicist and glass-designer. Other artists drawn into the *art nouveau* movement in France included Gallé, the great vase and glass-maker of Nancy, where a group of extremely talented decorators and furniture designers, of whom the most famous were Majorelle, Prouve and Vallin, also adopted the style with great success. By the end of the century, their swirling, curvilinear furniture and other craftsmen's objects which ranged from ash-trays and lamp-holders to combs and screens had become popular with dilettanti and in many fashionable households. One of the most popular craftsmen whose work was much appreciated by elegant ladies was the jeweller and vase-maker Lalique, whose reputation became world-wide. He had won a triumph in the 1895 Salon des Champs-Elysées where he had exhibited his latest jewellery including some pieces specially made for Sarah Bernhardt. Critics and Symbolists and Parisian personalities led by Jean Lorrain came to admire his work and were ecstatic in their praise of the lightness and refinement of his highly ingenious designs. Lalique's jewels were virtuoso creations in which he combined precious and semi-precious stones, pearls, ivories, enamels and metals to make fantastically intricate brooches, pendants, and diadems, exquisitely simple combs and pins, as well as jewellery imitations of dragonflies, butterflies, beetles and small reptiles which would have delighted Des Esseintes.

Art nouveau in Paris was most successful in small objects. It made its way into drawing-rooms, on to ladies' dresses as brooches, on to sideboards and tables as vases, into furniture and clocks; but there was little sign of its influence in architecture. Although it was used in the construction of a few private houses in Paris and in the decoration of some shops and cafés and notably in Maxim's restaurant in 1899, it did little to modify the outward aspect of the city until Hector Guimard created his famous entrances for the underground railway, thus giving the style a new nickname: the *style métro*.

Guimard was one of Paris's most forward-looking architects at a time when architecture was lamentably retrograde in the whole country and mainly characterised by its obsession with past French styles of the 16th and 17th centuries—as could be seen by looking at almost any public building of the period. Guimard had studied at the conventional Beaux-Arts school in Paris but had become a keen follower of Viollet-le-Duc, the great architectural theoretician and restorer of medieval monuments. He had been to Brussels to meet the architect Victor Horta whose buildings were among the most boldly modern in Europe. From Horta, Guimard had learned how to use the lines of *art nouveau* with elegance and simplicity; he was influenced by the former's axiom concerning the imitation of plant forms in nature: banish the leaf and the flower and keep only the lines of the stem. Inspired by this style, known as the "Belgian line", Guimard built one of Paris's very few *art nouveau* buildings, the Castel Béranger in Passy, for a wealthy modern-minded widow. He puzzled the public and other architects by his apparent hatred of any straight lines, by the building's lack of symmetry, his systematic use of wide curves and parabolas, and the design of the interiors.

In 1896, the newly formed Paris metropolitan railway company held a competition for designs for entrances to the underground railway. The *métro* had been planned more than ten years previously and it had always been agreed by the city's officials that any underground transport system which Paris might have should be as decorative as possible, and in aesthetic harmony with the city's streets. There were some twenty competitors. A mediocre designer called Durruy was awarded the first prize for his designs of glass-paned shelters for the entrances, but the president of the company's board overruled the decision, and chose Guimard, whose *art nouveau* designs he greatly admired. Guimard decided to use cast-iron which was cheaper than forged ironwork and far more suitable for his plant-like forms. In a short time, strange green stalks began to sprout out of the Paris pavements, blossoming into flower-forms, bearing lamps in their "mouths" and joined over the entrance by enamelled plaques with the inscription *Métropolitain* in lettering designed by Guimard himself. These bone- or plant-like structures and Guimard's high-glass roofs to cover the entrances were a sensation. People compared them to dragonflies spreading their wings, or to carnivorous, exotic flowers. Even the colour was a subject of controversy for the ultra-patriotic objected to green as being a German shade while the aesthetes, who were delighted by the way Guimard had decorated the yawning entrances to Paris's new underworld, loved it. The elongated, tormented aspect of Guimard's lettering had also worried the upholders of official taste and the critic of *Le Temps* declared that, for "the honour of the French taste" and to avoid "stupefying foreign visitors any longer", the "ridiculous inscriptions must go". Once again, one of the most usual reproaches made against *art nouveau* was that it was "un-French".

The Czech artist Alphonse Mucha, whose posters became so popular in France, was certainly un-French, but his own style, which has frequently if not always correctly been linked with that of *art nouveau*, achieved fame in Paris from the time he became associated with the country's most adulated woman idol, Sarah Bernhardt.

By the 1890's Bernhardt was at the peak of her fame and acclaimed the world's most famous actress. Her scandals, eccentricities, jealousies and tastes were talked about all over Paris. The great, the rich and the famous all vied to pay her homage, and she practically had her own accredited playwright, Victorien Sardou, who had dominated the theatrical scene for years with his well-made, highly coloured melodramas providing vehicles for her impassioned style of acting. Whether she was playing Cleopatra, the fiery Tosca, the Byzantine Theodora and Gismonda, or the Russian Fedora, Bernhardt was always Bernhardt, the supreme incarnation of the ideal woman of the time. She became almost an institution. The fact that many of the plays written for her were false, artificial, bombastic and dramatically crude did not matter to her adoring audiences although some critics, both in France and abroad, echoed Jules Lemaître's own opinion of her when he wrote: "By dint of expressing violent sentiments and of playing, in Sardou's sanguinary dramas, scenes in which people scream, roll on the ground, are tortured, kill, kill themselves or are killed, Sarah Bernhardt has lost the faculty of understanding and expressing the normal sentiments of everyday life."

In 1893, Bernhardt bought the Théâtre de la Renaissance, near the Porte Saint-Martin and made her début there with a play by Jules Lemaître, *Les Rois*. Her association with Mucha was the result of her manager's urgent need for a poster to advertise another Sardou play, *Gismonda*, in December 1894. So far, no poster artist had ever done justice to Bernhardt, although Grasset had won fame for his *Jeanne d'Arc* design. Alphonse Mucha was working for the printing firm of Lemercier at the time, having made a precarious living in Paris for several years by drawing illustrations for books, papers and magazines. After his employer had been telephoned by the manager of the theatre, Mucha was suddenly asked if he would try his hand at a poster, and he agreed. He began by making a few studies of Bernhardt in the theatre, set to work and produced a design ready for the hoardings on New Year's eve. The poster delighted Bernhardt and came as a great surprise to the public for it was quite unlike all other previous theatrical posters. Mucha's design, which he repeated later, was a long, vertical composition in which he combined traditional Slav decorative devices with a *fin de siècle* Byzantine sumptuousness and the floral patterns that became so much a part of *art nouveau* decoration. Bernhardt had already been idolised by the written word, the painting and the photograph: now Mucha idealised her in the poster. By choosing a vertical composition, he suggested that Bernhardt was taller than in real life. He portrayed her in a majestic standing pose, clothed in a heavy, sumptuously jewelled and embroidered robe with heavy folds, her idealised face crowned with leaves and set against a Byzantine-style mosaic pattern with the letters of her name making a halo for her head against a mass of soft blues and golds. It was a rich and luxuriant piece of work full of detail, avoiding the harsh reds and swirling lines which characterised other posters like those of Chéret. Employing shades of green, violet, pink and gold, it had a refinement and exoticism which expressed the striking personality of the actress and the gaudy splendour of her melodramatic vehicles. The "mosaic on a wall", as it was called, became a collector's piece almost at once and led to Mucha signing a six-year contract to design other posters for Bernhardt. Every year, new posters, nearly all similar in composition and style, followed and made the image of the actress inseparable from that of her posters. Whether he was portraying Bernhardt as Medea, Lorenzaccio, the Woman of Samara, Hamlet or the Lady of the Camellias, Mucha always presented her as a majestic or meltingly seductive ideal woman, and there can be little doubt that Bernhardt's already considerable ego was flattered still further by the way in which Mucha depicted her (it is interesting to compare a contemporary photograph of Bernhardt with the posters). Mucha's success soon brought him many other commissions and he became one of the most sought-after designers in Paris, producing posters for various firms, calendars, stained-glass designs, book illustrations and decorative panels. The review *La Plume* held an exhibition of his work and published a special number devoted to him in 1897, he was made a Chevalier of the Legion of Honour in the same year, conceived designs for jewellery and even for the interior of Fouquet's fashionable jewellery shop in 1901. He became friends with Sardou, Scribe, Rodin, Maeterlinck, Rostand and many leading actors and actresses. In 1903 he moved for some time from Paris to the United States before returning home to his first love— painting scenes from the history of his own country.

Mucha was not essentially an *art nouveau* artist. According to his son Jiri, when asked how much he owed to the movement he merely said, "I did it my own way". He also admitted his debt to Japanese art which he had studied very closely and to Eugène Grasset's bold, stained-glass-style outlines, and he combined what he learned from them with his own brand of Slavic-neo-Byzantine art. For several years, while the fashion for *art nouveau* objects was at its height, Mucha had a considerable influence on taste in Paris. His head of Bernhardt in the poster for *La Princesse*

Lointaine, with its wreath of lilies, became a kind of trade mark for the actress and was repeated with variations in many ornaments and pieces of jewellery. His female figures had a rather un-Parisian, Slav solidity and his posters lacked one of the first essentials of *art nouveau* design: a sense of movement. Instead, with their flower patterns, their luxuriant detail, heavy sumptuousness, and delicate choice of colours, they represented the taste of the *fin de siècle* aesthetes.

Where Mucha's work did have marked affinities with *art nouveau* was in his erotic stress of womanly curves, the flowing vertical linearism of his posters, and in his treatment of women's hair. He shared what seemed to be a virtual hair fetish with other artists of the decade, such as Toorop. The way in which they elongated the tresses of their female figures and made them into long, wandering tendrils and arabesques which coiled across the composition became a pictorial cliché. The style was exaggerated by less talented artists so frequently that it helped to create a widespread impression that it was mainly an affectation, disparagingly known as the "vermicelli" or "noodle" style.

The erotic suggestion of *art nouveau* was strong. Its swirling lines and drooping curves echoed those of elegant ladies and their costumes, but such feminine, provocative contours were not the monopoly of the style. There was a general mania for curves, well-rounded shapes and S-shaped feminine silhouettes. The woman sex-symbol of the time was usually represented in a sensuous, spiral pose when standing. Her bust and face would be tilted up slightly in one direction while the folds and hem of her dress would fall and flow gracefully in the other direction like a wave unfurling around her legs and feet. When she moved, she would do so with an undulating elegance and each movement would be stressed by the sway of her dress. The two most famous, living examples of this ideal woman whose physical charms were so heightened by this serpentine sinuous quality that other *Parisiennes* tried hard to adopt were Sarah Bernhardt and Loie Fuller.

Loie Fuller was an American who had abandoned life as an actress and entertainer in the United States to take up a career in Paris as a dancer. She had invented her own, extremely original style of dancing in which her graceful, whirling movements were enhanced by the soft, floating fabrics of her costumes and a constant change of coloured lighting effects. It was an ethereal sylph-like, poetical form of dancing, in which she seemed to become a flower or a flame as she pirouetted and spun amid a mass of changing lights and a flare of gauzy veils. She had had a sensational success first in New York and then repeated it at the Folies Bergère in 1892. She was the perfect example of the flower- or lily-woman so beloved by the Symbolists and Decadents and she was a constant source of inspiration for the feminine representations of *fin de siècle* artists and designers. Loie Fuller's dancing was a theme that was repeated countless times in statuettes, posters, prints, jewellery, bronzes, lamp-holders and ash-trays. The rippling forms of the 1890's woman were to be seen reflected everywhere, not only in *art nouveau* but in traditional architecture with its flourishes and scrolls, in the neo-baroque buildings and the Alexandre III bridge built for the 1900 Exposition, in furniture and interiors. As one French writer on the period—Louis Chéronnet—has remarked, to enter a 1900-period apartment was to be received by a woman no matter what the general period style might have been. Feminine influence was predominant in decorations. The line was feminine and expressed the legendary elegance of the *Parisienne*. In this society portraits of Parisian ladies, Boldini evolved his own nervous, shimmering linear style, the famous "whiplash" which not only expressed the vivacity and attraction of his sitters but could flatter them when their physical charms were not all that could be desired. By inventing a linear, springy, sinuous pose and by making the sitter subordinate to it, Boldini could endow every woman with what were held to be the main aesthetic attributes of the Parisian female.

If Edmond de Goncourt and other like-minded critics had not been so prejudiced, they would have seen that, besides being a brave attempt at a genuinely modern style, *art nouveau* at its best had quite as much curvaceous charm and elegance as that of the much-beloved French 18th-century furniture and architecture of the Rococo period, and could be quite as feminine. It was also to be noted that one of Paris's most famous and elegant restaurants, which became a favourite rendezvous of the elegant *demi-monde*, was Maxim's where the décor was completely *art nouveau* in spirit and style.

It was when the curvilinear style no longer seemed to reflect the alluring lines of pretty women but to degenerate into gratuitous arabesques and tormented writhings, that it became attacked as something perverse and alien to the French sense of measure and gracefulness. Inferior imitators and over-emphasis of its linear characteristics brought it into disrepute in Paris, and the fact that the movement was known to have originated abroad only encouraged its detractors.

With the coming of *art nouveau*, the ultra-nationalists and conservatives, whose chauvinism had been stimulated to so great a degree during the Dreyfus affair, had yet another pretext for showing their irritation and exasperated resentment against the foreign and the modern. But even while the art movement was reaching its climax in Paris, the theatre and, more particularly, a playwright who had become closely associated with Bernhardt, provoked a fresh outburst of jingoism and seemed to herald a return to a "healthy" French drama after the soulfulness and mysticism of Symbolist and Scandinavian theatre. The disturbances that broke out at the Théâtre de l'Oeuvre, the Mecca of the "Nordic-maniacs" in Paris, and the fact that many anarchist sympathisers supported it exacerbated nationalistic reactions among the theatre-going public. Jules Lemaître was only one of many hostile critics who complained that the foreign playwrights were alien to French taste and that what little originality they might have could only come from French sources of inspiration. Charles Maurras had gone even further by declaring that writers like Ibsen and Strindberg were "barbarians" who were corrupting French souls. What the nationalists wanted to see was a return of the "French spirit" to serious drama and to all the arts generally. Sardou might be a more popular dramatist than any foreigner whose work had been imported from abroad but despite his tremendous success there was nothing particularly French in his melodramas about Italian opera singers and Byzantine princesses. The man who was to bring "Frenchness" into the serious theatre was a far younger playwright, Edmond Rostand, who, like Mucha, knew how to please.

Rostand became one of the most successful playwrights in France at an early age. He had begun play-writing in his early twenties and in 1891 he had a one-act play refused by the Comédie Française although the jury had made some encouraging comments about it. Three years later, Rostand had a full-length play accepted and performed. It was called *Les Romanesques* and was a charming, delicate piece of romantic fantasy about two young lovers and their tribulations. It also had a certain 18th-century note of elegance and restrained passion. It was very well received by the public and the critics and won a prize from the Comédie Française. Encouraged by this sudden success, Rostand then wrote a mystical verse play after the manner of the Symbolists, *La Princesse Lointaine*, about the frustrated love of a medieval princess and a troubadour. Rostand took the play to Sarah Bernhardt who declared that she thought it superb and would put it on the stage with herself in the leading role even if it did not make a penny. The play had a lukewarm reception and only ran for thirty performances, losing Sarah Bernhardt some 200,000 francs. But she still had faith in Rostand and in 1896 he wrote another play for her, based on the biblical story of the Woman of Samara, *La Samaritaine*. There was a vogue for biblical dramas at the time and the play was a success at the Théâtre de la Renaissance.

Rostand then turned his attention to French history and decided to write a play about the little-known but strange poet-swordsman-writer Cyrano de Bergerac whose face was disfigured by an abnormally large nose. After studying the historical character, Rostand decided to make him into a great-hearted but unsuccessful lover and endow him with all the qualities of wit, exuberance, ebullient heroism and love of fine words which were considered to be typically French characteristics. He showed the play to France's greatest actor, Coquelin, who liked it and agreed to stage it at the Théâtre Porte Saint-Martin. It was a romantic verse drama in the great tradition of the early 19th-century Romantic school and Dumas's swashbuckling novels. Nothing could have been further in spirit from Sardou's mechanical melodramas, the naturalism of the Théâtre Libre or the pensive poetry of the Symbolists.

Shortly after *Cyrano* was accepted, Rostand began to have misgivings. It was not the kind of play that had a built-in appeal for any coterie—be it a fashionable society audience or the bourgeois middlebrows who loved the farces and light comedies of Feydeau and Courteline—and he was still little known. All that the public knew about the play was that it was an historical drama about a strange poet in the reign of Louis XIII and that their great Coquelin had agreed to play in the leading role. This last factor was a great advantage for Rostand but unfortunately his play had to compete with two others in the same week. At the Odéon, another great actor, Porto-Riche, was appearing in a new play and, to make matters even worse, Rostand's friend Sarah Bernhardt was playing in the near-by Renaissance theatre in a new play by Octave Mirbeau, *Les Mauvais Bergers*, which had its première on the same night. In view of such competition, even Coquelin had fears for the success of the play.

Cyrano made theatrical history on December 27, 1897. It hit exactly the right note with the audience and it came at the right time. The Dreyfus affair was about to explode and was already dividing the nation and raising doubts about the loyalty of many Frenchmen to their country; the activities of the *avant-garde* had disconcerted many critics and theatre-goers and the charity bazaar fire was still casting a gloom over high society. Rostand's play had heroism, self-sacrifice, poetry, noble gestures, duels, tremendous histrionics and pathos. At first the audience were cool but after Cyrano's long "nose" speech, which Rostand had thought of deleting, they began to clap; the duel scene made them enthusiastic; the love scene when Cyrano speaks for his rival under the heroine's balcony had them in raptures; and after Coquelin had spoken his last line in the death scene, there was an explosion of joy and wild applause in the theatre. There were forty curtain calls, the audience refused to leave for nearly an hour, Rostand and Coquelin were deliriously acclaimed. Crowds gathered on the pavement outside the theatre while Sarah Bernhardt came dashing from her own theatre to congratulate Rostand and tell him that she had been so anxious for his play's success that she had "galloped" through her own performance. The newspapers were almost unanimous in their enthusiasm.

The conservative critics led by Sarcey could not find anything but praise for *Cyrano* and hailed Rostand for having revived all the old glory of the French stage. Sarcey's comments were typical: "It is a work of charming poetry but, above all, it is a work of the theatre. Everything is there on the stage, we have found a dramatic author, a man who has the gift . . . What happiness! What happiness! At last then we are to be rid of the Scandinavian mists, of over-detailed psychological studies and the deliberate brutalities of the realistic drama. Here is the joyous sun of old Gaul rising again above the horizon after a long night." Rostand's sun was rising fast as well. On New Year's Day 1898, he was made a Chevalier of the Legion of Honour and, five days later, President Faure and his family came to the theatre to bestow official consecration on the play. Rostand had become a patriot of the French theatre.

The end of the century in France also saw a rise of Napoleonic nostalgia. The Emperor became hugely popular again with a vast public and inspired many books and historical studies. Rostand combined again with Sarah Bernhardt to give Parisians another patriotic treat on the stage. He had been interested in the story of Napoleon's son, the young king of Rome who had died an exile in Austria at the age of twenty. The part appealed greatly to Bernhardt who had already played men's parts as Hamlet and as Musset's Lorenzaccio. A play on the same subject called *Le Roi de Rome* had been made out of a novel and given in Paris in January 1899 but it was an inferior work and Bernhardt had refused the lead in it. Instead it was agreed that she would star in Rostand's play which would have the more resounding title of *L'Aiglon*, the "young eagle". Such a subject could hardly fail to arouse the enthusiasm of Bonapartists and ultra-nationalists who longed for a return to the glorious days of the Empire instead of the prosaic Republic. Although both Rostand and Bernhardt had been on Dreyfus's side during the "affair", friends begged Rostand not to allow himself to be used by the right wing who were ready to forget his political sympathies and present him as one of their propagandists. Rostand inserted a little verse in the printed edition of the play to say it was only the "story of a poor child" and not one of a cause to be defended or attacked, thus disclaiming any political motive for writing it. When it was performed on March 15, 1900, at the Sarah Bernhardt theatre before a brilliant audience, it had an overwhelmingly enthusiastic reception and coincided with a new feeling of intense nationalist pride aroused by the Universal Exposition that was soon to open. Like the great exhibition, *L'Aiglon* was seen as something which could restore patriotic Frenchmen's faith in themselves and their country and remind them of past accomplishments after the years of doubts, quarrels and anxieties.

VIII

1900

THE GREAT Universal Exposition of 1900 came as a happy
ending to the troubled 1890's decade in France. It was the
last of a series of Paris world fairs and exhibitions which
were held at eleven-year intervals since 1867 and it was intended
as a gigantic, international celebration of the whole century's
achievements and progress in every branch of the arts and
sciences. It was supposed to promote sales and trade, improve
public taste and, while making much of the need for world peace
and goodwill among nations, to improve France's prestige in the
world by impressing people with evidence of French intellectual,
industrial, scientific and artistic activity and successes. It was also
seen by its organisers as something which would raise national
morale and, after the Dreyfus affair, as something which would
help to restore the country's unity, and appeal equally to the
nationalists and the progressive radicals of the Left. It was also a
gigantic distraction for the country and it brought the atmosphere and gaiety of a carnival and fun-fair to Paris after recent
strife and bitterness.

The proposal to hold another exhibition in the capital was
first made only two years after that of 1889 and had been greatly
inspired by its success. Added support for the idea came from
Frenchmen who had become alarmed by the growing industrial
and military might of Germany. The jealousy and anger of the
nationalists was provoked when it was widely rumoured that
Germany was about to prepare a world's fair in Berlin in 1896
or 1897. There were fears that the enemy across the Rhine would
try to show that the main event of the century had been the rise
of Germany. The *Figaro* and a powerful lobby of interested industrialists and businessmen urged the government to prepare
a 1900 exhibition which would outshine all others that had been
held anywhere in the world.

On July 13, 1892, the government published a decree announcing that a new universal exhibition would be held on an unprecedentedly magnificent scale from April to October 1900. A commission was appointed to study the problems of organising the project and, in 1896, the necessary legislation required for it was passed in the Chamber of Deputies after the hostility and reservations of some members had been overcome with appeals to their patriotism. The Nationalist deputy Ernest Roche seems to have echoed the general feeling in the Chamber with his sonorous declaration that "France owes it to herself as the Queen of Civilisation to hold a great exhibition which will become one of her many claims to glory". A propaganda campaign to make the project acceptable to all Frenchmen was started by enthusiasts. In the words of its official sponsor, the planned Exposition would be the highest expression of "the philosophy and sympathies of the century". It would combine the qualities of "grandeur, grace and beauty" and, although it was stressed that it would display the fruits of collaboration between all civilised countries, one of its essential aims would also be to "reflect the refulgent genius of France and show that, as in the past, we now stand in the vanguard of progress".

The government granted a huge sum of money to transform these noble dreams into reality, a similar amount was voted by the Paris municipality and three times as much again was raised by issuing ticket vouchers to the public who were also offered reduced rail fares to and from Paris and passes giving them reduced admission rates to the various side-shows which were planned. A preparatory commission of fifty members headed by an engineer named Picard started to plan the exhibition, invitations were sent to other countries and work began. But the project still had many hostile critics.

Apart from the proposed transformation of a large part of Paris, the speculation encouraged by the allotment of ground for side-shows, booths, cafés and restaurants aroused resentments. Many objections were puritanical and moral. Maurice Barrès declared that the Exposition would weaken French moral fibre and lure the virtuous and hard-working youth of the countryside to Paris with disastrous results. Paris would be spoiled by too many foreigners, by an increase in vulgarity and prostitution and by the large-scale destruction of old landmarks, trees and buildings. Octave Mirbeau also attacked the project in a series of witty articles and accused the bourgeois of exploiting the whole idea of a world exhibition to line their own pockets. The conservative critics, who had already become suspicious when they learned that a leading sponsor of the exhibition was Millerand, the Socialist Minister of Commerce, also found all kinds of moral objections. As they remembered the more garish attractions of the 1889 Exposition, they asked for what moral purpose was this new sham city to be built in the heart of Paris? Their answer was: "So that Paris might become even more than before the city of cosmopolitan pleasure, the rendezvous of revellers and the world capital of a kind of perpetual belly-dance."

After various sites had been considered and rejected in turn, the preparatory commission decided that the exhibition would be kept to the centre of the city like its predecessors, although there would be an annex in the Bois de Vincennes for agricultural displays and sporting events. The site would be more or less the same as that of the 1889 Exposition although larger: it would cover the Champ de Mars, the Trocadéro and its hill, the Esplanade des Invalides, the Cours de la Reine, and the banks of the Seine between the Pont de l'Alma and the Place de la Concorde. Further space would be obtained in the Champs-Elysées and several small and narrow streets near the river would be pulled down. As far as architecture was concerned, the designs of buildings and decorative features would be left in the hands of the conservative architects of the School of Fine Arts, so that the exterior aspect of the whole exhibition would be dominated by the styles of the academies. Another proposal was for the building of a reconstruction of old medieval Paris, and it was agreed that part of the left bank of the Seine would be transformed into a "Quayside of the Nations" in which the main exhibiting nations would be able to put up their palaces and pavilions in their own national styles.

The plans aroused several new controversies. One of the most ambitious projects was the piercing of a new boulevard which would open a vista for pedestrians from the Champs–Elysées across the river to the Hôtel des Invalides. Two new permanent buildings would be set up as palaces of art and would flank this new thoroughfare. There would also be a new bridge, named like the boulevard, after the Russian Tsar Alexandre III, as another sign of Franco-Russian friendship. The plans made necessary several important demolitions including the ugly Palace of Industry which had often been reviled since its erection in 1855 and which now suddenly seemed to have become a familiar and much-loved feature of the Paris landscape. There was fresh criticism that Paris would lose many trees and green spaces although Picard had declared that the number of new trees to be planted would more than make up for those lost. One parliamentary deputy suggested that as the Eiffel Tower had been the most conspicuous feature of the 1889 Exposition, the main feature of the 1900 exhibition should be Paris without the tower.

About half the space on the site was reserved for French displays, the rest being divided among the other exhibiting countries, and soon new quarrels broke out. None of the foreign nations received the amount of space they had requested. The planned Quayside of the Nations as an international anthology of architectural styles aroused angry disputes, with America, Great Britain and Germany all unhappy about the space they had been allocated, by the Seine. Despite everything, work progressed. An army of builders, decorators and labourers began to set up a new city on both sides of the Seine in the heart of Paris, the Eiffel Tower was given a new coat of paint, crowds of sightseers came to watch the work, distinguished foreign visitors were escorted around the site and posed for photographs, and French publishers brought out series of lavishly illustrated and bound volumes devoted to the exhibition, its preparation and many of the more fanciful architectural and engineering projects that had been commissioned or rejected. There was another argument over the use to which the larger of the two new permanent buildings, the Grand Palais, should be put and it was eventually decided that it would house a collection of French art since 1800.

Another public controversy centred on the design of the gigantic main entrance gate to the exhibition area; called the

Porte de la Concorde. Its design was by the architect René Binet and it was supposed to be "modern", but there was very little in its exaggerated curves and decorative exuberance to suggest any advance over the styles of the Second Empire. Its most disputed feature was the statue of a tight-skirted and attractive young woman, elegantly coiffured in the latest manner, which would be perched on top of a gold sphere on the cupola which crowned the gate. This highly coloured, provocative female figure was officially called "The City of Paris". It was soon known as *La Parisienne* to the public, and critics complained in the newspapers that it was far too sensual and frivolous for an exhibition which was supposed to be serious-minded and idealistic. However, the *Parisienne* remained above the gate and work was already far advanced when the whole question of foreign participation was threatened by the Dreyfus affair.

A successful great international fair or exhibition in Paris would certainly help to restore French prestige abroad which had been suffering for some years from scandals, like that of the Panama affair, several humiliating diplomatic defeats and setbacks, and internal political instability. The Dreyfus affair had a very damaging effect on France's image abroad during preparations for the Exposition. The *Figaro* pointed out that many foreigners were afraid to travel to France as they feared an imminent civil war, and that there was a slump in the number of tourists who came to stay in the Paris hotels and to shop in the great department stores and fashion houses. There was enormous sympathy for Dreyfus abroad. The verdict after the second trial at Rennes in 1899 had incensed public opinion in many countries. A feeling of outrage was expressed by many leading newspapers in Europe and the United States; there were huge public protest meetings, Jewish businessmen and art patrons announced that they would have nothing to do with France or her exhibition, and calls were made for a general, international boycott of the Exposition until France had ceased to "murder Justice". The only French newspaper which seemed unperturbed by the prospect of France's isolation was the *Libre Parole* which remarked joyfully that at last there would be a purely French exhibition! But once President Loubet announced a pardon for

Dreyfus—as much for reasons of political expediency as for any other—the foreign officials and commissioners concerned with the exhibition were able to reassure their worried French counterparts that the countries they represented would take part as agreed some years previously.

Another great question that remained to be answered was: would the Exposition be ready on time for its announced opening? Many of the larger structures were still incomplete by January 1900 although the Alexandre III bridge had been finished in July 1899. The extreme muddiness of the site was making progress difficult. Months before the scheduled inauguration ceremony, French and foreign dignitaries had been arriving in Paris to supervise the preparation of the foreign pavilions and the installation of exhibits; the hotels were filling up, and a seemingly endless round of official and privately sponsored receptions and banquets had begun.

The day of the opening ceremony was April 14, 1900. Paris was in a relaxed mood and the weather was warm and sunny as President Loubet set out from the Elysée Palace in his state carriage, to drive with his escort, members of the Cabinet, high military officials, and soldiers from crack regiments to the huge Salle des Fêtes where the ceremony was being held. As the procession came near its destination, a small group of ultra-Nationalists who had gathered at one end of the Alexandre III bridge tried to demonstrate by shouting "Long live the Army!" and making a sudden dash towards the exhibition entrance; but the crowds merely laughed and continued to cry "Vive Loubet!", "Vive Picard!" and "Vive la République!"

At the ceremonial hall, Picard and the Minister for Commerce, Millerand, greeted the President and made speeches which were as distinguished by their progressive, republican sentiments as they were by the wealth of florid rhetoric which such occasions usually inspired. Millerand became even more lyrical than Loubet as he ended his oration with a fervid invocation to: "Industry! Liberating and sacred Industry! Thou, the consoler, under whose steps ignorance is banished and evil routed! By thee is Mankind freed from the servitude of night as it rises, rises ceaselessly, towards that serene and luminous region where the ideal and perfect harmony between power, justice and kindliness wait to be achieved . . . "

For some foreign observers like the correspondent of the London *Times*, who had called the ceremony "a festival of glorified and victorious democracy", such effusions were "somewhat laboriously lyrical" and a "premeditated celebration of materialism". He went on to warn his readers that "an omission which might be noted was that this official ceremony . . . seemed to have left no door open to the idea of religion, and one asked oneself what was the supreme power the thought of whom hovered over this national fête".

Not only God was absent from the ceremony. It was boycotted by some right-wing deputies who had been torn between their desire to attend the official consecration of French genius, and their fears lest their presence be interpreted as approval of the triumph of the Republic which they had tried so hard to overthrow in the recent past. As was expected, the Church was absent and because of the tension between the two countries and French sympathies for the Boers in the South African War, the British delegation was composed of only minor officials. The President of the Royal Commission appointed to administer the British section had been the Prince of Wales, but an outbreak of anglophobic propaganda in France had made it unthinkable that any member of the Royal Family should attend the event. The Paris press had not only been attacking British policies abroad with great violence, but so many insulting and even semi-obscene caricatures of Queen Victoria and her ministers had been displayed for sale in shops and newspapers kiosks that the British Ambassador had been temporarily recalled from the capital a short time before the opening day of the Exposition.

Although there had been some fears of attempts to disrupt it, the ceremony passed without incident, and Loubet then left with his party to tour the still incomplete site on the Champ de Mars and then to sail in an official barge past the Quayside of the Nations to the Alexandre III bridge where more speeches were made, before leaving the workmen to finish their preparations for the next day's opening to the public. The exhibition promised to be an enormous success and officials were confident that no less than sixty million people would come from all parts of the world to see it. The British visitors might be comparatively fewer in numbers compared with those of other countries but any loss of English support for the Exposition would be more than compensated for by the influx of Americans. The only people who seemed to be leaving Paris as the opening day drew near were some of the more conservative upper-class and aristocratic families who showed their disapproval of such a popular event by disappearing into the countryside for a while, leaving their city to the lower classes, the provincials and the foreigners.

The 1900 Paris Exposition was not only one of the biggest and most ambitious of its kind ever to have been held anywhere in the world. It was also an extraordinarily heteroclite affair in which the cheapest and gaudiest attractions of a country fairground were mingled with the most lavish and costly pavilions exhibiting the most recent scientific and industrial marvels, all amid a mass of some of the most strikingly out-of-date, showy architecture and decoration ever displayed on such a scale in the city. It was a gigantic hodge-podge of an exhibition and although its planning had taken years, the general impression it gave was one of a bewildering variety of architectural styles, contents, side-shows, cafés, official pavilions, fairground booths and halls for lectures and congresses.

As visitors made their way through the main entrance gate on the right bank underneath Binet's notorious *Parisienne*, the first great sight that greeted them was that of the two "palaces" on either side of the Avenue Alexandre III, both built in the most exuberant neo-baroque late 19th-century style. The larger of the two, the Grand Palais, offered what had been chosen as the best modern painting and sculpture from the exhibiting nations although, in this case as in the other sections, half the space had been kept by the French. They could admire its enormous portico decorated with opulent statues, the soaring horses and chariots on the corners of the roof representing "Harmony routing Discord" and "Immortality vanquishing Time", the great entrance on the Champs-Elysées side decorated with bas-reliefs illustrating such themes as "the Arts and Sciences rendering homage to the new century", and a lavishly decorated interior with a sinuous staircase of wrought-iron arabesques in a kind of *art-nouveau*-cum-Louis-XV-style twisting up towards a landing suppoted by porphyry columns adorned with metal creepers and steel scrollwork. The Petit Palais had a splendid iron doorway and a tympanum over the portico featuring the allegorical figure of Paris surrounded by the Muses, the Seine, the Ocean and the Mediterranean, a florid cupola painted in the interior with frescoes by Albert Besnard, a master of the rhetorical-academic school of the Salons, and inside, a well-laid-out retrospective display of French art of the century which later became one of the most popular features of the whole Exposition. The view, between the two buildings, of the façade and dome of the Invalides across the river, which Picard had proudly considered to be one of the most brilliant features of the exhibition's lay-out, was greatly admired as a permanent addition to Paris's beauty although the temporary, lavishly decorated buildings that lined each side of the Esplanade des Invalides and contained decorative and applied art exhibitions somewhat crowded the landscape.

The Palace of the Trocadéro, built for the 1878 Exposition, and the gardens on the hill that sloped down between it and the Seine, contained the colonial pavilion which illustrated the spread of Western civilisation and science in primitive countries, with more than half the space again being devoted to French achievements. The section was a strange medley of pavilions, huts and palaces with Moorish minarets rising above African huts, Polynesian cabins, a reconstructed Algerian Casbah, Indo-Chinese temples and pagodas, a model of the recently restored temple at Angkor Wat, all enlivened by Oriental and African musicians and dancers who competed for the visitors' attention. The most serious and industrial exhibits were to be seen by crossing the Pont d'Iéna to the Champ de Mars where great glass and iron halls exhibited achievements and inventions in engineering, mining, chemistry, textiles, armaments, machine tools and transport. The exhibition was the first in Paris to show automobiles and bicycles as well as demonstrations of X-rays, wireless telegraphy and motion picture devices, and it was there that

Frenchmen could see—sometimes with anxiety—the tremendous technological progress made by Germany, the United States and Great Britain.

Although one of the main aims of the Exposition was declared to be that of exalting the triumph of material progress as the great unifier of civilised nations, another less openly declared intention of the organisers was to show France's supposed superiority in technical achievements. As the lion's share of the space was again retained by the French, they were able to overwhelm rival entries with the sheer size and quantity of their products. As the introduction of the official catalogue stated: "Never before has our country better displayed the fecundity of its resources, the power and greatness of its servants, workers, craftsmen and artists as they all unite to accomplish the same great task". But even if many French visitors took for granted their country's lead in science and industry, other more thoughtful spectators were noticing the superior and more modern designs of some American and German exhibits. Some observers remarked on the high quality of Germany's products and the superior design of her pavilion in comparison to the stodgy and often unimaginative English stands, but they also had to concede that Germany was also often ahead of France in the style of her displays. Foreigners were able to point out that it had been France and not her former foe across the Rhine who had staged the larger display of modern armaments, and it was also noticed that the Japanese were ahead of the Russians—France's great ally—in many designs and innovations.

The final great official feature of the Exposition was the Street or Quayside of the Nations on the left bank of the Seine where the pavilions of the wealthier nations had been grouped together to provide a spectacular ensemble when viewed from the river or from its far side. While the architecture in the rest of the exhibition was French, the Quayside of the Nations displayed the national—or supposedly national—characteristics of various countries. One of the largest pavilions was that of Russia; but instead of being set by the river, it had been placed in the Trocadéro, partly to give it greater prominence because of the official love affair between Republican France and Tsarist Russia. Its

design was a jumble of styles and the building included a colossal
ikon, a Russian Orthodox tabernacle, a pagoda made of metal
tubing and samples of rich raw materials. One of the main
attractions was a huge map of France made by the jewellers of
the Imperial Court, in which cities were represented by jewels
and the different departments and regions by precious minerals
and metals. There was also a mock Trans-Siberian railway in
which visitors sat inside a railway carriage which was made to
simulate motion by means of rollers while panoramic paintings
of Russian landscapes were rolled past the window on long
strips of canvas.

Back on the quayside, the British pavilion was built as a dignified late-Tudor-style country manor house of real stone. It was
one of the more restrained architectual compositions compared
with many others among the twenty-three nations represented.
The only country that seemed unable to make up its mind on a
national style was the United States, which had settled for a showy
and riotously overladen, florid, neo-classical domed structure
covered with architectual flourishes and allegorical figures like
some badly designed wedding cake. The German pavilion was a
medieval town hall that might have come out of a set for the
Mastersingers of Nuremberg and had the highest spire of any building;
the Italian entry was a plaster pastiche of Tuscan cathedral style
with Venetian-Byzantine; Turkey was content with a mosque
and Spain was represented by a severe structure after the manner
of a Castilian castle. Only one building was distinguished by its
modernity and that was the Finnish pavilion. It was praised for
being both modern and traditional in its design and for being
the most authentically national in spirit. It was the work of Eliel
Saarinen, father of the Eero Saarinen who was to become so
famous in the 20th century.

Parisians who wished to live up to their legendary reputation
for frivolity could escape from the more arduous, educational
side of the Exposition by going to the many side-shows, amusements and popular entertainments. Most of these commercial
attractions were to be found between the Alexandre III bridge
and the Trocadéro on the right bank. They included architectural reconstructions of Swiss and Spanish-Moorish villages, the

"Old Paris" with strolling actors in medieval costume, theatres and cabarets, a "House of Laughter" built in a grotesque parody of official architecture and *art nouveau*, performances by Japanese, Javanese and Spanish dancers and a little theatre for Loie Fuller. There were also some very expensive cafés and branches of Paris's best restaurants, brasseries, bars, tea-shops, a great Ferris wheel, boating trips and a side-show offering simulated naval battles between model warships.

The Exposition was also famous for the displays of two of the most recent and popular inventions—the cinema and the phonograph—and for the various attempts made to combine the projection of moving pictures with mechanically reproduced sound. The most famous of these was the Phono-Cinéma-Théâtre in the Rue de Paris on the exhibition site. It was presented by Clément Maurice, the man who had bought the concession to show Lumière's *cinématographe* films in Paris's Grand Café. As he was a fashionable photographer specialising in portraits of well-known singers and actors, he had been able to enlist the cooperation of some of the city's most popular entertainers and actors. His poster advertised "talking" films of the clowns Footit and Chocolat—Toulouse-Lautrec's favourites—Madame Cossira of the Paris Opéra singing an aria from Gounod's *Romeo and Juliet*, the English comedian Little Tich and the duel scene from *Hamlet* performed by Sarah Bernhardt and Constant Coquelin. The reporter of the *Figaro* was warmly enthusiastic after the show and wrote that "Sarah Bernhardt . . . has been admirably rendered in the famous duel scene from *Hamlet* and the reconstitution of this scene is a marvel of art as well as a masterpiece of exactitude". Other newspapers including *The Times* were also impressed and several writers prophesied that one day it would be possible to record for posterity all the great theatre performances in both sound and image and also form historical archives of great importance thanks to the motion-picture camera and phonograph.

The Lumière brothers set up for their shows a colossal screen, twenty-five metres long and fifteen metres high, in the enormous Gallery of Machines where people could watch the films from either side of a screen which was made transparent by being kept moist. Even more spectacular was Grimoin-Sanson's Cinéorama. This was one of the world's first attempts at "cinema in the round" in which a circularly disposed battery of ten projectors simultaneously threw moving pictures upon a circular screen around them. The audience were given the impression that they were travelling in a balloon by being placed in a large nacelle over the projection cabin, realistically furnished with bags full of ballast, anchors and ropes while carefully draped folds of cloth representing balloon fabric hung from the roof of the hall. Grimoin–Sanson had filmed his pictures from a real balloon, and in his printed handsheets offering a "balloon trip across Europe and Africa" for the price of one or two francs, he promised that the spectators would "experience every impression and every surprise of a trip through the unknown, without fatigue, and without expense: first, the ascension, the wonderment of space, the living panorama of the great city, then an exodus towards far-off countries . . . In a few minutes, you will pass from the grandiose spectacle of the high seas lashed with storms to the vast horizons of the desert with caravans tracking across their vast expanses . . . "

Unfortunately only three balloon trips were accomplished as the projectors made the cabin unbearably hot and, ever mindful of fire risks since the Charity Bazaar disaster, the Prefect of Police ordered the closure of the Cinéorama. But the Exposition still had many other simulated trips, panoramas, dioramas and other shows using mechanical devices and projections to create illusions of movement and travel. If people did not want to see but only to hear, they could go to the very popular Théâtrophone which, for a fee, allowed a listener to hear a performance direct from the stage of a theatre a few miles away.

The Exposition had so many attractions for all tastes that it could hardly fail. But although the authorities had assumed that sixty million people would come to see it during the seven months of its life, the numbers admitted in the first few weeks were disappointing. A month after the official opening, workmen were still removing scaffolding and making finishing touches to pavilions and stands. There were some mechanical failures and the very hot weather in July and August deterred many people from joining the crowds. British visitors were often afraid to come in case they were given a hostile reception and their fears were increased by alarming newspaper accounts of anglophobia in the city. Only two rulers came—the Shah of Persia and the King of Sweden. There had been fears of anarchist outrages against royal visitors and one anarchist did hurl a bomb at the Shah although it failed to explode. Later in the summer months, attendances went up. The organisers of the Exposition decided to hold a series of lavish festivals which culminated in September with a monster banquet to which all of France's 36,000 mayors were invited, the exception being the Paris municipal council which was dominated by the Nationalists and which refused to have anything to do with the Prime Minister. The council decided to hold its own banquet at the Hôtel de Ville and sent out invitations including one to the Lord Mayor of London as well as to other foreign notabilities. The Lord Mayor and a few officials accepted at first, unaware that they were being used to further a right-wing manoeuvre, but the haughty refusal of the Mayor of Lyons and hundreds of other mayors in the French provinces killed the project and made the Paris council look ridiculous.

More than 22,000 mayors arrived for the official feast, many of them wearing their regional costumes, and they were entertained by President Loubet in two giant tents which had been set up in the gardens of the Tuileries. It was a very successful and well-organised occasion and, with cooler weather after the heat wave, it did much to attract a greater number of visitors during the final months. Congresses were also held; scholars and scientists from many countries inspected exhibits and met one another; the new *métro* carried people quickly and cheaply between the Porte Maillot and the Bois de Vincennes; international juries ceaselessly met and awarded thousands of prizes, medals and certificates of merit.

Although the autumn weather was bad and rain made many of the exhibition's gaudier, more ephemeral structures warped and discoloured, the closing date was put back to November, the number of banquets, receptions and fêtes increased and there was a last-minute rush of visitors. The Exposition closed down at last on November 11 after an extra day, at the end of which the whole site was illuminated in a spectacular display of electricity. It had been Paris's most ambitious attempt ever to hold an international gathering and a display designed to illustrate the latest progress made in every conceivable aspect of human creative activity. Even if the target of sixty million visitors was not reached, over fifty million did come—the largest attendance at any world's fair to date—and it was therefore a success. It had also raised doubts in some thoughtful minds. One of the most frequent criticisms heard was that the Exposition was disappointing aesthetically and had failed to present the best in French art.

In some respects, the 1889 Exposition had been more modern in spirit, and particularly in its architecture. The 1900 Exposition produced little in the way of modern, advanced architecture and design. It did leave three enduring additions to the city—the Grand Palais, the Petit Palais and the Alexandre III bridge—but if they had a certain grandiloquent charm and the bridge was undeniably both graceful and romantic, their styles showed little if any advance since the days of Garnier's Opera House. Many critics were inclined to call the overall external aspect of the Exposition an aesthetic monstrosity and several of its buildings were condemned as frankly hideous.

There was no unifying style throughout the Exposition, merely a confused and bewildering mêlée: the most disparate materials and pseudo-historical styles had been crowded together willy-nilly with Oriental, medieval, academic and North African architecture, with decorations assembled amid examples of bourgeois taste and décor at their most overloaded and vulgar. A great part of Paris had been transformed into a make-believe city of plaster, wood, cardboard and papier-mâché characterised by an endless succession of spires, domes, towers, and minarets. Buildings had cornices dripping with excessive decorations, their façades writhed with unnecessary stucco ornaments and they were inflated to elephantine proportions. Their designers seemed to have an uncontrollable mania for cupolas, huge doorways and staircases, neo-baroque entrances and terraces. Colossal plaster friezes, huge allegorical figures, weirdly-shaped pavilions, vague copies of *art nouveau* lines, and all the worst excesses of academic municipal architecture combined with surrealistic pleasure domes, pagodas and such monstrosities as the Tower of All the Nations, with its combination of Chinese pagodas, Moorish mosques and Renaissance towers, to give the impression of stylistic indigestion and an architect's nightmare.

The only really new and authentic modern style was that of international *art nouveau*; what little there was was mostly swamped by the aesthetic pot-pourri around it and it was perfectly possible to go through the exhibition without becoming aware of it. Like the best modern art, it was isolated from the main displays. Bing had stated that *art nouveau* was "not only a style of ornament but an attempt to bring to light every manifestation within the sphere of Modern Art that exemplifies the needs of contemporary life" and he had participated in the Exposition to express his views and theories with his pavilion, the "House of Art Nouveau Bing" as it was called. Here, people could see products of the movement at their best and most inventive instead of the pastiches and commercial exaggerations which were bringing it into disrepute in Paris. Bing's pavilion was on the Esplanade des Invalides and consisted of six rooms specially designed and furnished by his three most gifted colleagues—Eugène Colonna, Eugène Gaillard and Georges de Feure. Together with Gallé's popular glass and vases and Lalique's dazzling jewellery, it represented the best of the new art and although ignored by many of the French was greatly admired by German and English critics for art magazines. A typical reaction of the Paris press came from the *Figaro* which seemed to share the popular idea in France that *art nouveau* was associated with moral decadence by saying: "We are not as neurotic, as hallucinated, as opium-smoking as we may appear to be . . . The modern style is a bad *genre* we are giving ourselves . . . " It was also noticed by some visitors that the most genuine and modern forms and interpretations of the new art were to be seen in the German, Austrian and Hungarian pavilions, and that little attention was paid to them by most French reporters.

The most advanced French painting and sculpture to be seen were represented by the Impressionists and Rodin. Although collectors and connoisseurs abroad were beginning to compete for his work, Rodin had no official display. He had preferred to hold his own retrospective exhibition in a private pavilion near the Invalides which had been built with the financial aid given by some rich, appreciative bankers. It was here that he received the homage of many admirers who could hardly fail to note the contrast in quality between his display and that in the official sculpture rooms.

The young painters Marquet and Matisse took part in preparing the Exposition by stencilling a frieze in the Grand Palais, but there was hardly any sign that modern painting had got past the stage of Impressionism. Despite the efforts of the *Revue Blanche*, poster designers, some art galleries and several other periodicals which had made Bonnard, his friends and Toulouse–Lautrec fairly well known to the Paris public by this time, there was little to be seen of their work. All that the French painting section had to show of the work of the revolutionaries of the past decade were an early landscape by Gauguin, one canvas by Seurat, and three by Cézanne. While some Manets were an important addition to the retrospective display of French painting, a separate room was reserved for paintings by Monet, represented by fourteen landscapes, Sisley, Degas, Pissarro and Renoir. The Impressionists had been the subject of a great many controversies and attacks in the previous twenty years, but they now aroused few hostile reactions and were studied seriously by many discerning art lovers who had only read about them before. Now that they could see them, they found little to support the charges of wilful distortion, anarchism and the cult of amateurishness which had been flung at them in the past. Only one violent protest had been made at the inclusion of the Impressionists in the exhibition. On the day of the official inauguration in April, the old academician and member of the Institute, Gérôme, conducted President Loubet around the "Palace of Painting". As they came towards the doorway of the Impressionist room, he rushed forward, barred the entrance and cried: "Go no further, Monsieur le Président, here France is dishonoured!" It was a brave but futile gesture. Henceforth, the Impressionists had become respectable. They began to win popularity with the public who found their light, colour and refinement to be in the best French tradition, and their prices were beginning steadily to rise on the international art market.

The scarcity of good modern art in the Exposition, compared with the monumental display of bad taste and obsession with the past, made some French critics wonder if the exhibition had been worth while. The whole Exposition had been a huge, lavish show, a great popular distraction, an industrial and scientific display and also a colossal funfair. But was it anything else? It had been meant to reinforce French prestige but in this it had failed as far as art and even science were concerned for they were certainly no more advanced in France than in several other industrialised countries. Many observers noted that the public often seemed more interested in the exhibition's frivolous and commercial attractions. It was attacked for its lack of unity and deep moral purpose. Its promoters could say that one of its tasks had been to illustrate and glorify the French national genius but critics were able to reply: where did this genius really lie?

The answer was that it lay elsewhere. The Exposition had been a distraction for the country. It had taken people's minds away from their disputes and political discords, it had strengthened the Republic's prestige at least, and it had sealed the truce that followed after Dreyfus had been pardoned—a truce made even more durable in the last month of 1900 by the announcement of an amnesty for offences relating to the crisis. For many people, the Exposition had encouraged their hopes that the new century would bring them greater peace and prosperity and unprecedented material progress to the country. It had been a vast party to celebrate a century which had seen the world being transformed by human ingenuity, but in another way it had been a backward-looking occasion. France's true genius in the 20th century was to be found in her cultural achievements—in the arts that could be seen at their most vital and progressive in Paris for many years to come—and yet it was precisely in the French arts that the Exposition was at its weakest.

It would be both wrong and unfair to say that the 1900 Paris Exposition had been inspired mainly by narrow patriotic sentiment. Many of its organisers were sincerely idealistic and internationally minded. But it did take place when there was an upsurge of nationalism and jingoism in the country, after three decades of troubles and frustrations. It was intended as another glorification of Paris and yet, by a curious paradox, Paris's true claim to glory in the years ahead was to be strengthened as never before by a great influx of foreign talent. In 1900, Picasso first came to Paris. New art colonies were to spring up in Montmartre and later in Montparnasse and some of the most famous new Parisians were to be Guillaume Apollinaire, a Pole; the Catalan Picasso; the Russian Stravinsky; the Russian Chagall, and the Italian Modigliani. By 1900, Paris was not only the world's unrivalled centre for pleasure and entertainment, it was the world's most stimulating centre for the arts. The climate in which they were to reach such great heights and astound the world with their modernism and audacity had been prepared in the 1890's.

The return of comparative political and economic stability made Paris a pleasant city to live in. The fierce conservatism of the old guard in the arts, and even political strife and controversy, had encouraged cultural liveliness and a spirit of comradeship and adventure among the *avant-garde*. Because of the combativity, the polemics and revolts of the 1890's, there was no more exciting and promising battleground for new ideas against the old than Paris. The very fierceness with which the battles had been fought attracted new allies for progress and innovations from other countries, and these were to thrive in the atmosphere that had been nurtured.

The Paris of the old century's last decade has become a legend. But the period deserves fame for more than its gaudy night-life, its elegance, Maxim's and the Folies-Bergère, Toulouse-Lautrec and Aristide Bruant. It was the time when Paris was becoming increasingly cosmopolitan and slowly but surely conditioned to accept and even welcome experiment. From the "mauve Nineties", Paris was to emerge as the most stimulating cultural centre in the world, inseparable from the idea of artistic revolution and creation. Henceforth, to be "Parisian" meant much more than being French. To artists from the whole world, Paris was to become *their* capital.

SELECTED BIBLIOGRAPHY

Paris topography, social life, amusements and pleasures, high and low life, memoirs, reminiscences.

Baedeker, Karl, *Paris and its environs*, Ninth revised edition, Leipzig, 1888; Thirteenth revised edition, Leipzig, 1898; Fourteenth revised edition, Leipzig, 1900.

Bataille, Albert, *Causes Criminelles et mondaines*. Paris, 1881–1898.

Bercy, A. de and Ziwès, A., *A Montmartre . . . le soir. Cabarets et Chansonniers d'hier*. Paris, 1951.

Bertaut, Jules, *L'Opinion et les moeurs sous la troisième République*. Paris, 1936.

Bertaut, Jules, *Secrets d'un siècle*. Paris, 1957.

Bijvanck, W. G. C., *Un Hollandais à Paris en 1891*. Paris, 1892.

Blanche, Jacques-Emile, *Portraits of a Lifetime*. London, 1937.

Blavet, E., *La Vie parisienne, 1889*. Paris, 1890.

Bluysen, P., *Paris en 1889*. Paris 1890.

Bourgeois-Borgex, L., *La fin d'un siècle. Des Frères Lumière à Aristide Bruant* (Les Oeuvres Libres, no. 195), Paris ,1921.

Braibant, Charles, *Histoire de la tour Eiffel*. Paris, 1964.

Burnand, Robert, *Paris 1900*. Paris, 1951.

Casteras, R. de, *Avant le Chat Noir*. Paris, 1945.

Charles, J., *Cent ans de Music-hall*. Paris, 1956.

Child, T., *The praise of Paris*. New York, 1893.

Clarétie, Jules, *La Vie à Paris, 1800 etc.*, 12 vols. Paris, 1881–1901.

Coquiot, G., *Les Cafés concerts*. Paris. 1896.

Crussol, M., *Souvenirs de la duchesse d'Uzès*. Paris, 1939.

Daudet, Léon, *Souvenirs des milieux littéraires, politiques, artistiques et médicaux*. 6 vols. Paris, 1914–1921.

Debans, Camille, *Plaisirs de Paris*. Paris, 1889.

Derval, P., *Les Folies Bergère*. Paris, 1955.

Donnay, Maurice, *Autour du Chat Noir*. Paris, 1926.

Englishman (anon.), *An Englishman in Paris*. London, 1892.

Fosca, F., *Histoire des cafés de Paris*. Paris, 1935.

Gheusi, P. B., *Cinquante ans de Paris.* 2 vols. Paris, 1939.

Gilbert, E., *Autrefois-Aujourd'hui.* Paris, 1895.

Guiches, G., *Le Spectacle.* Paris, 1932.

Hare, Augustus, *Paris.* 2 vols. London, 1900.

Henry, S., *Paris days and evenings.* London, 1896.

Huddlestone, Sisley, *Paris, salons, cafés, studios.* Philadelphia, 1928.

Keim, Albert, *Le Demi-siècle.* Paris, 1950.

Krakowski, E., *La Société parisienne cosmopolite au XIXe siècle.* Paris, 1939.

Lanoux, Armand, *Amours 1900.* Paris 1961.

Lesourd, Paul, *La Butte Sacrée—Montmartre des origines au XXe siècle.* Paris, 1937.

Lorrain, Jean, *Poussières de Paris.* Paris, 1902.

— *La Ville empoisonnée.* Paris, 1936.

Macdonald, John F., *Paris of the Parisians.* London, 1900.

Mandell, R., *Paris 1900; the great World's Fair.* University of Toronto Press, 1967.

Meyer, Arthur, *Ce que mes yeux ont vu.* Paris, 1911.

— *Forty years of Parisian Society.* London, 1912.

Montorgueil, Georges, *Paris dansant.* Paris, 1898.

— *Paris au hasard.* Paris, 1895.

— *La Vie des Boulevards.* Paris, 1896.

Morand, Paul, *1900.* Paris, 1931.

Morrow, W. C., *Bohemian Paris of today.* London, 1899.

Platel, F., *Paris-Secret.* Paris, 1889.

Robertson, W. Graham, *Life was Worth Living.* New York, 1931.

Roman, Jean, *Paris fin-de-siècle.* Paris, 1958.

Romi (pseud.), *Maisons closes.* 2 vols. Paris, 1958.

Rothenstein, Sir William, *Men and Memories.* London, 1931–1939.

Simond, C., *La Vie parisienne à travers le XIXe siècle.* 3 vols. Paris, 1900–1901.

Symons, Arthur, *From Toulouse-Lautrec to Rodin.* London, 1929.

Taxil, Léo (pseud.), *La Corruption fin-de-siècle.* Paris, 1891.

Uzanne, Octave, *La Femme à Paris.* Paris, 1894.

Vasili, Count Paul (pseud.), *Society in Paris.* London, 1890.

Virmaître, Charles, *Paris documentaire, moeurs, trottoirs et lupanars.* Paris, 1897.

— *Paris Impur.* Paris, 1889.

Vizetelly, Ernest A., *Paris and her People under the Third Republic*. London, 1919.

Warnod, A., *Les Bals de Paris*. Paris, 1922.

— *Ceux de la Butte*. Paris, 1947.

Whiteing, R., *The Life of Paris*. London, 1900.

Wilhelm, Jacques, *La Vie à Paris sous le deuxième Empire et la troisième République*. Paris, 1947.

Artistic and literary tendencies and movements, political events and controversies, and occultism in Paris.

Baju, A., *L'Anarchie littéraire*. Paris, 1892.

Billy, André, *L'Epoque 1900*. Paris, 1951.

Blum, Léon, *Souvenirs sur l'affaire* (the Dreyfus case). Paris, 1935.

Bois, Jules, *Les Petites religions de Paris*. Paris, 1894.

— *Le Satanisme et la Magie*. Paris, 1895.

Boisson, Marius, *Les attentats anarchistes*. Paris, 1931.

Bonnamour, G., *Le Procès Zola*. Paris, 1898.

Boutet, Frédéric, *Mages noirs, messes noires* (Les Oeuvres Libres, no. 51). Paris, 1925.

Byrnes, R. F., *Antisemitism in Modern France*. Rutgers University Press, New Brunswick, 1950.

Carter, A. E., *The Idea of Decadence in French Literature, 1830–1900*. University of Toronto Press, Toronto, 1958.

Chassé, Charles, *Le Mouvement Symboliste dans l'art du XIXe siècle*. Paris, 1947.

— *Les Nabis et leur temps*. Paris, 1960.

Crespelle, J. P., *Les Maîtres de la Belle Epoque*. Paris, 1966.

Delhorbe, C., *L'Affaire Dreyfus et les écrivains français*. Neuchâtel, Paris, 1932.

Dinar, A., *La Croisade symboliste*. Paris, 1943.

Dumesnil, R., *L'Epoque réaliste et naturaliste*. Paris, 1946.

Fierens–Gevaert, H., *La Tristesse Contemporaine*. Paris, 1899.

France, J., *Autour de l'affaire Dreyfus*. Paris, 1936.

Herbert, Eugenia W., *The Artist and Social Reform. France and Belgium, 1885–1898*. (Yale Historical Publications. Miscellany no. 74). Yale University Press, New Haven, 1961.

Humbert, A., *Les Nabis et leur époque, 1888–1900*. Geneva, 1954.

Jackson, Arthur B., *La Revue Blanche, 1889–1903*. Paris, 1960.

Johnson, Douglas, *France and the Dreyfus affair*. London, 1966.

Joll, James, *The Anarchists*. London, 1964.

Knowles, Dorothy, *La Réaction idéaliste au théâtre depuis 1890*. (Bibliothèque de la Société des Historiens du Théâtre, tom. 4). Paris, 1934.

Lea, Henry G., *Léo Taxil, Diana Vaughan et l'Eglise romaine. Histoire d'une mystification*. Paris, 1901.

Lethève, J., *Impressionistes et symbolistes devant la presse*. Paris, 1959.

Lillie, A., *The Worship of Satan in modern France*. London, 1896.

Madsen, S. T., *Sources of Art Nouveau*. Oslo, 1956.

Maillard, F., *La Cité des Intellectuels*. Paris, 1905.

Maitron, Jean, *Histoire du mouvement anarchiste en France, 1880–1914*. Paris, 1951.

Mauclair, Camille, *l'Art independant français*. Paris, 1919.

Mellério, A., *Le Mouvement idéaliste en peinture*. Paris, 1896.

Nattier-Natanson, E., *Les Amitiés de la Revue Blanche etc.* Paris, 1959.

Nordau, Max, *Degeneration*. London, 1894.

Praz, Mario, *The Romantic Agony*. London, 1933.

Raynaud, Ernest, *La Mêlée Symboliste 1870–1890. Portraits et souvenirs.* 3 vols. Paris, 1918–1922.

Rewald, John, *Post-Impressionism*. New York, 1956.

Robichez, J., *Le Symbolisme au théâtre. Lugné-Poë et les débuts de l'Oeuvre.* Paris, 1957.

Sanborn, Alvan F., *Paris and the Social Revolution. A study of the revolutionary elements in the various classes of Parisian Society*. New York, 1905.

Sergent, A. and Harmel, C., *Histoire de l'anarchie*. Paris, 1949.

Shattuck, Roger, *The Banquet Years: the arts in France 1885–1918*. London, 1959.

Swart, K. W., *The Sense of Decadence in Nineteenth-Century France*. (Archives internationales d'histoire des idées, no. 7). The Hague, 1964.

Viau, Raphael, *Vingt ans d'antisémitisme*. Paris, 1910.

Vizetelly, Ernest A., *Republican France, 1870–1912*. London, 1912.

Waite, A. E., *Devil Worship in France*. London, 1896.

Weill, Georges, *Le Journal*. Paris, 1934.
Wilenski, R. H., *Modern French Painters*. London, 1963.

Books on some Parisian personalities, artists, writers etc. particularly mentioned in this book.

Anna, L. D., *Francisque Sarcey*. Paris, 1919.
Antoine, André, *Mes souvenirs sur le Théâtre Libre*. Paris, 1921.
Aubrun, R. G. *Les célébrites d'aujourd'hui. Péladan*. Paris, 1904.
Baldick, Robert, *The Life of J.-K. Huysmans*. London, 1955.
Barrès, Maurice, *Un Renovateur de l'occultisme. Stanislas de Guaita, 1861-1898*. Paris, 1898.
Billy, André, *The Goncourt Brothers*. London, 1960.
Bricaud, Joanny, *Huysmans occultiste et magicien,* etc. Paris, 1913.
— *Huysmans et le Satanisme*. Paris, 1913.
Bruant, Aristide, *Dans la rue*. 2 vols. Paris, 1889-1895.
Champion, E., *Le Souvenir de Jehan Rictus*. Paris, 1934.
Chassé, Charles, *Gauguin et son temps*. Paris, 1955.
Chastel, Guy., *J. K. Huysmans et ses amis*. Paris, 1957.
Cladel, Judith, *Rodin*. London, 1938.
Coquiot, G., *Toulouse-Lautrec*. Paris, 1913.
David, André, *Rachilde*. Paris, 1924.
Donnay, Marie-Thérèse, *Le Paul Fort que j'ai connu*. Paris, 1961.
Fort, Paul, *Mes mémoires*. Paris, 1944.
Gauthier, P. L., *Jean Lorrain*. Paris, 1939.
Germain, André, *Les Fous de 1900*. Paris, 1954.
Gide, André, *Journal*, Vol. I. Paris, 1947-1949.
Guilbert, Yvette, *The Song of my Life*. London, 1929.
— *Yvette Guilbert*. Paris, 1910.
Hanson L. and Hanson E. M., *The Noble Savage. A Life of Paul Gauguin*. London, 1954.
Jullian, Philippe, *Robert de Montesquiou*. London, 1967.
Kovaćević, M., *La Vie, l'oeuvre, l'influence et le prestige de André Antoine* etc. Paris, 1941.
Laver, James, *The First Decadent. Being the strange life of J. K. Huysmans*. London, 1954.
Le Rouge, G., *Verlainiens et décadents*. Paris, 1928.
Lugné-Poë, Aurélien, *Acrobaties 1894-1903*. Paris, 1931.

Mirbeau, Octave, *Des artistes, 1885–1896*. Paris, 1922.

Normandy, G., *Jean Lorrain*. Paris, 1907.

Péladan, Josephin, *Josephin Péladan* (special number of the *Nouvelle revue du Midi*, no. 10, Dec. 1924). Nîmes, 1925.

Perruchot, Henri, *Gauguin*. Paris, 1948.

— *Toulouse-Lautrec*. London, 1962.

Pouquet, J. M., *Le Salon de Madame Arman de Caillavet*. Paris, 1926.

Rachilde (pseud.), *Alfred Jarry, ou le Surmâle des lettres*. Paris, 1928.

Renard, Jules, *Journal inédit 1887–1895*. Paris, 1925–1927.

Rewald, John, *The Ordeal of Paul Cézanne*. London, 1950.

— *Paul Gauguin*. London, 1938.

— *Pierre Bonnard*. New York, 1948.

Ripert, Emile, *Edmond Rostand. Sa vie et son oeuvre*. Paris, 1968.

Schwarz, M., *Octave Mirbeau. Vie et oeuvre*. The Hague/Paris, 1966.

Shercliff, J., *Jane Avril of the Moulin Rouge*. London, 1952.

Tharaud, Jérôme and Tharaud, Jean, *La Vie et la Mort de Déroulède*. Paris, 1925.

Vaillant, Annette, *Pierre Bonnard*. London, 1966.

Vollard, Ambroise, *Recollections of a Picture Dealer*. London, 1936.

Zevaés, A., *Aristide Bruant*. Paris, 1943.

Index

NOTE: For reasons of space, many of the painters, singers, cafés, hôtels, etc., mentioned in the text only once or twice are entered cumulatively under appropriate headings; works by persons named are entered under the appropriate name. An 'f' after a number indicates that the name occurs on two, 'ff' on three, 'fff' on four consecutive pages; mentions on more than four consecutive pages are indicated, e.g., '64–8 passim', or the first page is given, followed by 'et seqq'. When a person or subject is discussed over several pages, first and last pages, linked by a hyphen, are given.

354   INDEX

Guitry, Jean, 303
Gyp (pen name of Sybille Gabrielle
Marie Antoinette de Riquetti de
Mirabeau, Comtesse de Martel et
Janville, 1849–1932), 60, 212, 266,
288f

Halévy, Daniel, 288
Halles, Les, 35, 63, 153
Hare, Augustus, 32, 44; *Paris*, 32, 44
Hauptmann, Gerhart (1862–1946),
136, 176; *Solitary Souls*, 176; *The
Weavers*, 136
Haussmann, Georges Eugène,
Baron (1809–91), 29, 35, 148
Haussmann, Boulevard, 30
Helleu, Paul Caesar (1859–1927),
217, 261, 266
Henri IV (1553–1610), King of
Navarre from 1572, of France
from 1589, 44
Henry, Émile, 165–6, 168, 173, 234
Henry, Hubert Joseph (1847–98),
276
Hérard, Angèle, 59
Hérédia, José Maria de (1842–1905),
242
Hermann-Paul, 172, 286
Hippodrome, the, 50
homosexual bars and clubs, 63
Horta, Victor, 310
Hôtel de Ville, the, 21, 30, 96, 106,
334
hotels: Brighton, 33; Claridge's, 34;
Crillon, 38; Meurice, 33; Oxford
& Cambridge, 33; Rivoli, 33;
Saint James & Albany, 33
Houssaye, Arsène (1815–96), 186
Hugo, Victor Marie (1802–85), 129,
141, 148, 184, 272; *Hernani*, 182,
272
Huysmans, Joris Karl (pen name of
Charles Marie Georges Huys-
mans, 1848–1907), 40, 60, 66, 141,
170, 195fff, 215f, 218, 220, 224, 228f,

232, 238, 261, 263; *Certains*, 263;
Là-Bas, 195ff; *see also À rebours*
Hydropathes, Les (society), 71f

Ibels, Henri Gabriel (1867–1936),
172, 236, 260, 286, 307
Ibsen, Henrik Johan (1828–1906),
143, 175, 177, 208fff, 233, 316; *The
Enemy of the People*, 177; *The Master
Builder*, 177; *Peer Gynt*, 179; *Pillars of
Society*, 177; *Rosmersholm*, 175
Impressionism and Impressionists,
107ff; exhibitions, 109, 114; 111–14
passim, 118f, 122, 126, 220, 232, 241,
246fff, 253, 261ff, 337
Impressionist Synthetist Group,
118
Indépendants, Salon des, 109, 111,
127, 191, 232, 239, 247, 251
Industry, Palace of, Champs Ély-
sées, 96, 324
Indy, (Paul Marie Theodore) Vin-
cent d' (1851–1931), 274
Interior, Ministry of, 24; Minister
of, 296
Invalides, Hôtel des, 36, 324, 329,
337; Esplanade des, 323, 329, 336
Italiens, Boulevard des, 31ff

Jaeger's 'sanitary woollen clothing',
Dr., 33
James, Henry (1843–1916), 236
Japan, 212, 306
Japanese art, 216ff, 305f; design, 330
Jardin de Paris, the, 50, 55f, 70
Jarry, Alfred (1873–1907), 178–84,
233, 236, 241, 252; *see also Ubu-Roi*
Jaurès, Jean Léon (1859–1914), 289
Javanese dancers, 29, 332; village,
121; for Gauguin's half-Javanese
model, *see* Anna
Jérôme Napoléon, Prince, 243
Jesuits, 27, 204
Jews and Jewry, 21, 41, 278, 288, 295;
see also anti-Semitism